HONEYMOON COUPLES

and

JURASSIC BABIES

HONEYMOON COUPLES *and* JURASSIC BABIES

Identity and Play in Chennai's Post-Independence Sabha Theater

KRISTEN RUDISILL

SUNY
PRESS

Cover art: Photograph of Cho Ramasamy and R. Neelakanthan in a performance of *Campavāmi Yukē Yukē* (*I Appear Age after Age*), 2004. *Source:* Courtesy of R. Neelakanthan, from the author's collection.

Published by State University of New York Press, Albany

Printed in the United States of America

For information, contact State University of New York Press, Albany, NY
www.sunypress.edu

Library of Congress Cataloging-in-Publication Data

Name: Rudisill, Kristen, 1975– author.
Title: Honeymoon couples and Jurassic babies : identity and play in Chennai's post-independence sabha theater / Kristen Rudisill.
Description: Albany : State University of New York Press, 2022. | Includes bibliographical references and index.
Identifiers: LCCN 2021057554 | ISBN 9781438489759 (hardcover : alk. paper) | ISBN 9781438489773 (ebook) | ISBN 9781438489766 (pbk. : alk. paper)
Subjects: LCSH: Amateur theater—India—Chennai—History. | Tamil drama (Comedy)—20th century—History and criticism.
Classification: LCC PN3169.I42 R83 2022 | DDC 792.0954/82—dc23/eng/20220611
LC record available at https://lccn.loc.gov/2021057554

10 9 8 7 6 5 4 3 2 1

This book is dedicated to the memories of all those
who helped shape it and are now gone.
Thank you for being part of this project and of my life.

*Sankaran Radhakrishnan, Norman Cutler, J. Bernard Bate,
Oscar Brockett, Neil Englehart, Martha Rudisill, K. Balachander,
C. Nagesh, R. Neelakanthan, Cho Ramasamy,
Mrs. Y. G. Parthasarathy, Crazy Mohan, N. Muthuswamy,
V. S. Raghavan, Cheenu Mohan, N. Mathrubootham, Girish Karnad,
R. S. Manohar, Purnam Viswanathan,
Ambi Rajagopal, Visu, T. S. Sridhar (aka Marina)*

Contents

Illustrations

1. Halwa is a type of sweet. S. Ve. Shekher says that "Doing jackal tricks on others to cheat is called as ALWHAA as local slang" (email to author, March 1, 2022).

Acknowledgments

This project has been a long time in the making and so many people and organizations have helped me along this journey in one way or another that I couldn't possibly name them all. I sincerely apologize if I have missed anyone who helped to make this a better book.

Those who first inspired and encouraged me to enter into this field include Michael Sells, Steven Hopkins, Wendy Doniger, Norman Cutler, and Barney Bate. I can never say enough to thank Martha Selby and Kathryn Hansen for their insightful comments and generosity of spirit and time. S. Radhakrishnan's influence is found everywhere throughout this work and I am heartbroken that he never got to see it published. S. Bharathy, Sam Sudhanandan, and many AIIS teachers also helped me with language questions. Thank you to those faculty from the University of Texas who read parts of this work in earlier reincarnations: Ward Keeler, Sumit Ganguly, Kamran Ali, Charlotte Canning, Monika Mehta, Veena Naregal, and Oscar Brockett.

The bulk of this research was undertaken thanks to a Fulbright-Hays DDRA that allowed me to spend twelve months from June 2003 to June 2004 in Chennai. It started in 2001 with a Foreign Language and Area Studies Scholarship as I studied at the American Institute of Indian Studies in Madurai. The writing was supported by a 2005–2006 Hemphill-Gilmore Fellowship from the University of Texas, Austin and a 2012 Institute for Culture and Society Fellowship from Bowling Green State University. Further research trips were supported by Eileen O'Neill and Karen Stoddard's fund as well as a Fulbright-Nehru Senior Research Fellowship. In Chennai, I need to especially thank Pritham Chakravarthy, Nandini Ramani, S. Maheswari, S. Ve. Shekher, Kaladhar, Sridhar, Telephone Mani, R. Neelakanthan (Neelu), and their families. Special thanks to Neelu for supplying the cover image.

S. Ve. Shekher and the members of Natakhapriya opened an amazing number of doors for me. Comedian Kathadi Ramamurthy and playwright Raadhu (S. Radhakrishnan) also provided friendship and assistance with this project. They went to a great deal of trouble to introduce me to people like the late K. Balachander, the late C. Nagesh, the late T. S. Sridhar (aka Marina), and Kamalhasan, and even though I was never able to parlay those introductions into interviews, I very much appreciated them. Raadhu's daughter Priya was very helpful with my questionnaires. I would also like to thank Dr. S. Gopalie for sharing his lifetime of knowledge about the Chennai theater scene with me.

Over the course of the year in Chennai I interviewed many people. Here I name a just a few of those I spoke with most extensively and thank them for their time and generosity: Mouli, Venkat, K. S. Nagarajan, Bosskey, Crazy Balaji, Y. G. Mahendran, T. K. S. Pughagherti, M. B. Murthy, Malathi Rangarajan, Kausalya Santhanam, A. R. Srinivasan, all the members of Natakhapriya and Crazy Creations, many members of United Amateur Artists, V. Sreevatson, K. Vivek Shankar, S. T. Baskaran, Pravin, Mangai Arasu, Pritham Chakravarthy, Kovai Padhmanabhan, K. S. Narayan, S. L. Naanu, Thillairajan, Delhi Ganesh, Manager Cheenu, Kamala Kamesh, R. S. Srinivasan, Dr. Mathrabootham, Girish Karnad, V. Rajendran, E. V. R. Mohan, Kalai Ravi, Kishore Subramanian, Priya Kishore, P. Muthuswamy, Mr. Prasad, K. P. Arivanantham, S. Thirukkonam, Bombay Gnanam, T. V. Sundararajan, Karur Rangarajan, Nalli Kuppusamy Chettiar, Murali, Bombay Chanakya, and Padmini Natarajan. I also had the good fortune to interview several giants of the Tamil stage who are no longer with us. R. Neelakanthan (July 20, 1936–May 10, 2018), Mrs. Y. G. Parthasarathy (November 8, 1925–August 6, 2019), N. Muthuswamy (1936–October 24, 2018), V. S. Raghavan (February 18, 1925–January 24, 2015), Cheenu Mohan (May 17, 1956–December 27, 2018), R. S. Manohar (June 29, 1925–January 10, 2006), Purnam Viswanathan (July 4, 1921–October 1, 2008), Crazy Mohan (October 16, 1952–June 10, 2019), Girish Karnad (May 19, 1938–June 10, 2019), and Cho Ramasamy (October 5, 1934–December 7, 2016) all gave generously of their time, and this book would be far less without their input. I hope to honor Cho in the future by continuing to publish my English translations of his witty and entertaining plays. I also have to thank the many actors, writers, technicians, sabha secretaries, volunteers, and audience members that I spoke to at performances.

Colleagues in Chennai and Madurai who asked some of the right questions and listened to me attempt to clarify my thoughts were incredibly valuable. Thank you for that and your companionship, Gardner Harris, Alison Mitchell, Kristin Bloomer, Aparna Balachandran, Bhavani Raman, Ajay Rao, Blake Wentworth, Nate Roberts, Rupa Viswanath, Kate Zubko, Frank Cody, Gillian Goslinga, Raj Arunachalam, Whitney Cox, Rick Weiss, Gita Pai, Nana Yaw Boaitey, Rachel Weiss, Shanti Pillai, Amy Allocco, Melanie Dean, Amy Tang, Rekha Viswanathan, James Hicken, Wendy Singer, Uma Vangal, and R. Radhakrishnan. I especially thank Katherine Ulrich, who shared a room with me in India for many months and whose friendship I value so much. She also copyedited this book, produced the index, and provided much valuable input.

Over the years I have presented parts of this research at conferences and would particularly like to thank Aparna Dharwadker, Susan Seizer, Davesh Soneji, Hari Krishnan, Kausalya Hart, Janet O'Shea, Lakshmi Subramanian, Haripriya Narasimhan, Amanda Weidman, Lisa Mitchell, Ritu Khanduri, Mona Mehta, Nusrat Chowdhury, Erin Mee, C. S. Lakshmi, Anushiya Ramaswamy, Sreenath Nair, Kat Lieder, Arnab Banerji, Jennifer Goodlander, Emily Wilcox, Neilesh Bose, Paula Richman, Fawzia Afzal-Khan, Arya Madhavan, David Mason, Rumya Putcha, Dheepa Sundaram, David Jortner, A. R. Venkatachalapathy, and Francesca Bremner, who have offered comments and encouragement at various points in the project. Portions of chapters 3 and 5 were published in the *Asian Theatre Journal* in 2012; an earlier version of chapter 4 was published in *South Asian Popular Culture* in 2009; and a portion of chapter 7 was published in *Text and Presentation* in 2008.

I would also like to thank Susan Wadley for organizing the invaluable AIIS workshop for turning dissertations into books. Thanks to my fellow participants Laura Brueck, Amit Ahuja, Kristin Bloomer, Michael Baltutis, Niharika Dinkar, Pavitra Sundar, Varuni Bhatia, and especially Tarini Bedi and to our moderators and leaders Geraldine Forbes, John Echeverri-Gent, Kalyani Menon, and Karline McLain. Thank you to Kathy Foley at the *Asian Theatre Journal* and those who selected my article based on this work for the Association for Asian Performance Emerging Scholar's Award and helped me prepare it for publication.

My colleagues and friends at Bowling Green State University have been incredibly supportive, and I would like to thank several of them for reading or listening to parts of this work. Jack Santino, Scott Magelssen, Bradford Clark, Angela Nelson, Esther Clinton, Jeremy Wallach, Becca Cragin, Jeff Brown, Marilyn Motz, Radhika Gajjala, Vibha Bhalla, Neil Englehart, Dan Shoemaker, Khani Begum, Montana Miller, Joe Demare,

Akiko Kawano Jones, and Candace Archer. And thanks to my father Stan Rudisill, siblings Kevin Rudisill and Lynne Sadler and their families. Most of all, thanks are due to my husband, partner in life and Tamil film dance, and sometimes research assistant Vagish Vela, and to our sons Elijah Marx, Sivaji Vela, and Surya Vela, for our family dance parties and never letting me forget how to play and have adventures.

Note on Transliteration

I follow the Madras University Tamil Lexicon scheme in the transliteration of Tamil words and phrases. There are, however, many names, places, and words that are more familiar in their Anglicized forms (for example, Carnatic rather than Karnāṭik, sabha rather than *sapā*, dravida rather than *tirāviṭa*, kazhagam rather than *kaḻakam*). I have included those in the text without diacritics. I have also included some names and play titles without diacritics as they are found in the English-language press in Chennai.

One peculiarity of this project is that many of the texts I am working from are in the spoken form of Tamil. They are spelled out phonetically in Tamil and will look wrong to anyone who knows the correct spelling (for example, *māpḷē* instead of *māppiḷḷai*, *sombu* instead of *sembu*). I have transliterated these faithfully. When English words have been transliterated into Tamil, I have generally chosen to transliterate them back into proper English (for example, *dear* rather than *diyar*, *Washington* rather than *Vāsiṅkṭoṉ*) for ease of reading. Anything in English in the original will be in italics in my translation.

Introduction

Discovering Sabha Theater

SABHA SECRETARY SHANKAR: There's no need for you to *worry*, Doctor. Your daughter's dance *arangetram* will be in our sabha only.

DOCTOR: What, Shankar? You have been saying this same thing for three years. You won't give a *chance*.

SHANKAR: As soon as you return from your *foreign trip* the *arangetram* will happen. *Definite*. When you are coming back from *foreign* could you please bring me one small *radio*? Please try . . . (he exits)

***

DOCTOR (to Nurse Parvati): Listen. I'll tell you one thing. Don't let your daughter learn *dance*. If she learns, it's all over. Whether the *arangetram* happens or not, your prestige will sail away on a boat. You'll have to go begging to all the sabha people in town. Otherwise, your daughter . . .

PARVATI: I'm not even married.[1]

—From *Cāttiram Co<u>n</u>natillai* (*The Scriptures Don't Say So*) by Cho Ramasamy

This joke, from Cho Ramasamy's 1979 play *Cāttiram Co<u>n</u>natillai*, demonstrates the amount of power wielded by cultural organizations called sabhas in the city of Chennai (formerly Madras), India. Doctor Kailasam has been trying to schedule a debut performance, or *arangetram*, for his young daughter for three years, with no success. He has put a lot of time and energy into cultivating a relationship with Shankar, the secretary of one of these sabhas, in the hope that he will commit to a date. The play makes it clear that Shankar will never commit, because he enjoys exploiting the leverage he has over the doctor too much. As Nurse Parvati says to the doctor later in the scene, "you are giving that sabha secretary an awful lot of leeway . . . He is accomplishing everything in this *nursing home.*" As a cultural gatekeeper in the true sense of the word, Shankar helps determine which dancers are allowed a platform for performance and thereby sets the standards for dance in the city. Those decisions, this joke implies, may be based as much on personal networks, favors, and connections as they are on the skill and training of any individual dancer.

Defining Sabha

The word *sabha* simply means "association" or "organization," and it was commonly used all over India in a manner similar to the words *majlis*, *mehfil*, and *jalsa* to convey the general sense of a public function, recital, or performance. In the late nineteenth and early twentieth centuries another use of the word *sabha* became popular with reference to drama. Not only were the performances referred to as sabhas, but the plays themselves. The most famous of this genre was the *Indar Sabha*, a play designed to be a performance within a performance. The audience in the theater watched the character of Indra, king of the gods, enjoying musical performances at his court ("sabha"). The play, written entirely in verse, had no divisions of acts or scenes and was basically a collection of songs held together by a thread of a story. The *Indar Sabha*, as printed text, stage drama, set of recorded songs, and film, was popular for more than one hundred years in a number of different languages and inspired many other plays based on the same principle. This genre of plays was referred to as *sabhai natak* ("sabha drama") in Urdu literary history[2] and differs greatly from the sabha dramas I discuss in the context of post-Independence Tamilnadu, traces of which can be found in the historical narrative of Tamil drama as amateur theater, modern theater, and metro theater.

The word *sabha* was associated not just with particular plays, but also with Tamil drama *troupes* well before India's independence and the beginning of the sabha theater. Troupes such as the Mangala Bala Gana Sabha, N. S. K. Nataka Sabha, Sakti Nataka Sabha, and the Devi Nataka Sabha[3] would remain at a single theater and stage several plays over a fixed period of time. They took advantage of being in one place by using elaborate sets. "Sabha theater," in the sense that I (and M. Tangarasu) use it, refers to sabhas as private cultural organizations in Chennai that organize and sponsor classical music and dance performances along with some dramas and the occasional film, debate, or religious discourse. They have been the dominant patrons of the arts in the city since the 1928 founding of the Music Academy of Madras.

Sabhas organize entertainment for their members, whose fees vary based on the hall that they use for their performances,[4] where the seats are in the theater, and how long a commitment the member makes (e.g., seasonal, one year, lifetime membership). Chennai's sabhas have earned an international reputation for quality performance arts based on the annual music festival they organize, which typically involves well over 2,500 classical music and dance performances within a month-long period (see Fuller and Narasimhan 2014, 202). Less well known is that they have also dictated the style and content of the popular Tamil drama for the past seventy years. Each sabha has its own identity and focus based on the tastes of the founders and response of members to each year's schedule. "At the beginning of the twenty-first century," writes Amanda Weidman, "this idea has been carried to such an extreme that many concert-goers identify the type of music-lover they are by the sabhas whose concerts they attend; even though for the most part all the sabhas feature the same musicians, one makes a social statement by choosing where one goes to hear them" (Weidman 2006, 80–81). The same is true for theatrical productions.

"Sabha Theater" (or "Metro Theatre" as S. Gopalie calls it) is a genre of Tamil-language commercial theater that started in Chennai in the period following India's 1947 independence from British colonial rule. Its name comes from the fact that these amateur drama troupes rely on the sabha patronage system for survival, but the theater also has a very specific aesthetic and narrative style. The plays are part of a multilingual world of folk and experimental theater, classical music and dance, and Tamil-language television and film. The sabha theater crosses over with each of these, sharing writers, actors, and narratives in varying combinations.

I went to my first sabha play on July 24, 2001, the day of Tamil stage and film star Sivaji Ganesan's funeral procession.[5] It was one of S. Ve. Shekher's, at the Narada Gana Sabha. Shekher talked about how he had been up since six that morning and had followed the funeral procession on foot all the way from Sivaji's house in T. Nagar to the cremation grounds near my flat in Besant Nagar (approximately eight kilometers). I remember the hilarity, and how hard it was to catch any of the jokes, when the audience was laughing so hard they drowned out the punch lines. But most of all, I remember the minute of silence for Sivaji, when I could have heard a pin drop in that theater.

Intrigued, I went to see Crazy Mohan's hit play *Jurassic Baby*, where the children and adults in the audience roared with laughter as the actor playing Cheenu (the late "Cheenu" Mohan) dressed in a diaper and acted like a baby on stage. I was fascinated by the sabha plays from the start; even though I didn't catch many of the jokes, I could see how much the audiences loved them. The experience was markedly different from other performances I'd attended in India. It wasn't the absorbed concentration of a classical performance; the casual, distracted attention of a folk performance; the shouting at the screen, singing along, and catcalls of a film; or the turn-off-the-mobile-phone polite focus of a modern (I use this in the sense of Aparna Dharwadker, 2019) or English-language drama.

I was hooked, and full of questions about everything. This book is the result of twenty years spent trying to answer those questions, to uncover the history, give a name, and sketch the generic boundaries for this type of theater as well as to analyze and interpret particular plays and to seriously consider what they mean for those who produce and consume them. I don't answer all these questions, and am oftentimes left with more, but I am also left an audience member and fan, happy to pay a few hundred rupees to enjoy the clever humor and insider camaraderie of a sabha play.

Development of Sabha Theater

The most numerous, visible, and popular plays staged in Tamilnadu's capital city of Chennai today bear little resemblance to the stereotypes of Indian performances that most people are familiar with from folk theater, classical dance, or commercial film. The costumes, make-up, stage settings, and language are actually quite quotidian, and there is little spectacle, song, or dance to draw in viewers. Additionally, individual tickets are relatively expensive, but few in the academic or modern drama worlds have any respect for these plays or consider them real "theater," as I learned when contact after contact suggested I change my research topic.

Sabha theater was one of the new dramatic traditions that started in the post-Independence period that favored dialogue over other aspects of production. It fits nicely into Susan Seizer's fourth stage in the "history of the development of modern Tamil drama" that culminates "in the development of two distinct styles of drama, the elite amateur style of the sabhas, private social organizations that sponsor theatre and music concerts, spurred by 'self-consciously modern elite sensibilities' and the popular professional style of the commercial theatre companies who put on 'company dramas' " (Seizer 2009, 78). Lawyer and judge Pammal Sambanda Mudaliar (1873–1964) is widely known as the "Founding Father of Tamil Theatre" (Muthiah 2003; Sundaram 2014). He started the Suguna Vilas Sabha in 1891 as a theater company to promote amateur Tamil-language drama in Madras.[6] It continued through the Second World War and then transformed into a social club. The Suguna Vilas Sabha and the genre of theater it inspired borrowed more from the British theater than from the Parsi, which isn't surprising given that sabha theater actors come from elite backgrounds and have western-style educations, steady incomes, and secure social statuses. They choose to take up participation in dramas as a hobby, rather than as a career. They take pride in being from "good families" and thus free from the commercial need to please the public and earn money, instead describing themselves as having the freedom to serve the art and create.

Elite amateur drama was not a new phenomenon in the post-Independence period; elites have been translating and adapting western dramas as early as the 1860s in Chennai, as Theodore Baskaran (1981) has discussed in detail, but it was new for sabhas, functioning as a patronage system, to support this type of drama in this period. Although sabha theater shares elite creators and audiences with modern and experimental theater traditions, most scholars of Tamil drama employ the common analytical strategy of contrasting them, always to the detriment of the popular plays. Ramanujam (2003a), Perumal (1981), and other like-minded scholars favor the work of Tamil playwrights such as N. Muthuswamy and Indira Parthasarathy, who spent time in Delhi and are concerned with theater and stagecraft theory. These playwrights are part of a national theatrical tradition that Aparna Dharwadker (2005, 2019) has described as "modern" Indian theater, as I discuss further in chapter 7.

Very few scholars, in either Tamil or English, have addressed the genre of sabha theater, even those who wrote at the time when sabha plays were at the peak of their popularity (1965–1985). I suggest that the lack of critical attention is due to the plays' highly specific target audience, status as entertainment, and focus on humor. These plays do not fit the definition of "theater" that many intellectuals use and are thus ignored in favor of the experimental theater with its leftist politics and potential for social reform. On October 4, 2003, *The Hindu*, Chennai's major English-language newspaper, did a spread called "On the Stage in Chennai" that discusses the history of theater in the post-colonial city from about the 1950s. It says very clearly that "[t]here was a time when the only theatre group in Chennai was the Madras Players." That troupe, known for their performances of Shakespeare, celebrated their fiftieth anniversary in 2005—shortly after sabha theater groups like the United Amateur Artists (2002; see figure I.1) and Viveka Fine Arts (2004; see figure I.2) celebrated theirs.[7] The article completely ignores, and in its selective telling of history, erases, the most visible and popular theatrical tradition Chennai has seen in the post-Independence period.

Figure I.1. Cover of United Amateur Artists Golden Jubilee souvenir. *Source*: Author's collection.

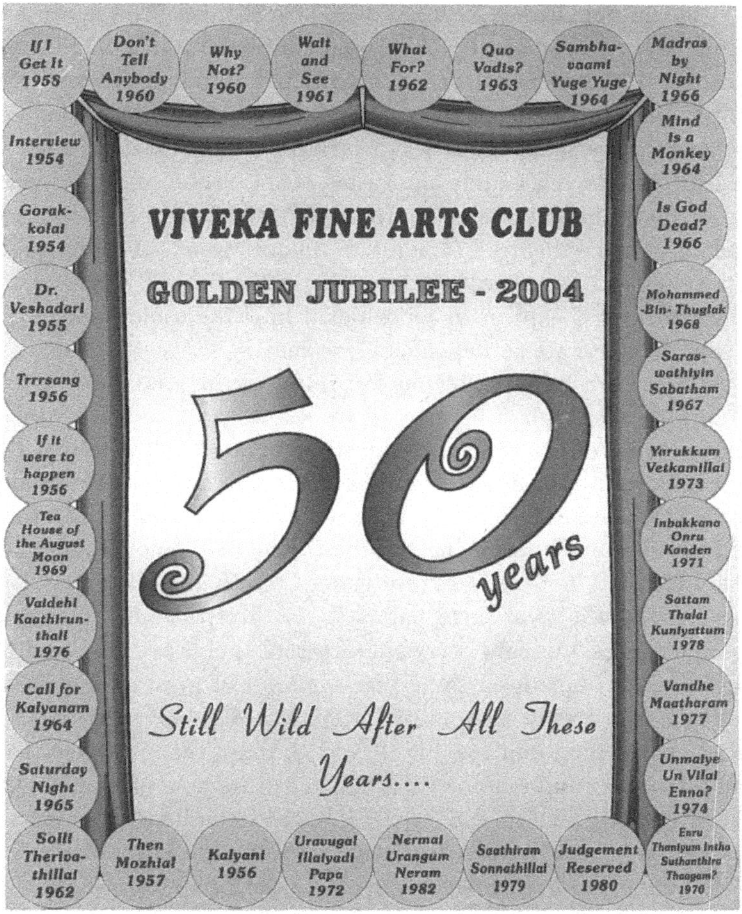

Figure I.2. Cover of Viveka Fine Arts Golden Jubilee souvenir. *Source*: Author's collection.

Sabha plays tend to focus on light-hearted entertainment, and they have a recognizable formula, like all popular culture genres, that continues to draw audiences to the theater. Audience members are individuals who each bring different experiences and interests to their viewings. However, the viewers of a particular genre such as this do represent a community whose interests and values form distinct clusters. Seeing a number of sabha plays and recognizing the structural, aesthetic, and thematic similarities, audience members come to hold certain expectations when they go to the theater. Farley Richmond and S. Shankar have both argued that the homogenization of the plays is an unfortunate but inevitable by-product of the sabha patronage system. Richmond, for example, writes that "[i]n the late 1960s and early 1970s it became apparent that a theatre group needed the Sabhas in order to survive . . . The theatre groups were forced to cater to the whims and tastes of the Sabha office bearers and their membership. Plays with controversial themes or productions with unique or unusual themes or staging techniques were out of the question because they did not appeal to the tastes of the Sabhas" (1990, 431). In the first chapter, I explain in more detail how the sabha system works and why the plays are so dependent on them.

When I arrived in Chennai for fieldwork in June 2003, I started attending as many plays sponsored by sabhas as I could in order to develop a sense of what sabha theater is all about. I estimate that I have now seen around 150 such performances. I would go backstage and meet the artists, which in the sabha world often translated into an invitation to attend any future plays as a guest of the troupe with automatic backstage access. I checked *The Hindu's* event listings (see figure I.3) every day for a year and showed up at some hall or other three or four nights a week for performances. I bought every audiocassette, published play, and DVD I could find and borrowed some that were out of print or unpublished, spending hours on my own and with Pritham Chakravarthy or S. Radhakrishnan listening and reading. I read through years of issues of *The Hindu* newspaper and searched through artists' scrapbooks for published criticism in both English and Tamil. I talked to audience members and visited artists at their homes, backstage, and on tour in India and in the US (see figure I.4 for a poster advertising a performance of S. Ve. Shekher's in Dubai).

The more performances I saw, the deeper my questions became. I began to notice the striking similarities that connected the artists and audiences in terms of education, caste, class, region, and religion, and started studying patronage patterns. I learned that this is, above all, an insider theater.[8] I went into the field asking questions about globalization and the purpose of regional-language theater for this elite group of Chennai-ites, most of whom are educated in English. But as time went by, I slowly realized that the audiences and performers were bound not only by their language, religion, and class, but also by their high-caste status as Brahmins. This book is about a particular genre of theater and

Music Dance Drama

Abbas/ Prabhat, 9840051463

Today 7-00 p.m., Narada Ghana Sabha Hall A/c, The Great Comedy Thinker Crazy Mohan's Record created, Masterpiece, Decent Comedy, Crazy Mohan, Balaji in MARRIAGE MADE IN SALOON. Gather to laugh together. Bkg. 9-00 a.m. at Hall: 24990850. Spons: MY TVS QUALITY USED CARS, MARS — MIOT ACCIDENT RESCUE SERVICES.

Abinaya/ TVK, 9840354779

Today 7 p.m. Narada Gana Sabha (Mini Hall) A/c, Comedy King S. V. Shekher's superhit hilarious non-stop comedy "YAMIRUKKA BAYAM YEAN". Bkg. 9-01 a.m. Ph: 24993201.

Arasu Arts/ Priya

Today at 7 p.m. at Rani Seethai Hall. Comedy King Basky in "OHO" By: T. D. Balu. Booking at the hall 5 p.m. onwards.

Bharat Kalachar

Prog. for Feb. 04. 8th Feb. 9 a.m. sharp under the Endowment of Sri P. OBUL REDDY & Smt. P. GNANAMBA — THIAGARAJA ARADHANA CELEBRATION and Group singing of PANCHARATHNA KRITHIS lead by Senior musicians; As a homage and in memory of former Chairman, Advisory Council, Bharat Kalachar awards Dr. SEMMANGUDI SRINIVASA IYER VET-

Bharat Kalachar

In association with Vision Care, 21st Feb. 6-30 p.m. at Dr. Rama Rao Kala Mandap (A/c), Habibullah Road, T.Nagar, Inauguration of U.A.A.'s new drama "UBHADESAM SEIVATHU UAA" — written by Venkat; dramatized and directed by Y. Gee. Mahendra; A Five in one Comedy rich with purposeful humour through unique stories told by Sri Sathya Sai Baba, Osho, The Gita and Zen Buddhism; Hon'ble Justice Sri K. S. Bakthavatsalam lights the Kuthuvilakku; website: www.ygeem.com

Brahma Gana Sabha (Ph:56106425)

At Rani Seethai Hall. 13th Feb. NALLATHORE VEENAI SAITHEY. 21st Feb. Rail Priyas Anniversary — Two fully hilarious Comedy Skits. 28th Feb. Kathadi's New Play ORU KODI ASAIGAL. Limited membership available.

Esther Fine Arts, 32857997

Today 6-30 p.m. at Rajaannamalai Mandram A/c, Nanjil Nee Manimaran in PUTHIYA BHOOMI, Cine Dance Programme. Bkg. 10 a.m.

Hamsadhwani (Regd.), 24915555

14th Annual February, March, April mega festival of 80 concerts commences on Wednesday, February 18 (Mahasivaraathiri day). Watch out for details. New members enrolled.

Hums and Drums, Phone: 26600985

To-day 2-30 p.m. SAINT THYAGARAJA SWAMIGAL ARADHANA PANCHARATNA KRITIS followed individual performances by Musicians at Maharishi Vidya Mandir, 28, Dr. Guruswamy Road, Off. Poonamalle High Road. Musicians Rasikas welcome.

Kalarasana

On 7th: Gitanjali's PENN BIMBANGAL by Augusto.

Kartik Fine Arts (Regd.), Ph: 24997788

Performance for Feb. 2004. 2nd PURANDARADASAR DAY — Music by CHARULATHA MANI — Tiruvarur Balam, Papanasam Kumar, Nanganallur Swaminathan. Talent promotion programme dances with financial aid from Tamilnadu Eyal

Hindu Feb 1, 2004

Figure I.3. "Music Dance Drama" events listing from *The Hindu*, February 1, 2004. *Source*: Author's collection.

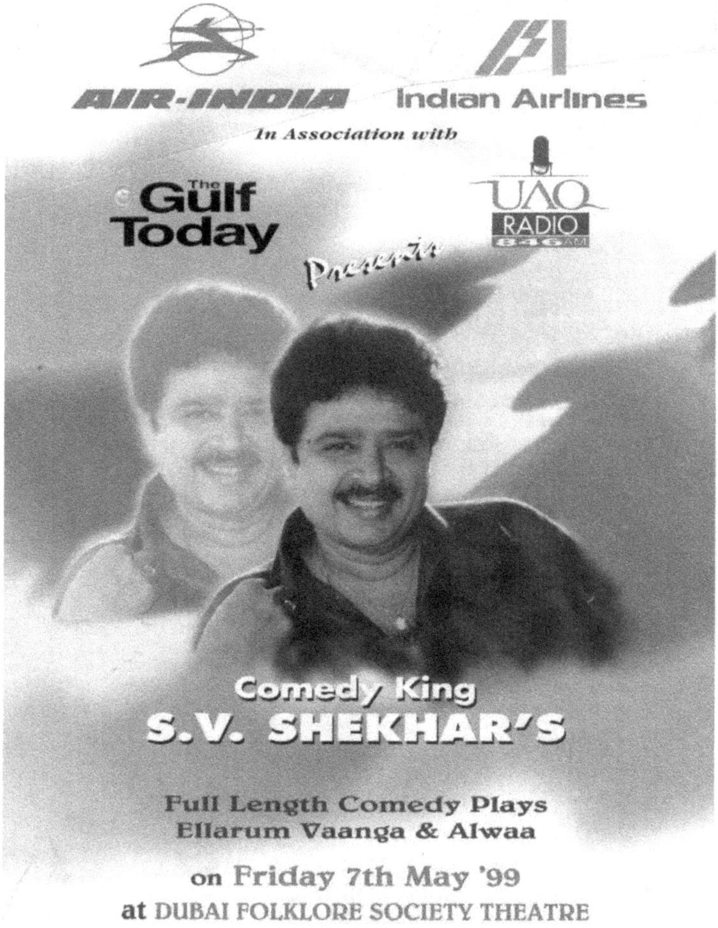

Figure I.4. Poster for S. Ve. Shekher's plays *Ellarum Vānga* (*Everyone Is Welcome*) and *Alwaa* (*Halwa*) held at the Dubai Folklore Society Theater on May 7, 1999. *Source*: Courtesy of S. Ve. Shekher.

the specific, urban, elite Brahmin community that has used it to construct and project its own superior identity.

Part I provides a general analytical framework for the discussion of sabha theater in context. In it, I describe sabha theater as a genre, contextualizing it historically, politically, and aesthetically so as place it within the wider history of the Tamil stage. In this section, I discuss the way that this theater expresses a Tamil Brahmin identity that struggles with being simultaneously traditional and modern, counteracts the negative public image of Brahmins that is projected by the Dravidian movement, and distinguishes these plays and their viewers from the so-called vulgar arts of film and professional theater while connecting them to the respected classical performing arts. I also detail the critiques of the theater, which include lackluster aesthetics, repetitive formula, undemanding content, and the fact that it is socially exclusive. Part II then offers examples in the form of case studies of particular plays that illustrate and elaborate upon the key arguments set out in Part I. These chapters analyze sabha theater as an expression of a complex Brahmin identity, using the humor displayed in the genre's plays as a tool to access and reveal this identity. I also point to specific examples within the plays that are meant to serve as markers of a superior Brahmin identity such as the absence of song and dance, the use of Brahmin dialect, and the limited participation of women. The area studies approach combines ethnography with performance studies as well as historical and literary analytical methodologies in order to view these arts and communities from a multidimensional position. Ethnographic information obtained through questionnaires, interviews with performers, writers, and audience members as well as the observation of rehearsals, performances, and television and film shootings helps present a complex view of a theatrical genre that is simultaneously patronized and dismissed by its viewers.

Brahmins became the most powerful taste-makers (in Pierre Bourdieu's sense) in Chennai through a combination of factors involving long-standing privilege, colonialism, law, and nepotism.[9] These structural advantages have made them disproportionately influential in shaping middle-class culture in the city. They dominate not only the sabhas, but also the press and the universities, which means that it has been difficult to find perspectives on sabha theater from outside this insider group's feedback loop. As an outsider myself, with no caste affiliation, I have tried to be cognizant of this fact and to not only introduce and nuance critiques where I find them, but also to consider from whom they are coming. In contrast to other scholars (Singer 1972; Hancock 1999), I argue that Brahmin identity is not best visible in tradition and ritual, because performances of the classical arts and the response of connoisseur audiences to them reveal an ideal that is frozen in time. Unlike classical music and dance, which are valued because of their adherence to "tradition," sabha theater is a relatively recent development that reflects shifts in the political and social identity of the elite Tamil Brahmin community in Chennai.

I look to something fluid, spontaneous, and contested: humor. Jokes are cued, but it is common for them to fall flat, lose relevance over time, and appeal to limited groups. Marx and Sienkiewicz point out that "[c]omedy . . . has a powerful capacity to create in-groups and out-groups. It ruthlessly sorts individuals by whether or not they have the requisite background experience to understand and enjoy that which is making everyone else laugh. This is particularly important at the level of nation. Nations, regardless of how natural and eternal they may feel, are products of social convention and require constant upkeep" (2018, 239). Caste has been around in some form or another for several thousand years, so feels even more natural and eternal than the nation, in spite of the work that has been done to dismantle the system. Comedy creates inside jokes that help to keep these societal divisions current, and those who find it funny, belong; those who either don't get it or don't think it's funny can be excluded and "be argued to not 'properly' belong to that community" (Marx and Sienkiewicz 2018, 268). So, when audiences actually laugh and find intended jokes funny, they are signaling their belonging to what they consider to be a desirable, exclusive, and elite group. These performances and jokes can thus offer insights into the non-idealized self-conceptions of the community of observers who are responsible for the creation of taste in Chennai.

Chapter 1 takes an in-depth look at the community of patrons through the sabhas themselves. It considers what they are, how they became popular, the kinds of entertainment they promote, and the effect these organizations have on the form and content of the theatrical genre that bears their name. Using Bourdieu's theories of distinction, I look at the sabhas as a space in which the classical arts are promoted alongside often-disparaged comedy plays and how the entertainment schedules distinguish these viewers from, particularly, film audiences. Chapter 2 situates sabha theater and its Brahmin patrons in the political context of Tamilnadu during the period when it emerged and examines the importance of caste identity to this particular genre. Chapter 3 is designed to give a closer look at the quantifiable characteristics of the genre. It answers questions such as the following: What does sabha theater look like? What are the conventions of the genre and where is there room for invention and play? What can you expect to see and hear when you attend a play in terms of performers, aesthetics, style, content, language, and humor?

The individual plays in part II serve as case studies for detailed analyses that examine the way Brahmin identity is constructed and how the exclusion or negative treatment of female characters as well as members of lower-class communities reassert Brahmin male superiority. Chapter 4 analyzes the play *Washingtonil Tirumaṇam* (*Wedding in Washington*) from the early 1960s. This play offers a very detailed description of a perfect Brahmin marriage . . . in Washington, DC. It clearly delineates the role of good Brahmins in society and the proper way for family relations to work by describing every item of food, clothing, and ritual in detail for the characters of the clueless Americans. Chapter 5 moves from marriage to two other life-cycle rituals: going on a honeymoon and having a baby. Kathadi Ramamurthy's *Honeymoon Couple* (1979) and Crazy Mohan's *Jurassic Baby* (2001) express cultural values and expectations through circumstances designed to be funny as well as include individual jokes, which reveal instances of belonging and inclusion. Chapter 6 looks at two plays from very different time periods where the heroes masquerade as servants in order to think about issues of class relations and purity/vulgarity, both of which are central to the self-construction of this Tamil Brahmin community, which Fuller and Narasimhan argue can be described as a "middle-class caste" (2014). Purnam Viswanathan's *Undersecretary* from the 1950s and S. Ve. Shekher's 1993 *Ciṉṉa Māpḷē, Periya Māpḷē* (*Younger Son-in-Law, Elder Son-in-Law*) reveal differences in the ways that Tamils thought about these issues in the post-colonial as opposed to the post–economic liberalization periods. Chapter 7's analysis of Cho Ramasamy's 1968 political satire *Mohammed bin Tughlaq* looks closely at the divide within the Tamil Brahmin community as it projects itself as both regional and pan-Indian, both traditional and modern. Here, I probe the blurred boundaries between the sabha theater genre and the pan-Indian modern theater genre, which appeals to many Tamil Brahmins as cosmopolitan urban intellectuals. This chapter thus encourages the development of a more fluid and modern understanding of a multi-faceted Tamil Brahmin culture, which is heavily influential both in India and abroad.

PART I

SITUATING SABHA THEATER

CHAPTER ONE

The Space of the Sabha

Art Patronage and the Reinforcement of Taste in Chennai

> INTERVIEWER: *What are your extracurricular activities?*
>
> MADHU: *Extracurricular activities? Sir*, I am a *basketball player, Sir.*
>
> INTERVIEWER: Really? . . . . How many people are on a *basketball team?*
>
> MADHU: What, *Sir*? Are you asking how many players? There are eleven on this side and eleven on that side; this man is an *umpire* and that one is an *umpire.*
>
> INTERVIEWER: (pause) Isn't that a *cricket team*?
>
> —from Crazy Mohan's *Aladdin and the 100 Watt Bulb*

In this joke from Crazy Mohan's 1979 play *Aladdin and the 100 Watt Bulb*, the character Madhu tries to impress a man interviewing him for a job by saying, using the English phrase, that he is a "basketball player." He clearly thinks that this will improve his chances of getting the job, but it backfires. The interviewer doesn't take his word for it but follows up with a specific question about the mechanics of this American game. In his response, Madhu unwittingly reveals that the only sport he knows is India's most popular: cricket. A June 21, 2010, *New York Times* blog links basketball quite solidly to the Indian middle class when it says "Basketball is largely considered a sport for the wealthy. . . . The sport has grown in popularity along with the country's economy" (Belson and

Timmons, 2010). To get the joke in this play, one has to be familiar with both basketball and cricket, and to be familiar with basketball, one needs to either have connections to an elite school or college that offers it, have traveled abroad to the US or have friends or family who have, or subscribe to ESPN or Star Sports, pay television channels. The joke predates the 1998 Bollywood film *Kuch Kuch Hota Hai* that introduced basketball to the popular Indian imagination by nearly twenty years and reveals that basketball in India, unlike in the US, remains a marker of middle-class status as well as possesses some cosmopolitan cachet due to its novelty as a markedly American sport. This joke, like much of the humor in sabha theater, makes it clear that these plays are by and for the middle class, and highlights the importance of, at the very least, understanding those things designated as contributing to the creation of good taste and culture.

Cultural organizations such as sabhas are key players along with the press and the academy in creating a notion of "good" taste in Chennai, and all three are dominated by the high-caste Brahmin community, which thus both constructs and embodies the idea of good taste dominant in the city.[1] Ideas about good taste are determined in a substantial way by the performances that find their way into the sabhas, so the entertainment-centered dramas favored by sabhas offer an essential counterpoint to classical music and dance performances, with which they are in rotation.[2] Each sabha has its own unique identity and calendar of events, but are best known for their December–January music festival, though many operate year-round. Although each organization is distinct from the others, there is still an identifiable "sabha aesthetic" for each art, which I articulate for theater in chapter 3. This chapter focuses on the historical context and effects of this patronage system to illustrate the mechanisms by which taste is created through the sabhas.

Before there were formal sabhas with paid memberships, tickets, and performance halls with proscenium stages, there were neighborhood associations that gathered in homes and community halls to sing devotional songs (*bhajans* or *bhajanas*). Most sabhas started this way, as "community organizations, established by groups of concerned citizens, usually Brahmins, with the idea of providing music to the neighborhood" (Weidman 2001, 104).[3] The Parthasarathy Swami Sabha, for example, was founded in 1900 by a Mandyam Iyengar named Manni Thirumalachariar, who "felt the need for an association to conduct *bhajans* and Harikatha regularly for the local community" (Iyengar 2003). There were fifty original members, most of whom lived on Thirumalachariar's street in Triplicane.

The focus on music performance in Madras began as early as 1883, when a branch of the Gayan Samaj was founded for the "improvement and revival of Indian music" (Weidman 2001, 6). Even at this early stage, audiences were linked to and distinguished by their tastes in "classical" and "vulgar" music, terms borrowed from discussions about language that were ongoing in this period. The British were actively recruiting Brahmins instead of members of the non-Brahmin land-owning Vellala caste for civil service positions after 1858, so members of this community flocked to Madras city and began gaining in political and social influence. Not surprisingly, discussions flourished in the Brahmin-founded and run music colleges, sabhas, and press, which framed Carnatic music "within a thoroughly culturalist discourse where it operates as a sign of culture, tradition, refinement, and Brahmin middle-class identity" (Weidman 2001, 110). In addition to the Gayan Samaj, the Madras of the 1880s saw the founding of the Indian National Congress, the Madras Mahajana Sabha, and the Theosophical Society, all of which were dominated by Brahmins. The proceedings of the Gayan Samaj articulated that the organization desired "to distinguish between the 'disgusting songs sung by low castes' and 'Hindu music,' the system of music elaborated in Sanskrit treatises, and to teach the latter scientifically" (Weidman 2001, 6). A further goal, shared by most of the above organizations, was to revive regional arts and project them as pan-Indian.

Chennai's influence in the arts and its predominance on the Indian performing art scene have been acknowledged for many years, at least since the city began to grow in the eighteenth and nineteenth centuries as a center of colonial administration and commerce. It attracted merchants, landholders, and Brahmins, and with the subsequent increase in wealth, the city also became a center of musical patronage. Musicians moved to Madras city from princely states, particularly from Tanjavur, in great numbers between 1850 and 1920 as the monarchs lost power and money, and with them the ability to support the arts. This trend continued so that today, Carnatic music is, as Kathleen and Adrian L'Armand once put it, "almost entirely centralized" (1978, 115) in the city of Chennai.

The project of providing music to Chennai neighborhoods became more formal than the small gatherings hosted by neighborhood sabhas when, in 1912, Brahmins began sponsoring music conferences every few years in a conscious attempt to "define and standardize" the classical music of India. Not surprisingly, these discussions were held among members of the middle and upper classes who considered themselves refined and their musical tastes "classical," while music popular among members of the lower classes was categorized as "vulgar" and looked down upon. Audiences heavily favored the elite because the sabhas required an audience "of a certain economic class, one that not only had the concept of music as a leisure-time activity (part of 'culture' and 'tradition,' not a money-making career), but could also afford to pay for it" (Weidman 2006, 104). Although music was being promoted as a universal language of aesthetics by "the Brahmin music establishment,"[4] it was in actuality divided into several different types such as classical, vulgar, devotional, and later, film. Through this and similar processes, Brahmin middle-class identity has been linked to national ideas of culture, tradition, and refinement. Furthermore, these "cultural policy makers," as Milton Singer calls patrons, organizers, and critics of performance arts, helped to set the standards of public taste and criticism, and eventually created an atmosphere where, as Lakshmi Subramanian has demonstrated, "consumption of classical music became an integral element in their [Brahmin] cultural self-definition, a marker of status and taste and a cementing agent of a collective identity and presence" (Subramanian 2006, 166).

Many of the earliest sabhas were in the northern part of Madras known as Sowcarpet, Mint, Georgetown, Black Town, or just "Town," which was "the business and commercial heartland [of Madras] until the 1960s" (Ramachander 2004).[5] After that, however, the scene began to change as wealthy Telugu Chetti music patrons moved out of the Mint Street area and Brahmins from rural areas who had been affected by the 1961 land reforms moved to the city and became prominent patrons of classical music. In the decade following the land reforms, the population of Madras City increased by almost 800,000 (42.8%) (Hancock 1999, 47). The new Brahmins tended to congregate around the large temples in the city in areas such as Triplicane and Mylapore that were already Brahmin-dominated or settled in developing outer suburbs such as Adyar and Besant Nagar (figure 1.1). Mylapore and Triplicane were already centers of culture with a number of sabhas, but new ones sprung up in those areas during the 1960s as others relocated there or simply closed in Georgetown. These areas of the city thereafter "monopolised all commerce, art, culture, media, civil administration, economic prosperity and public life in the city" (Ramachander 2004). It is difficult to ascertain the Tamil Brahmin population of these neighborhoods, but Fuller and Narasimhan, drawing on Weinstein and Auclair, estimate that they make up 13.9% of Chennai's population totaling approximately 390,000 people. Their 2005

Figure 1.1. General map of Chennai, 2007. *Source*: Google, Europa Technologies.

survey found the percentage to be 47.3% in Thyagaraja ("T.") Nagar, though Auclair estimated 64.5% of that neighborhood, 62.6% of Adyar and 74.5% of Mylapore. At any rate, Brahmins clearly have the power in terms of both numbers and money to set cultural precedents in these areas of the city (Fuller and Narasimhan 2014, 236).

Sabhas are still neighborhood organizations, as members usually live near the performance hall and often know many of the other members in advance of joining. The Brahmin-dominated neighborhood of Mylapore was an early home to many sabhas such as the Thyagaraja Sangeetha and Vidwat Samajam and is where they continue to be concentrated. The small geographic area of Mylapore is currently home to the Mylapore Fine Arts Club, the Rasika Ranjani Sabha, Narada Gana Sabha, Bharatiya

Vidya Bhavan, and Rani Seethai Hall, just to name a few (see figure 1.2). Triplicane used to be another drama hotbed in the city, but its prominence has faded. The Parthasarathy Swami Sabha is still there, but Triplicane Fine Arts and others have folded. In the mid-1940s and '50s the wealthy neighborhood of T. Nagar became the other major theater neighborhood in the city with the founding of such organizations as the Sri Thyaga Brahma Gana Sabha and Krishna Gana Sabha. The number of sabhas in that area continues to expand and now include Mrs. Y. G. Parthasarathy's Bharat Kalachar as well as many that utilize the Vani Mahal as a performance space. There are a handful of other halls scattered throughout the city (such as the Annamalai Mandram near Parry's Corner, the government-run Kalaivanar Arangam on Warangal Road, and new ones popping up in Nanganallur), but the venues are heavily concentrated in Mylapore and T. Nagar.[6] These two neighborhoods are the theater and classical performance neighborhoods of the city in the same way that Kodambakkam is the center of the Tamil film world.

Many sabha secretaries have noted a cultural divide in Chennai between the northern (Georgetown) and southern (Mylapore) parts of the city that illuminates part of what is unique about the post-Independence sabha theater. There was a substantial shift in the content and style of the plays performed on sabha stages around the time of independence, and the reasons for that shift are many, including cultural, political, and financial explanations. Sabhas are concentrated, as stated above, in "South Chennai,"[7] and the audience found in these Brahmin neighborhoods was very different from the non-Brahmin audiences found, for instance, near Parry's Corner at the Annamalai Mandram. S. Gopalie, theater artist and former producer of Doordarshan's drama series in Chennai (a job he held between 1974 and 1992), addresses this phenomenon and the consequences it has had on the content of sabha dramas in the introduction to his thesis:

> The South Madras Sabhas were mostly Brahmin-oriented, both at the level of administration and at the level of audience. Since most of the plays were with the Brahmin audience, the plays were more readily accepted. The North Madras Sabhas were of another kind. They held an advantage of a floating population who might visit theatre till it got the next train or bus to return to their village or town.
>
> There are certain plays that are more readily acceptable by the South Madras audience, which simply fail with North

1. Annamalai Mandram
2. Kalaivanar Arangam
3. Vani Mahal
4. Krishna Gana Sabha
5. Bharat Kalachar
6. Rani Seethai Hall
7. Narada Gana Sabha
8. Music Academy
9. Mylapore Fine Arts Club
10. R. R. Sabha
11. TAMBRAAS main office
12. Tughlaq offices
13. Alliance Française
14. Max Mueller Bhavan
15. Museum Theater
16. Kamaraj Memorial Hall

Figure 1.2. Detailed map of Chennai showing major sabha drama halls and other places of interest, 2007. *Source*: Google, Europa Technologies.

Madras audiences. While the South Madras audience identified in a way with the family represented on the stage (Brahmin) the North Madras audience watched it as a piece of curiosity. (Gopalie 2002, 14)

Gopalie, a 1963 graduate of the National School of Drama in Delhi and an active member of the Chennai theater scene, affirms that the majority of these post-Independence plays, unlike the more universally known mythological and historical plays, were "Brahmin-oriented" and represented Brahmin families on the stage. I will address the Brahmin orientation of sabha theater in depth in the next chapter.

Tamil Brahmins and "Classical" Good Taste

In his essay on the neighborhood *bhajana* groups in Madras, which mushroomed in Mylapore around the turn of the century, Milton Singer discusses one that was highly organized, in a similar manner to sabhas: "The group elects officers, solicits donations, prints announcements and invitations, and issues an annual report with an audited account of its revenues and expenditures" (1972, 214). In addition, this particular group was instrumental in founding an association of Madras *bhajana* groups and devotees. Although Singer argues that these groups were "integrative," the breakdown of identifiable donors he lists for the 1959 annual festival is at least 80% Brahmin. Many group leaders told him that they saw their role as "democratizing," but only insofar as they sought the improvement of "non-Brahman speech, attitudes, and behavior that come[s] from association with Brahmans" (229). A. Mangai and V. Arasu, in their study of pre-Independence Tamil drama notices, discuss how the early ones (dated between 1892 and 1915) explicitly denied entry to Dalits (2009, 117). I have found no evidence of this with sabhas, but it may have been a rule that didn't need to be spoken, given the identity of the organizers. Although most sabha memberships remain primarily Brahmin, this is not something that is openly acknowledged or discussed. As it is now politically incorrect to express superiority on the basis of caste, people do not do so publicly although the attitudes are still present to some extent and they may do so in private (see Fuller 1996). This is not to say that the patrons for classical music and dance or even sabha theater are entirely Brahmin. Many Chettiars, Pillais, and Mudaliyars also patronize these arts; Nalli Kuppusamy Chettiar, of Nalli Silks, is currently one of the biggest sponsors of sabha plays in Chennai. However, because Brahmins so dominate the Chennai elite, the rhetoric of modernization and the arts that they promote tends to invoke what Lakshmi Subramanian refers to as "the trope of tradition, especially its spiritual dimensions" (2006, 100).

Many scholars and critics have noted the correlation between high social status and what is considered to be "good" taste (Bourdieu 1984; Radway 1997; Gans 1999). In India, consumers, and often producers, of these classical cultural performances tend to have high social status that is usually accompanied by high caste and class statuses. As Fuller and Narasimhan put it, Carnatic music "epitomizes middle-class Brahman social respectability and cultural refinement" (2014, 204). Tamil Brahmins set the standard not only within Chennai, but in the nation-state of India more broadly, as evidenced by the performances and discussion of Kuchipudi at the first All-India Dance Seminar in 1958.[8] It therefore makes sense that those who aspire to higher status would alter their entertainment choices and professed tastes to be in closer accord with those arts patronized by recognized elites. The sabhas are, on one hand, "aimed at people . . . who want[ed] desperately to present themselves as educated, sophisticated, and aesthetically articulate."[9] On the other, they are aimed at the actual elite and provide a forum in which "quality" performances can be seen. Sabhas, like book clubs and other cultural organizations, give their members a schedule that they can follow throughout the year to become more cultured, although the sabhas usually state their goal as improving the state of the arts, not their members.

This patronage structure allows powerful members of the community to define taste according to their own standards by becoming sabha secretaries and organizers and arranging entertainments in that capacity. Their focus is on the construction of high-brow Indian culture through the classical music and dance performances they offer. Through their theatrical offerings, however, they also tap into an audience that desires performances that combine the internationality of a "world class" with an "Indian touch" (Brosius 2009, 182). The plays use an Indian language and inside jokes, but also require competence in the English language and American popular culture to understand some of the humor. The plays, therefore, appeal to regional and national pride as well as to the allure of the "foreign" and the class-based privilege that accompanies it (Fernandes 2000: 616), signaling the way that ideas about "being middle class have increasingly begun to include global discourses about transnationalism, privatized services, and (post) modernist urbanism," as Henrike Donner and Geert De Neve put it (2011, 15).

The Brahmin community's dedication to the promotion of the arts as part of a nationalist agenda was evident in the founding of the sabhas and the "classical" performances they sponsored, the success of the Bharata

Natyam school Kalakshetra (founded by Brahmin Rukmini Devi in 1936), and the community's support of Hindi as a national language. Those who were invited to perform in the sabhas and for All India Radio as classical musicians were also primarily of Brahmin caste. The Tamil music performance community was divided as early as the fifteenth century into ritual temple specialists, singer-composers of devotional poetry, and the professional singers who were attached to the courts. Each had their own musical tradition, and the project of consolidating a "classical" music that Lakshmi Subramanian dates to the eighteenth and nineteenth centuries privileged the court singers "who had a grounding in musical grammar and belonged to the upper castes, mostly Brahmins, who combined knowledge of the scriptures, Sanskrit with a reading of conventional musical texts" (2006, 9) over the others, particularly over the temple ritual specialists, the devadasis and the Oduvars, who were of low social status. One solution, just as in dance, was to try to attract performers of higher social status. The English daily *Swarajya*, edited by T. Prakasam, for instance, "urged that the precious art be separated from its evil association, but added that this would be possible only if an increasing number of votaries of the art imparted to it something of the purity of their own lives. It was a call for girls from 'respectable' families to take up the dance" (Arudra 1997, 8). All India Radio actually barred "singers and musicians from the courtesan culture—anyone 'whose private life was a public scandal.'"[10] The station also discouraged performers from "non-respectable" communities by using an elaborate audition system by which performers were graded not only on performance but also on music theory, something that only the new amateur Brahmin performers, who had academic as well as performance training, were learning to the satisfaction of the station.

Classical music and dance performances appeal both to a local audience and to the cultural tourists who come to Chennai for the festival. Performers come from all over the world because "[c]oncerts in Chennai bolster the credibility of dancers as performers, teachers, and choreographers within their local communities" (O'Shea 2007, 155). Music season concerts are also the best publicized, attended, and reviewed. Locals as well as Indian and foreign tourists flood the city at that time of year to see some of the many concerts and dance performances that take place each day.

Sabha theater is more directly targeted at a local (Tamil-speaking) audience than the classical performances. Visitors to the city may not understand Tamil, and even if they do, many jokes allude to local issues or events with which they may not be familiar. Consequently, there is much more flexibility with scheduling dramas than is the case with the classical arts, whose performances tend to be clustered around the festival. Amateur drama on the urban stages lasts year-round, and actors typically head straight to the theater from their offices, with no time or tolerance for drinking, unlike the professional commercial popular theater genre Special Drama with its flexible schedule, fixed drama season, and every-actor-for-himself organization, which is "better adapted to the vagaries of the alcoholic tide of an actor's life" (Seizer 2005, 61). Additionally, many sabhas such as Karthik Fine Arts, the Mylapore Fine Arts Club, Sri Parthasarathy Swami Sabha, Bharat Kalachar, Brahma Gana Sabha, and the Nataka Academy hold drama festivals at other times of the year (see figure 1.3 for an example) and honor the contributions of theater artists at those times, exonerating them from the necessity of including dramas in their festival schedule.

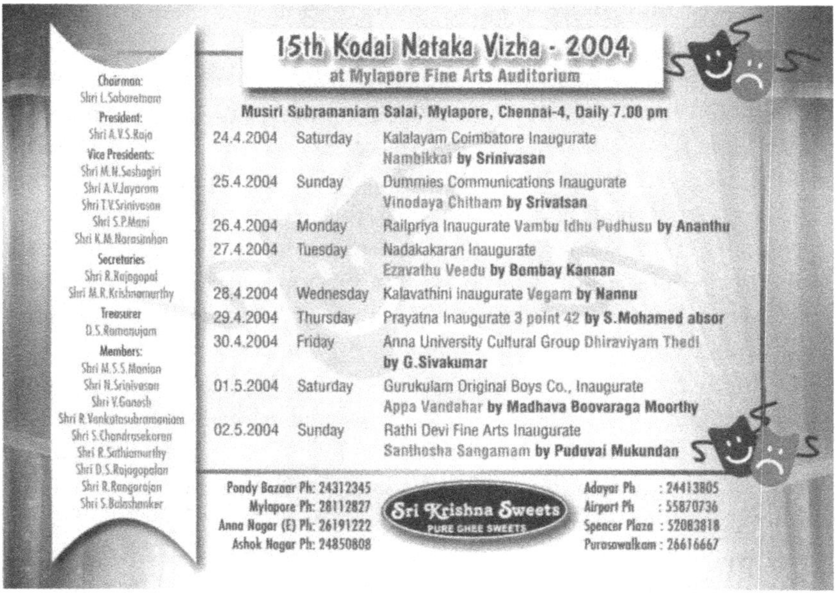

Figure 1.3. Schedule for the 15th Kodai Nataka Vizha at the Mylapore Fine Arts Auditorium, 2004. *Source*: Author's collection.

Kausalya Santhanam wrote an article in *The Hindu* in 2003 called "Is Drama Left Out of the Celebration?" It is a series of interviews with "a few leading names of Tamil theatre" to ascertain their views "not only on the status of Tamil theatre during the festival but also its position overall in the perception of the people, the sabha organizers, and State authorities." The responses of the artists to this question are diverse and closely related to the type of theater each one performs and to his (or her) level of popularity. R. S. Manohar, famous for his historical and mythological dramas complete with elaborate costumes and stage settings, and founder of what was previously one of the most popular troupes in the city, "can't understand why drama does not form part of the festival in a substantial measure." "Crazy" Mohan, an extremely popular "pure comedy" artist, on the other hand, spoke as an apologist for the sabhas' attention to music during the festival season: "Music concerts are held only during the December season while drama is staged throughout the year. Even during the season, quite a few sabhas host plays." He understands Manohar's viewpoint, but says that it is only certain types of plays that are not booked during the season: "Serious theatre and the classics may not appeal to everyone today in Tamil Nadu. . . . I feel it is in good taste to like humorous plays, it is a healthy trend. . . . So viewers come to the theatre to see something different [from the tragedy and conflict they can see in TV serials] and novel like [my plays] 'Jurassic Baby' or 'Crazy Ghosts.'" S. Ve. Shekher, whose genre and popularity are similar to Mohan's, agrees with him that "[s]ome sabhas honour drama artists regularly during the festival. In Chennai, the regular sabha is in fact only oriented to the music festival." Artists who perform plays that are more likely to appeal to visitors from outside of Chennai (N. Muthusamy, Bombay Gnanam) tended to side with Manohar in asserting that the sabhas need to do more to encourage drama during the season.

Another reason that the annual festival has featured mainly music and dance may be the fact that many critics and sabha leaders agree with critic K. N. Subramanyam (1967) that the quality of dramas in the city is very poor compared to the quality of music. Sabhas base their reputations on the classical music and dance performances they offer, and the festival is their opportunity to share that schedule with the world. Sabha plays are patronized by the same core elite audience as the classical arts, but are not interesting to the non-Tamil-speaking tourists who attend the festival and are willing to pay for tickets to individual performances.

Sabhas and Finances

Most sabha concerts are ticketed, which naturally limits access to those who can pay for either a membership or a ticket, but even the free events are primarily attended by Brahmins who consider themselves to be middle-class (see figure 1.4). Many sabhas only earn money from ticket sales during the music/dance festival season and are able to exist for the rest of the year on these earnings and their meager membership fees;[11] there are others that only exist during the festival season. The Priya Cultural Academy, in fact, no longer has any actual members. They used to have as many as three hundred, but now rely entirely on sponsors and gate collection. Even without members they are usually able to sponsor two shows a month, but that number varies with funds.[12]

When sabhas in Chennai first began sponsoring theater in the early 1930s, they worked with professional troupes who put on mythological and historical plays, modeled on the popular Parsi Theater of nineteenth- and twentieth-century Mumbai, with extravagant costumes, stage settings, props, spectacles, and songs.[13] Both sabha theater and Special Drama (see Seizer 2005) branched off from that professional drama company model.

Figure 1.4. Ticket from a performance of S. Ve. Shekher's *One More Exorcist* at the Kalaivanar Arangam, 2001. *Source*: Courtesy of S. Ve Shekher.

NARADA GANA SABHA (Regd.) CHENNAI - 600 018

Income & Expenditure a/c for the year ending 31st March 2003

	31-3-2003 Rs.	31-3-2002 Rs.
Income:		
Subscriptions	377,000.00	361,600.00
Gate Collections	36,610.00	14,645.00
Advertisement	3,000.00	6,000.00
Music Festival Receipts	1,686,991.00	1,382,381.00
Donations	12,975.00	15,000.00
Interest on Fixed Deposits	270,759.00	240,969.00
Misc. Receipts	230.00	0.00
	2,387,565.00	2,020,595.00
Expenditure:		
Remuneration to Artists	107,550.00	117,850.00
Hall Rent & Electricity Charges	185,500.00	162,000.00
Music Festival Expenses	1046,594.35	956,034.00
Publicity Charges	49,465.00	45,110.00
Printing and Stationery	41,697.95	34,313.00
Dance Lighting	2,400.00	5,150.00
Postage and Telegrams	31,588.00	30,326.00
Refreshments	6,220.00	7,217.00
Music Competition Awards	24,250.00	25,500.00
Music Competition Expenses	3,224.00	3,150.00
Volunteers	5,045.00	4,005.00
Pooja Expenses	5,600.00	5,850.00
Bank Charges	411.00	400.00
Endowment Prizes	14,610.00	14,085.00
Miscellaneous Expenses	6,242.00	1,813.50
Pension to Musicians	18,000.00	18,000.00
Depreciation	21,498.00	7,710.00
Donations for Cultural Endowments	400,000.00	1,00,000.00
Cultural Sponsorships	53,001.00	16,000.00
Photos	300.00	0.00
Salaries and Wages	25,085.00	13,775.00
	2,048,281.30	1,568,289.00
Excess of Income over Expenditure transferred to General Fund	339,283.70	452,306.00
	2,387,565.00	2,020,595.00

R. Krishnamoorthy
President

R. Surianarayanan
Honorary Treasurer

R. Krishnaswami
Hony. Secretary

Examined and found correct
For Fraser & Ross
K. N. Ramasubramanian
Partner
Chartered Accountants

22-06-2003
Chennai

25

Figure 1.5. Narada Gana Sabha Income and Expenditure Report for the year ending March 31, 2003. *Source*: Author's collection.

Sabha theater grew out of the work of Sambanda Mudaliyar, whose contribution "feeds that stream in Tamil drama of an elite, modern 'social' theater by and for middle-class society" (Seizer 2005, 54) while Special Drama developed into a "regionally attuned form[s] of 'hybrid theatre' that [is] neither purely commercial nor ritual, neither urban or rural; they are, rather, both" (Seizer 2009, 85–86). This is Seizer's fifth stage of Tamil modern drama development, where hybrid forms like Special Drama and Kattaikkuttu[14] (which she refers to as Music Drama) "inaugurate a reverse trajectory to the usual teleological story of the progress of modernity in South Asia" (Seizer 2009, 85) and challenge the urban middle-class's ownership of "modern theater." The Mudaliyar model, where amateur, middle-class performers put up Tamil translations of Shakespeare and plays about contemporary social issues on evenings and weekends, sharply contrasted with the Sankaradas Swamigal model that inspired Special Drama, where the artists are professionals and the plays based on puranic and court themes. Dheepa Sundaram's work on the Tamil "protest" theater in the late colonial period provides an example of a genre that is an interesting hybrid of these two models, and which evolved into the Dravidian political plays of the post-Independence period, with which sabha plays are occasionally in conversation.

It was sabha theater, Farley Richmond argues, and not the film industry, that "hastened the demise of the old-style commercial theatre of Madras" (1990, 431), which had dominated proscenium stages in Chennai in the early twentieth century. Mudaliyar eliminated or greatly reduced most of the markers of the professional theater such as music, elaborate trick sets and stage properties, and spectacular costumes. This was done in an attempt to compensate for the not-so-respectable reputation of professional theater artists by distinguishing his troupe and their productions from those of the professionals in every way possible, including style, content, language, sets, and costumes, but also had the effect of being far cheaper to produce.

The professional companies became increasingly expensive to run, and most had folded by the end of the 1940s, unable to compete financially with the new cheap amateur productions and therefore unable to attract the necessary sponsorship of sabhas.[15] Their mythological and historical extravaganzas had given way to low-budget amateur comedy plays concentrating more on dialogue and plot in the style of western theater by the early 1950s. The film industry was also a factor, and there was a surge of films during the 1940s and 1950s that borrowed stories, techniques, and actors from the popular theater and also included excellent music and dance performances.[16] Films cost less for individual audience members to attend, but received more return on investment than the stage plays since the films could be distributed all over the state and played simultaneously in multiple theaters. Today's sabha plays take pains to distinguish themselves from film, as the following joke beautifully demonstrates. In this sequence from Cho Ramasamy's 1964 *Mind Is a Monkey*, film producer Jagadish pitches his film to Malathi, whom he wants to be his heroine, and Gopinath, her upper-class drama director friend. Gopinath's voice is dripping with sarcasm and Jagadish's with enthusiasm:

> JAGA: *Sir!* Listen to the story. It is a rare and wonderful story. There is a woodcutter. . . . it's a very modern story . . . A poor woodcutter.
>
> GOPI: A poor woodcutter . . . very modern *type*.
>
> JAGA: The woodcutter cuts wood.
>
> GOPI: Tso! Tso!
>
> JAGA: I haven't started any more of the story. This is only the opening *scene*, then there is one good song.
>
> GOPI: Really!
>
> JAGA: He is continuously cutting wood—one crow flies by—immediately he sings:
>
> "He created the wood;
> He created me to cut the wood.
> He created the wings;
> Who did he create to cut the wings?"
>
> GOPI: Wonderful, *Sir*! What an *idea* . . . what an *idea*! Good theme. Yes, what is the *role* for her? The woodcutter, the wood, or the crow?

JAGA: Wait, *Sir*, you're a fine one! He went to the woodcutting shed. He cuts wood in that woodcutting shed.

GOPI: Does the crow fly?

JAGA: No; the *heroine* comes. He cuts a piece of wood. One chip flies. It falls on her. She turns and looks. The woodcutter then has an *idea*! This man stands here; she stands there. In the middle there is a balance scale; one plate is touching the ground. He has an axe in his hand. What? Do you understand the meaning?

GOPI: How? . . . How?

JAGA: We show the balance. One plate is standing touching the ground. This man has an axe in his hand.

GOPI: *Oh*! Okay, this is just Tamil *cinema*. He stands holding an axe in his hand thinking, "Should I put this on the scale, or not?"

JAGA: No, no. Society's habit is to weigh people into rich and poor. We will show how to cut that.

GOPI: *Oh! I see!*

JAGA: Listen to the story.

GOPI: Won't you leave it?

JAGA: The woodcutter will see the *heroine*. Love!—a *drama scene*.

GOPI: Will they see and just stand?

JAGA: Yes—modern *type*. He will stand on one plate of the balance; this girl on the other plate. Balance *dance*.

GOPI: Good *idea*—I understand. You are showing that for a man to be like a Tamil *cinema hero*, he needs to stand in a balance perfectly for the weight of the Tamil *cinema hero*. Right?

JAGA: No *sir*! There is no difference between the poor man and the rich man. We are showing that. *Duet* song. The story goes that way. There is good *scope* for the *heroine*—the dialogue is written by our Samikkan. That is "Compromise" Samikkan. The dialogue is full of good themes. Her *dialogue* is very good.

GOPI: Listen—Malathi! Here is the *dialogue* you need to speak.

JAGA: Listen—looking at the woodcutter she will say—and this is a good theme—"he may be a woodcutter—it may be a woodshed—there will be wood . . . to boil the marriage rice you need the marriage fire: for the marriage fire the wood of friendship is necessary." You, Malathi, are that wood, and that is the woodcutter!

(Malathi is astonished.) (trans. Rudisill 2002, 54–56 from Ramasamy 1997)

There are several levels of criticism about films embedded within this sequence. First, the film producer thinks his story is rare, wonderful, and modern, but it is clearly none of those things. There is very little of it developed at this point, as he has only the first scene, but he thinks it's really deep; Gopi laughs at him. It's full of symbolism that is at once obtruse and too literal, which is an impressive balance in itself. The film has barely started and already there are two songs and a dance with a gimmick. Also, the hero and heroine fall in love the second they see each other. And the crow seems to exist only for the literalism of the first song. The implication is that sabha plays offer something different (and better) than the gimmicks, song-and-dance sequences, haphazard planning, and overly literal symbolism of film.

Actors also make a distinction that favors those who act in theater over those who work in film. This is ironic because many of them act in both mediums, so it is sort of a criticism of themselves. It is certainly difficult for actors to perform in film and theater simultaneously due to the uncertainty of film shooting schedules and the need to commit to times and dates for live theater, but many of them manage. Many more will do work for television, which has a relatively regular schedule compared to film and is less likely to conflict with evening theater performances. It is true that film or television scenes can always be shot again and that they are done in short takes that require very little memorization. In fact, they require no knowledge of Tamil since an actor can memorize one line at a time for the camera or actually have the voice dubbed in later by someone else. The true amateur theater actors who work for a bank or the railways during the day do not have time for more than the occasional play, but actors who are trying to make a living need to work in the better-paying mass media industries to do so. Live theater is still a stepping stone to those industries, although not nearly on the scale that it used to be, for example in 1965, when K. Balachander moved his focus from theater to film and provided the opportunity for many sabha actors to perform on the big screen. The other contrasts Brahmins draw between sabha theater and popular film are often based on differences in the perceived audiences of the two forms.

Sabha plays also distinguished themselves from company dramas. In an interview with S. Gopalie, Karthik Rajagopal, former secretary of the Mylapore Fine Arts Club and founder of Karthik Fine Arts, told a story about the professional theater troupe T. K. S. Brothers.[17] The troupe, related Rajagopal, demanded higher and bigger stages from the sabhas in order to accommodate large sets and stage properties, then canceled all sabha shows when told this wasn't possible. As a representative of the sabhas, Rajagopal says that this incident "opened our eyes. And at this moment Y. G. Parthasarathy with his partner Pattu the playwright, K. Balachander, [V. S.] Raghavan, and others came forward to do plays right in our Sabha premises." For the sabhas, he continued, these new artists were "most convenient in financial terms and what the amateurs gave us was absolutely fresh to our audience, that is our members" (Gopalie 2002, 375, 376). These amateur troupes keep their overheads low with minimalist requirements for salary, costumes, and staging, and can afford to appeal to only a small cross-section of the population in the city,[18] unlike the elaborate professional performances[19] or expensive ventures such as film and television, which are popular with broader audiences.

Considering the financial pressures faced by sabhas, it is important for them to promote the shows that can earn them the most money. Jon Higgins, an ethnomusicologist and Carnatic musician, wrote in 1976 that "[a] threefold increase in the number of sabhas in Madras within the past fifteen to twenty years has heightened the competition to produce performances which will draw the biggest receipts. The effect upon classical music is predictable concerts are gradually being replaced in sabhas by premiere screenings of new Tamil films and the ubiquitous social drama (the South Indian equivalent of North America's afternoon TV soap-serials). Faced with angry criticism from the minority of music lovers, a sabha secretary simply shrugs his shoulders with the standard disclaimer: 'It's what the public wants' " (22–23). The implication, of course, is that the "ubiquitous social drama(s)" (what I am calling sabha dramas) that the public "wants" are clearly inferior to the classical music that the public "should" appreciate and support. Sabhas need to maintain their financial viability and therefore tend to sponsor entertainments that the public "wants" and will pay money for. In 1976, before the advent of the television serial in India, sabha dramas attracted far more viewers than they do today and were quite lucrative for sabhas to stage.

In contemporary Chennai, however, the financial incentive has reversed: it is more financially rewarding for sabhas to support the classical arts than even the comedy plays of sabha theater. Only a very few drama troupes are popular enough to attract the public and earn gate collection for the sabha. The sabhas' expenses are high, especially for those who rent the big air-conditioned halls for the evening, even though they may pay little for the actual performances. Sabhas may "sponsor" music and dance performances, but that does not necessarily mean that they pay money to the artists for their work. Because Chennai performances provide so much cultural capital and the city is such a desirable place for artists to perform, many sabhas have either reduced or eliminated remuneration for artists. There are so many excellent classical performers in the city, especially during the music season when they travel there from all over the world, that it is impossible for the sabhas to attract viewers—and therefore funding—for them all.

This trend of "insufficient honoraria," in Janet O'Shea's words, has led to what some call "a stagnation" in the Chennai cultural landscape where " 'newcomers' don't get a platform to perform—unless they are prepared to turn their pockets inside out and let their money do the talking" (P. Dhananjayan, quoted in Muthalaly 2003a). This is the situation hinted at in the joke that opened the introduction to this book, where Cho Ramasamy's character of a sabha secretary gets all his family's medical treatment for free and requests expensive electronics from the doctor's trip abroad simply because he is promising to someday set a date for the doctor's eight-year-old daughter's classical dance debut in his sabha. The more established sabhas have boxes filled with elaborate applications from dancers and musicians who are willing to pay ("make a donation") to be placed on their performance schedules. These performers spend incredible amounts of money to print colorful booklets with their biodata, photographs, and previous performances and wait for sabhas to contact them.

The result of this trend is that many talented artists in the city never get a chance to perform. In order to compete with the financial advantage of international artists, many Chennai-based artists "supplement intracity concerts with outside ones, frequently turning to the better-paying international venues to support their career in Chennai because of the discrepancy between their payment policies and those of their Chennai counterparts" (O'Shea 2007, 156). Without reliable funding, Chennai continually presents the same performers to its audiences, leading to a decline in attendance. The hope that many of the local performers hold is that if the audiences won't pay, perhaps corporate sponsors will. The trouble with this idea is that if there is no proof of demand and a guaranteed audience, companies won't spend the money to sponsor performances, wanting a higher return for their advertising dollars. So again, the cycle continues and the big-name performers can both attract corporate sponsors and sell tickets, but everyone else—in music, dance, and theater—struggles.

The financial problems clearly affect all the arts promoted by the sabhas. Shonali Muthalaly's October 23, 2003, article "Fine Arts, But No Future?" in *The Hindu* highlighted some of the funding issues for promoters of the arts that apply equally well to sabhas as to the Marga Festival she is discussing. An organization called "Marga" put together a three-day festival for the "unrecognized cultural treasures of dance, theatre, and music" in Chennai, but hardly got anyone to come to the Bharatiya Vidya Bhavan show. Muthalaly laments that this poor turnout was "in spite of the fact that the organizers roped in an array of talented performers at a considerable expense, ensured that the show was professionally executed with dramatic lighting, powerful orchestras and lavish costumes and set it all in an air-conditioned, comfortable auditorium located in Chennai's cultural heart, Mylapore." The reasons for this problem are many, and the audience is both partly responsible for and negatively affected by the trend. Most programs organized by sabhas, especially classical music or dance programs during the non-festival season, are not ticketed. The members, of course, have paid their annual fees and can attend, but these events are also open to the general public and do not require those attendees to purchase tickets unless it is a big-name performer. The reason for this is that, as Dhananjayan, a well-known Bharata Natyam teacher and performer in Chennai, laments in the same article, "People are unwilling to buy tickets in Chennai. This is a sad situation existing only here" (in Muthalaly 2003a). Someone, however, has to pay for these performances.

Although many amateur classical musicians and dancers are willing to fund their own performances to build resumes, get exposure, or have an outlet for their years of training, this is not often the case for amateur theater troupes, though it is becoming more common. Usually an unknown troupe will fund one performance of a new play themselves to which they will invite the sabha secretaries and the press, hoping to get some good reviews and shows booked for the rest of the year. They are, however, amateurs, and most do not expect to earn money from their drama performances. They are aiming only to not operate at a loss, though many will make up financial shortcomings with money earned at their regular jobs at the bank, railway station, or small business. Krishnamoorthy of Dummies Drama described these difficulties, saying that "[a]t a time when there is a lack of interest in theatre, we find it necessary to have innovations on stage with lights, sets and projections. Every time we think creativity, we are forced to think of cost. We spend thousands of rupees and find it difficult to break even merely through gate collections" (Narayan 2004).

It is unlikely that sabhas will pay theater practitioners in Chennai more for their performances, so although artists are distressed by the lack of audiences, they don't have any financial motivation to alter their style or humor in order to appeal to broader audiences. Kathadi Ramamurthy told me that his plays generally run a deficit of a few hundred rupees per performance, and he draws many more people to the theater than most troupes, which must operate at even bigger deficits.

Shri Srinivasan of Kala Niketan, a north Chennai sabha, discussed with S. Gopalie his hesitation to book the plays of Y. G. Parthasarathy or Cho Ramasamy because of the excessive use of English in their plays. This is an indirect reference to the Brahmin orientation of the plays, since members of that community are usually highly educated in English-medium private schools. Srinivasan says that "it is all right with the Mylapore, T. Nagar, Triplicane audiences. But North Madras audiences believed in pure, unadulterated Tamil."[20] The Mylapore sabhas were assured that their members would attend all sorts of plays, be they Brahmin- or film-star-oriented, and the legacy of that is that most amateur plays were then and are now inaugurated by Karthik Fine Arts at the Mylapore Fine Arts Club. The north Chennai sabhas are much more cautious, waiting to book a play until it has been proven to be a success in south Chennai. Kala Niketan's Srinivasan says,

> [w]e never sponsored any Tamil amateur play on our own. Our principle was different. Let the amateur inaugurate and do [the] first few shows anywhere. We will watch and discuss. If the amateur's play is acceptable to us, we invite the group and we fix the fee.
>
> If it is a group with a film star, we give what the other sabhas offer. Here again the remuneration may vary. We believe in gate collection, and if it is not good we do not encourage such groups. (Gopalie 2002, 37)

This attitude was severely criticized by many, including playwright Venkat, who blames it for the plight of Tamil theater today, saying that "business-men Sabha secretaries,"

> booked popular plays of Crazy Mohan, S. Ve. Shekher, Cho, why even R. S. Manohar, and made money. They never bothered to encourage up and coming, struggling playwrights. . . . If there had been organizations to put up only plays, theatre would have taken roots. But only Sabha secretaries grew up, made money, bought cars and homes. Theatre never grew. It is my feeling that the sabha secretaries earned more than Cho and Manohar.[21]

This image of the self-serving sabha secretary out to earn money through performances is contrary to the principles of most sabhas, as any money earned through gate collection should ideally be reinvested in the organization by the secretaries or donated to a worthy cause. Sabha secretaries are usually elected by the general membership for fixed-term appointments and can gain the popularity necessary for re-election by using profits to procure better performances for the following season or to do charity work, a heavily publicized objective of many organizations (see figure 1.6 for a photograph of S. Ve. Shekher at his fiftieth blood donation).[22] Additionally, sabhas are now registered under the 1975 Tamilnadu Soci-

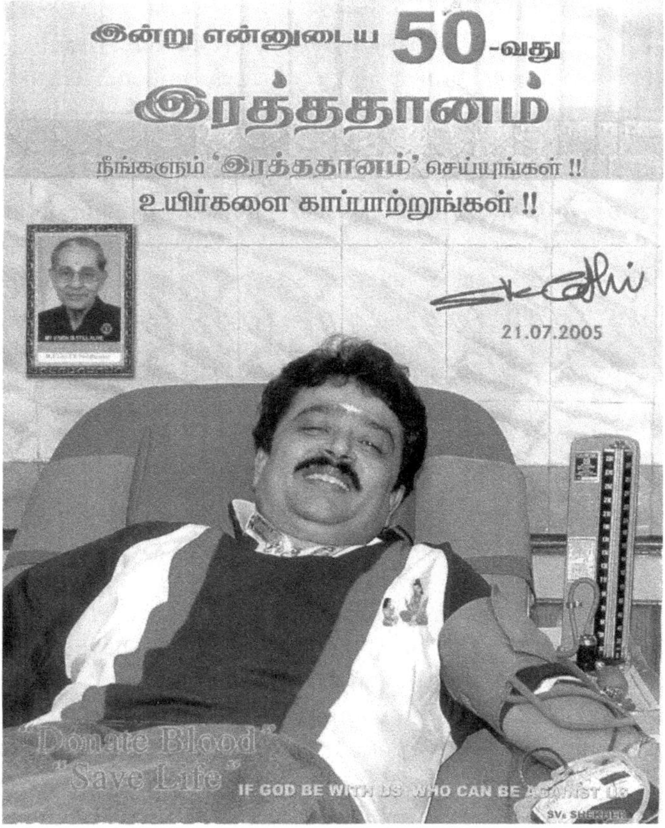

Figure 1.6. Photograph of S. Ve. Shekher at his fiftieth blood donation. *Source*: Courtesy of S. Ve. Shekher.

eties Registration Act, which explicitly forbids members and officers from receiving bonuses, dividends, honoraria, or other payment for service (see Government of Tamilnadu, Chapter 3, section 25).

One of the major issues faced by sabhas and amateur artists alike over the years has been that of remuneration. How much should each group be paid per play? Should it vary by sabha or troupe or what? The sabhas are of different sizes, some with very small memberships, some with large; some theaters have air conditioning, while others make do with fans and poorly working generators. If there is a large hall to pay for, can they fill it for one show? For two shows? Will they be able to sell any tickets outside their members? Could they partner with another sabha to sponsor the show? How many actors are in the troupe? How elaborate and expensive are their sets and costumes? How many professional female actresses do they need to pay? Can they accept part of their payment in the form of tickets to the performance? All of these factors need to be considered in order to make the performance, if not a winning, at least not a losing proposition for either troupe or sponsor.

Discrepancies and in-fighting about appropriate remuneration prompted the founding of the Federation of City Sabhas and the Association of City Sabhas. The idea behind these organizations, which soon combined, was to "fix fees and regulate theater."[23] The sabha secretaries would convene after the initial performance of a new play held for this express purpose and after deciding whether or not to add a play to what quickly became known as "the sabha circuit," would fix the fee for a performance of that play. This fee could be difficult for smaller sabhas to pay, and their failure to do so was part of what led to the collapse of the organization. Another major problem was that many actors and troupe leaders (notably Komal Swaminathan) accused the sabhas of being arbitrary and believed that they should be paid more. The Federation no longer serves the function of fixing standard fees, but the website does list current objectives, which involve things like education, funding performances, collecting books and recordings, providing scholarships, organizing lectures and discussions, publishing, and teaching. Overall, "with the ever-changing needs of institutions and persons involved in the arts, the Federation hopes to create and maintain a conducive atmosphere for the propagation and growth of Indian Arts and Culture" (citysabhas.org).

Because of the sabhas' almost exclusive access to resources and performance spaces, the predominantly Brahmin middle-class members of the sabhas have dictated the style and content of the popular Tamil drama over the past seventy years. The sabhas' position was that the troupes should be appreciative of any remuneration at all since acceptance onto the circuit provided exposure for their work by guaranteeing the troupe around seventy performances throughout the city for a play. This type of exposure is no longer available. Gopalie writes that "[b]etween the years 1965–1985 one can choose from a dozen plays in an evening. But that dwindled from 1980 onwards. The reasons are far too many. The sabhas dwindled from a little over a hundred to a mere dozen."[24] What this means is that today, a popular troupe with an extensive active repertory, like S. Ve. Shekher's Natakhapriya or Crazy Mohan's Crazy Creations, will perform around six to ten plays a month,[25] but the majority of troupes are lucky to get ten sponsored performances over the course of a year. V. Sreevatson, whose Dummies Communications was five years old at the time, with one play inaugurated each year, told me in an interview in 2003 that if they couldn't get ten sponsored shows in a year they would sponsor some themselves in order to reach that number.

Distinction, Motivation, and Audience/Performer Status

One reason that sabhas are willing to operate at a loss for certain performances is that they consider themselves to be doing a service to the art and to the community by sponsoring quality artists. Critics and sabhas are to some extent both instruments of the Brahmin community and as such consciously consider part of their agenda to be to raise the level of taste in the city. Many Tamil journals, including *Āṉanta Vikaṭan*, *Kalki*, *Bharata Mani*, and *Kaveri* had regular columns of music criticism by the 1930s and 1940s. "It was the responsibility of the music critic . . . to help ignorant audiences develop their 'taste' in music" (Weidman 2006, 84). Sabhas have been associated with the classical arts from the beginning of the twentieth century, and these arts are firmly at the top of the accepted hierarchy of available entertainments in Chennai, especially Carnatic music.

Pierre Bourdieu's argument about "distinction" is helpful in considering sabha plays, but does not answer several key questions, even taking into account the rule that the status of a performance art and the status of the class of the patrons of an art are reciprocal. The status of an art is raised by attracting high-class patrons *and* people can raise their status by preferring art that is accepted as "high-brow." In Bourdieu's view, "[n]othing more clearly affirms one's 'class,' nothing more infallibly classifies, than tastes in music. This is of course because, by virtue of the rarity of the conditions for acquiring the corresponding dispositions, there is no more 'classifactory' practice than concert-going or playing a 'noble' instrument . . ." (1984, 18). Bourdieu sees music as the most "pure" of all the arts because it is the most personal and internalized. The idea is that while people can learn to appreciate different kinds of music, there will always be some that touch them more than others, and this personal preference, as a function of many internalized characteristics, most notably educational level and social class, is difficult to change. For Bourdieu, nothing classifies more than taste in music, which allows for infinite social distinctions due to its numerous divisions and sub-divisions marked by genre, period, style, artist, and so on, and is, he argues, not as inextricably tied to the aesthetic and political as a necessarily social art like theater. Music, an art he views as representing "the most radical and most absolute form of the negation of . . . the social world" is therefore least likely to contaminate determinations of how classifications of art are linked to taste as a way of marking the hierarchical classifications of people (Bourdieu 1984, 18–19).

Bourdieu contrasted music, whose consumption he saw as an individual predilection, to theater, which has a social message and only works when it has "an immediate and profound affinity with the values and expectations of its audience" (1984, 19). This is, of course, an overly simplistic view of both arts. Music making and consumption are often political and communal, while theater audience members can have individualized and even contradictory experiences of a performance. Additionally, it is not the case that all theatrical performances need live audiences; Stuart Blackburn's excellent book on the lack of audiences for shadow puppet performances is only one example. These exceptions do not render Bourdieu's contentions useless, however, especially in the case of something like sabha theater, which is especially bound to the values and expectations of its insider community, in both form and content. Identification with the insider community takes place in a viewer's imagination, and comedy can seamlessly confirm or contradict that person's belonging. Stuart Hall writes that identities are "the product of the marking of difference and exclusion . . . identities can function as points of identification and attachment only *because* of their capacity to exclude, to leave out, to render 'outside,' 'abject' " (1996, 4). Andy Medhurst relates a story demonstrating the power of comedy in this regard: he was at a comedy show (Roy "Chubby" Brown) and the audience laughed at a joke referencing AIDS, which made him realize he was uneasy and "feeling excluded, being targeted as the object of communal ridicule, being informed that I was a queer interloper in an overwhelmingly heterosexual environment" (Medhurst 2007, 25). The immediate feedback of these moments of unease at a joke or simply not understanding why it's funny mark the boundaries of the insider community.

Sabha theater is thus an excellent tool for learning more about the tastes of the Tamil Brahmin community and the distinctions that it makes between itself and others, even if part of that distinction is explicitly linked to musical taste within the sabha system. Classical Carnatic music, as complex as it is, can be appreciated on many levels and is more accessible to outsiders than sabha theater, as it is bound by neither language nor culturally based humor (as evidenced by the growing trend of sabhas without memberships, dependent solely on ticket sales, usually functioning only during the music season). Following Medhurst, I argue that the theater, bound to the strictures of the tastes of the local Tamil Brahmin community that are made visible through the humor, is a better measure of that community and its generalized notions of good taste than the music.

Rather than being an art based on tradition, like Carnatic music, sabha theater is dependent upon the desires of the current membership. Some plays have remained popular through the years while others have gone out of vogue entirely or had to be updated. In the process, the plays reveal continuities and changes in the themes and jokes that have been considered funny by the core Tamil Brahmin community in different time periods. Recent themes include consumerism, globalization, and the rise of the IT industry in Chennai, while earlier plays were more likely to include reference to joint families, dowry, and the importance of horoscopes. My project differs from Bourdieu's in that rather than trying to determine how a wide range of tastes reflects many different economic and social classes, I am trying to determine the boundaries of acceptable tastes within a narrow elite community. For this project, it is not the "pure" musical selections, but the "contaminated" theatrical (and even more specifically comedic) selections that by definition resonate with the values and expectations of that community, that reveal the most about the sabhas' (and through them the broader Tamil Brahmin community's) idea of good taste.

Bourdieu has divided musical genres into three "zones of taste," which he finds "roughly correspond to educational levels and social classes" (1984, 16). The zone that is the most "classifying," as he puts it, is "legitimate" taste (as opposed to "middle-brow" and "popular") because preference for works in this category is highest "in those fractions of the dominant class that are richest in educational capital" (13–18). Carnatic music, as a "legitimate" art, is very scientific and exact (notwithstanding the wide scope for improvisation), and therefore best appreciated by connoisseurs (listeners educated in its system).

Two of the stereotypical characteristics of these connoisseur sabha audiences are silence and discipline. In 1944 P. Sambamoorthy wrote an essay titled "Our Concert Programme: Some Underlying Principles," which advised performers and audience members about proper behavior at a concert. Amanda Weidman quoted him as saying, "members of the audience should particularly take care that they do not talk with each other or become restless, when the tambura or some other instrument is being tuned. Nor should a member of an audience make an entry or exit during the middle of an item" (Weidman 2006, 83). She has also drawn attention to a 1940 *Āṉanta Vikaṭan* cartoon that illustrated the discipline expected of classical music audiences, saying that they should not come late, cough or sneeze, talk noisily, or bring crying children. As Weidman's analysis of an advertisement for a water pump that promises "music hall silence" demonstrates, the space of the concert hall was ideally an awe-inspiring place, set apart from other spaces. The over-explanations, however, indicate that the silence and discipline of audiences were a far-from-realized ideal. The connoisseurs of Carnatic music distinguish themselves from listeners of "vulgar" folk or film music in the same way that Bourdieu's sample of Parisians who prefer the *Well-Tempered Clavier* do. So with regard to music, Bourdieu's classifications and ideas, from the context of twentieth-century Paris, are applicable in today's class-conscious Chennai. The picture, however, is much more complicated with regards to theater. Since sabhas are usually joined on the basis of their music selection, the plays have little effect on the perceived cultural status of the viewers. The dramas, which are not considered classical or high-brow, are offered for a different reason, which I discuss in the next chapter.

The Carnatic-music sabha audiences may not meet the ideal of silence, but the drama audiences most certainly are even further from that model, though it is the cinema audiences that are notorious. K. S. Rajendran wrote that Kalki, in his weekly column "Drama Āṭal Pāṭal" ("Drama, Dance, Song") in *Āṉanta Vikaṭan,* which contained performance accounts of Tamil popular dramas from the early 1920s, described in great detail "[t]he noisy auditorium full of women with children, drunkards and lumpen elements of those days."[26] I did not notice any drunkards during the course of my fieldwork, but I did find a new annoyance in the ubiquitous mobile phone. I kept count of the phones that rang loudly at each performance and found it to be an average of ten or twelve, but on occasion I heard more than twenty over the course of a two-hour play. Several times I heard people answer their phones and carry on personal conversations at a volume that drowned out the actors on stage. S. Ve. Shekher, improviser that he is, made a joke on stage that called out the offender; Y. G. Mahendran actually stopped his play and reprimanded a young man from the stage. Crazy Mohan mentioned the constantly ringing cell phones to me before a show of his in Houston in November of 2004, expressing his distaste for the disrespectful Chennai audience members as opposed to the polite, attentive American ones who "concentrate and enjoy the jokes." Never once, however, did I hear a pre-performance announcement to turn them off, though that was standard at all the non-sabha plays I attended in Chennai.

The audiences may not be trying to improve themselves, but many will watch the plays with some of the same connoisseurship that they bring to the classical arts, evaluating them on such criteria as creativity, timing, execution of jokes, and quality of acting and production. While there are new plays every year, many of those presented on Chennai's stages are favorites from previous years. I found that audiences often know the dialogue by heart either from seeing a play performed many times, seeing the televised or film version, or listening to the audiocassette recording of the dialogue (see figure 1.7). With the exception of new plays, nearly everyone at least knows the story in advance of viewing the play in the theater. This makes it difficult for first-time viewers to follow the jokes, because audience members anticipate them and laugh *before* they are told. Part of the appeal of the cassettes and, in turn, of repeated viewings of the live performances, is that one picks up new things with each hearing.

Sabha theater audiences tend to notice differences in performances such as updated jokes, improvisations, and asides. These are what make each performance a special, unique experience, and the audiences notice and appreciate the effort and expertise. Even so, there is debate within the community concerning the plays, one side of which suggests that they are actually detrimental to both the art of drama and the psyches of the audience members. The merit of individual performers of classical music and dance may be debated, but never the status or inherent value of the genre itself. Although the sabha audience may define itself as high class based on its musical choices, its theatrical choices contribute to the sabha's identity in a different way. Rather than being based on tradition, the theater it presents is dependent upon the desires of the current audience (that is, membership).

It is very difficult to talk about something as nebulous as taste and the reasons why certain types of music or performance or visual art appeal to different people. There are so many factors that go into determining an individual's taste, including upbringing, education, age, gender, and economic status, that it is difficult to pinpoint any one thing to explain entertainment tastes. The sabhas are a particularly fruitful place to study the combination of entertainments that constitute "legitimate" good taste (in Bourdieu's sense) in Chennai because the community that belongs to these organizations is in actuality quite homogenous.[27]

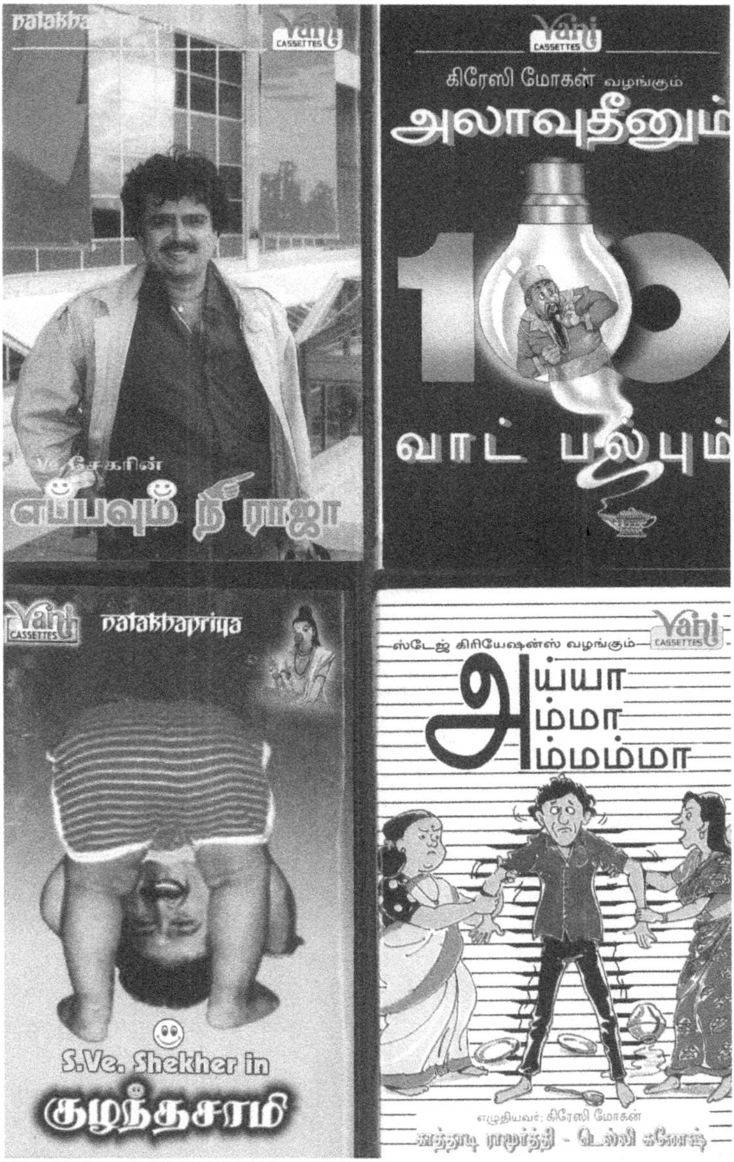

Figure 1.7. Audiocassette covers of S. Ve. Shekher's *Eppavum Nī Rājā* (*You Are Always a King*) (top left), Crazy Mohan's *Alāvutīṉum 100 Vātt Palpum* (*Aladdin and the 100 Watt Bulb*) (top right), S. Ve. Shekher's *Kuḻantacāmi* (*Child Guy*) (bottom left), and Stage Creations' *Ayya, Amma, Ammamma* (*Father, Mother, Grandmother*) (bottom right). *Source*: Author's collection.

In this book, I expand ideas about the taste of that Brahmin community by looking not to the respected and traditional classical arts, but to the humor of sabha theater. Susan Seizer has moved in a valuable direction with her work on village comedy, successfully convincing her readers "that humor is a good site for the study of culture" (2005, 21). I take this one step further and argue that more than being a *good* site for studying culture, humor is one of the best. It offers insights into identity construction without the added complication of conferring status on the observer. Sabha theater in particular assumes that the observers already have high status, so the plays take that for granted and make jokes that reveal the inconsistencies inherent in it, such as the joke about basketball that opened this chapter. Participating as a performer or audience member in classical performances allows individuals to partake of the symbolic cultural power associated with them. This reputation for good taste and social status that they thus enjoy may or may not represent their actual taste or financial situation.

Decline

The number of sabhas that sponsor Tamil-language plays has drastically declined in number since the 1980s. All of the theater personalities I interviewed noticed that there are far fewer sabhas now than in the past, and much discussion and debate in the field revolves around the reason for this decline, attributing it to such factors as the rise of television; the overcrowding of the city and subsequent transportation difficulties; and the stabilization of Tamil politics into a virtual two-party system, where both parties are Dravidian in origin and thus both court the Brahmin vote, making anti-Brahmin rhetoric obsolete and negating the need to combat it. Part of what gives the sabha theater its strength and perseverance also restricts its growth and appeal: it targets a limited audience and relies on insider humor.

I studied *The Hindu* events listings from 1992 and found eighty-four sabhas that regularly sponsored dramas,[28] two troupes that sponsored their own dramas,[29] nine organizations that sponsored a drama as a one-time special event,[30] and several other groups that sponsored non-Tamil-language dramas (in English, Gujarati, Malayalam, and Sanskrit).[31] In 2004, however, there were only forty-two sabhas (fully *half* of what there was in 1992) regularly sponsoring Tamil dramas[32] and two special events open to the public,[33] but nine troupes now sponsored their own plays on occasion[34] and the number of English-language dramas in Chennai had significantly increased.[35] There is a new website called "Music of Madras" that has listings of music, theater, and dance in the city. I looked at all available data from January 2019–January 2020 and found that out of 263 listed sabhas, only twenty-six are sponsoring dramas (down 40% from 2004 and less than 10% of the total), so that number is continuing to drop.[36] Another seven are the troupes themselves or trusts in their name that are sponsoring shows.[37] English dramas are still well represented, along with one French play. Koothu-p-pattarai is also very active, even after the 2018 death of founder N. Muthusamy (see Ramaswamy 2001 for more on this troupe). Across all three years, businesses, schools, and temples continue to organize one-off performances for employees, students, or the public on special occasions, and these shows may take place in more remote areas of the city.[38]

It is important to note that while sabha theater is declining, it is not "dead" as so many intellectuals and journalists in the city claim. The relevance of these plays to an educated, middle-class audience both in India and the diaspora is ample proof of their importance, and while the dedication of artists and enthusiasts may not lead to a revival, it certainly indicates a continuation of live Tamil-language sabha theater in Chennai. Another sign is the entrance of new troupes into the field, as many of the older artists retire or die.[39]

S. Ve. Shekher told me that back when there were 170 sabhas it was hard for new groups to break in. His strategy was to skip the sabhas and go straight to the public through the press and then use popular demand to get onto the sabha circuit (Author interview, May 12, 2004). This seems counterintuitive, that it would be difficult for that many sabhas to fill their schedules with quality performances, which is exactly the argument that K. N. Subramanyam used to explain why sabhas began sponsoring dramas in the first place in the 1930s. In an article he wrote for the *Sangeet Natak Akademi Journal* in 1967, Subramanyam said that "by the end of the thirties, the *sabhas*, being unable to command a regular supply of good music, began to patronize plays and theatre troupes, both amateur and professional" (34). He then went on to say that

> [i]n nearly 25 years, the *sabha* approach to entertainment of an evening has entrenched itself in the consciousness of the middle-class audience, which, while it was familiar with good

> music, was not familiar with good drama. It mistook any entertainment on the stage as worthwhile and often compared even a tolerably good drama with a bad film and began to find it wanting. So that under the patronage of the *sabhas*, the film stars were vicariously called on to act in plays and those who acted in plays to large audiences, hoped for cinema chances sooner or later. Bad art flourished and is flourishing under and [in the] guise of the popular. (1967, 34)

The dramas, unlike the classical performances, rarely attracted any academic attention or critical acclaim, which worked both for and against them. Because sabhas depend on their reputations to attract members, most were hesitant about adding dramas to their performance schedules. However, as the plays attract little critical attention, especially compared to the financial gains, they do little to damage those reputations and have proved instrumental in raising the funds necessary for other initiatives.

The Hamsadhwani Sabha, founded by the late R. Ramachandran, operates out of Adyar (which, like neighboring Besant Nagar, is an area of the city with a high percentage of Brahmin residents). Ramachandran told Fuller and Narasimhan that he was unable to involve non-Brahmins in the organization because "they just assumed it had nothing to do with them" (2014, 207). The sabha holds performances on the outdoor stage of the Youth Hostel and continued with only classical music for thirty years. It is unusual because in 2003 the organization, at the request of its members, chose to include the occasional play in their annual schedule. Instead of sponsoring plays on that year's sabha circuit, however, Hamsadhwani chose to sponsor single performances and revive several classics from the 1960s such as Cāvi's *Washingtonil Tirumaṇam* (*Wedding in Washington*) and Raadhu's *Kalyāṇattil Kalāṭṭā* (*Marriage Fiasco*). They fixed the remuneration separately with the troupes for these one-time performances of old favorites that would be certain to draw crowds. These individual negotiations can be much simpler than those, discussed earlier, that take place with new plays.

The decline in the number of sabha plays performed in Chennai is usually attributed to television, which was becoming accessible and popular at the time the decline started (the popular Doordarshan *Ramayana* serial, for example, aired in 1987), and has also been linked to a financial recession in the Bombay film industry in the 1980s (see Mankekar 1999). Many sabhas, in fact, had to change their drama schedules to accommodate television's film schedule. Once films were showing on Saturdays and Sundays, many dramas moved to the Friday evening time slot, good writers and actors moved to the television and film industries, and many former audience members found that they preferred to stay home and watch their favorite drama personalities on TV. This was especially true as transportation in the city became more and more expensive, and Chennai became less safe, more congested, and more polluted. There was also a population shift from the center of the city to more remote (sabha-less) neighborhoods in the Chennai of the late 1980s along with the marked gain in the popularity of classical dance noted by Anne-Marie Gaston (1996, 24–25). This last could be related to a renewed consciousness of what constitutes good taste. It also makes sense that this surge correlated directly with a loss of patronage for the theater, which shares producers and audiences with the classical arts through the sabha system.

Given all of this evidence for a decline in theatrical offerings in the last twenty-five to thirty years, I was surprised to learn that the actual number of sabhas is not decreasing at all. In fact, many scholars have found the exact opposite. Amanda Weidman, for example, wrote in 2006 that "the number of sabhas in Madras has increased astronomically, particularly in the last thirty years."[40] As a scholar of Carnatic music, Weidman tells a story of astounding success. The India Fine Arts Association, she reports, has quadrupled the number of performances they sponsor over the last thirty years, and this is a common trend. She finds that the sabhas are earning money, sponsoring more performances, and multiplying in number. The discrepancy between my numbers and Weidman's can be reconciled in part by the idea that it is only the sabhas that sponsor Tamil-language plays that are declining. Several of the sabhas from the 1992 list are in fact still active but have changed their focus to exclude dramas.[41] Augusto, a playwright in Chennai, adds further insight when he says that "[d]uring the festival season, sabhas mushroom just as shops spring up everywhere during a Thiruvizha [festival] and then disappear. The sabhas tie up with sponsors and wherever there is space for the parking of cars, concerts are held" (Santhanam, December 1, 2003). These seasonal sabhas may be growing in number and promoting classical music, but they are not regular players on the cultural scene in Chennai and almost never sponsor plays. This does not mean, however, that the theater doesn't contribute to conventional understandings of good taste and class. My argument in this chapter is that it does—precisely because of its connection to classical music and dance—and even the discourse from proponents of the classical arts that belittles the plays only underlines their importance in the popular imagination.

Conclusion

Tamil-language comedy plays may not have the same status as Carnatic music or Bharata Natyam, but they are central to insider understandings of Tamil Brahmin culture. The plays do not attempt to *create* identity or culture, but to reflect them. The sabha plays may not be known for their cultural capital, but their association with the classical music and dance traditions through the sabhas' patronage opens a space in which they can take advantage of the reputation of recognized elite arts. They use the sabhas' reputation for good taste and excellent Indian performance arts to promote Tamil-language comedy theater in addition to classical music and dance. Sahba plays reflect Tamil Brahmin culture and/or stereotypes of it, revealing much about the concerns of the conservative middle-class community that represents itself through the plays.

In the following chapter I look at where the Tamil Brahmin community fits into the social and political scene in Chennai in order to think about how its position has affected the sabha theater. Brahmins in Chennai dominate the press, the universities, and the sabhas, but they are a numerical minority.[42] This disjuncture and the political ideologies of the majority non-Brahmin community have led to both anxiety and pride, and this tension is visible in the plays performed on sabha stages.

CHAPTER TWO

Brahmin Humor

Caste Politics and the Rise of Sabha Comedies

> RAMANI: When I came to look at you for marriage you sang a song. A good song. A rare raga! What was it called? . . . Oh, yes! Bukhari!
>
> RUKMANI: Dear Lord! That's not Bukhari, some non-vegetarian raga. What are you babbling about? Go brush your teeth.
>
> RAM: No, really . . . Bukhari . . .
>
> RUK: Idiot. Not Bukhari. *Mukhari*.
>
> RAM: Oh . . . Mukhari.
>
> —From Kathadi Ramamurthy's *Honeymoon Couple*

In this joke, Ramani is reminiscing about the beautiful classical song that his wife-to-be regaled him with at their first meeting. It is a standard practice for girls to be asked to perform a song at this time, and many middle-class Brahmin girls will have trained in Carnatic vocals or instruments. This is a practice brought up in several plays, and can often be used to great humorous effect, for example, where the girl's father thinks he is being asked to sing instead of his daughter and breaks out in "Twinkle, Twinkle, Little Star." In this instance, however, the girl sang the song beautifully, but her musically illiterate husband remembers the name of the raga incorrectly, saying that that she sang a song of the "Bukhari" raga instead of "Mukhari." The Mukhari raga is associated with *bhakti* (devotion) and feelings of ecstasy and joy. Bukhari, on the other hand, brings to mind the *Sahih Bukhari*, which is one of the canonical collections of Muslim *hadith*, the sayings of the Prophet Mohammed. Muslims, in general, are non-vegetarian, as contrasted to Rukmani with her good (vegetarian) Tamil Brahmin family and training in classical music. This joke not only makes fun of Ramani's musical illiteracy, but also of his cultural and religious ignorance. As discussed in the previous chapter, there are classical music connoisseurs from a number of different castes in Chennai, but this group is largely dominated by Brahmins.[1] Additionally, it assumes vegetarianism is superior to non-vegetarianism, thereby marking Hindus (especially Brahmins, who are more likely to be vegetarian than non-Brahmins) as superior to Muslims.

In this chapter, I argue that the theatrical genre of sabha comedy plays not only developed partially as a response to anti-Brahmin sentiments but also functioned as an apology for the Brahmin community and a celebration of its culture. The Brahmin community responded in a variety of ways to the stereotypes of piety, prejudice, hypocrisy, and narrow-mindedness that "not only missionaries, but British civilians and even a few amongst Hindus"[2] espoused, and the dramas are one of them. The fact that the plays were comedies and not taken seriously in the press as either art or propaganda opened a space for Brahmins to laugh at themselves and confront stereotypes indirectly, as jokes. The plays, in their language, content, production, and consumption, are anchored by a preconception of Brahmin superiority that precludes the need for direct political confrontation without sacrificing the community's belief in its own self-importance.

I further suggest that the decline in the popularity of sabha dramas that accelerated in the late 1980s may be related to a shift in political thought from anti-Brahmin sentiments to a pro-Tamil ideology within the Dravidian parties, a gradual process whose completion was marked by the AIADMK party members' acceptance of Brahmin J. Jayalalitha as their leader after the 1987 death of Chief Minister M. G. Ramachandran.[3] These changes made affirmation of Brahmin culture through the arts a less compelling and urgent agenda. The loss of urgency and often relevance of these dramas to the lives of Chennai Brahmins also contributed to the loss of audiences, and required troupes that wished to remain commercially viable to rethink their work. Once Tamil nationalism ceased to be an urgent issue, campaign platforms in the state focused on more economic and local issues. The shared history of the two major parties, however, has had a lasting effect on the state and its politics.

Celebrating the Tamil Brahmin Community

In the early twentieth century, Tamilnadu was the home of a powerful anti-Brahmin movement. As early as 1954, when K. Kamaraj, a Dalit, was chief minister representing the Congress Party, Madras State became the first in the nation not to have a Brahmin in its ministry (Pandian 2007, 5). Dravidian party politicians like C. N. Annadurai and M. Karunanidhi spread anti-Brahmin rhetoric through literature, drama, and film (see Hardgrave 1965; Irschick 1986; Rajendran 1989), which Hardgrave has referred to as a "cultural offensive" (Hardgrave 1965, 30–31). Plays performed by the Dravida Kazhagam dramatic troupes helped solidify a sense of community and unique Tamil identity that was often contrasted to Brahmin cultural history, which was considered Sanskritic and thus distinct from that of the Dravidians. The cultural offensive of the Dravidian movement was then balanced by the Brahmin cultural defensive, of which the Tamil-language sabha dramas were a part. In the early post-colonial period, when discussions of Indian national identity dominated public culture, Tamil Brahmins chose to emphasize their regional and caste identity with Brahmin-dialect, Tamil-language plays. They were inspired to assert their authenticity as Tamilians and reaffirm their values by developing positive images through live theater targeted at their own insular community rather than using the mass media.

Non-Brahmin painter V. Santhanam's dismissal of the theatrical genre on the basis that it is a Brahmin genre (author interview with V. Santhanam and A. Viswam, March 8, 2004) is echoed by other critics, middle-class people, and intellectuals such as Kausalya Santhanam, who once asked T. S. Sridhar (a. k. a. Marina) whether his plays "cater[ed] to a niche Brahmin audience that belonged to a certain class and section of society" (April 16, 2004). Marina denied it despite the strident Brahmin dialect he uses, saying that "[a]n artiste has no caste," but it is clear that the few audience members and fans who value these plays are almost exclusively from that small community. Many of the sabha plays use this distinctive Brahmin dialect of Tamil,[4] but the feelings of kinship and connection with the other people in the theater goes beyond the language itself.

Sabha theater works to humanize a Brahmin community that has been demonized by political opponents and allow its members to maintain their self-respect and confidence. One of the major questions that arose from my research concerns the purpose of this type of theater. If it is not widely appealing and doesn't earn money, why do people continue to sponsor and participate in it? I argue that a lot of the pleasure that comes from attending these plays has to do with the self-affirmation and momentary realness created by and for this imagined community in the physical space of the auditorium. Benedict Anderson writes that "[a]ll communities larger than primordial villages of face-to-face contact (and perhaps even these) are imagined. Communities are to be distinguished, not by their falsity/genuineness, but by the style in which they are imagined" (2006, 6). Anderson has identified language as one of the primary tools by which a community is imagined, writing that "through that language [the mother tongue], encountered at mother's knee and parted with only at the grave, pasts are restored, fellowships are imagined, and futures dreamed" (2006, 154). Sabha theater is the product of a Tamil Brahmin community concerned with reifying local identity using language and inside jokes while simultaneously marking itself as cosmopolitan through both style and content choices. As a genre of popular culture that developed in the Brahmin community during a period of intense anti-Brahmin politics, sabha theater functions as a window into the identity formation of a community so often defined solely by religion and classical art.

This is an insider theater for a privileged minority community that has found it politically incorrect to talk about its own superiority, which they perceive to be natural and eternal. They can recognize, in this safely segregated comedic space, what it means to belong to the Tamil Brahmin community, especially at a moment of modernization and globalization, when that definition is under constant pressure to open and change. Andy Medhurst, writing about English cultural identities, says that

> it is exactly because identities are so disputed, so slippery, so rocky and so anxious that the celebration of belonging offered by comedy is all the more welcome. Belonging may be a fiction, but it is a fiction from which solidarity and sustenance can be drawn. Comedy is a brief embrace in a threatening world, a moment of unity in a lifetime of fissures, a haven against insecurity, a refuge from dissolution, a point of wholeness in a maelstrom of fragmentation, a chance to affirm that you exist

> and that you matter. Comedy's consoling fantasy is that however difficult life might be, however much forces way beyond your control try to rip you to pieces, there can still be moments where—right here, right now—you can join those who are like you in a celebratory rite of communal recognition. Comedy says to us: you're among friends, relax, join in. (2007, 19)

Sabha theater thus offers a place for Tamil Brahmins to come together and enjoy a performance that is directly targeted at them, speaks to their issues and worldview, and reinforces their values and deep sense of entitlement. I relate the feeling of belonging that develops as audience members sit next to one another and share in the laughter and the humor to the way Anderson thinks about particular phrases and songs as creating an impression of "unisonality, the echoed physical realization of the imagined community" (2006, 145). The simultaneity of this shared experience and the particulars of the content provide a way to perpetuate, define, and create a notion of that ever-changing and difficult-to-grasp concept of Tamil Brahmin "culture" that is equivalent to the culturally dominant community's ideas of good taste, even though the plays themselves may not be.

Anderson's imagined communities are limited because "even the largest of them . . . has finite, if elastic boundaries, beyond which lie other nations" (2006, 7). Comedy embraces some people and welcomes them into a space of belonging, but it is also designed to exclude. Herein lies the danger of comedy as well as the danger of a caste-based community. With regard to comedy, Medhurst writes that "it would be easy to . . . attack comedy as divisive, exclusionary, in league with prejudice, a weapon of the powerful, an activity dedicated not only to supporting inequalities but also to cloaking them in an aura of inevitability, a way of selling us bigotry in the name of entertainment" (2007, 19). As for caste, it is conceived in blood, not language or belief, which closes the community from conversions (religion) or naturalizations (nation). It is closer to race, so Anderson's statement that "[n]ationalism thinks in terms of historical destinies, while racism dreams of eternal contaminations" (2006, 149) partly explains why endogamous marriage is so very central to the idea of Brahmin culture. Like racism, casteism manifests within national boundaries and justifies domestic repression and domination. Caste-based comedy, thus, is a dangerous proposition. In the world of the auditorium, large portions of the poor and the variety of ethnic groups are eliminated from Chennai society due to financial and linguistic constraints effortlessly facilitated by the sabha patronage system. The few who appear as characters in the plays are stereotypes of these groups introduced to highlight the uniqueness and superiority of Tamil Brahmins.

While Tamil Brahmins' educational, economic, social, and cultural capital is significant and disproportionate, they are producing theater by and for a minority community that was formerly in a position of power, then watched the inevitability of that slip away with democracy as the majority non-Brahmin population gained political power. The older generation of Tamil Brahmins, who are the primary patrons of these plays, grew up owning land and property and being economically and educationally dominant and powerful. They look back to the earliest Hindu text, the Rig Veda, and read the Purusa Hymn, where the sacrifice of the Cosmic Man created Brahmins from his head and all others from lower and therefore inferior parts of his body. They remember or have parents who remember the colonial period, when Brahmin dominance was solidified, and they became the default leaders of the newly independent nation. Nicholas Dirks writes that "In the Tamil south . . . both colonialism and post-colonialism move offstage, to be replaced by a colonial theater of double mimesis, in which the Brahman plays the role—not quite, but well enough—of the British colonial ruler, and in which colonialism might be said to have ended not in 1947, but only in 1967, with the ascension to political power of the DMK" (1996, 293). These plays, which were created during the rise of the non-Brahmin movement that politicized the notion of a community of non-Brahmins while destabilizing Brahmin superiority, reveal a palpable nostalgia for earlier times, when there was a feeling of natural and eternal dominance of Brahmin culture. More recently, sabha comedian S. Ve. Shekher served as a member of the legislative assembly from 2006–2009 and advocated for Brahmins, even appealing to the chief minister of Tamilnadu for 10% reservations for the community (see figure 2.1, where Shekher is pictured with Hindu nationalist Indian prime minister Narendra Modi).

Sabha comedies were at the peak of their popularity between the 1960s and 1980s, when the Dravidian (non-Brahmin) parties won power from the Brahmin-dominated Congress Party, spread anti-Brahmin messages, agitated against Hindi and Sanskrit, gained significant increases in reservations for intermediate and lower castes in colleges and government jobs,[5] and began lessening their involvement in drama (see Rajendran 1989, 141). The sabha plays responded to these developments as well as to the non-Brahmin political dramas that were widespread in the post-

Figure 2.1. Photograph of S. Ve. Shekher and Narendra Modi. *Source*: Courtesy of S. Ve. Shekher.

Independence period. A few of these, such as M. Karunanidhi's *Poompukar*, have been translated into English, but there is yet to be a thorough academic study of these dramas. Theater scholar A. Ramasamy has suggested that sabha playwrights simply borrowed the form of the more broadly circulated and popular Dravidian dramatic texts and changed the content to shift focus to the Brahmin middle-class, but the differences between sabha plays and the Dravidian films of the period raise doubts about this.

Politics and the dramatic arts have been especially closely linked in Tamilnadu, even in comparison to most other Indian states. The trend of using the media to reach the people that started with dramatic troupes only intensified with the rise of the film industry and the contesting of elections by Dravidian political parties. Cinema facilitated maximum exposure for party agendas and the DMK in particular took advantage of actors and writers in its political campaigning. C. N. Annadurai, then leader of the party, was a writer, director, and producer who did many "openly propagandistic" films, to use Robert Hardgrave's terminology. Former chief ministers C. N. Annadurai and M. Karunanidhi were playwrights and screenplay writers. Former chief ministers M. G. Ramachandran and J. Jayalalitha were both famous actors on stage and on screen. There is a real theatricality to Tamil politics that influences both the press and the actions of the players, which even held true after Jayalalitha's death in 2016, when during the confusion over succession, members of the state legislative assembly were allegedly being held hostage at a coastal resort so they could not interact with one of the candidates for chief minister (see "AIADMK," 2017; "Sasikala," 2017; Lakshmana 2017). Certainly, all politicians are public people who know that they are in the public eye and stage various statements or actions with this in mind. But in Tamilnadu, the politicians are actually professionals, or at the very least experienced amateurs, in the drama and cinema fields.

The Brahmin/Non-Brahmin Divide

Because Tamilnadu's caste politics have had a significant effect on the art produced in the region, particularly on the sabha theater, it is important to look in depth at the history of the non-Brahmin movement in order to appreciate the scope of its influence. Robert Hardgrave has located the first string of non-Brahmin social projects and organizations in 1873 (Hardgrave 1965, 12), shortly after Robert Caldwell's 1856 *Comparative Grammar of the Dravidian or South-Indian Family of Languages* (Caldwell 1974). The goal of these organizations was to work with the colonial government to neutralize internal power differences and advance the non-Brahmin community through education, which would hopefully lead to desirable government jobs. In its early stages, the movement was dominated by wealthy elites from powerful communities such as the Vellala, Chettiar, and Mudaliar. "Urbanization and Brahmin dominance," as Marguerite Ross Barnett has argued, "were interrelated features of nineteenth-century social change resulting in the dichotomization of socio-economic elites into non-Brahmin and Brahmin segments" (1976, 16–17). Non-Brahmin elites challenged Brahmin preponderance in education[6] and posed a political and financial threat to that community, although there was an "interconnectedness," to use Lakshmi Subramanian's language, of scholarship and cultural transactions between Brahmins, Pillais, and Chettiars that is evident in the literature and performance arts of the late nineteenth century.

The non-Brahmin movement tended to conflate the different varieties of Brahmins into a single group that was conceived of as in opposition to all other castes, which were negatively identified as simply "non-Brahmin." As M. S. S. Pandian notes, this formulation has since become "taken for granted, self-evident, and naturalized in the Tamil region" (2007, 6). In the early twentieth century, most Brahmins in Chennai belonged to the Congress Party, while the non-Brahmin political position was best expressed through the Justice Party, also known as the South Indian Liberal Federation, which was founded in 1916 with the intention of influencing government policy in favor of the non-Brahmin community. The Non-Brahmin Manifesto that they released that year forced comment on the issue by members of the Brahmin community, who V. Geetha and S. V. Rajadurai have convincingly demonstrated "since the last quarter of the nineteenth century . . . had worked hard to present themselves as respectful and humble purveyors of the commonweal; as an honourable community of civic-minded citizens who could effectively mediate native concerns and represent native interests to an essentially alien government" (1998, 4). The responses to the manifesto, especially those of Annie Besant, revealed the extent of "brahmin self-pride and self-love" and further fueled a sense of entitlement and a will "to consolidate that power into definitive social, cultural and political authority" (Geetha and Rajadurai 1998, 33, 10).

The Congress Party's frequent non-participation in elections as a protest to colonial rule contributed to the Justice Party's electoral success. The Justice Party focused its campaign on proving the superiority of non-Brahmin, that is, native Tamil religion, language, and culture, specifically championing the Saiva Siddhanta tradition. This position appealed to "elite non-Brahmin castes with a tradition of orthodoxy," though some non-Brahmin elites "subscribed to brahminic ways and views" (Barnett 1976, 32). These elites were united with Brahmins "by professional, intellectual and cultural concerns" as well as "a set of cultural (and religious) preferments" (Geetha and Rajadurai 1998, 4). Many of them joined the Madras Presidency Association (MPA), which was formed in 1917 as "a forum for non-brahmins in the Congress" (Geetha and Rajadurai 1998, 4).

The non-Brahmin movement soon shifted to a more radical "anti-Brahmin" one. Narendra Subramanian describes the anti-Brahmin shift in this graphic language: "The Dravidian movement in Tamil Nadu began during the 1910s by raising militant demands for secession and virulently opposed the upper Brahmin caste with appeals which to some extent resembled those of Nazi anti-Semitism" (1999, 7). This agenda coincided with the strict social reform program of E. V. Ramaswamy Naicker, also known as "Periyar" ("Big Man"). Naicker left the Congress Party in 1922 upon determining that the party was a "tool of Brahmin domination" (Hardgrave 1965, 25). He had a strong anti-religious and anti-capitalist bent, and advocated for the rights of women. He wanted to see the destruction of the caste system in its entirety and encouraged disposing of the need for Brahmins, asking people to marry across caste lines without the use of a priest. He began what was known as the "Self-Respect Movement" in 1925 to encourage non-Brahmins to accomplish those goals. Most radical of all his strategies of undermining Brahmin domination, and the one that cut right to the heart of a Brahmin self-identity that was based, as stated earlier, on "a set of cultural (and religious) preferments," was the "inversion rite":

> Periar and his followers inverted religious orthodoxy through the denigration of Brahminical norms, the abuse of Hindu deities, epics and scriptures, and the derision of the acts of godmen who claimed divine inspiration. . . . Early Dravidianist inversion rituals included beginning ceremonies at inauspicious hours, garlanding idols with slippers rather than flowers, parading idols around town while beating them with slippers, breaking idols, ceremonially cutting (rather than putting on) the sacred thread worn by Brahmins, displaying placards depicting deities engaged in sexual orgies and, where the DK[7] was strong enough to permit it, beating up rather than honouring visiting religious mendicants. (Subramanian 1999, 113–14)

These incendiary and spectacular methods drew national attention to the movement and to Naicker himself.

Naicker took over leadership of the Justice Party in 1935, then reorganized it as the Dravida Kazhagam (DK) in 1944. Although the Justice Party had always allied with the British against the Congress, assuming that non-Brahmins were more likely to attain justice under foreign rule, the DK chose to ally with the British as a strategy for avoiding Brahmin domination in an independent India. This was a very real concern because politically, most Brahmins were supporters of the Indian National Congress, the party of Mohandas Gandhi and Jawaharlal Nehru, which ruled India for much of the post-colonial period. Members of the DK, a militant mass organization, wore black and vowed to purge South India of Brahmin tyranny and to achieve a sovereign independent Dravidian Republic. It was their goal to be independent, under the rule of neither the British nor the Brahmins.

In 1949, C. N. Annadurai split the DK, forming the Dravida Munnetra (Progressive) Kazhagam (DMK), and taking with him three-fourths of the DK membership, leaving the DK to stagnate and decline. Although it is true that Periyar's "politics of heresy remained a vehicle of protest rather than of social change" (Subramanian 1999, 116), his ideas, as well as his body of support, have continued to be influential in Tamil politics and the formation of Tamil identity, long after the ideal of Dravidastan had been given up. While Naicker protested Independence Day celebrations, the Indian flag, and the Indian Constitution as tools of Brahmin tyranny, non-Brahmin politicians from the DMK recognized independence from colonial rule as an all-India accomplishment and wanted a more democratized party leadership along with an emphasis on the issues of language, territory, and cultural identity instead of non-Brahminism and caste. In other words, the DMK shifted the focus from ties of blood to ties of culture.

The DMK cultivated a very different understanding of Dravidian identity, Tamil cultural history, and religion's social role than the DK had. The DMK actually made overtures to Brahmins and religious figures. They didn't break religious idols, but instead upheld Pillaiyar and Murugan as "indigenous" deities. It was at this point in history that the Dravidian movement shifted from an anti-Brahmin to a more Dravidianist platform. This shift was partly necessitated by the increased mobilization of backward castes in the 1940s that split the non-Brahmin community into backward and forward segments. Although they had different agendas with respect to other issues, the two were still able to come together on the concept of Dravidian community and identity. The 1950s was a time when the DMK was figuring out its own identity, and when it laid "the basis for broader cultural nationalist appeal and expanded mobilization," as Marguerite Ross Barnett puts it (1976, 56). It was not yet a party in power, but the policies and ideologies that it articulated at this time would become essential to understanding later moves and appeals made by the party. This was the period of the "emergence of the politics of cultural nationalism and the mass internalization of Tamil identity" (Barnett 1976, 89). It was also the period in which the sabha theater genre began, wherein Brahmins asserted their *Tamil* identity through use of the language in their dramas.

Even from the 1930s, there was a growing recognition in political arenas of the value of numbers, not just of wealth and ritual status. In contrast to the Congress, which was dominated by elite Brahmins, the DMK worked to solidify its populist appeal to the "common people," often intertwining it with ethnic appeals. Narendra Subramanian's 1999 book, *Ethnicity and Populist Mobilization*, is an attempt to reconcile the seemingly incompatible identities of the Dravidian parties as both populist and ethnic nationalist, contrasting Tamilnadu to the numerous historical cases where ethnic nationalism has led to violence, intolerance, and authoritarianism. Brahmins engaged the caste issue indirectly not by attacking non-Brahmins, but instead by reaffirming their language, values, and culture by creating a genre of theater as well as the *bhajana* groups mentioned by Milton Singer that were also popular in this post-Independence period: "At the same time, the Dravidian movement for linguistic regionalism, with its championing of Tamil against Sanskrit, Telugu, Hindi, and other Indian languages; of non-Brahmans against Brahmans; and of 'rationalism' against 'superstition' drives the orthodox Hindu, and particularly the Smarta Brahman, to a defense of his religion, his culture, and his caste" (Singer 1972, 240). *Bhajana* groups and sabha dramas were not directed at broad cross-sections of the Tamil population, but rather affirmed Brahmin culture to audiences that were predominantly Brahmin.[8] Producers and patrons of the sabha theater productions in the city assert their superiority, especially over popular genres such as commercial film and television, by extolling the *purity* of their plays, a characteristic I see as intimately linked to their Brahmin identity and discuss in detail in chapter 3.

The Congress Party, with its traditional appeal to voters of wealth and high ritual status, had little credibility with the backward classes, and the Dravidian parties, with their history of anti-casteism and anti-Brahminism, were able to capitalize on that and win votes. The success of the DMK's populist efforts is clearly demonstrated by these figures: in the 1957 elections in Tamilnadu, there was a 49.3% voter turnout; the 1962 elections, which took place after the DMK's voter registration drives, had a 70.7% voter turnout (Subramanian 1999, 171). In fact, since the DMK came to power in 1967, the Brahmin-dominated Congress Party has never again ruled in the state of Tamilnadu. Subramanian argues that "[n]on-Brahminism endured in Tamilnadu alone because it was linked to Tamil nationalism from the 1930s onwards in a populist discourse" (Subramanian 1999, 83).

Marguerite Ross Barnett has traced the changing identity the Dravidian parties have espoused as the movement has swung over time from being non-Brahmin to Dravidian and then to Tamil. Once the DMK and the (AI)ADMK ([All India] Anna DMK) became basically a two-party system in the state (after 1972 when M. G. Ramachandran split from the DMK and formed the ADMK), mobilization on the basis of caste was no longer necessary or profitable. Both parties pretty much agreed on the issue of Tamil identity and didn't want to alienate the Brahmin population, whose votes might prove the difference between the two parties. In fact, Jayalalitha, who served several terms as chief minister of the state until her death in 2016, occasionally emphasized her Brahmin (and therefore respectable) status in order to counterbalance public criticism of her as a modern film actress.

Although the division between Brahmins and non-Brahmins had been established long before, the statewide Tamil Brahman Association (TAMBRAAS), which specifically addresses Brahmin concerns, was not founded until 1980. That was the year that the Mandal Commission made its recommendation to reserve 27% of all central government jobs for backward castes in addition to the 22.5% already reserved for scheduled castes and tribes. These recommendations were not implemented until ten years later by Prime Minister V. P. Singh, a decision that led to violent protests and self-immolations particularly among higher-caste students. At this same time, M. S. S. Pandian noted "a revival of iconoclastic rationalism and anti-Brahminism" at the sixth state-level DMK conference (Pandian 1990, 1938). Mary Hancock's research has convincingly demonstrated that the Tamil Brahmin community in Chennai still felt victimized ten years after the implementation of the Mandal Commission's recommendations. Fuller and Narasimhan found elderly Brahmins recalling humiliating incidents and DK assaults particularly from the late 1950s and early 1970s and feeling the lingering resentment from non-Brahmin communities. These periods of heightened incidents happened during the peak of sabha theater. The rising resentment in the 1950s is marked by the start of the genre and the entry of a number of troupes, and the 1970s is when today's most popular troupes (Natakhapriya and Crazy Creations) were started. This again reinforces the connection between the plays and the need for both the affirmation of Brahmin cultural worth and the safe, insular cultural space of the sabha.

Mary Hancock found that most Chennai Brahmins worry about the effects of the reservations and believe that decisions about enrollment in educational institutions or employment in government jobs should be based on merit alone. In many interviews conducted by Hancock, "Brahmans also claimed that they were the recipients of day-to-day, informal discrimination—insults (including the degrading term *pārppaṉ*, which was sometimes used to refer to Brahmans), street harassment, and petty crime" (1999, 41). Fuller and Narasimhan mention the forced cutting off of men's topknots and sacred threads. Gopalakrishnan, then president of TAMBRAAS, told Hancock that "TAMBRAAS had been founded to combat the harassment and violence to which Brahman women were subjected by 'anti-Brahman rowdies and gangsters' " (Hancock 1999, 40; see also Jagadheesan 1991). The organization, in other words, was viewed as necessary to protect Brahmin culture, especially as it was embodied in its women, reinforcing once again the link between morality and class status. Now, they primarily run their horoscope matching center and provide funding for poor Brahmins to complete important rituals.[9]

Brahmin organizations such as TAMBRAAS do little political lobbying, but most members of the community tend to support the AIADMK over the DMK because of Jayalalitha herself, but also because of the more culturally conservative policies the party promotes (it typically allies with the Hindu nationalist Bharatiya Janata Party).[10] The sabha theater artists tended to support Jayalalitha not only because she was a Brahmin, but because she was once one of them. She got involved with politics through her film work with M. G. Ramachandran, but she got into film through the theater. Like her mother and her aunt, she acted with Y. G. Parthasarathy's United Amateur Artists for a while, debuting in their 1964 production of *Undersecretary* (which I discuss in detail in chapter 6) in the role of Kantha. Now that she and long-time DMK leader Karunanidhi (1924–2018) are both gone, caste and Tamil separatist issues have faded in regional politics, though the current political climate at the national level, with the ruling party proudly Hindu nationalist, has reinvigorated the Brahmins who align with them, such as S. Ve. Shekher. However, it is also true that after Jayalalitha's death, both proposed successors to the BJP-allied AIADMK party's leadership (and to completing her term as chief minister) were from the non-Brahmin Thevar caste.

Brahmins developed outlets, such as the sabha theater, which were outside of politics and the mass media favored by the populist Dravidian parties to affirm the worth and contributions of their community for their own benefit rather than as a justification for the majority population. This strategy has the benefit of consolidating feelings of identity and relationship as well as fostering the Tamil Brahmin imagined community, which can inspire great loyalty and emotion that later translates into political decisions. It also opens up the space for self-criticism, which is problematic, but tolerated so long as it doesn't reach the general public.

An excellent illustration of this phenomenon is Brahmin playwright Venkat's recollection of the fate of his 1986 play *Uyiril Kalanta Uṟavē* (*Relationships Mixed in Life*), which criticized Brahmin values such as feeding servants in the back yard instead of in the hall (as the living room is known to Tamils) and more generally attempted to "expose hypocrisies" within the community (author interview October 7, 2003). Many individual prominent Brahmin actors such as Major Sundararajan, S. Ve. Shekher, Srikanth, and Delhi Ganesh, spoke out against the play along with TAMBRAAS representatives and tried to have it banned. Venkat recalls that the controversy went on for two to three months in all the magazines and he was "excommunicated from the community for some time." He was eventually given police permission[11] to perform the play after removing some inflammatory dialogues and promising not to add new ones. At this point, he says that "[t]he Brahmins wanted me to do the play in their midst to reform the Brahmin society, but not to the public. I refused" (Gopalie 2002, 258). Eventually, TAMBRAAS paid him three thousand rupees for the rights to the script, which they never performed. He no longer has a copy of it.

Venkat believes *Uyiril Kalanta Uṟavē* is his best play, and he also sold it to the cinema, where it was produced as a film by K. Bhagyaraj in 1988 called *Itu Namma Āḷ* (*This Is Our Man*).[12] The main story concerns a graduate from a lower-caste barber community who pretends to be a Brahmin and puts on a "sacred thread" in order to earn money for his mother's eye operation. His masquerade is successful and gets him a job, a loan, and a Brahmin wife. The problem comes when the truth about his identity is revealed. The "rest of the film is on how he saves both the father and the daughter [his father-in-law and wife], thus making religion bow before humanity."[13] The film was just as incendiary among the Tamil Brahmin community as the play, but was seen by a broader cross-section of the population, which only added to its offense. Tamil film review website lolluexpress.com includes a page for readers to comment on various reviews and films, and the title of the page for *Itu Namma Āḷ* is "WAS BAGYARAJ HARSH ON BRAHMINS / IYERS ???" which was prompted by the fact that "our readers say that 'Brahmin community was insulted.' " Some of the readers thought the film was "hilarious" or "funny," but the overwhelming response from within the Brahmin community was that it was "irritating," "too much," "quite offensive," and "inflammatory" ("Ithu Namma Aal"). There's even an anecdote that when M. G. Ramachandran's Brahmin wife, Janaki, saw the film, she got angry and walked out.[14] There is a different tenor to the criticism of Brahmins in this play and film than in the many sympathetic sabha plays that also exaggerate Brahmin characteristics for the sake of humor. Perhaps it is because the undercurrent of Brahmin superiority that is present in the plays is missing in *Itu Namma Āḷ*.

Brahmin Conservatism

During the late nineteenth and early twentieth centuries there were ongoing politics in the region that privileged South India and its arts as more authentic and "Indian" than those from the north, which were believed to have been contaminated by Islamic and other foreign traditions. This theory was supported not only by proponents of the Dravidian movement, but also many from the Tamil Brahmin community. Brahmin scholars like U. Ve. Swaminatha Aiyer and Subramania Bharati were very involved in the Tamil Renaissance, which was then appropriated by the non-Brahmin movement. The Tamil Brahmin community shared some sympathies with the Dravidian cultural agenda of promoting Tamil arts and language as classical and distinct from those of Sanskritized North India, but the non-Brahmins often shut them out and tried to discredit them as not authentically Tamil. As early as 1891, C. R. Day wrote *The Music and Musical Instruments of Southern India and the Deccan*, where he argued that the southern musical tradition was pure in comparison to the northern Indian tradition. This argument was deeply influential to the (mostly Brahmin) project of what Lakshmi Subramanian refers to as "the making of the modern classical music tradition in south India" (2006, 1) as a separate "Carnatic" tradition deliberately opposed to the Hindustani tradition, which was deemed full of "alien influences."

The divide between westernized elites into Brahmin and non-Brahmin affected culture on all levels. The actors in Sambanda Mudaliyar's troupe were all westernized elites, mostly lawyers and bureaucrats of the British Raj from Brahmin and high non-Brahmin Hindu castes such as the Mudaliar and Pillai communities. Mudaliyar himself "was offered knighthood and enjoyed all the privileges of an English education" (Mangai and Arasu 2009, 126). The mixed-caste productions did not mean, however, that the troupe was free from caste strife. K. S. Rajendran has noted that "Pammal Sambandha Mudaliar admits that the Brahmin/non-Brahmin clashes ruined the functioning of his troupe" (1989, 94). Caste difference in audiences helped determine which plays were performed for which sabhas, generally correlating to the North/South divide discussed earlier. The educated Brahmin audiences of Mylapore enjoyed watching themselves on stage in plays that were complete with Brahmin dialect speech and jokes that turned on knowledge of English or Hindi, but the non-Brahmin Georgetown audiences preferred plays with film stars, historicals, and mythologicals.

The Brahmin community in Chennai is actually more cohesive than Brahmin communities elsewhere, as is evidenced by its remarkably high level of status summation (covariation of caste and class status) as opposed to that of Brahmins in the rest of India.[15] There has been, as Mary Hancock notes, a concerted effort within the community to "mitigate material inequalities" using mechanisms such as "kinship obligations, strategic deployments of social service, and the informal use of hiring preferences" (1999, 45). These mechanisms and their effects demonstrate the strength of the bonds between members of that community, which has the highest social status in the city and therefore the most to lose through any changes to the caste system. Reiterating entitlement and superiority in the theater is one more way to perpetuate the system and structure that keeps Brahmins dominant not only economically, but also socially and culturally, three types of capital that usually go together. Brahmin conservatism extends even to notably orthodox entertainment tastes in the Chennai community, where innovation and change to beloved classical arts face resistance.

Tamil Brahmins pride themselves on their traditional tastes and are often characterized by others as being "conservative."[16] Of all the cities in India, it is Chennai that is generally considered to be the most "cultured." It is well known as a center of the arts, which is another reason to study issues of taste in relation to it. Tamil Brahmins tend to define their culture and cultural value by the measure of tradition. In an article about modern dance choreography in India, Krishna Chaitanya lamented that "the situation in India seems to be solidly and stolidly hostile to the least innovation" and that Indian classicists are "fanatically orthodox," as evident in their reviling of the innovative dance choreographies of Chennai dancer Chandralekha (Chaitanya 1987, 6). Similarly, acclaimed dancer Yamini Krishnamurti recorded her doubts about performing in the Kuchipudi style in Chennai because the Tamil Brahmins, who saw Bharata Natyam as "the only worthwhile dance form," were sure to react with a "swift and cruel negative" to her performance (Krishnamurti 1995, 72).

Chennai Brahmins conflated Tamil nationalism with Indian nationalism and saw the revival of traditional arts as victories for the nation.

Their pride in Indian culture was evident in their attitude toward both culture and politics. As members of the Indian National Congress, many were active in the Indian independence movement as well as in the reform and revival of the classical arts. It is particularly interesting that the shift from sacred to secular (in music, dance, and theater) involved Brahmins, whose identity is so tied to religion, especially in Chennai. The community's penchant for "classical" arts such as Bharata Natyam and Carnatic music, as well as any art form with a religious influence, is well documented,[17] but far from exhausting the extent of this community's tastes.

In her work on classical music in South India, Amanda Weidman has analyzed how the term "classical" was used in the pre-Independence period in Madras city. Weidman argued that unlike western music, "Indian music . . . never had a classical period; from its first use, the term was a marker of cultural status and authenticity" (2006, 5). Looking forward to the present, many scholars of Indian performance arts, such as Anne-Marie Gaston and Kathryn Hansen (1992), have offered definitions of the "classical" arts that support this claim by stipulating that the classical arts enjoy the patronage of a dominant or elite social group. In pre-Independence Madras city, this designation unquestionably referred to a community of "notables," as V. Geetha and S. V. Rajadurai refer to them, who were mostly Brahmin (Tamils, Telugus, Deshastas, and Niyogis) though they included a handful of non-Brahmin "prominent merchants or bankers or respectable landlords who subscribed to brahminic ways and views" (1998, 4).

The more generations back a practice can be traced, the more "authentic" it is believed to be and the more status it confers, and this is true of the performance arts as well. This is one reason that so many people who were involved in the rather recent revivals of classical Indian performance traditions invested a great deal of time and energy into linking those traditions to ancient texts. Many scholars (see Singer 1972; Chatterjee 1993; Geetha and Rajadurai 1998; and Joshi 2001) have written about the conflict that this privileging of tradition has caused for Indians who are trying to be "modern" while at the same time retaining their high status by being "traditional." Milton Singer, in his analysis of Tamil Brahmins, explained that they compartmentalized, an idea that John Harriss found many today reject (2003, 349–51). Srinivas uses the language of "contextual variation" to explain the negotiation (1966, 123), and Fuller and Narasimhan suggest using the phrase "code-switching," but don't elaborate. I agree with them, however, that code-switching, as it is used in linguistics to mean toggling between languages during the course of a single conversation, is a great way to understand how "Tamil Brahmans have come to see themselves as both fully modern and authentically traditional" (2014, 27). Minelle Mahtani's idea of "mobile paradoxical spaces," which is developed in her consideration of multi-ethnic women, is helpful here as well because it "gets at the mobility and simultaneity of particular subject positions" (2001, 180). The multi-dimensional fragments of Tamil Brahmin identity place them in a variety of contradictory spaces (both modern and traditional, local and global) at the same time. Sanjay Joshi (2001) has also helpfully described the use of traditional hierarchies and religious beliefs in the construction of a modern Indian middle-class identity as a "fractured modernity," which captures the contradiction inherent in what he argues is a coherent project of self-empowerment.

Classical performance arts confer status on the viewers as well as performers and are considered to be embodiments of Indian/Tamil culture. Part of the project of this book is to broaden the limited understanding of Tamil Brahmin taste by contributing a study of sabhas, one space where the classical arts can be viewed side by side with popular, though often dismissed, comedy plays. Ganguly-Scrase and Scrase have shown that there are many different "middle classes" in India, and each has different tastes when it comes to entertainment and culture; the same is true even within the Tamil Brahmin community, which is far from monolithic. While many members of this community in Chennai enjoy both the sabha plays and the classical arts, other sub-groups align themselves with more intellectual factions and avoid these plays in favor of English-language productions and "modern Indian theater" in the sense that Aparna Dharwadker uses that phrase (2005; 2019; see also Dalmia 2006).

All the plays in Dharwadker's study, indeed in the canon of modern Indian drama itself, are *serious* plays, a term she uses without complication, although it has many connotations. In the sense that Dharwadker uses the word "serious" to describe modern Indian dramas, she implies that all these plays are by writers who are committed to the theater. The division is "between serious and commercial theatre" (2005, 84), and it is that chasm Dharwadker sees as limiting channels of publication and performance. Importantly, the division between "serious" and "commercial" cannot be mapped onto the dichotomy of "amateur" and "professional," which makes it much harder to distinguish between the "serious" theater that forms the modern Indian canon and the plays that are performed in Chennai's sabhas. As early as 1956, Indian theater discourse had developed specific meanings for the terms "professional" and "amateur" that are a bit counterintuitive. These meanings, as Dharwadker explains in the following passage, came to refer not only to the financial situation of the troupes, but also to the types of plays that they performed: "Because of its association with urban proscenium theatres and the Parsi stage, by the 1950s the term 'professional' had come to denote not just commercial or full-time activity but a theatre that was nonserious, superficial, inartistic, or merely popular, and hence not worth preserving. The counterterm 'amateur' referred occasionally to lightweight college and community productions, but it mainly denoted aesthetic and thematic seriousness, artistic boldness, and long-term commitment to the art" (2005, 43).

The other factor in the connotations of "professional" and "amateur" that specifically relates to sabha theater comes out of the discourse about classical dance. Dancers from traditional dance communities who made their livings by performing were considered to be professionals. This had a negative connotation in Tamil Brahmin circles because of the association of these women with prostitution that eventually led to the 1947 Anti-Dedication Bill, which made it illegal to dedicate girls to temples as *devadasis*. As part of the vast project to reform and revive the dance that is today known as Bharata Natyam, women from wealthy, high-caste communities began to perform. Their involvement gave respectability to the art, but one of the primary components of this prestige was their designation as *amateurs*. These women did not need to earn money by dancing or any other means. Their fathers (and occasionally husbands, though it was common for them to stop dancing publicly after marriage) earned enough money that these women could dance simply to glorify Indian culture, and Tamil culture, in particular. If tickets were sold, the performance was usually a benefit and the proceeds were donated to a worthy charity (see Gaston 1996, 67).

This discourse, which was taking place within the sabhas where Bharata Natyam was performed by respectable women, bled over into theater discourse as well. It was much more respectable to be an amateur performer, with income from another job, than a professional who depended on performance for a living. In the case of sabha theater, this has been one reason for the formation of troupes through friends and family and the disdain toward remuneration that many artists will express, though not necessarily sincerely. The amateur scenario also gives artists the freedom to produce the plays they think best, not the most profitable. It is still very difficult to make a living as a theater artist in India, and most urban performers would classify themselves as amateurs (see Banerji 2020 for Bengali perspective). This is certainly true in the context of sabhas, and Dharwadker mentions many of the forerunners of the modern Indian theater, Girish Karnad among them, who "have made the familiar compromise of making a living in film and television in order to pursue the theatre of their choice" (Dharwadker 2005, 122).[18] So sabha theater artists are just as "serious" in terms of commitment and time investment as the modern Indian theater practitioners, a discussion I take up in more detail in chapter 7.

The value placed on traditionalism has in the Indian case often been envisioned as a need to protect Indian culture from sexually suggestive scenes, lyrics, and dialogues. Monika Mehta's evaluation of letters written in protest of the song "Choli ke peeche kya hai" ("What Is Behind the Blouse?") in the 1993 Hindi film *Khalnayak* argues that "Indian culture" is part of a "vulnerable trio" (along with women and children) that needs this protection (see Mehta 2001). The letters cited by Mehta in reference to the *Khalnayak* debate are written by both men and women, but the connecting thread is their concern about the corruption of culture. Within India, one of the concerns of these debates about culture, which Mehta highlights, is "whether national prudishness in any way affected the state's (and a portion of the public's) much desired goal—to be modern and democratic" (Mehta 2001, 1). Mehta is dealing with mass media in her writing, and the mechanisms by which the state can or cannot control the content and imagery of audiocassettes, films, and television are very different from the limited distribution and rigorous self-censorship found in theater productions in Chennai.[19] In her discussion of state censorship, Mehta helpfully points out that there are three separate players participating in censorship debates—the state, the film industry, and the citizenry—each of whom has a different agenda and interest at stake. The debates are, she suggests, not purely academic but actually productive of discourse, sexuality, and the final version of the film in question.

Brahmins in Tamilnadu have been extraordinarily successful at balancing these two seemingly contradictory positions and have the reputation "of being very modern and adaptable because they have acquired modern education and have gone into the professions, business, and industry, although they are also regarded as representatives of Sanskritic Hinduism and the Great Tradition" (Singer 1972, 395). They have managed to reconcile these conflicting identities and to control others' perceptions of them through a variety of strategies, including their self-representation in sabha plays. These plays may reflect culture and/or stereotypes of it but they don't deliberately set out to *create* culture in the way that classical performances do. The plays reveal much about the concerns of the conservative middle-class community and prompted S. Shankar to write in his introduction to his translation of Komal Swaminathan's *Water!* that "[m]embers of the sabhas are predominantly urban and middle class, and are notorious for their narrow, conservative tastes and encouraged a conformity and superficiality that degraded both the form and the content of the play" (2001, xiv). The discussion about culture in Chennai circles is not just generically "Indian" but more specifically "Tamil," with marriage, morality, and language perceived to be its central components.

The word "culture" is such a complex concept in academic thought that Nicholas Dirks was asked to convene an interdisciplinary conference to discuss why "the word culture [is] used so frequently, so provocatively, and for so many different purposes" (Dirks 1998, 7). As it is generally used in Chennai, "culture" refers to the right way for things to be done and for people to behave and to be seen behaving, especially in relation to other members of society. Susan Seizer's informants believe "that only lifelong marital bonds of the proper sort constitute *true* 'Tamil culture' " (emphasis in original, 2005, 6), and I have also found marriage and family ties to be the primary components of "culture" in the contemporary Tamil context. "Culture" only expands to include religion and then classical music and dance after this primary definition has been exhausted. There is an air of "distinction," to use Bourdieu's term, about culture, and the concept also implies hierarchy: these components of culture are something that Matthew Arnold's "men of culture" follow, appreciate, and are capable of disseminating. The word "culture" itself carries connotations of high class and taste, and it is actually possible for an individual or group to lose "Tamil culture" (see Seizer 2005, 6). Members of society with "good taste" are those who adhere to and recognize performances of the unwritten rules of "culture," which are primarily constructed and modeled by the minority Brahmin community in Chennai.

Language, Theatre, and Politics

Drama had been used as a political tool in India by the late nineteenth century, long before the non-Brahmin plays that preceded sabha theater. Nandi Bhatia argues with reference to plays like *Nil Darpan* ("The Indigo Mirror"), *Gajadananda Prahasan* ("Gajadananda and the Prince"), and

Chakur Durpan ("The Tea Planters' Mirror") that "theater in India had indeed become an expression of political struggle against colonial rule and a space for staging scathing critiques of the oppression and atrocities inflicted upon colonial subjects by rulers . . . (2004, 1). In response to this tendency, the British government passed the Dramatic Performances Censorship Act in 1876. This led to the popular trend of staging representations of the *Mahābhārata* and other mythological stories in order to comment on sociopolitical events, "elude censorship and at the same time disseminate nationalist ideas" (Bhatia 2004, 43). The British, not wanting to interfere with religious performances, had a much harder time preventing the staging of these plays[20] than those not based on religious stories. Rakesh Solomon writes that audiences were familiar with the mythological subjects and "alert to their accumulated meanings, associations, and resonances" (1994, 327), but the British officials were not. Although they slowly decoded the political messages and banned production and publication, "the authors' allegorical strategies—at the minimum—bought enough time to propagate their ideas of cultural and political resistance for varying periods of time, and on occasion, to defend themselves successfully against the routine charges of sedition" (Solomon 1994, 327).

The use of the theatrical stage to spread nationalist messages seems to have reached the Madras Presidency quite late by comparison. What was taking place on Bengali and Marathi stages in the late 1870s didn't happen in Madras until the early 1920s with the work of S. Sathyamurthy, Suthanandha Bharathi, and Subramanya Siva. Their efforts were in response to particular events such as the Tinnevelly Sedition Case, the Rowlatt Act, the Jallianwala Bagh massacre, and the Non-Cooperation Movement (see Baskaran 1981, 28–42.). According to S. Theodore Baskaran, nationalist plays in Madras then declined in the late 1920s and only revived with the next "wave of political activism" that started with the execution of Bhagat Singh and other revolutionaries in 1931. This event led to plays such as *Desa Bhakthi* (*Patriotism*) staged by the Bala Shanmugananda Sabha and *Khaddarin Vetri* (*The Victory of Khadi*) staged by the professional troupe T. K. S. Brothers that inspired so many in the sabha theater.

Tamil actors were directly involved in political activity *off* stage from as early as the 1928 founding of the Tamilnadu Nadikar Sangam (Tamil Actors Association). This provided "an organizational framework for the political involvement of drama artistes," and resolved at a conference in December of 1931 "to give all assistance to the Congress and to intensify nationalistic propaganda through the stage" (Baskaran 1981, 38), to which the colonial government responded by requiring all dramas to receive permission from the district authorities before they could be staged. After the end of World War II and the promise of independence, nationalism virtually disappeared as a subject of dramas. Most of the drama companies folded and the personnel left for the cinema.

Language, in India in general but in Tamilnadu especially, has a history of politicization and association with regional identity. At the time of independence (August 15, 1947), India was divided into states based on Great Britain's "administrative units" in the former colony. The Madras Presidency was one of many of these units that crossed linguistic boundaries. The debate raged in the central government about whether to redraw the state boundaries along linguistic lines, but with Prime Minister Jawaharlal Nehru against the idea as a threat to national unity that would encourage disruption and disintegration, it remained only a debate until 1953. That year marked the creation of the Telugu-speaking state of Andhra Pradesh after the movement won the support of the Madras government and the Tamilnadu Congress Committee and one of its leaders fasted to death (see Mitchell 2009).

In addition to the linguistic problem of state reorganization, the greater one of a language for the nation also deeply affected Tamilnadu. There was a strong push in newly independent India to assert an indigenous linguistic identity that resulted in the 1965 decision to change India's official language from English to Hindi. Tamilians responded with two months of demonstrations, riots, and violence until the Official Languages Act was finally amended. The threat to the Tamil language was seen as a threat to Tamil identity and people.[21] The assertion of Tamil identity that has been manifested in the love and celebration of the language has remained strong as is evidenced by, among other things, the Tamil-language comedy drama troupes of the post-Independence period. Choice of language, in this heavily politicized linguistic atmosphere, always made a statement. As an illustration, K. Balachander, who moved from the sabha theater into the film industry, made a film in 1985 called *Sindhu Bhairavi*, which includes a character that "has strong feelings that South Indian classical music is not sung primarily in the South Indian language Tamil . . . [because] this has made it inaccessible to the general Tamil public in the state." The author of this review on the Internet Movie Database (imdb.com) laments that "this is a truth and such an elitism has pervaded south indian [*sic*] classical music for the better part of [the] last century" (learnnew 2003). Tamil, in this account, is the vernacular, the language of the people, through which they express their emotions and form their culture.

The Tamil language, however, is very complex. There are so many varieties that not only is the use of Tamil a political statement in itself, but a further statement is made by the *type* of Tamil used in a play, film, or any other artistic endeavor. The language is often referred to as "Tamil diglossia" because the written and spoken varieties are so different. For example, the verb *paṭittukkoṇṭirukkiṟēn* ("I have been studying") in written form would be pronounced *paṭiccukkiṭṭirukkṟe* in standard spoken Tamil. There are words that are only used in spoken Tamil, and words that are only used in written or "literary" Tamil. Kamil Zvelebil has been quoted as saying that "Colloquial Tamil and Literary Tamil will be considered as the two opposite poles of the same language" (in Deivasundaram 1981, 18). Different media use different degrees and combinations of the two. For example, newspapers tend to be literary, novels mix forms depending on the background of characters, and popular magazines will often print the spoken form (see Thirumalai 1983).

S. Arokianathan has documented the high (literary) versus low (colloquial) varieties of language used in the different types of radio programs broadcast on All India Radio. He concluded that when considering radio programs that were dramas, one had to take the target audience (women, children, farmers, et al.) into account in order to determine the language variety. The spoken language becomes especially important as more and more Tamilians, both in the diaspora and in Tamilnadu, attend English-medium schools. These Tamils can speak their native language but are often unable to read or write it. Their spoken Tamil, however, tends to be of a more literary variety than uneducated Tamils'. Spoken Tamil itself is not standardized but is actually broken into a vast number of dialects that are based on regional and caste differences, among other factors. Sabha dramas, even when they are written, are in a spoken Tamil format that gives the flavor of the dialect and indicates the rhythm of speech.

Language variety, even in political speeches, is used to differentiate between speakers. These speeches are in a form known as *mēṭaittamiḻ* or "platform Tamil," which is a performance genre of Tamil spoken on literary and political stages (*mēṭai*). The form is marked by poetic conventions and the status of the speaker, as John Bernard Bate has argued, corresponds to an "aesthetic distinction between 'refinedness' (*cemmai*), as marked by literary style and citation, and vernacular 'vulgarity' (*koccai*)" (2000, 5). He writes that "as socially typifying genres, the hierarchical arrangement of speech genres corresponds to definite and hierarchically ordered categories of people" (2009, 17) and identifies four types of distinctions signaled by speech (proper, civilizational, epochal, and political). The Justice Party and Congress politicians had made their speeches in English or in spoken Tamil, but the DMK, particularly Annadurai and M. Karunanidhi, brought about what Bate calls an "oratorical revolution" where speech was modeled on the written word and therefore required literacy. This revolution linked stage performances with politics, Tamil language, and cultural identity in a new way in the late 1940s and early 1950s, just as Tamil language sabha comedy plays began to emerge in Chennai. Those plays are deliberately written in a colloquial language that is very different from the more literary variety of Tamil found in the historical and mythological plays by professional companies that had come before or from the poetic language found in the plays written by Karunanidhi and other leaders of the DMK. The colloquial (low, by literary standards) language of the sabha plays has ensured that they receive little to no recognition as literature, but they simultaneously illustrate the superiority of the Brahmin language and culture through the interactions of the families in the plays.

Most of the sabha plays, with the exception of S. Ve. Shekher's, whose language I would describe as "Madras Tamil," are in a dialect commonly known as "Brahmin Tamil." The dialect is marked by its Sanskritized vocabulary and a difference in pronunciation of particular verb endings, among other things. This is the dialect spoken at home by the Tamil Brahmin community, and the writers and actors choose to work in the dialect most comfortable for them and thus mark their language in this way in the plays. An example would be ending imperatives with a long o sound rather than a short a. So "please come in and sit down" would sound like "vāṅgō. utkārangō" rather than the more standard "vāṅga. utkāranga." It is easily understood by Tamils of all communities, but it does tend to keep the audiences insular. Films, for example, may use the Brahmin dialect, but usually only to mark a particular character and for comic effect. Marina, Crazy Mohan, and Cho Ramasamy are representative of sabha playwrights who prefer this marked Brahmin language as the primary dialect in their dramas. They may play on other language characteristics and differences as part of the comedy by introducing other dialects of Tamil for comic effect in the same way that Brahmin dialect is often used in other media.

Conclusion

Originally a response to the anti-Brahmin sentiments espoused by the Dravidian movement, sabha comedy plays provide a space in which Brahmins can engage the caste issue indirectly by reaffirming their language, values, and culture through the characters and plots of the dramas. Even though the anti-Brahmin movement has lost its potency in recent years, it is clear that the Tamil Brahmin community in Chennai still feels its effects. The cultural commentary in the plays and their relevance to an educated, middle-class audience both in India and the diaspora provide ample proof of the importance and relevance of the plays to this community. The dedication of many artists and enthusiasts may not lead to a revival, but certainly to a continuation of live theater in Chennai. Some of the tools by which the community asserts its *Tamilness* include the use of colloquial, Brahmin dialect and the representation of "typical" Brahmin families on stage, depicted at home, worshiping, going to the doctor, and interacting with one another and their friends and neighbors.

As an insider theater, the sabha plays help to foster feelings of camaraderie, fraternity, and shared history and experience among audience members and fans. The plays, in their language, content, production, and consumption, are anchored by a preconception of Brahmin superiority, but their comic nature and dismissal by the press allow Brahmins to laugh at themselves and confront stereotypes indirectly, as jokes. The jokes are designed to point out contradictions between actual practice and ideals, and in doing so shape both the way Brahmins think about themselves and act as a corrective to inappropriate behavior. The following chapter looks at the elements that make up a sabha drama to create an overall aesthetic that projects and reflects Tamil Brahmin identity.

CHAPTER THREE

The Amateur Aesthetic

Two or Three People Just Standing on Stage

> Muthu (on phone): Hello! Yes, this is the National Gas Company. Head Clerk Muthusamy speaking. Who is this? What? I didn't hear you properly. Oh! Perumal? So are you well? It seems like I can see the God Perumal, but I can't see you, the person Perumal. What? Markandeyan? Or Mathrabootham? No. They haven't come yet. Today's Saturday, no? So even if he comes, today is Saturday, so it's a half day only, so he'll just sign a few papers hurriedly and dash off. Yes. All the horses in Guindy are waiting for him. What? It's not the season . . . mmm . . . has that occurred to him? Every week it is only him who is running; the horses won't run.
>
> —From *Parama Rahasiyam* ("Top Secret") by K. K. Raman

Many of the jokes of the sabha theater are simply slices of everyday life. This 1971 play is set in an office in Madras that has a managing director named S. S. Rajan who lives in Bombay. One of the clerks in the office is taking a correspondence course and is continually receiving packets in the mail from his course that are postmarked Bombay and stamped "S. S. Rajan." All of his bosses think that he is close with the managing director, whom he has never actually met or spoken to, and the packets are from someone entirely different with the same name. In the joke I have included here, the head clerk relates that Saturday is the big horse racing day at Guindy Race Course, so at least one of those employees will appear for a half day only, if he shows up at all, in his rush to get to the race track. When he finds out that it is not racing season (races are only held in the cool winter season), he quips that it must be his colleague who is racing, then. The humor is built around everyday occurrences: the phone doesn't work properly, there is confusion about the names of gods and men, employees are late to the office, and the excuses people make to get out of work don't stand up to the most cursory scrutiny.

Sabha theater, as I've mentioned, encompasses not only a political ideology and a patronage system, but also a structure and an aesthetic, which are dictated in part by the patronage system. Because audiences are linked to particular venues, sabha plays must shift venue for every performance—even when they run for decades. This precludes such things as elaborate sets, which are valued in many western plays (even in Chennai), but make sense only when a play can be linked to a particular theater in which the stage set can stay and to which audience members must travel. In the sabha system, it is the audience that remains in the theater while the various troupes and plays come to them along with all their sets, props, and sound and light equipment, a set-up that has had significant effects on the style of sabha plays.

These plays, which are by far the most numerous, visible, and popular in the city of Chennai today, exhibit the influences of commercial film, folk theater, English drawing room comedies, and regional caste-based political plays in addition to Pammal Sambanda Mudaliar's work, which responded to the popular Parsi theater and the Tamil Musical Dramas it inspired.[1] In his autobiography, Mudaliar credits the English-language plays staged by Europeans with giving him his first respect for the theatre and writes disparagingly of the Tamil plays performed near his boyhood home: "When I compared the costumes and make-up of the English actors with those of performers in Tamil plays, I could have no liking for either the Tamil plays or these performers" (Mudaliar 1996, 26). Many of these English plays were in the style of the comedy of manners, and in addition to the less extreme costumes and make-up, likely endowed the developing sabha genre with its emphasis on both witty dialogue and elite characters.

The three types of plays typically seen on the sabha stage over the years are "continuous non-stop comedy plays," "tolerable murder-mystery plays," and "historical and mythological plays" (Shankar 2001a, xiv), of which the comedies have been the majority by far. Themes and approaches vary widely to include horror (*My Dear Kuṭṭi Picācu* [*My Dear Little Evil Spirit*]), audience participation comedy (*Washingtonil Tirumaṇam* [*Wedding *in Washington*]), serious social themes (*Pass Mark*), comedy based on American culture (*One More Exorcist*), political satire (*In̲pakkanā On̲r̲u Kaṇṭēn̲* [*I Dreamed a Sweet Dream*]), and cross-dressing comedy (*Mīcai Ān̲ālum Man̲aivi* [*She's My Wife Even Though She Has a Moustache*]), but the plays share formal and aesthetic characteristics such as scene division, blocking, costume, sound systems, and acting style.

The sabha genre actually divides its plays into "comedy plays" and "serious plays." Within the sabha genre, "serious" plays tend to dominate the attention of critics but flop with audiences, while the comedies become the modern classics.[2] These comedies are derided in the press for their lack of seriousness and message, as the critics overlook the element of gravity in the subtle critiques of certain practices, attitudes, and affectations of the middle class that are revealed in the language and culture jokes and humorous situations. The comedies portray, in an exaggerated fashion, the "normal confusion" of culture for humorous effect, not social reform. This is in distinct opposition to the "DK/DMK plays [which] were an attempt to substitute perfect situations for the normal confusion of contemporary Tamil society" (Rajendran 1989, 138). The pure comedy plays that sabhas tend to favor as the most commercially successful consist of plots that simply string together a series of jokes. Many of these jokes are considered "kaṭi" jokes, which means they bite or sting. These one-line jokes are dismissed as having no content and the attitude toward them implies that they are "stupid" jokes. This type of humor is generally discussed in a dismissive manner in Tamil culture, but its cleverness and sharp wit are clearly appreciated by audiences, who continue to laugh.

Perhaps another reason for this penchant for comedy is that sabha audiences are connoisseurs of the classical music and dance traditions and are therefore trained in a way of viewing that detaches them from the action on stage. *Rasa* is the "savor" of an emotion that one experiences from, for example, watching a dance performance with its stylized gesture language. The sabha plays offer exaggerated views into typical family life to audiences that are ready to relax for the evening and enjoy some entertainment. Comedy is easily accommodated by a viewing style that favors intellectual detachment and connoisseur-like interpretation of the action. If the audience doesn't get involved with the characters, serious dramas can lose their power and appeal. Comedies, on the other hand, deliberately keep the viewer at a distance and allow writers, directors, and actors to slip in messages and allude to serious and political issues that may get through to the audiences, especially if they listen to the play more than once, as many do. The Chennai sabha audiences are so trained in viewing this way that satire and humor are perhaps the best ways to approach serious issues.

A Vulgar, Formulaic Theater

Many elites in the city lament the state of "Tamil drama today," reminiscing nostalgically about the plays that used to be performed in Chennai. Most are nostalgic for the professional troupes that staged mythological and historical dramas that were considered serious productions with intricate sets and costumes and scripted in a more formal language than the current plays.[3] Criticism of sabha theater in both common parlance and the press uses a language of disintegration or stagnation that distinguishes today's plays from those of the 1960s. In fact, when I returned to Chennai in 2008, I saw many more mythological and historical plays being offered than had been the case four years earlier. On my most recent visit, in 2016, I saw only old plays being revived. Kathadi Ramamurthy was celebrating sixty years in theater by performing old favorites and S. Ve. Shekher had revived *Crazy Thieves in Palavakkam* from 1976. There are new plays being produced, but they are few and far between. I'll discuss some of these in the epilogue. Critics suggest that the sabha plays have either gone downhill or not developed at all; that the artists are simply presenting audiences with basically the same play over and over. Kausalya Santhanam, *The Hindu's* theater critic, has written numerous articles to that effect. Her articles on the sabha theater genre are titled "When Will They Try to be Different?" (May 10, 2002) and "Caught in the Formula Trap" (May 18, 2001), for example. There have been some broad shifts in recent years, but there is certainly some truth to this assessment.

The other major criticism that crops up with reference to sabha theater is that it is "vulgar," an accusation that nearly all performance arts in India have dealt with at one time or another. Most actors and dancers in India face stigma because of their nature as public performers, because of the communities they are from, and/or because of the jokes that they tell. One way that producers and patrons of the sabha theater productions in Chennai assert their superiority over folk drama and commercial films is to focus on the purity of their plays, as discussed in the previous chapter. Purity is posited as the opposite of vulgarity, and in discourses about film sequences that "should" be subject to censorship, the vulgar is construed as "that which was corrupting, violent, and obscene; in short, sexuality" (Mehta 2001, 3). This definition of the vulgar links purity with prudishness or modesty, as the opposites of sexuality.

Middle-class families in Chennai, for the most part, are exemplars of Monika Mehta's "national prudishness" and like to pretend that sex doesn't exist and children are immaculately conceived. This tendency is exploited by a very well-received joke I discuss in chapter 6 from S. Ve. Shekher's 1993 play *Ci<u>nn</u>a Māpḷē, Periya Māpḷē* ("Younger Son-in-Law, Elder Son-in-Law") about the elder son-in-law Dog Narasimhan falling asleep on the first night of his marriage instead of consummating the marriage, then ten years into his unconsummated marriage expecting children to simply materialize at any second. First night is an obvious opportunity for artists to talk around sex without mentioning or alluding to it directly; mere mention of the first-night rituals is enough for adult audiences to understand the reference.

This issue of purity and prudishness evident in these discussions about the propriety of the arts was perhaps most explicitly visible in the reforms of Bharata Natyam carried out by Rukmini Devi and others in pre-Independence Madras. Rukmini Devi herself started the trend of Brahmin women, who were seen as inherently pure and modest, performing on stage. This had hitherto been the domain of lower-caste women whose reputations as prostitutes had tarnished the dance in the eyes of respectable society leaders, culminating in a ban of their performances in 1947. It wasn't just the performers, but also the performances that were at issue here. Davesh Soneji has described some of *devadasi* salon dances as "unabashedly sexual and undeniably modern" (2012, 11), which meant that they needed to be significantly reworked (music, movement, costume) in order to fit the religious nationalist agenda. Rukmini Devi's performance at first scandalized the Brahmin community,[4] but Brahmins soon began sending their daughters to her dance school Kalakshetra. By the 1960s, Brahmin women dominated the classical dance scene in Chennai.

Sabha plays are often dismissed as "just comedy" by the very same people who are both parodied in them and patronize them. It is interesting to note that this contradictory attitude toward a favored entertainment genre is found not only in the elite sabha viewing community, but also is prevalent among village audiences. Susan Seizer reports having heard the same trope that I did many times in the context of her research on the folk theater genre of Special Drama. When she asked about the story of one of the comedic scenes, she was "invariably informed, by audience and artist alike, that 'there is no story here, this is just *comedy*!' (*ingu kathaiyē illai, kāmeṭi tāṉ!*). *It was as though drama and comedy were antithetical terms.* 'Just comedy' meant that such performances have no touch with the more esteemed realm of the written story, verse, plot, or narrative" (2005, 203, emphasis mine). The juxtaposition of the serious and the comedic found in Special Drama is, in fact, a device found in ancient Sanskrit dramas and often in Tamil films. The comedy here runs on a separate "comedy track" secondary to the main drama and characters. Comic episodes will be inserted into the main drama, marked by characters of lower status that use a lower-status variety of language. Thus, the audience gets both drama *and* comedy in the space of a single performance.[5] The distinction, however, seems to be lessening and performances leaning more toward the comic. During her research in 1992–1993, Seizer found that 42% of Special Drama performances consisted of different mythological and historical dramas, but 55% were of *Valli's Wedding*, a play Seizer describes as "essentially a comedy" (2005, 129). The remaining 3% "were for an event of 'pure comedy' conducted in a vein of social farce known as *Kathambam*. . . . Performances so named consist solely of comedic scenes, performed by multiple sets of Buffoons and Dancers, with no roles for heroic actors. 'Kathambam' is an apt term to name what is perceived as a messily tantalizing excess of comedy—one that audiences clearly appreciate, even if no one else does (or will admit they do)" (Seizer 2005, 130). These increasingly popular *Kathambam* performances are much closer to what happens in a sabha drama, which, after all, is "just comedy."

The sabha genre favors comedies, and as Seizer has astutely discerned, "[t]he historiography of modern Tamil drama stresses comedy as the most vulgar aspect of drama" (Seizer 1997, 4). I see three separate fears associated with vulgarity in the arts that are visible in the dialogues about sabha dramas. One is the idea that people will imitate what they see on stage or screen and thus they will themselves be corrupted by these ideas and images. A second is that Indian "culture" itself will be corrupted. If "culture" is represented in such a way within the community, there is also the fear that the inappropriate behavior observed in the media will be imitated and become normative and accepted, thus actually changing the culture, whose composition and definition are dependent on the actions of its community members. The third and related fear is that the community that produced the offending film, play, or song will be represented to the outside world as vulgar or corrupt and thus lose status. It is therefore logical that modesty is an externally visible sign of both (good) taste and middle-class identity.

Sabha theater and its performers have not escaped the association of the performance arts with vulgarity. Being of high social status, these performers choose to get involved in theater as a hobby, rather than as a livelihood necessitated by poverty, and they respond not by going on the defensive as so many folk performers do, but by going on the offensive. S. Ve. Shekher has acknowledged that some of his jokes are considered to be in bad taste: "It is complained that my jokes are vulgar. Now, I do admit there may be a joke here or there, which may be described as vulgar. But, vulgarity takes its full form, not on the joke cracked, but on the reaction to the joke. The vulgarity will not manifest if the reaction is bland. I have a family audience. A whole family attends my show. I can't offend their values with my jokes, which are often referred to as 'vulgar'" (in Gopalie 2002, 233). He recognizes that he pushes the boundaries of good taste but argues that his jokes are not vulgar unless the audience interprets them as such, which children, for example, would not do. Therefore, these plays are in good taste and suitable for family entertainment and the burden of "vulgarity" is placed on the audience.

A Clean, Healthy Theater

To counter accusations of vulgarity, sabha drama fans consistently employ two lines of defense. The first is that these plays, especially in relation to other available entertainments in the city, are "clean," "healthy," and suitable for family viewing. The second is that sabha dramas are relaxing and remove working people from the stress of their everyday lives. The values that are repeatedly asserted—"clean," "healthy," and suitable for the entire family to enjoy—are central to the self-circumscription of this community of conservative, middle-class Brahmin fans. The labels are used to distinguish those who choose this sort of entertainment from those who enjoy humor based on sexual innuendo and double entendre, both common devices in films and folk dramas that are targeted at a broader (that is, lower) audience in terms of both caste and class. Upper-middle- and middle-class filmmakers interviewed by Sara Dickey tended to "portray the bulk of cinema viewers—the 'mass,' as they are frequently called—as having narrow, unsophisticated, and even prurient interests in movies" (Dickey 1993, 126). These filmmakers talk about their own aesthetic or creative fulfillment and their desire to do films with "clean stories" or "social messages," but because those films tend to flop, they feel forced to "compromise" and provide fantasy, comedy, and songs. Sabha theater actor A. R. Srinivasan understands that films need to do good business and feels fortunate to be in the theater, where they have a small but "decent" audience and therefore no compulsion to be vulgar or "pander to low taste."[6]

Even though sabha theater prides itself on its cleanliness, there are still jokes about sex in a few of these plays. In place of the "vulgar" and inappropriate banter between a bachelor and an unmarried "Dancer" character that dominates Special Drama or the elaborate courting and vamp characters of film (see Dwyer 2000) are jokes about the first night of a marriage. The main difference between sabha theater and the folk theater or cinema is the level of physical interaction between male and female actors. Susan Seizer writes that "[b]road physical comedy characterizes the Buffoon-Dance Duet" (2005, 203). This standard Special Drama scene is constructed around the highly improbable plot of an unmarried woman who is dancing alone in the middle of the road accidentally "bumping" into a young man. The humor relies on "exaggerated gestures, mockery, and extreme characterizations" in addition to the sexually suggestive language. These comic scenes are interludes in the otherwise very proper drama in which the actors stand fairly still at the front of the stage and direct their speech toward the audience. Film song and dance sequences are similar to these comedy tracks in that the characteristic of lacking discipline could apply equally to both. Film song sequences, like comic interludes, are often out of order, full of fantasy, unreality, and abrupt shifts. They also serve as a space in which to push boundaries of propriety, allowing the actor and actress more physical interaction than the regular story line. Both of these examples involve unmarried couples, and the story may end with a love marriage.

It is at this point in the narrative that sabha theater offers something different. The unmarried characters of film and folk drama may flirt and interact in a culturally inappropriate manner, but sabha drama instead promotes the middle-class domestic space as the one safe enough, and acceptable enough, to deal with the topic of sex. This is both on the level of audience, perceived to be middle-class families, and the characters, who are conceptualized the same way. These sequences are admittedly rare in the corpus of plays, but most frequently and explicitly found in the work of S. Ve. Shekher, a comedian who deliberately pushes the boundaries of Brahmin propriety. It is these "innuendoes of dialogue, mostly of an adolescent kind, [that] sustain their plays," writes K. S. Rajendran (1989, 160) in a clear exaggeration.

On the other side of the debate are those who take offense at these accusations of vulgarity and its association with the lower classes, defending the plays as clean, moral, and respectable to both view and create. The discussion between the two main factions of the Tamil Brahmin community about the value and propriety of the sabha theater reveals a lot about how this group constructs its identity. During Crazy Creations' 25th Anniversary function in the fall of 2003, two prominent Brahmin women, vanguards of tradition through the performing arts (respected Bharata Natyam dancer/scholar Dr. Padma Subramanian and founder/dean of the Padma Seshadri Bala Bhavan school Mrs. Y. G. Parthasarathy), praised the troupe for their efforts in keeping entertainment "pure." Praising the purity of the plays is the primary way that producers and patrons of the sabha theater productions in the city assert their superiority, especially over popular genres such as commercial film and television. At the Narada Gana Sabha on October 2, 2003, Dr. Padma Subramanian said that Crazy Mohan's biggest achievement has been to write comedy for twenty-five years without resorting to sex or violence, and her words got a standing ovation from the audience. She said that he includes "all innocent jokes" and lots of family relations themes that make for "healthy entertainment."

This phrase, "healthy entertainment," gets to the second line of defense for securing respectability and status for the sabha theater: the plays are relaxing and remove working people from the stress of their everyday lives. It also combines the two lauded characteristics of the sabha dramas: healthy and entertaining. Watching these plays, the audience members can laugh, forget their worries, and not think at all for two precious hours. These benefits of light-hearted laughter and relaxation are in opposition to the enjoyment derived from watching classical music or dance, which are never a laughing matter and require great concentration as well as education to properly appreciate. I interviewed a psychiatrist, Dr. N. Mathrabootham,[7] who prescribes sabha dramas to his depressed patients. He says that not only does it get them outside the house, among other people who are enjoying themselves, but it makes them laugh, which is surely the best medicine he can offer.

In her address, Dr. Subramanian reminded the audience of this medical need to laugh in order to remain healthy and credited Crazy Mohan's plays with being both medically and morally beneficial for viewers. She acknowledged the gargantuan nature of this task by thinking about her own medium of classical dance, saying that humor, "hasya," is by far the most difficult rasa to perform. Similarly, at the September 28, 2003, function for the same occasion at Rani Seethai Hall, Mrs. Y. G. Parthasarathy talked about the relationship between *tairiyam* (courage) and *paittiyam* (madness). Crazy Mohan's plays, she said, are examples of "healthy humor," and the audience feels good both during and after the play. He never employs double meanings and writes very clean scripts. She likened lead actor Crazy Balaji to her late husband, the founder of United Amateur Artists, calling him a "full dramatist" who sacrificed everything to devote himself to the stage. "Senseless comedy lightens our minds," she said in English, turning the primary criticism of this genre into a compliment.

Most intellectuals say that entertainment should be instructive to be worth watching. They claim to want to see messages and morals in their plays. This was, in fact, the principle of the early television serials that were known as "pro-development soap operas," and designed to promote various developmental initiatives such as family planning and adult literacy (see Singhal and Rogers 2001). Mrs. Y. G. Parthasarathy and others like her, however, see value in entertainment that simply releases the viewer from daily stresses. As long as the humor is clean and doesn't actually negatively affect viewers, they argue that there is nothing wrong with its being frivolous and senseless.

In addition, Mrs. Y. G. Parthasarathy praised Crazy Mohan's dialogues and the other actors in the troupe, saying that he puts pressure on the interpreter/actor. Because the stage is such a powerful medium, it is important that the jokes and the messages are healthy and appropriate, and Crazy Mohan's work is. For this reason, she counts herself one of his fans who love to see the plays again and again. She praised *Jurassic Baby* (which I discuss in detail in chapter 5) in particular as a fantastic play because it is so beloved by children, adding that it is wonderful for kids, so clean and healthy, and different from TV. It is also a very good way for families to spend time together, and she encouraged parents to take their kids to the theater and enjoy the medium. "We need these plays in these 'crazy times,'" she concluded, referring to the aesthetics and characteristics of sabha dramas in general, not just Crazy Mohan's. This discourse attempts to legitimize this genre of theater as a fitting complement to the classical performances that usually take place in these spaces and to mark it as appropriate entertainment for middle-class audiences.

Now that I have addressed how fans and critics talk about sabha theater, I analyze the basic characteristics of the genre in order to address the structure, content, and aesthetics of the plays themselves. The characteristics of sabha drama that are visible in these plays—patronage by *sabhas*, with their middle-class, usually Brahmin, audience base; a central theme concerning marriage alliances and/or married life; scripted witty dialogue with a thin plot and one-liner jokes, often including language jokes that code-switch between Tamil and English; a socially conservative message; and an "amateur aesthetic" that involves minimal sets, costumes, lighting, and two-hour evening or weekend matinee performances—help to define the genre.

Scripts, Plots, and Themes

Sabha plays, in general, are scripted, not improvised. Most troupes are organized around a central figure who may be either the playwright (Crazy Mohan's Crazy Creations, Cho Ramasamy's Viveka Fine Arts, Marina's [T.S. Sridhar's] Rasika Ranga, K. S. Nagarajan's Kala Nilaiyam) or the lead actor (S. Ve. Shekher's Natakapriya, Kathadi Ramamurthy's Stage Creations, Y. G. Mahendran's United Amateur Artists, Purnam Viswanathan's Purnam New Theatre). New troupes generally start when an actor or writer who has been part of another troupe becomes famous enough to earn a chance from the sabhas to draw audiences on his own. They may take with them some actors from the old troupe and also find friends and family members to join them in their new endeavor. Appendix E includes a family tree of sorts, showing some of the relationships between troupes. Occasionally, as in the case of Rail Priya or Dummies Drama (also known as Dummies Communications) (see figures 3.1 and 3.2), a troupe of all unknowns will appear. V. Sreevatson, the certified accountant who started Dummies Drama with his business partner and a group of friends, loved theater but felt that Tamil theater had started going downhill in the 1990s. He wrote his first play, *Women's Rea*,[8] and produced it with a group entirely made up of first-time actors in 1999. Things were difficult for this troupe, which without a big name behind it, has had to pay for everything independently and work very hard to earn the support of sabhas.[9] This is an unusual scenario, however, and most troupes begin with either an established lead actor or writer.

One constraint on writers is that all scripts for dramas performed in Chennai needed to be cleared by the police until the 2013 High Court ruling that some provisions of the Tamilnadu Dramatic Performances Act of 1954 (a relic of the 1876 British Dramatic Performance Act) were unconstitutional (see Sangameswaran 2013). The 1954 Act was set up by the state government after a play by M. R. Radha[10] "led to a law and order problem" (Shankar 2001a, xvi). There were a number of issues involved

Figure 3.1. Advertisement for Dummies Communications (side 1). *Source*: Author's collection.

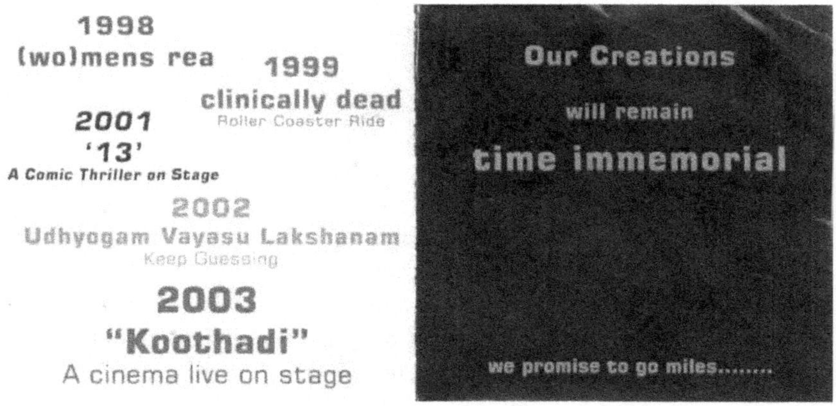

Figure 3.2. Advertisement for Dummies Communications (side 2). *Source*: Author's collection.

in the implementation of this law. One is illustrated by this funny story related by Shonali Muthalaly:

> Every theatre group has to get permission from the local police station before they perform a play, irrespective of where they are performing. To obtain permission, the script has to be passed by the police and the play signed by the playwright.

> One director, who recently staged the "Twelfth Night" [*sic*] was repeatedly asked to get its author's signature at the police station. When the bewildered, and rather shaken, director stammered that it's a play by Shakespeare, who was dead, the unflappable policeman said "Oh . . . Ok, Sir. Ask Mr. Shakespeare's close relative to sign then" (2003b).

The second big issue was that in addition to the playwright's signature, every page of an approved script must be officially stamped, and this needed to be done at least one month before the inauguration date. This means that because scripts tend to go through many incarnations in rehearsal, the final product may bear little relation to the originally submitted script. Most writers had their doubts about whether anyone actually read their work. In fact, the police hardly ever suggest deletions of scenes or lines for sabha plays, so the few instances where it has happened are significant. Cho Ramasamy, with his overtly political satires, has had more trouble with this than any other sabha playwright, which I will discuss in detail in chapter 7.

Even with an approved script, and notwithstanding pre-performance edits, there are comedians like S. Ve. Shekher who do not follow a written script very closely but will improvise jokes to keep the play updated with regard to current events and audiences returning to the theater. In general, playwright-centered troupes tend to adhere much more closely to the written script than actor-centered troupes. Actor-centered troupes generally own the rights to plays by several different writers and have a great deal of freedom to improvise or to change the dialogue or the play as they like. These insertions, deletions, and/or alterations are completely unregulated by the state.

Producers and audiences, who both represent the very specific community of middle-class urban Tamil Brahmins, also play a role in these debates about appropriate topics and jokes, and since they are more directly involved than the state, their concerns actively affect the format and content of sabha plays. One reason, perhaps, that the state feels little need to censor sabha plays is that this community exercises a great deal of self-censorship that is stricter than any law would require. Unlike the strict rules governing film releases, no state official will view the final version of the play to determine whether or not the approved script is being followed. Now that the law has been overturned, these issues are no longer a concern.

Reading, Viewing, and Listening to Plays

Most sabha plays are meant to be heard and/or seen, not read, so very few are published. S. Ve. Shekher, Marina, and Cho Ramasamy are the notable exceptions, along with a few famous plays from other playwrights.[11] These plays are a troupe's security in the sabha theater world. No one else can perform the plays, and they tend to be very possessive about them, which is also a characteristic of *terukkūttu* and other folk theater genres.[12] In 2012, Cho allowed T. V. Varadarajan to perform one of his plays using the published script and recorded a video that was shown before the play praising the troupe and saying he was happy that his play was still relevant. Rumor is that he regretted it after, and the permission was not renewed or extended to anyone else. Occasionally, a writer will retain the rights to his work (Mouli, K. K. Raman) and the troupe will pay for each performance. This does not mean, however, that the plays are published and the writers are trying to earn money by selling rights or books. Mouli, for example, is simply too busy with films to stage any of his own dramas and doesn't want them published because sequences from them could be useful for him in later film work or lifted by other filmmakers (author interview with Mouli, August 19, 2003).

This possessiveness about a troupe's cultural property is not the main reason, however, that sabha plays are not published. The main reason is that the writers and actors believe that their work is only effective *in performance*. They don't publish their plays simply because they don't believe anyone would read them. Most looked surprised at the very idea of publishing. These are *dramas*, I was told again and again; they are meant to be performed in order to be appreciated. There is no habit of reading dramas in Chennai, and the few Tamil dramas that are published are printed in very small runs. Most dramas are not considered worth spending time on. Attending a performance is social; it is an enjoyable escape, but why would anyone read a string of jokes on a page? I was asked. Of course, many people read jokes on a page, as there are published joke books as well as the popular magazines that Gabriella Eichinger Ferro-Luzzi talks about in her 1992 book *The Taste of Laughter*. Another issue is that more and more young people are not learning to read and write Tamil. They may be fluent in speaking and listening, but study in English-medium schools and never learn the Tamil script.

A much more common way to fix a Tamil sabha play for posterity has been to record a performance text on film. While it is clear from the cultural and linguistic references that the target audience is educated and wealthy, the actual audience may be broader thanks to the mass media. The Doordarshan drama series produced by S. Gopalie in the 1970s and 1980s included many sabha dramas, including most of the work of Purnam Viswanathan and Kathadi Ramamurthy, among others. There are many examples of films that are not much more than filmed play performances, and there are directors like Mouli, Visu, and K. Balachander who moved to film directly from the theater. Balachander is famous for films that "analyse unusual or complicated interpersonal relationships and social themes" (http://www.answers.com/topic/k-balachander, viewed May 28, 2007) and made Komal Swaminathan's *Water!* and many of his own plays such as *Etir Nīccal* (*Swimming Upstream*) and *Nāṇal* (*Reed*) into films. Cho Ramasamy has several plays such as *Mohammad bin Tughlaq* and *Maṉam Oru Kuraṅku* (*The Mind Is a Monkey*) that were made into films. Even some of the full-length comedies have been made into films such as Crazy Mohan's *Marriage Made in Saloon* and S. Ve. Shekher's *Atiruṣṭakāran* (*Lucky Guy*).[13] Since about 2005, it has been common to sell DVDs of recorded plays, and Kalakendra, based in Chennai, has been the leading producer.

Dialogue is the most important component of the sabha comedy plays, and the intonation and timing that accompany it are what keep the jokes alive. This means that it is important for the audience to be able to hear, and a poor sound system can ruin a play, which I saw happen at a 2004 Rasika Ranga play at the Narada Gana Sabha. It was practically impossible to hear the actors, audience members kept jumping up and shouting for them to be louder or to fix the mikes, and it was quite an embarrassing show for this established and respected troupe. Most of the sabha actors are amateurs who are not particularly trained in voice projection (two notable exceptions being R. Neelakanthan and Karur Rangarajan), so the dramas are well-miked. Most of the sabha troupes use three long, low microphones across the front of the stage. These are less intrusive to the performance, but also less effective than a set-up like S. Ve. Shekher's where there are four standing microphones into which actors speak directly, impeding their ability to interact physically with one another. Critic M. Tangarasu has lamented that with these plays all the techniques designed for theater are excluded. Tamil theater is at the sad state, he wrote in 2000, where it is enough for two or three people to stand on stage and say lines that the (not particularly discerning) audience can laugh at (2000, 93).

Instead of being divided into three or five acts, which are further divided into scenes the way most western plays are, these plays are divided into lots of small scenes. A typical play will have between twenty and forty individual scenes. In production, the scenes are separated by a brief period of darkness and some recorded music. Sometimes a set change will take place during the break. There is a longer break of about ten minutes for an intermission about halfway through the play, unless there's a long function before the play begins that necessitates eliminating it. This is a time for the audience to get snacks, use the restroom, and chat for a few minutes.

The plays, which are known for having extremely thin plots, include many jokes about how ridiculous film plots are, often complete with mock summaries, as demonstrated in Cho's joke about the woodcutter film I referenced in the first chapter. In these instances, the plays emphasize the quality and veracity of their plots and characters, implying that however bad these two things may be in the play, at least they are superior to what is found in film. This distinction and the critique of films is found not only in the plays themselves but also outside of the theater, where the sabha artists are happy to be associated with the classical performance genres, but they make a point of being "distinct" (in Bourdieu's sense) from film.

It is important to note that the plays *do* actually have plots, despite many accusations to the contrary. And while individual scenes within those plots can toy with challenging social norms, in the end the message of the play must affirm traditional values, especially with regard to marriage alliances, but concerning everything from generational norms to gender roles and class, caste, and regional divisions. These are performances designed to amuse and entertain, not to teach, and should resolve noncontroversially. The Mahalakshmi Ladies Drama Group run by Bombay Gnanam addressed controversial social themes in their earlier plays and avoided this issue by developing a strategy of including multiple perspectives on a topic. They would then leave the ending of the plays open, with no resolution, so that no particular point of view would be identified as the right answer and privileged. Instead, as long-time member Padmini Natarajan puts it,

> Quite a bit Gnanam leaves it to the audience to decide whether you want to . . . You know, the ending was what you would like it to be. You know? Sometimes it's a question. She just throws a question. And she says, you decide. You tell me. And very often, after the performance, when the curtain calls are on, people in the audience get up and give an answer . . .

> We've had arguments, we've had fights from the audience. How could you do this? You know? It's been very interesting, the way that the audience gets worked up about this whole issue, whatever the issue is that you have been handling or talking about. (Natarajan, 2015a)

For this troupe, part of the strategy for staying within the conservative values of the audience, and those of the affluent, educated, middle-class families of the performers themselves, was simply to not take sides. The plays thus always align with the values of the audience if each member of it can write his/her own ending. For example, in *Ārambam* (*Fresh Beginnings*, ca. 1998) on widow remarriage, audiences expected that Gnanam would come out in favor of widow remarriage. Instead, she leaves it open. At the end, the widow turns to the audience and says "Is it necessary for me to marry? Is there no life without marriage, without a partner? What should I do? You tell me what should I do?" (Natarajan, 2015). There is no sense of what the playwright believes to be the right thing for this character, or for any other woman in her situation. This is unusual, however, and most plays resolve storylines, not requiring the audience members to do that work.

In contrast to sabha plays (with plots), there are comedy shows in Chennai that really are nothing but jokes. For example, the Humour Club International, which has several branches in Chennai, is often "invited by many organizations, both private and government, to stage humour shows for their staff members tied down by hectic schedules."[14] These programs usually run about thirty minutes and consist of "jokes, humour music, miming, magic, skits and ventriloquism" (Vijayalakshmi 2003). There are also people like M. T. Vedantham who conduct hour-long humor shows that consist of "50–60 non-stop jokes" (Bhuvaneshwari 2003), which are gleaned primarily from Tamil magazines. In this environment, the recent rise of standup comedy is no surprise.

Although the plays may include jokes similar to the ones found in magazines and humor shows, the difference is that they have a connecting thread that can keep audiences interested for the two-hour show, even though the plot resolution is usually obvious within the first ten minutes (as is true of most popular culture genres based on formulas). The most common plot line is organized around the Tamil proverb, "Make a marriage, even if you tell a thousand lies."[15] The most common themes are marriage alliances and/or married life, which have continued to resonate with middle-class urban audiences. Traditional notions of marriage and family are still central to modern imaginings of Tamil culture (Trawick 1990), and this has been fodder for the dramas. Farley Richmond, writing in 1990, commented that "[i]n Madras one may find plays that are concerned primarily with family and social issues. The generation gap is a favorite theme among Madras playwrights. Many of the contemporary plays show older, tradition-bound parents attempting to come to grips with the new lifestyles and changing values of their children" (1990, 402). Twenty-six years later, Stage Creation's 2016 play *Nīyā Nāṉā* (*You or Me?*) by S. L. Naanu deals with these issues; its central theme concerns the increasingly rare joint family versus independent families.

The jokes and comic themes of these plays can be very revealing about the cultural values of the Tamil Brahmin community. The audience response to these performances involves a spontaneity that is absent in classical and religious cultural performances that have pre-scripted responses. Connoisseur audiences of the classical arts are expected to respond to performances in particular ways coded by years of tradition.[16] Although there are cues in the dramas (a pause or music) to indicate intended jokes, it is difficult to script comedy. Marx and Sienkiewicz say that "[a] joke is an invitation that comes with a test. If you closely follow its movements, grasp its logic, and laugh at the right moments, you become part of a club—those who get it" (2018, 102). This is why comedy writer Crazy Mohan believes that the audience must be taken into consideration in this type of performance in particular: "Comedy is the only form of performing arts which is a duet between the audience and the performers—the rest are all solos," he says (Santhanam, September 8, 2003). When the audiences laugh, when they find intended jokes funny, these performances offer insight into the *actual*, not idealized, anxieties, concerns, and self-conceptions of this elite community of observers. Even S. Ve. Shekher, who deliberately tries to appeal more broadly than other troupes, and has both young and non-Brahmin fans, still roots his plays in a specific audience base. In an interview with S. Gopalie, former producer of Doordarshan's drama section, he said, "I do not have much belief or faith in some groups, calling themselves special, doing plays that were hits in Broadway or London. I must do a play, say to a Mylapore audience, focusing on the Mylaporean problems. Where is the need to project to my people somebody else's problem? There is little point in it" (Gopalie 2002, 229). The typical Mylaporean audience is reasonably cohesive and has a recognizable, though unstable, identity that allows him to say this and to target his work.

In the full-length comedy plays sponsored by elite urban sabhas, every scene includes jokes and comic characters as well as colloquial language. The salient features of sabha dramas, which have little literary merit according to K. S. Rajendran, are "contrived plots, unnatural developments, thrills and suspenses, hilarious comedies" (159–160). The "serious" sabha plays are rarely lightened with any humor at all, but these are seldom performed, poorly attended, and often outdated. An example is Prayatna's *3.42*, which though it included critically lauded innovations such as ventriloquism and an all-male cast, is non-stop tension for two straight hours. The play concerns an injured athlete who is jealous of his young protégé and attempts to sabotage him, eventually driving the boy to suicide. The emotion and tension are "tedious" and "unendurable after a point," according to well-known drama critic Kausalya Santhanam (May 14, 2004). Serious plays are sometimes supported by sabhas in part due to a regional nationalistic effort to encourage Tamil language and promote artists who work on dramas in that language that address serious social reform issues. This benefit may outweigh considerations of profit potential or audience predilection. The serious/comedy contrast in the sabhas needs to be drawn not within the plays themselves but between dramas and performances such as classical music and dance.

Chennai's urban audiences have revealed a preference for comedy over serious drama, whether in Tamil or in English, on stage or on screen. In a 2003 article for *The Hindu* titled "Hooked on Humour," Kausalya Santhanam writes that "[f]or quite a few years now, the monopoly of success on the Tamil stage has been that of the experts with the appealing pun," and a large percentage of the experts she names (S. Ve. Shekher, Crazy Mohan, Cho Ramasamy, Kathadi Ramamurthy, Mouli, Nagesh, Thangavelu, Bosskey, the United Amateur Artists) are from the sabha theater. Tamils are incredibly proud of their language play, and those who master it are much appreciated. Santhanam, a Tamil herself, says without reservation that "Tamil Nadu has some of the best comedians/ennes in the country. For, this is a city where even the cab driver and the rickshaw man are masters of the ready quip and the instant retort. The Tamil people have a talent for the right word" (Santhanam, September 8, 2003). The paradox is that although most Tamils agree with this self-aggrandizing representation of themselves as funny, they will also decry the sabha comedies with that familiar derogatory slur "just comedy." In recent years, at least twenty clubs and sabhas supporting standup comedy as well as sketch and improv have appeared in the city, forms that appeal more to the youth of a global Indian new middle class than to the older generation of Brahmins targeted by sabha theater.[17]

Santhanam respects comic traditions in Tamil and understands the hard work behind them, saying "Comedy is hard work. A good director must have a sense of humour apart from being able to hold the balance so that it does not become mere hamming" (September 8, 2003). Even so, she has little to say about the sabha dramas that is positive. She believes that today's comedies rely too much on recycled jokes and have little to offer the "discerning viewer" and that performers are more concerned about neither offending nor insulting the audience than they are about challenging or engaging them, and this contributes to the repetition of tried and true jokes and themes (January 24, 2003). Comedian S. Ve. Shekher, in a disclaimer meant to compliment viewers, told Santhanam that "[t]hose who come to view plays are well educated. So even in a socio-political satire . . . I only give my opinion" (September 8, 2003). The resulting conservative reliance on the familiar is the same as in the commercial cinema that this performance genre attempts to distinguish itself from, but the rhetoric and motivation are different. Shekher is worried that audiences will be engaged with the performance and feel offended or insulted; the typical mass media fear is that audiences will become passive absorbers and imitators of what they see on screen (see Gans 1999).

The actual response of intellectuals to these "safe," formulaic sabha plays is, as exemplified by Santhanam, to be bored. She rarely reviews any of the comedies, from which she cannot expect innovation, preferring to attend and review the few serious dramas staged. She is continually disappointed by the lack of originality even here, however, and expressed her boredom with the serious plays in a 2003 article titled "Outdated Ideas, Antiquated Scenes":

> In various permutations and combinations, this theme is played out again and again in mainstream Tamil theatre. The conflict in familiar relationships—between father and son, mother-in-law and daughter-in-law and among brothers. And of course the Montague-Capulet like feud between the families of two young people in love. The situations are developed through the clashes and misunderstandings that take place. But invari-

> ably everything turns out right in the end. Copious tears of regret are shed with the patriarch of the family, who is usually considered infallible, flashing forgiving smiles or delivering a long speech on the need for togetherness and understanding.

Other intellectuals in the city agree with her assessment and thus either avoid the stage altogether or attend the English-language comedies (usually Indianized adaptations of western plays), which are growing in frequency and popularity, or foreign comedies translated into Tamil.

The problem of staleness in the arts is one that has a long history with regard to Tamil culture, even extending to classical music. While for the most part, this is a genre valued for its adherence to tradition, the famous nationalist poet Bharatiyar wrote an essay in 1916 in which he said that the Tamils had lost their feeling for music: "Go to any district, any village, . . . whichever vidwan [scholar] comes, it will be the same story. Because Tamilians have iron ears, they can stand to listen to the same seven or eight songs over and over and over and over again. In places where people have ears of flesh they would not endure such a thing" (quoted in Weidman 2006, 174). This complaint is echoed by today's Tamils when they discuss sabha dramas. Part of the reason the Chennai audiences stopped paying attention to Crazy Mohan, informants tell me, is that although he claims never to repeat a joke, there are many repetitious instances. Having seen many of his plays, written for Crazy Creations and other troupes, I sympathize with the criticism that Crazy Mohan's plays are "formulaic." Tired jokes that Chennai audiences hear every week, however, can seem new and exciting to audiences in the U.S. or other diasporic communities, who only have the opportunity to see plays once every few years.

This accusation of unchanging formula has also been a common criticism of Indian films as well as of most popular culture products. The formulas need to evolve and producers innovate just enough to keep their audiences coming back to see/read yet another installment. Some formulaic conventions, as put forth by John Cawelti in his influential 1976 book *Adventure, Mystery, and Romance: Formula Stories as Art and Popular Culture*, include ways of treating specific characters or things, plot types and story patterns, cultural stereotypes, and stock characters. All of these can be found in commercial cinema in India as well as the sabha plays, but the intents of the film and sabha drama formulas are diametrically opposite. The cinema formula is aimed at appealing to broader audiences, while the theater formula targets a very small minority population in the city. Films are crowded with music, dance, and fight scenes, elements that are included primarily to appeal across generations, classes, and regions. Sabha theater, on the other hand, is generally designed to appeal to a particular Chennai-identified Brahmin community that prides itself on intellectualism and eschews most of the signature "masala" elements of commercial film. Actor A. R. Srinivasan told me in an interview that the professional theater was in the same style as film, with songs and everything. The amateur theater that he counted himself part of as an early member of the United Amateur Artists, deliberately distinguished itself from the professional theater and film worlds, and one strategy was to remove all the elaborate costumes and sets as well as the music (author interview, May 14, 2004).

There are many joke themes that recur in the sabha plays over and over, thus offering a glimpse into what makes Tamil Brahmin audiences laugh. It is useful in thinking about both the genre and the community that produces and views it to take a look at a few of Tamil theater's most popular jokes. I will analyze some of this dialogue in depth in part II of this book as I look at individual plays. Some of the community characteristics revealed by my analysis include language, a concern with caste and class status, gender and generational roles, status symbols and anxiety about money, and the value of good names and reputations, doctor/patient relationships, and generosity.

Language

Jokes and dramatic themes are one window into the self-identity of the Tamil Brahmin community; language is another. While Dravidian politicians were agitating against Hindi and Sanskrit, these Brahmins were writing and enjoying plays in *Tamil*. The Tamil that was predominantly used, and still is by many troupes, is marked by the Brahmin dialect. Cho Ramasamy, Marina, and Crazy Mohan, for example, all use this distinctive Sanskritized dialect, which reaffirms the identity of this community as simultaneously Tamil *and* Brahmin. The speech in these plays is, as Arokianathan claims of radio plays in general, "normal day-to-day speech forms . . . 'recreated' in a controlled environment" (1988, 2). This familiar, nostalgic language, in fact, is one reason why many diasporic Tamil Brahmins say that they prefer Crazy Mohan over the more broadly popular S. Ve. Shekher, whose comedies are in a dialect commonly called "Madras

Tamil." The plays may have little to do with making the members of the audience more "cultured," but many of the jokes *assume* a certain level of education and cultural competence, including knowledge of English (and often Hindi and Telugu), current events, and classical performance arts as well as mass media.

S. Ve. Shekher realized that Brahmin dialect and subject matter would severely limit his audiences and so made a point of having his plays written in everyday Madras Tamil and keeping the themes and families in his plays as generic as possible. Although he himself is Brahmin and proud of it, S.Ve. Shekher understands that the population of Tamil Brahmins who enjoy theater is not large enough to sustain a troupe at the level he wants and has spoken many times about the insular way other troupes use Brahmin dialect and culture in their plays. Marina, in response to criticism of this kind, said defensively during an interview that "[t]here is nothing wrong with people using the language that they are familiar with and writing about the society they know."[18]

By extension, sabha theater troupes also tend to hire actors and actresses that they know from their own community. They find actors through family, co-workers, and friends, who are part of the same social circles as themselves and their audience members. Fittingly, these troupes often refer to themselves as "family."[19] Shekher, in contrast, employs non-Brahmins in his troupe, approaching good performers whom he has seen in other troupes or on television and inviting them to join. His actors are rarely permitted to perform with other troupes, though they are free to do television and film roles, provided they don't interfere with show times and rehearsals. Their success in the mass media brings more recognition and publicity to his stage troupe.

Tamil-language theater, like the Marathi-language theater that Apte (1992) discussed, demonstrates ethnocentrism and the pride in language and culture that both Tamils and Marathis are famous for.[20] Even though sabha theater is entirely a Tamil-language theater—and this characteristic is central to the genre and therefore to the identity of the writers, performers, and viewers—there was a very popular trend for a while of using English titles for Tamil plays. A few examples are *Honeymoon Couple*, *Jurassic Baby*, *Madras By Night*, *If I Get It*, *Lights On*, *One More Exorcist*, and *Flight 172*. When asked about his practice of titling plays in English, Cho Ramasamy responded by saying, "I did a number of plays and for some reasons I can't recall now why I gave the titles in English. T. K. Shanmugam, a reputed professional, was so annoyed with my titles in English for Tamil plays, and made public comments when he presided over one of our plays. I promised him my next play would not bear an English title. He looked pleased. I called it 'Quo Vadis' " (Gopalie 2002, 53). It is easy to see the source of T. K. Shanmugam's annoyance with this trend. This was a period of intense Tamil pride that came with the rise of the Dravidian movement. Why disguise Tamil literature with an English title, thus masking its true nature?

Middle-class urbanites have a conflicted relationship with the English language. English is a marker of education, class, and wealth in India, thus the English titles introduce an element of snobbery onto the stage. However, just because something is in English doesn't mean it automatically confers status on the viewers. In fact, several of the academic articles that refer to sabha theater (Ramanujam 2003b; Arakappan 1999) focus on this trend and imply that having English titles for Tamil plays is misleading and somehow dishonest. While there is a thriving market for both domestic, regional-language literature and imported English-language literature, choice of language is never unmarked by class biases. Paul Brians estimates that only about three percent of the Indian population can read English with enough fluency to enjoy the high literary novels that he addresses in his work (2003, 4). The post-Independence generation grew up reading Nancy Drew, Enid Blyton, and other English-language fiction, and English is today considered an Indian language, despite the historical postcolonial context. Sanjeev Sanyal writes that "the new middle-class is both more casual and confident of both its English—and its Indianness" (2008, 181). Writing in Tamil, as discussed in the previous chapter, is a deliberate political choice, but also a celebration of the vernacular.

The two major political parties in Tamilnadu are both regional parties that often campaign on Tamil nationalist issues. Cho Ramasamy wrote a play called *Cāttiram Connatillai* (*The Scriptures Don't Say So*) that includes the character of a politician who educates his son in English-medium schools. He claims that he made a "sacrifice" (*tiyākam*) in terms of his career and reputation by doing so:

> I've sacrificed. Whatever other people have said, I sent this boy to study in *English medium* schools . . . Everyone from the other parties keep saying, "He talks 'Tamil, Tamil' on the stage but sends his son to study *English medium*." Haven't I worried? If I had sent him to *Tamil medium* what would this

> boy's fate have been? Isn't this a sacrifice I've made? (Rudisill forthcoming 2022, 35)

This character parodies former chief minister M. Karunanidhi, a celebrated Tamil writer and orator who lobbied for Tamil education but educated his own children in English-medium schools.

English also introduces an element of pretension, which does not command respect and is always a good source of humor. In his 1969 Tamil adaptation of George Bernard Shaw's *Pygmalion*, Cho Ramasamy explained the place of English in middle-class India through a conversation between Marudhayi (the vegetable seller trying to raise her social status by learning to behave like a middle-class girl) and Gopinath (her teacher). Marudhayi is nervous about the party Gopinath is throwing, where she will be expected to pass as a London-educated doctor, because she doesn't speak any English. Gopinath reassures her with this speech:

> GOPI: How many modern girls can speak English to a person without mistakes? If you know four phrases in English, that is enough—only four phrases! You can manage if you can remember them when moving around high-class people.
>
> MARU: Four phrases?
>
> GOPI: Yes: Thank you; I am sorry; How nice; How lovely.
>
> MARU: Is that all?
>
> GOPI: But one more thing you need to remember: before saying all these phrases, you need to make the sound, "Oh!" Modern girls' knowledge of English is only this much. Oh! Thank you!; Oh! I am sorry!; Oh! How nice!; Oh! How lovely!—That's all.
>
> MARU: What if I suddenly forget all four?
>
> GOPI: Not to fear! "Oh!" by itself is enough—if you go to a party that's all you need to know! Half the time these women will just shout, "Oh! Oh!" In truth, you don't need even that. Whatever they say, you just need to smile, and that is enough.

> A modern girl! It is enough to show your teeth. In this society, many high-class people will show their teeth.
>
> MARU: I don't understand anything. (Ramasamy 1997, 30)

Cho never answered the unspoken charges of T. K. Shanmugam, simply writing off his English titles as insignificant.

The Amateur Aesthetic

Sabha theater relies heavily on dialogue and jokes for its appeal, but there are also audio and visual components to the plays that can add significantly to the humorous effect. These can include costumes, gesture, sets, music, and physical comedy. The plays are designed to be fast paced and elicit quick laughs from the audience. The structure and aesthetic of the performances are based on the premise that both performers and audiences are working people who participate in the occasional drama for fun. Instead of lasting all night like most folk dramas, sabha performances (of dance, drama, or music) are limited to approximately two hours.

The general aesthetic of sabha dramas is about speed and convenience. When the actors work all day in an office, it is difficult for them to spend a lot of time rehearsing, applying makeup, or dressing in elaborate costumes. This distinguishes them from most genres of professional and folk theater in India. Kathakali, in nearby Kerala, for example, requires several years of rigorous training in expression, dance, gesture, and martial arts before an actor is ready to perform in public. The make-up and costume requirements for a single performance may take several hours of preparation (see Zarrilli 2000, 57–58). Rajendran has suggested that sabha actors and actresses "all learnt how to act by watching films" (1989, 158), but they certainly also learn by watching each other and by doing.

Most sabha dramas concern the lives of everyday families and thus allow for quotidian language and costumes. M. Tangarasu remarked derogatorily that one of the conveniences of sabha theater is that people can rush straight from the office and onto the stage in the evening. This is part of what distinguishes this type of theater and these actors from "professionals" who need to earn their living on stage. The "costumes" say very clearly that acting is something these people do as a hobby, not a profession. The actors are dressed as everyday members of a family, with the men in pants and shirts, veshtis, and the occasional lungi. The women mostly wear saris or salwar kameez, with the occasional nightdress or more modern jeans and a shirt. For the most part, the characters of sabha plays are ordinary folk and they dress in ordinary clothes, though perhaps slightly more flamboyant than usual, with louder patterns on their shirts or lungis than are typically worn.

There are some exceptions, usually in plays that are set in mythological or historical times or that involve time travel to either the past or the future (for example, *Kātula Pū*, *Mahābhārtattil Maṅkāttā*, *Crazy Kishkinda*). Particular characters, especially film stars and priests, also have special costumes that can be funny. Additionally, there are often characters that are in disguise for one reason or another, and these costumes can be ridiculous. The most common disguises include large moustaches and men in drag.

The acting style, like the costumes and the language, contributes to the quotidian aesthetic of sabha theater. There is no elaborate training required for actors, who can go from no acting experience to rehearsing casually a few times, to performing on stage. Rehearsals do not involve any practice of acting techniques or voice projection, the way most professional theater productions would. They learn new plays from written scripts,[21] but if it is a revival of an older play they will often use audio recordings of previous productions. In the latter case, there are usually only a few troupe members who are new and were not part of the previous production. Farley Richmond described the sabha acting style as "realistic acting" with a "melodramatic tendency" (1990, 415). Like America's popular TV sitcoms, Tamil sabha plays show the interactions of an everyday family in which viewers can recognize themselves. These fictional families are, however, funnier, exaggerated versions of the everyday who often become involved in situations that are ludicrous, yet barely believable with an elaborate set up of lies and coincidences.

The sets in sabha dramas are also very uniform. All of the troupes rent their sets from the same two designers (Padma Stages and Kumar Stage) so the same generic living room will be seen at different plays by different troupes. It usually consists of a painted backdrop with a door to the back and possibly a window. The troupes decorate the walls differently with posters of deities and plastic flowers, but there is not much that is distinctive about the sets, which cost about six hundred rupees to rent for an evening performance. They will put two plastic chairs in the center of the stage and occasionally a small table with a phone. Some troupes

(Stage Creations and Natakapriya are good examples) will special-order painted curtains to use as backdrops representing a garden, a bus stop, or another location.[22] The most popular set after the living room is the doctor's office. This set usually uses the same setting as the living room, but with a change of furniture. The doctor has a desk with one chair behind it for him to sit in and one chair beside it for the patients. Other common sets include a road or park, a police station, and a temple.

As far as lighting goes, this amateur theater uses only focus lights. A. R. Srinivasan told me that they only light the stage from the front because they do not have enough lights to do more. He told me that early on the United Amateur Artists attempted different lighting, but it created problems with their sets because the measurements of the different theaters were so different.[23] So now the sabha plays are only front lit, and the stage is full of shadows.

Women on Stage

The stigma of women performing on stage was one that affected both the film and stage industries. The connection between film and live theater was very close when the sabha genre of the full-length Tamil comedy play started in the 1950s. Famous film stars drew audiences to the theater where fans were excited to see them perform live, and theater actors, directors, and plays moved into the film world. Films are much more widely disseminated among more varied publics than sabha plays, and in its early days one of the claims to purity that this Brahmin-dominated theater had over film was the absence of actresses. Anna Morcom phrases it beautifully when she writes "That a woman performs in front of men tends to mean that she will be seen erotically, and as sexually available, whether her performance is erotic or not" (2014, 6). Despite a stigma against actresses due to this association of prostitution with the performing arts,[24] they were common in films at least since D. G. Phalke cast his daughter Mrnalini in the role of Krishna in his 1919 production of *Kaliya Mardan*. From about the 1920s, "The emerging star system was key to building prestige, showing female performers as glamorous and beautiful on-screen; and off-screen, as rich and modern. The cinema was then able to gain real moral capital from the presence of women" (Morcom 2014, 114). Stage plays could gain viewers, but there was no claim to morality to be gained from having female performers. Early films often divided female characters into a heroine and a vamp, so that heroines could maintain a level of respectability and decency with more modest costumes and more classical dance movements. Vamp characters, who could be shown drinking, wearing western clothes, and and performing more erotic dance movements, were typically played by Anglo-Indians or women from hereditary performance lineages.[25] The vamp character had disappeared by the 1990s, when space was made for heroines to wear western clothes and dance western movements.

The reluctance of women to perform on stage in front of live male audience members lasted much longer in theater than in the film medium, where performances could be recorded in a studio or on a set. S. Ve. Shekher argues that theater is actually safer for women's reputations than film or television because it is easy to quit and there are no recordings (author interview, July 8, 2003), but few see it this way, focusing instead on the greater access viewers have to the actress's physical body in a live performance as opposed to their image on a screen. Another factor adding to the delay of female stage actresses was that the families of these respectable young men did not want their sons to be in contact with corrupting actresses, as both Mouli and R. Neelakanthan informed me in interviews. Neelakanthan told me that there was a time when Viveka Fine Arts was the only troupe that did not allow ladies to participate but would use the two best-looking men for these female roles. They chose to do this because they were afraid of their families' reactions and didn't want the stigma. People thought that boys might get spoiled if they were working with lady artistes.[26] Male artistes such as Cho Ramasamy, Karur Rangarajan, A. N. Radhakrishnan, and P. N. Kumar played the women's roles in the 1950s and '60s, a trend that lasted until the early 1980s for the especially orthodox (see cover image of Cho in a female role performing with Neelakanthan). Neelu suggested that the reason Viveka Fine Arts originally had difficulty getting opportunities to perform in north Madras sabhas was not the use of English or the Brahmin orientation that I discussed earlier, but simply that they didn't have any lady artistes, and audiences wanted that.[27] They were successful in the more conservative south Madras sabhas, however, and eventually Cho's plays became popular with audiences all over the city and even began including female actresses. Actor S. Ve. Shekher shared an anecdote about a Natakhapriya performance in the early 1980s, when "*Kumudam,* a Tamil weekly, wanted us to perform in their campus for their employees. It was on a big condition that no lady should participate in the play. We agreed. We asked one of our boys in the group to do the lady's role. The play went off very well" (Gopalie 2002, 220–21). It is true, however, that this same orthodox Brahmin community allowed their daughters to learn and perform the classical dance Bharata Natyam on stage. Practitioners of this art could also claim to be preserving a valuable aspect of authentic Indian (Tamil) culture, unlike stage actresses of the very recent performance genre of sabha theater.

There are still very few female actresses in the sabha circuit, and that has been one of the biggest challenges of that genre over the years. Plays never have more than three female characters, and one or two are far more common because good actresses are expensive and hard to find. Even established troupes with regular female artistes are rarely able to keep them for more than a few years. Some playwrights choose to craft plays with no female characters in order to avoid this problem. Female sabha theater performers, unlike the men, are often professionals and are therefore better compensated than their male counterparts.[28] They are still paid far better in television or film than theater, and S. Ve. Shekher commented that if their names are going to be spoiled by acting they will usually decide to take the higher paying jobs (author interview, July 8, 2003), and it is true that many of these women also work in film and television. The amateur male actors are rarely paid more than transportation fees for Chennai performances, but women can be one of the biggest expenses of a troupe. Farley Richmond explained that in "Madras, for example, an amateur group is made up entirely of actors who are not compensated for their efforts, yet the women must be paid and are considered 'commercial' artists. More than one director has complained that competent actresses cannot be found to play the female characters in a play" (1990, 414). Male actors tend to be exclusively associated with one troupe, while the women take roles where they can get them, often performing for several different troupes at the same time. Shubha Ganesh, for example, acts for Kathadi, Rail Priya, Bharatirajan, Gitanjali, and others.

Brinda Venkatraman is a professional actress who was born in the temple town of Srirangam and started learning classical dance (Bharata Natyam and Kuchipudi) when she was young. She has now been honored with a long list of acting awards including a Kalaimamani Award from the government of Tamilnadu, a Vani Kala Nipuna award from the Sri Thyaga Brahma Sabha, a Lifetime Achievement award from the Parthasarathy Swami Sabha, and Bharat Kalachar's Nataka Kala Bharati. Journalist Malathi Rangarajan writes that, "Versatile Brinda has worked with all the Tamil troupes" (2017), and she is not exaggerating. Brinda's first theater role was with Nawab Rajamanickam Pillai, who founded the professional Tamil theater troupe Devi Bala Vinoda Sangeetha Sabha in 1934 to produce mythological and historical plays. Since moving to Chennai, she has worked with theater greats such as R. S. Manohar, Heron Ramasamy, Kathadi Ramamurthy, Crazy Mohan, and Y. G. Mahendran. She says that "In Kathadi's 'Dowry Kalyana Vaibogamey' I've played all three female parts—Uma, Gowri and Rushyendramani" (quoted in Rangarajan 2017). She mostly does theater on the weekends and television serials during the week. "An A Grade artist with AIR and Doordarshan, theatre actor and dubbing artist in films and serials, Brinda also gives voice-overs for audio recordings of agencies like Santhome Communications" (Rangarajan 2017). For the past fifteen years or so, the only theater group she works with is United Amateur Artists, and she has traveled the world performing with them.

Although many female performers are professionals, some are amateurs and have an arrangement to act exclusively with a particular troupe, very similar to the model of the male actors. These troupe members earn their livings by working at banks, for the railways, or in other jobs with fairly flexible schedules. They may also be housewives, but are then likely to be the wife or daughter or niece of a male actor in the troupe, who is always present to protect their reputation and marriage prospects, in the case of an unmarried woman. I translated one of Kathadi Ramamurthy's plays called *Paṭi Tāṇṭiya Pati* ("The Husband who Crossed the Threshold") by Gajendra Kumar and was confused the whole time about whether one of the characters was supposed to be male or female. The verbs and terms of address just did not match, then at the end there was a whole scene that required a female character. When I asked Kathadi about it, he told me that the play was written with a female character in mind, but they had a performance one night that they could not get an actress for. She was there, but the preceding function lasted so long that she would not be able to stay until the end of the play. Instead of getting one of the men to play her role dressed as a woman, like most troupes would have done, Kathadi rewrote the whole character. This also had the added benefit (given the lengthy function) of shortening the play significantly, since it eliminated an entire subplot.

The roles available for women are severely limited and are all supporting roles. The stock characters of the mother, mother-in-law, wife, love interest, and maid pretty much cover it. Films are starting to have woman-centric plays with female characters who are subjects, not objects (recent films starring Jyotika and Nayantara are good examples), but that has not really translated to the sabha stage, where there is an almost absence of women. I've discussed how this has happened structurally, based on the history of female performers, but it also tells us something about Tamil Brahmin identity and humor. With the single exception I discuss below, there are no female playwrights or directors involved in sabha theater. The female roles, as we've seen, can often be written out by being moved off-stage or converted into male characters. They exist primarily to play straight woman for the star's jokes, to be the object that drives his actions, or to be the butt of the jokes. Occasionally a female character will work, which we know because that's where the love interests meet, or because she and the hero clash at work, such as in *Yāmirukku Bayam Ēn?* ("Why Fear When I am Here?") where the hero and heroine are rival lawyers on a case.

Even now when women regularly perform, sabha theater is still a male domain. It prides itself on its cleanliness and decency, and therefore avoids such taboos as men and women touching on stage. Another phenomenon is the troupe made up entirely of women. The best-known troupe of this type in Chennai is the Mahalakshmi Ladies Drama Group (MLDG) founded by Gnanam Balasubramanian, or Bombay Gnanam as she is commonly known, in 1989. The story is that she read a comment in a newspaper article in which leading Tamil theatre practitioners in Chennai like R. S. Manohar and Komal Swaminathan stated that it was "not possible" for women to write, act, and be fully involved in Tamil theatre and took it as a challenge (Santhanam, May 23, 2003). This group of mostly housewives has made a niche for themselves in the very male-oriented sabha theatre scene in Chennai. Elsewhere, I discuss the story of the Mahalakshmi Ladies Drama Group and argue that their own identities as affluent middle-class Brahmin women along with strategic storytelling and staging methods has allowed them to not only avoid censure but also to become popular with the conservative, traditional Brahmin community in Chennai while bringing to the stage all manner of controversial topics (Rudisill 2016). These women address various social issues in their work, and there are no male actors allowed. The women dress as men and play all the male roles, a reversal of the earlier trend, but in keeping with the purity principles of not mixing male and female performers on stage.

Conclusion

Sabha plays employ what I call an "amateur aesthetic" that is based on the premise that both performers and audiences are working people who participate in the occasional drama for fun. Characteristics of speed and convenience are elevated in the minds of writers and performers. Production aspects from the sets to the props to the lighting are minimal and serve to direct audience attention to the actors. The fast-paced dialogue is filled with jokes, puns, and allusions, and the caste identity is implicit in the performances, apparent in the dress, the speech, the terms of address, and the little rituals both among actors in the theater and on stage during performances. The specificity of these markers shows the rooting of humor in a particular cultural context.

The following chapters move from surface jokes to a deeper understanding of Tamil Brahmin culture. My intent with these in-depth analyses is to gain insight into issues of identity and taste within the sabha drama system. *Washingtonil Tirumaṇam* (*Wedding in Washington*) from 1963 is considered a classic of the genre. The reading of this story and its presentation in the media of novel, drama, and television program that I present in the following chapter clarifies the connection between local politics and the emergence of this dramatic and theatrical genre in the post-Independence period. The play is self-consciously Brahmin in a way that many of the later plays are not and provides a good entry into both the theatrical genre and the self-identity of the Tamil Brahmin community.

PART II

SABHA COMEDIES IN FOCUS

CHAPTER FOUR

Wedding in Washington

Performance of Brahmin Culture

On April 13, 2004, I walked into the outdoor theater at the Indira Nagar Youth Hostel in Chennai, right when Goodwill Stage's production of the play *Washingtonil Tirumaṇam* ("Wedding in Washington") was about to begin. Despite their large number, all of the folding chairs were taken, mostly by elderly women, so the organizers took one from behind their table and placed it front and center for me. This was a play that I had heard about from many sources: my Tamil teacher, friends, actors, writers, and audience members at other plays, and I felt very fortunate to see a revival of the much-acclaimed forty-year-old drama. It was one of the "classic" plays that Hamsadhwani, a long-time classical music organization, had chosen to resurrect while considering whether to add dramas to their entertainment schedule (they eventually decided against it). During the intermission function they announced that they selected plays based on such factors as the former reception of the play and its family-oriented values. In this chapter, I compare the unapologetically Brahmin-oriented *Washingtonil Tirumaṇam* play to the novel and the television serial and identify ways that this versatile story has been adapted for multiple media and enjoyed by viewers of several generations, who have taken pleasure in the elaborate and ritually perfect traditional marriage function it depicts.

The story tells of the wealthy American Mrs. Rockefeller, who heard her friend describe a South Indian marriage, then decided that she must see one for herself. Accordingly, she arranged for an orthodox Tamil Brahmin marriage to happen right there in her hometown of Washington, D.C. By portraying the actions of good Brahmins and the proper way for family and community relations to work in an ideal society as a cultural performance[1] put on for the benefit of an audience comprising culturally ignorant tourists (the Americans in the story), *Washingtonil Tirumaṇam* functions to educate the spectators and readers, who are actually cultural insiders. The cultural misunderstandings the narrative is designed to exploit create great comic effects and allow audience members to identify with different characters and participate in the marriage on different levels.

Washingtonil Tirumaṇam was originally a serialized novel by Cāvi (1916–2001), which was published in the Tamil language weekly *Āṉanta Vikaṭan* the early 1960s. It was adapted as a stage play by the now-defunct Triplicane Fine Arts in 1963, a radio play around the same time, and produced as a television serial in 1995. The novel was finally published by Narmada Publishers in book form in 1999, and the Apple podcast appeared in 2018. This history is a clear indication of *Washingtonil Tirumaṇam's* continued popularity.[2] The play celebrated its five hundredth performance in May 2001 with a function sponsored by the Nataka Academy and Goodwill Stage at the Narada Gana Sabha and has now been performed more than six hundred times (Padmanabhan 2008), packing theaters in April 2008 (Sreelalitha 2008) and as recently as October 2019 (*Music of Madras*). The story is obsessed with the conservative, traditional ideals of the Tamil Brahmin community, and offers a very elaborate description of a perfect Brahmin marriage, with careful attention paid to every small detail, foodstuff, and ritual, often using highly technical ritual and culinary terms specific to Brahmin culture. What makes this marriage so unusual is that it takes place in Washington, D.C., a place that author Cāvi "had not visited before writing the story" (Swaminathan 2001).

Washingtonil Tirumaṇam comes out of a period that Itty Abraham has referred to as "the 'long' 1950s." He and the other organizers of the 2006 "Long 1950s" pre-conference event in Madison, Wisconsin, use the term to mark the period from about 1945 to 1965 "when a radically new set of political, economic, and socio-cultural institutions were being set in place across this region." The play was part of the new socio-cultural institution of sabha comedy plays that was becoming popular in the Chennai of the 1960s. The dramas are indicative of a new social and cultural trend in Tamilnadu as in other parts of the country to move from a pan-Indian focus to a more regional one. The universally known mythological and historical dramas that previously dominated India's stages yielded to narratives that were rooted in specific languages, regions, and communities. The humor and the versatility of the story have clearly appealed to Tamils over the years.

Given its colonial history, it is no surprise that, just as Marilyn Ivy argues about Japan, India is "literally unimaginable outside its positioning vis-à-vis the West" (1995, 4). The post-colonial period followed colonial trends of reflecting on indigenous culture in relation to western cultural norms. These reflections often developed into cultural performances that mediated the conflicting ideals of modernity and tradition. The novel *Washingtonil Tirumaṇam* was a place where Tamil Brahmin identity was constituted and negotiated in the long 1950s, and it continues to fill that role for later generations of readers and spectators.

Cultural Narcissism

As the novel sets up the narrative, Mr. and Mrs. Hari Hops have taken a trip to India where they were fortunate enough to witness a traditional four-day Tamil Brahmin marriage in Tanjore. Upon their return to America, they shared their experience with their very good friend Mrs. Rockefeller. After viewing countless pictures, reading notes, and listening to their detailed descriptions for "four full days without a break" (Cāvi 1999, 22), this wealthy woman decided that she must see a South Indian marriage for herself.[3] "Yes," said Mr. Hops, "however much we describe it, you won't be able to understand all of that. Having brought a marriage party from South India, if you conduct the marriage right here, you can understand everything perfectly" (Cāvi 1999, 22–23). Mrs. Rockefeller immediately picked up the phone and began planning, saying that to make the marriage perfect, she would go to any expense, bringing not only the family members to Washington, D.C., from Chennai, but also guests, priests, and cooks. This is an important point, because marriages are notoriously expensive in South India. The bride's family typically pays for the wedding (and usually a dowry as well), and it is common for families to go into a great deal of debt in order to marry their daughters properly. For this reason, marriages can be a serious source of stress for all of the family members involved.

The narcissism of the author about his culture is evident in the very set-up of the narrative. The South Indian marriage, which is obviously considered to be the pinnacle of culture, is too rich and complex to be described, even with the help of notes and photos, over a four-day period. Only by conducting it herself and being intimately involved in the planning and details could Mrs. Rockefeller, an outsider, have any hope of grasping the intricacies of culture inherent in a traditional marriage. Additionally, it is obviously a venerable and worthy goal to wish to learn about South Indian culture. No one seems to think that this is a strange undertaking, and it is clearly the most interesting thing happening in Washington, D.C., at the time. Journalists and photographers are continually following the marriage party around asking questions and snapping photos so that they can explain this wondrous foreign culture to their enthusiastic readers. The smallest things draw huge crowds and headline the American newspapers.

Cultural Anxiety

The set-up of the *Washingtonil Tirumaṇam* narrative reveals not only cultural narcissism, but also cultural anxiety. If the traditional Brahmin marriage rituals were alive and well and projected to remain so, why record them in fiction? In fact, drama critic Kausalya Santhanam suggested in 2005 that this was quite repetitive and boring for Chennai viewers when she wrote of the play that "it appeared dated . . . to stage an [Brahmin] Iyer wedding in Chennai is like bringing coals to Newcastle . . . the Sastrigal [ritual] portions could have been trimmed." This wedding tells the story of two separate (national and community) cultural anxieties that were triggered by the momentous events of the long 1950s, which included such things as India's independence, the formation of a national cultural identity, the rise of the non-Brahmin movement in Tamilnadu, the growing popularity of cinema, and the very real lure of an exotic, wealthy, and modern America. The impulse didn't fade when the times had changed, and the 1995 television serial followed closely on the heels of the 1994 mega-hit Bollywood film *Hum Aapke Hain Koun* (*HAHK*), which has a very thin plotline and resembles a marriage video with its fourteen song-and-dance sequences. The nearly three-hour film shows many rituals associated with North Indian marriage in great detail, but *Washingtonil Tirumaṇam* goes even deeper by introducing a self-consciously didactic tone.

The basic structure of the story is that the Tamils are teaching Mrs. Rockefeller and the other Americans about their culture by not only performing, but also explaining their marriage rituals. The narrative offered an original way to preserve a record of the strict Tamil Brahmin cultural prescriptions that were quickly becoming impractical due to urban living, work schedules, and financial restrictions. It is an example of what I call "pre-emptive nostalgia," where a cultural practice is perceived to be endangered and is thus recorded both for the present generation to enjoy and for future generations to refer to.[4] *Washingtonil Tirumaṇam's* popular comedic form ensured its longevity.

The exotic locale of Washington, D.C., as a setting for this marriage allowed readers and viewers to move into a fantasy world free from financial restrictions where every obstacle could be overcome simply by wishing for it. The same is true for *HAHK* and films like *Dilwale Dulhania Le Jeyenge* (1995), which was set in the West and offered what Anjali Ram describes as "a slickly designed Global North fantasy world replete with all the signifying metaphors of western affluence . . . as a backdrop" (2014, 78). While *Washingtonil Tirumaṇam* explains the fantasy through the wealth of Mrs. Rockefeller, the Bollywood films are silent about finances, and the wealth of the characters is simply assumed. Patricia Uberoi found that with *HAHK*, even those of her informants who had little money and could never afford to conduct the rituals on such a lavish scale, believed the film gave the "overall impression of the verisimilitude of representation" (336) in its celebration of the marriage functions. *Washingtonil Tirumaṇam* provides minute ritual details set in a fantasy world far from viewers' everyday lives. Cāvi's story "literally transported the Madras readers and audience to Washington with his realistic description of the place" (Swaminathan 2001). The lavishness of the wedding, thanks to the Rockefellers, reveals the lofty financial aspirations of Tamil Brahmins. The fantasy here serves a deeper purpose than when exotic locales are used in film song-and-dance sequences because the exotic locale of the novel came complete with a whole cast of characters that interact with the marriage party. The presence of Americans who are ignorant about Tamil culture invites detailed explanations of rituals that any good Tamil Brahmin would be embarrassed to admit ignorance of. *Washingtonil Tirumaṇam* is not just entertainment, which is the charge so often leveled at sabha theater. It also serves to revalue "South Indian" culture and (humorously) expose differences between it and American culture.

One of the reasons this play has continued to appeal to insider audiences over the years is that viewers and readers from different generations can appreciate it in different ways and for different reasons. For the older generation, the performance has all the pleasures of nostalgia; for the younger generation it is a record of a more "authentic" cultural milieu full of prescriptions from which they are free. Discourse about Tamil youth is often critical for this very reason. They are trying too hard to be "modern" and are "losing" their culture by aping films and American youth, lament the cultural conservatives of the older generation. *Washingtonil Tirumaṇam* allows for a displacement of tradition onto the past or onto ideal selves to which contemporary Tamil Brahmins need not even aspire. This play removes some of the pressure felt by today's Brahmin community to be both modern and traditional. Conservative Brahmins perform *tradition*, not modernity, and they define their culture and cultural value by the measure of tradition (see figure 4.1). Through *Washingtonil Tirumaṇam* they can revel in comic stereotypes of themselves and displace modernity onto the American characters and by association onto their modern selves. Self-reflexivity and the valorization of traditional cultural practices can be vocalized in this context because of the American characters.

For example, the characters of the two priests in *Washingtonil Tirumaṇam* proudly display their ignorance of modern life and America as

Figure 4.1. Close-up of three actors facing audience in a 1992 Goodwill Stage performance of *Washingtonil Tirumaṇam*. *Source*: Courtesy of Kovai Padmanabhan, from the author's collection.

opposed to the more cosmopolitan family members. Religion and tradition reveal them to be backward and thus objects of humor. The play doesn't necessarily privilege this worldview and is full of nostalgia and a desire to do things in a traditionally correct manner.

Different Media, Different Messages

Washingtonil Tirumaṇam offers a unique opportunity for the researcher because it is available in three different media, and each adaptation has a different agenda and audience. The discrepancies and variations among the three versions of the story reveal much about what works conceptually and narratively within each medium's limits as well as about their intended audiences. The television serial, coming so long after the novel and the play, must be analyzed in terms of the younger generation of viewers to whom it made the story available. Being directed at a broader audience, this version lost some of the technicalities of the novel and the play, but it still used the Brahmin dialect of Tamil and added other emphases (such as the newly conceived character of the marriage broker) that kept the story directed at local viewers.

Washingtonil Tirumaṇam first appeared during the long 1950s, which was a period of intense reflection about the nature of newly independent "India" and "Indian culture." Following Arjun Appadurai's argument in *Modernity at Large* (1996) that people can imagine and actualize more and more different lives *because of* media and geographic mobility, it becomes clear that globalization doesn't necessarily mean homogenization of culture. The increasing exchanges of culture and population between India and America during the 1960s inspired discussion, emotion, and comparison, and *Washingtonil Tirumaṇam* is one crucial site where this exchange is registered and validated. In fact, K. S. Nagarajan said that when he directed the play for Kala Nilayam, "we had some Americans appearing as guests for the wedding" (Santhanam, October 10, 2003), an instance of actual cultural exchange facilitated by the play.

Washingtonil Tirumaṇam doesn't portray Americans as hippies in search of enlightenment, but instead as people amazed by and interested in the things that this particular group of Tamil Brahmin Indians were proud of and identified themselves with such as ritual and propriety. The magic of the novel is that it takes everyday things from Tamil Brahmin life and makes them wonderful in the eyes of the Americans, thus revaluing them in the eyes of Tamil readers who may have taken them for granted. For example, a new well is built behind Mrs. Rockefeller's "summer house" so that the *pāṭṭis* (grandmas) can bathe in fresh well water. The sound of the un-oiled rope squeaking along the pulley sounded so melodious to Mrs. Rockefeller that she engaged two watchmen to make sure no oil could be applied, as was the norm. She raved so much that American musical experts, Hollywood orchestras, and music researchers converged on the summer house in order to research this fabulous music machine. After much discussion it is decided that either moving the instrument or trying to reconstruct it in the studio might be unsatisfactory, so recordings are made right there at the summer house to be used for background music in Hollywood films.

Most sabha plays are targeted at Brahmin audiences, and that is certainly true of this play. The theatrical version of *Washingtonil Tirumaṇam* naturally had to be much shorter than Cāvi's novel. It is impossible to show the full four days of ritual and celebration in a two-hour production, so jokes and episodes had to be carefully selected (see figure 4.2). Two main features of the stage play have stood out to audi-

Figure 4.2. Scene with priests and umbrella in a 1992 Goodwill Stage performance of *Washingtonil Tirumaṇam*. *Source*: Courtesy of Kovai Padmanabhan, from the author's collection.

ences over the years. First, this is the only sabha play that I know of that invites audience participation with the exception of the post-performance discussions encouraged by the Mahalakshmi Ladies Drama Group. At the end of the play the marriage procession actually leaves the stage and walks around the theater among members of the audience. Many audience members will stand up, congratulate the couple and their families, and perhaps offer a small gift. The play brings the audience into the fictional family and gets them personally invested in bringing the marriage off successfully. Purnam Viswanathan, who acted the role of the bride's father more than three hundred times, related that the audience automatically got involved, to the point of following the actors up onto the stage. He said there was a time when they were performing *Washingtonil Tirumaṇ am* almost daily and the audience would come dressed as elaborately as if it were an actual marriage (author interview, May 20, 2004). Many theater enthusiasts lament the fact that its innovative structure never took off in the genre or inspired others to follow its model.

Second, there is an audience expectation for entertainment and amusement that must be met for a play to remain popular. There are humorous situations built into the narrative of *Washingtonil Tirumaṇam*, but the play's humor is really driven by the steady stream of short jokes based on cultural confusion and language play (such as when the sweet *payasam* is misheard as "poison" and the fried cracker-like treat *appalam* as "apple-ham"). This is not the situation in the novel. Although it includes many jokes, the novel also includes long explanatory sections and detailed descriptions of Washington, menus, and other things. The play also includes jokes that are not explicitly told in the novel but fit easily into the story.

The character of Mrs. Rockefeller is central to both the novel and the play, but she is portrayed very differently in the two media. The play has only two hours in which to convey what the novel has 176 pages to do. There are also limits on the number of characters, especially female characters that can be portrayed on stage. The drama troupe creates the illusion that they are part of a very large cast because several actors play more than one role. They even expand the number of female characters beyond the number of available actresses by having at least one (the blouseless, appalam-making grandmother) played by a male actor, which has the added benefit of intensifying an already humorous episode. The play, unlike the novel, also includes the characters of Mr. Rockefeller and their young daughter. The very costumes of the Rockefeller family are used to poke fun at Americans in a way that the novel never did.

There is never any indication in the novel that Mrs. Rockefeller looks ridiculous or inappropriate, but that is certainly part of the stage play. In the performance I saw, the elder Rockefellers sported these horrible very fake-looking orange wigs and Mrs. Rockefeller wore a green velvet suit (see figure 4.3). The daughter, who I estimated at about twelve years of age, wore a green velvet dress that was *very* short along with a bright pink wig.

The play also updates some of the traditional rituals of the novel for a more modern audience. For example, the Janavasam ritual is the ceremonial arrival of the bridegroom. In the past and in the world of the *Washingtonil Tirumaṇam* novel, this procession was held on foot. The ritual has not disappeared in modern times; it is still held in some token way by Tamil Brahmins that value their culture and consider this to be an integral part of it. What this means today is that the bridegroom and his entourage usually arrive by car. When K. S. Nagarajan directed the play for Kala Nilayam, he said that he "engaged Nari koravas[5] to carry hurricane lamps during the Janavasam scene in 'Washingtonil Tirumanam'

Figure 4.3. Scene with the Rockefeller family members in a 1992 Goodwill Stage performance of *Washingtonil Tirumaṇam*. *Source*: Courtesy of Kovai Padmanabhan, from the author's collection.

and a car was brought to circle the auditorium" (Santhanam, October 10, 2003).

The drastic change made by the television serial is the erasure of the character of Mrs. Rockefeller, who is so central to both the novel and the play. She is replaced by two characters: Margaret, the American wife of Hari Hops (who in the novel is Mrs. Rockefeller's friend but in the serial is a friend of the bride's father), and Katherine, the college friend of Vasi, the bride, who in this version is a US permanent resident attending Columbia University in New York City. Additionally, the journalists of the earlier versions are replaced by a variety of random Americans who encounter the priests here and there and ask questions that allow for explanations of things like the tuft of hair that they sport and the *takḷi* (Indian-style supported spindle) they use to make thread.

The absence of Mrs. Rockefeller meant that the marriage budget, unlike in the earlier versions, was not unlimited. In the novel, when two lakh (200,000) coconuts were requested she said, "Is that all? I'll fly in one million from our large estate in Hawaii." The play upped this offer to two million. Everything cheerfully and in excess is the theme of the novel and the play. In the television serial, however, money suddenly becomes an object. This shift allowed the groom's mother, who was previously a very minor character, to take on her traditional role of being demanding and trying to extract as much money from the reluctant bride's family as possible. Her husband is overwhelmed by everything they have done and enjoys seeing Washington; she angles for an all-expenses-paid trip to Niagara Falls, as well. In addition, the bride's family, well-to-do permanent residents in the US, can only fly twenty-five people over from India for the marriage. This means that there is much negotiation over who makes that cut, as the list has to include cooks as well as priests and family members. There are entire episodes devoted to these negotiations, which are not an issue in the novel, where Mrs. Rockefeller is chartering four flights a day between Madras and Washington, D.C., and bringing in everyone she can think of, including distant relatives and unrelated older village women who are contracted to make the appalams.

The novel and the play focus on anecdotes about Americans who don't understand Indian culture, while the television serial does the opposite. There are long sequences in the serial with no dialogue, and sometimes no visible characters, that do nothing to advance the narrative, but simply show the many tourist sites of Washington, D.C., that the characters visit. The opening credits are, in fact, a montage of these scenes. Many of these, such as the NASA Preview Research Center and the Statue of Liberty (which is *not* in Washington) are not part of the original novel. The television program takes the opportunity to show Indians viewing at home the exciting attractions of Washington, D.C. This footage, which really makes the viewer feel well-traveled and cosmopolitan, is not possible either in the novel or on the stage. In those media, the specific attractions are mentioned in so far as they are either important settings for the action or in order to make a joke. A good example that appears in all three versions of the story is the visit to the Lincoln Memorial. The priests hear that they are going to see the "Lingam Mandapam"[6] and get very excited. They happily prepare to perform puja (daily worship rituals) there until someone kindly explains that "Lincoln" is the name of a former US president and has nothing to do with the god Siva.

The television serial is more realistic than the novel or the play. By 1995, there were so many diasporic Indians in Washington that a few women putting a kolam[7] in front of a house would not draw the huge crowd described in Cāvi's novel, which was written before 1965, when changes to US immigration policy caused the Indian population in the country to swell. Instead, the serial shows only the bride's friend Katherine, her boyfriend, and her mother watching from a nearby vantage point and commenting to one another about how beautiful the design is. Likewise, it is outside of the realm of belief that the priest would be invited to give an exhibition of thread-making from the top of the Washington Monument, or that there would be headlines in the newspapers about some guy making thread. The television program transforms the huge crowd of journalists into a single interested neighbor who flippantly suggests that the priest take his *takḷi* to the top of the Empire State Building (again, *not* in Washington) and asks if she can do a write-up for their neighborhood publication. This allows the screenplay writers to use Cāvi's wonderful English-language rhyming headline "Spinning Man from Gandhi Land" and wax poetic about Gandhi.

Authentic Ritual Performances

The theatrical version of *Washingtonil Tirumaṇam* is a "ritual" in two different ways. First, the play is repeated over and over, following the same script and stage directions. Second, it is a play about a marriage ritual, which is the ritual that conservative Tamil Brahmins hold most dear.

This play is unusual because it publicly stages for both the live Indian audience and the American characters the usually behind-the-scenes marriage preparations along with the conducting of all the small rituals associated with the marriage, to which most guests would not be privy. It is common for people to perform culture through rituals or dramas that are designed for tourist audiences, but this is a tourist performance once removed, where even the tourists are characters performing for locals. Tourist performances highlight those elements of a culture that can be easily understood across cultures and also work as a spectacle tourists will pay money to watch. They are understood as being selective representations and no tourist performance (though it may claim to be) is believed to be "authentic."

Washingtonil Tirumaṇam is not designed for tourists: this cultural performance is geared toward the same insular audience as a real marriage ceremony, which explains Santhanam's "coals to Newcastle" comment in her critique. This play offers a way for the Tamil Brahmin community to define itself internally as well as to the outside world on its own terms. The identity that Tamil Brahmins both embrace and struggle with is *traditional* and *conservative*. These characteristics are both celebrated and mocked in the world of *Washingtonil Tirumaṇam*. For example, in the television serial, when Margaret Hops offers to read the palm of one of the priests, he declines, saying that he cannot touch any woman except his wife, even in this innocent fashion, in an exaggerated display of modesty. This scene has the added effect of painting the American Mrs. Hops as immodest, even though she is dressed in a nine-yard sari[8] and the palm reading was her husband's suggestion.

Washingtonil Tirumaṇam revels in the conservative stereotype without losing its sense of humor. Tamil Brahmins of the 1960s may have been traditional with regard to their culture, but they were also educated and cosmopolitan. The narrative includes many jokes that require knowledge of both American culture and the English language. All of Mrs. Rockefeller's lines are in English but are written in the painstaking transliteration that is so difficult to read that many writers actually chose to publish their work in two separate scripts. A good example of cultural competence is the joke that when the Americans hear that there is "oil" in some little seeds that the priest has, they assume it is oil for their cars, not for cooking, and hail him as a genius for discovering it.

The part of the Tamil marriage ritual that most perplexes the Americans in *Washingtonil Tirumaṇam* is something called the "campanti caṇṭai" ("the in-laws' quarrel"). No marriage can be perfect, or to put it another way, a perfect marriage includes a fight between the groom's family and the bride's family. No one is really bothered by this development except for the Americans who can't stand to see people fighting and fear that the marriage may actually be called off. The Tamils understand that there must always be a crisis in married life, and this ritual is a way of dispensing with that crisis *before* the marriage in order for the couple to enjoy a peaceful married life. In the end, Mrs. Rockefeller understands the important role that the groom's uncle played by expressing his dissatisfaction and causing trouble. Out of gratitude for his troublesome but necessary actions, she presents him with a car at the end of the story.

Modernity and Authenticity

The pleasure of the younger generation in this story from the 1960s begs the question of how authentic Tamil Brahmin traditions reconcile with modernity. The concepts of authenticity and modernity are both contested and defined in various ways depending on their context. My forthcoming article on Japanese Bollywood dancers identifies multiple criteria these dancers turn to in determining the level of authenticity in a performance. Scholars like E. Patrick Johnson (2003), Paul Gilroy (1994), and Stuart Hall (1996) interrogate the usefulness of the term and identify some of its contradictions. Anthropologist Louisa Schein's work (1999) on the Miao minority in China and the traditional/modern conflict visible in the performative aspects of actual wedding rituals raises some interesting questions and issues with regard to the Brahmin minority in Chennai and their performances of marriage. The rural Miao are constantly faced with a reputation for being "backward" as compared to the urban Han majority. They perpetuate this stereotype by continuing their drinking rituals and using elaborate Miao dress for the bride, but bring a taste of the "modern" to the proceedings by including the wedding gift of a beautifully framed poster of a "blonde model in a hot pink G-string bikini reclined atop a snazzy racing car" in photos with the bride and youthful urbane guests wearing T-shirts and carrying beepers ("despite the fact that there would be no phone on which to return calls") (Schein 1999, 374). Tamil Brahmins, on the other hand, are extremely well-educated and many have traveled. They may wear western clothes and watch English movies on a regular basis, and mobile phones are everywhere in Chennai.[9] The marriage ritual, however, is not the place to display these transgressions of traditional culture. Instead, it is the time for all the women (even those who wear jeans to college on a regular basis) to dig out their fancy silk saris and put jasmine flowers in their hair.

Washingtonil Tirumaṇam glorifies tradition and a strict adherence to the proper rituals. The question is whether it allows for the possibility that shortened and simplified rituals can still be authentic. Louisa Schein writes that "[t]hrough nostalgia, traditions were historicized, consigned to the past. Through mediation, culture was rendered as a slick surface of images. Through commodification, culture was alienated from embedded social process. And through formal staging—whether for tourists or for themselves—rituals became transactions between spectators and performers" (1999, 367). *Washingtonil Tirumaṇam* certainly mediated the marriage ritual for Tamil mass audiences through television, commodified it through the novel, and staged it for years as a drama. However, its billing as "entertainment" and its tenor as humorous have kept its championing of lengthy, expensive ritual prescriptions squarely in the realms of fantasy and nostalgia.

Most sabha plays are about the all-important life-event of marriage. The narratives either end in marriage or immediately follow one. The staging of the marriage ritual itself, however, is usually very perfunctory. The audience might hear a recording of a nadaswaram[10] playing or see the couple exchanging garlands. These are sufficient markers for them to understand that the marriage has been completed. A few famous plays such as Kathadi Ramamurthy's *Dowry Kalyana Vaibogame* ("Dowry Wedding Celebrations") and Raadhu's *Kalyāṇattil Kalāṭṭā* ("Wedding Fiasco") focus on the negotiations and family relations that are involved in the arranging of a marriage and everything that needs to be done to keep the two parties happy and committed to the match. *Washingtonil Tirumaṇam* is actually a non-efficacious marriage ritual performed on stage encapsulated into a two-hour block of entertainment. Additionally, it is cheap to attend and stage, the politics are never personal, and mistakes and misunderstandings are funny, not tragic, in a fictional setting.

Conclusion

In this chapter, I argued that *Washingtonil Tirumaṇam* has remained relevant to audiences for so many years because it offers different things to different generations of viewers. The narrative displaces tradition onto the past or onto ideal selves to which contemporary Tamils need not aspire and allows them to associate themselves with modernity. *Washingtonil Tirumaṇam* serves as a place where Tamil Brahmin identity can be continually re-constituted and re-negotiated through its transfer to different media. The staged performance is partitioned off from everyday life and the disjunctions and continuities between the two can reveal a lot about a community's self-perception.

The following chapter analyzes two plays that are representative of the genre in terms of themes and topics of jokes. The 1977 *Honeymoon Couple* and 2001 *Jurassic Baby* are both written by Crazy Mohan, so there is a lot of similarity between them. The chapter works from the humor found in these two plays to a deeper understanding of Tamil Brahmin culture and its values.

CHAPTER FIVE

Honeymoon Couple and *Jurassic Baby*

Belonging and Respect

> TEACHER: Let's start a lesson. First English. Pay close attention. A is for *eli*. *Eli* means *rat*. B is for *bigel*. *Bigel* means *whistle*. (He wolf whistles in demonstration.)
>
> BOY: Rowdy Uncle.
>
> TEACHER: C is for *singam*. *Singam* means *lion*. . . .
>
> MADHU (boy's dad): You need to say if is this English or Tamil. I'm confused.
>
> TEACHER: Nothing is confusing. This is like, I'm doing one technique. Both at the same time.
>
> —From *Jurassic Baby* by Crazy Mohan

This joke from the 2001 play *Jurassic Baby* blends English and Tamil and requires understanding of both. The teacher is doing a technique to teach both languages at the same time, though he starts by calling this an "English" lesson. The letter A in English is a homophone for the letter *E* in Tamil. *Eli* is a Tamil word that starts with *E*; then he gives the meaning, rat, in English. The same pattern continues through the ABCs, where he says the English letter is the start for the Tamil word, which he then gives the meaning for the Tamil in English. The two languages and alphabets are so intertwined that to get the joke, the viewer would need to understand the way the sounds work in both alphabets. While it's common to blend languages to produce Tanglish in the contemporary context, with a Tamil ending added on to an English word, for example, they usually remain more distinct at the level of alphabet. Language jokes come in all varieties, but the sabha comedies are particularly fond of what are called "code-mixing" jokes like this one that blend two languages and require competency in both. The second language is usually English, as here, but occasionally it is Hindi or Telugu. All the language jokes say something about this audience. The Tamil ones reiterate the fact that they are Tamils above all else, and proud of it. The code-mixing ones say that they are also cosmopolitan and multilingual.

This book is part of a larger project to use humor to access Tamil Brahmin identity and adds to the work Gabriella Eichinger Ferro-Luzzi has done on the cartoons and jokes in popular Tamil weekly magazines favored by Brahmins (Ferro-Luzzi 1992). This chapter analyzes two plays that are representative of the genre in terms of themes and topics of jokes. The 1977 *Honeymoon Couple* and 2001 *Jurassic Baby* are both written by Crazy Mohan, so there is a lot of similarity, though there are twenty-five years between them, and they are associated with different lead comedians and infused with those personalities. Both plays have English titles, though this is more essential to the humor in *Honeymoon Couple*, where "honeymoon" is not just a foreign word but also a foreign cultural concept. Through these two plays, I make concrete some of the more general themes and jokes types I discussed in chapter 3, locating specific instances of humor in Tamil Brahmin culture. According to Ferro-Luzzi, who analyzed verbal Tamil humor that had been "gathered in written form," including jokes and cartoons from magazines, comedies, folk stories, and humorous literature, and categorized them thematically, language jokes are the most popular type of Tamil joke (see Ferro-Luzzi 1992). Her general categories work within the sabha theater world as well. After language and logical fallacy jokes, some of her categories are husband and wife, courtship and marriage arrangement, elders and children, in-laws, food, school, medicine, law and order, beggars, the economy, technology, politics, and cinema. Most of these come up in these two plays, as well as a few others.

Milton Singer and Mary Elizabeth Hancock studied the "everyday invention of culture" (Singer 1972; Hancock 1999, 9) among the Tamil Brahmin elite in Chennai; I focus on the identity construction of this particular community as constituted by their representation of themselves on stage. These plays are an example of what Victor Turner has called "performative reflexivity," when a sociocultural group or its members "turn, bend or reflect back upon themselves, upon the relations, actions, symbols, meanings, codes, roles, statuses, social structures, ethical and legal rules, and other sociocultural components which make up their public 'selves'" to produce "a deliberate and voluntary work of art" (1988, 24). The families depicted on the sabha stage are alleged to be representations of ordinary people in extraordinary circumstances, but often include exaggerated examples of various stereotypes. The plays directly confront public perceptions of Brahmins and, by using humor, writers and comedians are able to go a step beyond the socially acceptable, and thus simultaneously challenge and reinforce the public face of the middle-class Tamil Brahmin community. This strategy of self-representation is one way that Tamil Brahmins have managed to reconcile their conflicting identities of both traditional and modern and to control others' perceptions of them.

Kathadi Ramamurthy's 1977 *Honeymoon Couple*[1] is one of the most popular of the "pure comedies" from the peak of the sabha theater genre. This is when there was a formula that worked, new troupes were splintering off from the old ones as well as starting with all newcomers to the field, and all of them were flourishing.[2] It was written for Kathadi's drama troupe Stage Creations by comedy writer Crazy Mohan, who was trained as an engineer but started writing plays and humorous short stories at an early age, soon turning that hobby into a career after finding success with the 1976 play *Crazy Thieves in Palavakkam* written for S. Ve. Shekher.[3] S. Prabhu writes that

> Crazy Mohan was groping for success in those early days (he was still in his 20s). He says Kathadi gave it to him on a silver plate with his outstanding dialogue delivery in *Ayya Amma Ammamma.* He says that without doubt it was Kathadi who taught him writing (and his brother Balaji acting) . . . Crazy Mohan goes on . . . "[I] used to show every script to him and in no time, he would get back to me with the edits . . . Since I was occupied with office work (Crazy Mohan worked in Sundaram Clayton—his first and last job), Kathadi even used to play my role as an actor in my plays. He was instrumental in the development of my troupe. Looking back, Kathadi was my Gateway to success in the world of theatre. He taught me first to crawl and later to walk on stage. It was he who helped

me raise the bar in my script writing. Truth told Kathadi made me fly high." (2014)

Mohan wrote three plays for the man he referred to as Kathadi "Dramamurthy," and *Honeymoon Couple* has been popular over the years as a live performance staged over 350 times and on television as one of Doordarshan's "Sunday Dramas," produced by S. Gopalie in the early 1980s. This play is still regularly performed, and I saw it several times over the course of my fieldwork and noted that it was sponsored by Almighty Sree Vaari Fine Arts as recently as November 2019. It was also being sold in DVD format at bookstores in Chennai and online from 2007 (see figures 5.1 and 5.2). It is truly one of the classics of Tamil comedy theater, thanks to both Crazy Mohan's writing and Kathadi Ramamurthy's acting.

Two years after this play, Crazy Mohan started his own troupe, Crazy Creations, for which he has written all the plays. He also acts, but the main comedy is usually between the duo of his brother Crazy Balaji and Cheenu Mohan. Balaji's character is usually called Madhu, while

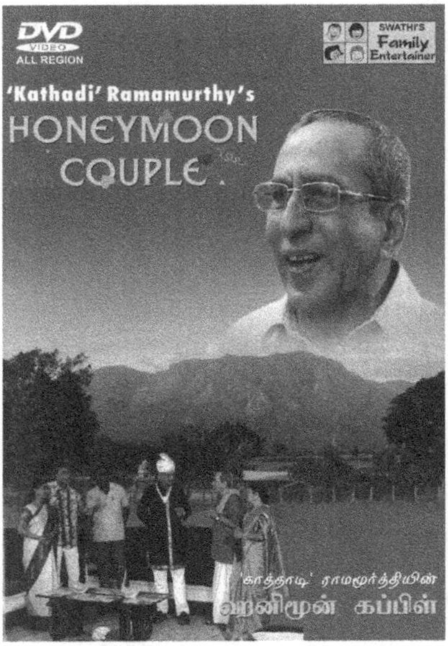

Figure 5.1. DVD cover for Kathadi Ramamurthy's *Honeymoon Couple*, 2007 (front). *Source*: Author's collection.

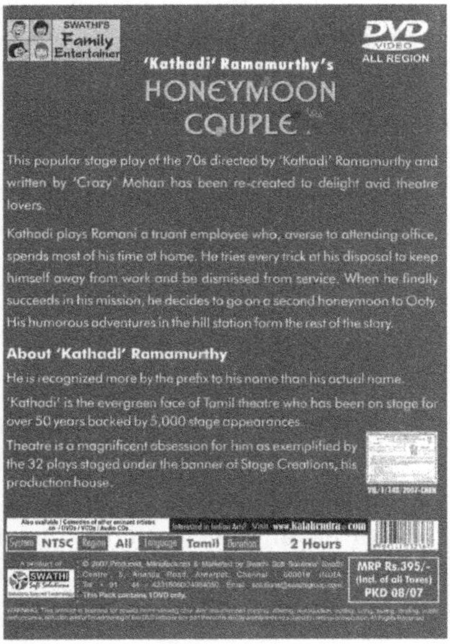

Figure 5.2. DVD cover for Kathadi Ramamurthy's *Honeymoon Couple*, 2007 (back). *Source*: Author's collection.

Cheenu's is called Cheenu, and the Madhu-Cheenu pairing is a signal for hilarity. They have an excellent chemistry. The 2001 *Jurassic Baby* is a classic example of this, with Cheenu playing a double role such that he is both Madhu's brother-in-law and son (see figure 5.3).

Kathadi Ramamurthy and *Honeymoon Couple*

Likte many post-Independence amateur actors, Kathadi got involved with theater in earnest when he started participating in productions with college friends in 1954 (see figures 5.4 and 5.5 for his Golden Jubilee celebration

Figure 5.3. DVD cover for Crazy Mohan's *Jurassic Baby*, 2006. *Source*: Author's collection.

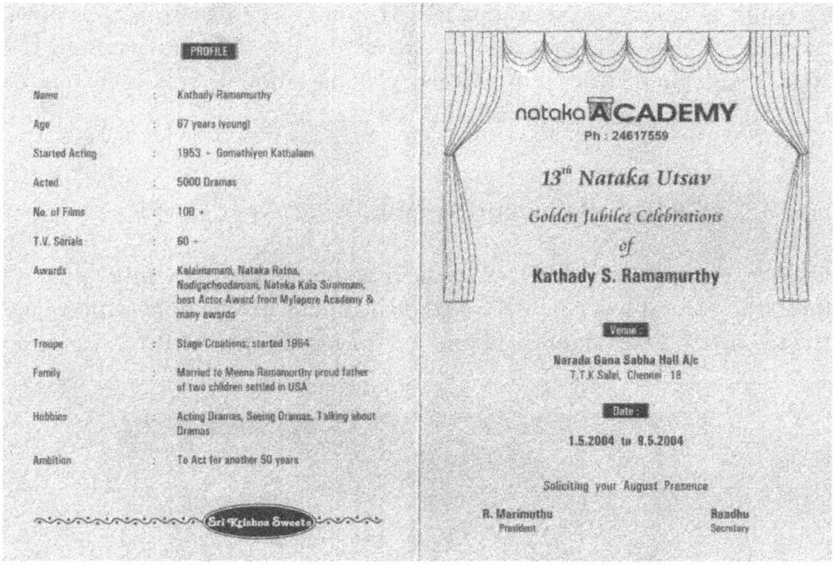

Figure 5.4. Golden Jubilee celebration program for Kathadi Ramamurthy, 2004 (front/back). *Source*: Author's collection.

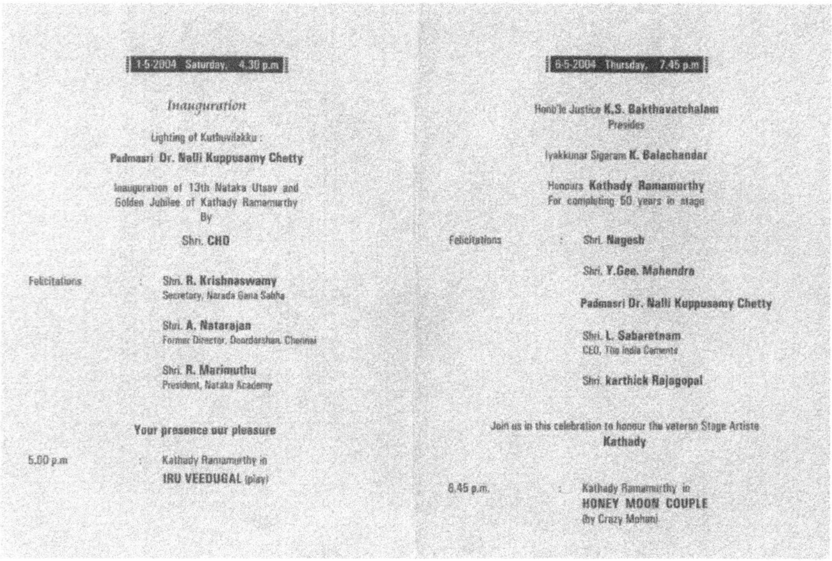

Figure 5.5. Golden Jubilee celebration program for Kathadi Ramamurthy, 2004 (inside). *Source*: Author's collection.

program from 2004), though his father, S. Sundaresan, set the example earlier by acting for Vani Vilas Sabha in Kumbakonam while holding a full-time job as a manager at the municipal office (Prabhu 2014). Kathadi himself worked a full-time job as a manager at Jenson and Nicholson's. He got his nickname ("Kathadi") from a character he played in Cho Ramasamy's 1958 play *If I Get It*, back when he was performing with Viveka Fine Arts. He split off in 1966 to form his own troupe, Stage Creations, with Shivaji Chaturvedi, T. D. Sundararajan, and Bobby Raghunathan. Kathadi is very proud that Stage Creations "has introduced several playwrights and actors who have shone in cinema, saying "We've staged 47 plays so far. After every two or three plays I bring in a new writer to lend variety and fresh perspectives" (Prabhu 2014). He has now given more than 6,500 stage performances.

Working with a variety of writers with their different voices makes it easier for Kathadi to avoid the repetition of jokes that has been a real problem for someone like Crazy Mohan, who writes all of Crazy Creation's plays. It is still difficult to keep variety in the plays and retain the audience's interest, and Kathadi says that "[o]nce they [the writers] succeed with us, they get to know the artists and their potentialities. This is the problem. Once they know this they begin to write for the artists to exploit their talents, and fail to tell a story. Here and this way [*sic*] the play fails. The audience begins to feel that they are seeing the same character over and over again" (Gopalie 2002, 107). This is, in fact, a problem that Kathadi in particular has faced over the years. While some plays were written expressly for him and maximized his particular talents, music and dance critic Charukesi offers another explanation for the trend: "It is a mystery whether the script writer wrote the dialogues to suit Kathadi's style or Kathadi converted it to suit his style of delivery to make it natural" (Charukesi 2017). Either way, there is a consistency in the characters and humor within the group of plays featuring this veteran actor that goes beyond the sabha aesthetic.

One of Kathadi's most famous roles, Tuppa̱riyum Cāmpu (Detective Sambu), originated from a late 1940s serialized detective series by Devan in the popular magazine *Āṉanta Vikaṭan*[4] that fits seamlessly into the sabha genre. Sambu is "a not-very-intelligent bank clerk in middle age, who solves difficult crime puzzles out of serendipity . . . sometimes considered to be a comical version of Sherlock Holmes. Sambu is described by Devan as having a bald fringe, a prominent nose and a weak chin. Along with a generally bewildered stare his appearance invariably invites people to term him asadu (stupid), an assessment not far from the mark. This becomes an asset for Sambu as criminals often underestimate him" ("Thuppariyum Sambu," 2022). Kathadi's person has become conflated with Detective Sambu, whose illustrated figure the actor uncannily resembles. When he revived the role as part of a celebration of his having been in theater for sixty years, drama critic Roshne B described the actor as "Dressed in a high-waist dhoti, white shirt and a black coat, the versatile Ramamurthy looked every inch the Sambhu as described in the book" (2016).

Three of Kathadi's plays have been made into films, the best-known being *Pattina Pravesam* (1977), directed by K. Balachander, and *Dowry Kalyanam* (1983), written and directed by Visu in a film that catapulted both Visu and actor Delhi Ganesh to fame. Delhi Ganesh says that "I owe a lot to Kathadi . . . *Dowri Kalyana* . . . made me a known face on the theatre circuit" (Prabhu 2014). He was able to move successfully from stage to screen, but still works with Stage Creations, which he told Malathi Rangarajan from *The Hindu* when she attended a rehearsal of that very play for the sixtieth anniversary celebration. It "is an integral part of my life. So here I am. We are never driven by ego or jealousy. If somebody from Stage Creations becomes popular, Kathadi is only too happy. I've been a part of the troupe for very long and despite film commitments I join them whenever possible" (Rangarajan 2016). This is also beneficial for the troupe, as audience members like to come to see film stars live on stage.[5]

Kathadi Ramamurthy is widely respected as a performer and a man, and is considered to be one of the best comic actors the Tamil language has ever seen. Even S. Ve. Shekher has said that he was the "best" in comedy.[6] He has a sense for his audience and a humorous manner that keeps them laughing. Kathadi's timing is perfect and his interaction with Sri Lalitha, the actress who usually plays opposite him, had been polished over the thirty-nine years she had been with his troupe as of 2019, especially in plays like *Honeymoon Couple*, which they have performed together hundreds of times. S. N. Parvathi and Prema Sadasivam are the other two actresses that have worked with Stage Creations on a long-term basis. Kathadi is not an improviser like S. Ve. Shekher, tending to stick to his scripts pretty closely, though he knows where he can cut if necessary and when jokes have lost their relevance and need to be deleted or updated. The scripts are not published, and he keeps a cupboard full of unpublished plays in his living room, handwritten in long notebooks, covered with marginal notes, and stamped with the seal of police approval.

Honeymoon Couple has a plot with a slight twist on the standard: it is okay to tell a thousand lies if they result not in a marriage, but in a honeymoon. The marriage, in this case, occurred twenty years ago, but the honeymoon did not follow. This allows for some great humor that works because of the inversion of roles and a clarification of what is appropriate for people of different ages in Tamil culture with regard to love, sex, and romance. It is the aged, forty-five-year-old man, wearing dentures, who is longing for a honeymoon with his mortified and reluctant thirty-eight-year-old wife, while their children stay chastely at home to attend college.

I have translated a great deal of *Honeymoon Couple* from Kathadi's handwritten and much-annotated notebook, and it is clear that like many of his plays, it has undergone a lot of changes over the years although the basic plot and main characters have remained constant. Ramani in *Honeymoon Couple* is one of Kathadi Ramamurthy's most reprised and best-beloved characters. Ramani hates to work and spends all of his time trying to get out of it by making up lies and excuses to tell his wife, his boss, his colleagues, his creditors, and anyone else who will listen. Instead of working, he wants to go on a honeymoon. The idea is so crazy that he tells his wife Rukmini that it came to him in a dream.

> RAM: Nothing . . . Rukku . . . You asked why I was smiling in my sleep this morning . . . I dreamt that you and I were going on a honeymoon.
>
> RUK: You have a daughter who's old enough to be married! Don't you have any shame? Dreaming about going on a honeymoon!
>
> RAM: Why is that so crazy? It just came to me in a dream. (trans. Rudisill 2004, 3 from Mohan 1977)

He goes on to tell her all the details of their dream honeymoon including what they wore while sitting in their air-conditioned room in the cool hill station of Simla eating ice cream.

Although Ramani wants to go on a honeymoon and argues that this is a perfectly natural desire for a middle-aged man, he still feels the deep-seated cultural pressure against it. Rukmini is mortified by the whole idea, and he is not immune. Even when he first tells his wife about the idea, he says that he feels "embarrassed" about it (trans. Rudisill 2004, 8 from Mohan, 1977). Later, when he is getting excited about the prospect and shouting about the new pants and shirt he has bought for his honeymoon, he is shushed by his wife. She says yes, they are going on a honeymoon but that they should do it without noise because she feels ashamed (*mā<u>n</u>am pōra<u>r</u>a*) (trans. Rudisill

2004, 31 from Mohan, 1977). Even though there is plenty of evidence of his own embarrassment on the subject up to this point, Ramani scolds his wife, saying that it's not as if she's eloping, since she's going on honeymoon with her own husband. "What's there to be ashamed about in that (*Atula e<u>nn</u>a avamā<u>n</u>am*)?" The manager of the Ooty (a hill station west of Chennai and a popular honeymoon spot) bungalow, who does not know that Ramani and Rukmini are "honeymooning," makes it clear that the idea of an older couple on a honeymoon is not just laughable, but actually offensive to the general public. He says that the mind changes with the person and while it may be possible to enjoy a honeymoon at a later age, what would the world say (*Ulakam e<u>nn</u>a collum*)? He answers his own question: they would say you were a rascal without modesty (*vekkala keṭṭavan*), a rascal without shame (*mā<u>n</u>ala keṭṭavan*), and that you were loose in the head (*lūsu*). In fact, with a daughter of marriageable age "wouldn't they stone you?" (*kallai viṭṭu e<u>r</u>iya māṭṭāṅka* . . .), he asks rhetorically (Mohan 1977, 128). At the very end of the play, Ramani and Rukmini decide to come clean: "[n]ow that everything is revealed, why should we hide just this? We came on honeymoon." The play ends when the raja, who has come to the bungalow (see figure 5.6), grabs his chest and screams as if they've given him a heart

Figure 5.6. Screenshot from *Honeymoon Couple* DVD. *Source*: Author's collection.

attack with their confession of honeymooning, but in a replay of an earlier scene, it is only an ant bite.

Crazy Creations and *Jurassic Baby*

Jurassic Baby reveals how important it is for Tamil couples to have children. Madhu and Mythili have been married for a while but seem to be unable to have children. She is thirty years old and they have tried all the usual ways to get pregnant, with no luck, so they finally resort to calling in a faith healer, played by Crazy Mohan. He makes a concoction for her to drink and she gets pregnant. Cheenu plays Mythili's younger brother, who is a stereotypical lazy guy with no work, and they make fun of him. Madhu, in contrast, works a lot and at the end of her pregnancy has to travel for his job. While he's gone, she goes to the hospital to have the baby, and Cheenu gets a call from a friend with a job offer in Singapore and leaves before the delivery. The baby, it transpires, grows very quickly. He's a "Jurassic" baby, which seems to mean large, in this case, and unrelated to the second period of the Mesozoic era. By the time the baby is ten days old, he's the size of a grown man with a remarkable resemblance to his uncle and is played by the same actor. When Madhu gets back, he mistakes the baby for his brother-in-law, as does everyone else who knew him. The parents have all kinds of worries about their son, who is mentally far behind where he is physically. He looks like he is thirty-five years old, next to his father's thirty-seven years and his mother's thirty.

They name the baby Cheena, which is close to Cheenu but not quite, and also a homonym for the country China, which prompts several jokes. *Jurassic Baby* exposes the way parents and children relate to one another and presents it in a humorous manner. Cheena, for example, has a habit of hitting people, usually his father, but his teacher and others as well, when he feels too much pressure, which audiences find funny. It's a reversal of the acceptable, as rules of respect would normally forbid a son from hitting his father. Because he is very young, they let him get away with it and instead go to great lengths to avoid the things that trigger him. This is similar to the humor in the *adipidi* scene that Susan Seizer (2005, 232–73) talks about with Special Drama, where the humor is found when the wife is beating the husband, which is seen as the inverse of the natural order.

There's an element of humor in watching this grown man behave like a child, but it may also be a commentary on Indian men, who are stereotypically over-dependent on their mothers. Because of the traditional joint family system, where a man brings his wife into his mother's house, there are a lot of jokes and characters based on this. A lot of times, it is about the mother, jealous of the son's relationship with the wife, but it is also about the son, who can't (or won't) make any decisions without his mother's involvement. Cheena, appearing five years older than Mythili, wants to sit on his mother's lap and begs her for special sweets. While this might be cute in a small child, it is not in a grown man, so audiences laugh, especially children.

On the Boundaries of Culture

Honeymoon Couple and *Jurassic Baby* are good examples of the hypothesis that although techniques, genres, and certain themes may be cross-cultural, humor is rooted in particular cultural contexts. In his work on humor in Marathi theater from 1970–1990, Mahadev Apte argues that "[w]ithout the shared cultural knowledge and conventions one cannot appreciate humor even by oneself, nor can one communicate it to others" (1992, 38). There are, of course, different degrees of appreciation, and the relationship between culture and humor can work in both directions. It is possible to understand and appreciate humor after gaining cultural competency, but it is also possible to work from the humor to a deeper understanding of culture. My analysis of the humor in Tamil plays is like Apte's in that both are designed to offer insights into these particular communities and cultures, and they work because "humor functions as a barometer, albeit a rough one, of what makes a society tick and what its major sociocultural attributes are" (Apte 1992, 14).

It is made clear in *Honeymoon Couple* that marriages, honeymoons, and babies are appropriate only to the young in the specific world of Tamil culture because people traditionally get married early and have children right away. It is still common to see the family planning slogan that "the marriage age for a girl is twenty-one" on the back of lorries and rickshaws, testifying to the fact that many girls are married younger. It is natural for these young couples to have children, not older people. When Ramani's fifty-year-old co-worker Tanikatchalam announces the birth of his eleventh child, all his workmates chide him, saying "[d]on't you have any shame? Having babies at age fifty!" (trans. Rudisill 2004, 21 from Mohan 1977). Only Ramani supports him, scolding the others: "Che! You are all so conservative. In America they have new marriages at age fifty and go on honeymoons. You are still so old fashioned" (trans. Rudisill 2004, 20 from Mohan 1977). This argument, that Americans are progressive and Indians backward, is not particularly effective in conservative Tamil culture, which often criticizes the practices of a corrupt America where young women flirt with boys and dress immodestly and people marry and go on honeymoons late in life only to get divorced ("die-vorce" as it is pronounced in Tamil English). The fears of western cultural imperialism and the spread of these "modern" practices make up a large part of the objections that middle-class Tamils voice about film and television (see Butcher 2003, 14–15) and that sabha dramas refer to in distinguishing themselves and their values from those media.

A honeymoon is designed for a newly married couple to travel together for a short time in order to get to know each other in every way, including sexually, apart from their families. This is when they establish themselves as a couple, and the characters in this play are obviously uncomfortable with the whole idea. Tamils have not been following the tradition of honeymooning for long and are very conservative about sex, especially among those who have reached an age where they are no longer trying to have children. There is something shameful and inherently funny, this drama assumes, about a middle-aged man desiring pleasure, and particularly the sexual pleasure associated with the honeymoon. The joke is made explicit in an exchange between Ramani's wife and son, where Rukmini tells her son Dilip that "[t]he son is at an age where he should know what a honeymoon is, but doesn't. The father is at an age where he should forget it." Dilip replies that the "[o]pposite house boy and his wife went on honeymoon and immediately had a baby," prompting his mother to scold him: "[d]on't say that in front of your father or he'll start planning for that, too" (trans. Rudisill 2004, 31 from Mohan 1977). Of course, in order to have another baby after the honeymoon, they would have to have sex during it. This theme is still relevant and clearly pan-Indian, as the 2018 Hindi film *Badhaai Ho* demonstrates. This film features an older couple getting pregnant, even though they already have one son in high school and one in college that has a girlfriend and is thinking about marriage himself. Their sons are embarrassed, and their family, friends, and neighbors are disgusted and ashamed. It finally resolves with the mother-in-law and sons at least accepting the baby and arguing that it's better that the husband is sleeping with his own wife than with someone else's wife or a prostitute.

Babies are a source of shame for older couples who have passed the appropriate time for that stage in their life. Pregnancy basically reminds everyone that the couple is having sex, something that is seen as shameful and private. For younger couples, however, babies are eagerly awaited by not only the couple, but also by their parents, who long to be grandparents. People continually ask them when there will be good news, and companies go out of their way to make it possible for women to continue working after having children (see Fuller and Narasimhan 2007). Madhu and Mythili's seeming inability to have children is a constant source of shame and frustration, such that they are willing to go to any lengths to have a child. The faith healer they hire, however, accidentally gives them the wrong concoction. While she does get pregnant, it transpires that the stuff she drank was actually intended for a dwarf, so that he could grow to a normal height. The lesson does not seem to be about the dangers for yourself or your unborn child of drinking mystery potions from random witch doctors. Crazy Mohan's character mixed up the formulas, but he doesn't realize it until he comes back to check on them several months later and meets Cheena. This prompts him to follow up with his other patient and realize what must have happened. In the end, he is able to fix it, and Mythili ends the play with a normal-sized ten-month-old baby in her arms.

There is also an element of cruelty towards those with disabilities that is evident in this play. First, the dwarf also goes to desperate measures, requesting an unknown potion from a shady witch-doctor type because he is ashamed of his body. And the joke is furthered when Crazy Mohan's character wonders whether the potion for a baby that was intended for Mythili might have made the unfortunate man even shorter. Further, while it is important to have a baby, there are also restrictions on the *kind* of baby that is acceptable. Parents want a child they can be proud of and it is not uncommon to disown a child who has brought shame on the family. Regarding this particular baby, the parents and the faith healer have the following conversation:

> MADHU: How do we keep this large kid? People on the road say we should put him in a mental hospital.
>
> PRIEST: Do that then.
>
> MADHU: We are ashamed to call him our son. (Mythili looks sad.)

PRIEST: Is this really a big issue? If it is hard to call him your son, then call him your brother-in-law. (Shock on the faces of the parents.) Say it is the Mythili's brother.

MADHU: Brilliant idea. My brother-in-law is in Singapore. Mythili, say it is your brother.

MYTHILI: How dare you say our son is my brother? My stomach is burning.

Their child does not look just like every other child, and the two ways they think of to handle it are to (a) get rid of him by hiding him out of sight in a mental institution, or (b) lie to everyone about who he is. The faith healer offers to make another potion for him, but they decline, afraid of the effects it might cause given their latest bad experience with his potions. Eventually, they decide to have the baby call them older sister and brother-in-law in front of other people, which naturally confuses the child because they seem to want him to call them mom and dad when they are alone. He keeps messing it up and calling them both at the same time, then telling people about the plan. This is just like a small child, who will repeat everything you say and has no instinct about which information should or should not be kept quiet, so it is funny.

The boundaries of culture revolve around notions of shame and honor. In both plays, the focus is on conformity and when people deviate from the norms of society, it is funny. These moments may be big or small, but thinking about culture and the reactions of other people within the society help explain embarrassment and boundaries of acceptability. Rukmini, for example, scoffs not only at the idea of a honeymoon, but more generally at her husband's dreams for romance after twenty years of marriage. He is always saying that he wants to take leave from work so that he can take her to the movies and enjoy life with her.

RUK: Isn't there a proper age to enjoy specific things?

RAM: What is all this big deal about age?

RUK: A big age . . .That's what I am saying. By this November you will be 45 years old. How much did you desire to go on a

> honeymoon when you were young and couldn't! But can you go for a honeymoon now? . . .
>
> RAM: We can. Definitely we can. I know that the only obstacle to our honeymoon was your father. He's not here now. (trans. Rudisill 2004, 18–19 from Mohan 1977)

Ramani's argument is that if a man can get married later in life, as many do if their first wife dies, why can't he go on a honeymoon? The logic is sound, except that he is proposing a honeymoon with a woman he has been married to for twenty-odd years, not one that he's just married and needs to get away from everyone with in order to get to know. Another instance of shame is present in *Jurassic Baby*, with all the discussion about the baby's personal hygiene and grooming. When he first sees him, Madhu assumes he is looking at his brother-in-law Cheenu. He tells him he looks weird without a moustache and asks why his hair looks like he showered in a washing machine. Later in the play, we see Madhu shaving his son's face, as the child is not coordinated enough to do it. He may have a man's body, but he does not have a man's education, experience, or well-developed gross and fine motor skills, so must be taken care of like a baby.

Although *Jurassic Baby* takes place after marriage and mostly deals with pregnancy and a first baby, it still goes back to the proverb about it being okay to tell a thousand lies to make a marriage. The most disturbing scenario in this play has to do with the character of Janaki. Janaki and Cheenu fell in love before he went to Singapore, though they had not told each other how they felt. Janaki shows up at the house, mistaking Cheena for Cheenu, and it is clear that she is interested in marrying him. Rather than telling her the truth about the child's identity or informing Cheenu in Singapore that Janaki has stopped by looking for him, Madhu's idea is to marry her to their son instead of to the man she loves. He's worried they would never be able to find a match for his man-child, and here's this woman, ready to marry him, and they should take advantage of that, even though the boy is only six months old at this point. Madhu never considers what Janaki's life would be like, having to raise her husband like a son. Cheena would not be able to support her financially or in any other way. And going back to the start of this play, newly married couples are supposed to want and to try to have children. This person, though appearing as a man, is a child himself and clearly in no position to raise someone else. And it is unclear how long the effects will continue. Will she be thirty and married to a man in an eighty-year-old body if he keeps growing at an accelerated rate?

Madhu never considers Janaki in any of his deliberations, and even Mythili goes along with it. As audience members, we are convinced that Janaki has married Cheena while Cheenu is upstairs, ignorant of the proceedings. It is only *after* the marriage has taken place that Madhu finds out that the faith healer had informed Cheenu about the cruel trick Madhu was playing on him and Janaki so that he would have time to substitute himself in and marry the woman he was in love with all along. He even pretends to act like a baby, adopting some of Cheena's signature mannerisms during his wedding so that his sister and brother-in-law won't interfere. There's a level of selfishness and cruelty on their part that I find disturbing. Tell a thousand lies to make a marriage, even if those lies would ruin lives. The audience, though, given the genre, knows that the play has to end with Cheenu and Janaki together, and everything resolved, so they are not concerned.

Crazy Mohan was new at writing plays when he wrote *Honeymoon Couple*, and his original version included four female characters, too many for sabha theater. *Jurassic Baby* has only two female characters, Mythili and Janaki, which is far more standard for the genre. *Honeymoon Couple* had to undergo some changes in order to get the number of actresses needed down to the more manageable number of two, Rukmini and the Maharaja's daughter-in-law Janaki. Originally, there was also Ramani and Rukmini's daughter Nandini and a woman named Julie that they met while on honeymoon. The daughter's role was eventually made an entirely off-stage role. Any lines she needed to be on stage for were rewritten for her brother Dilip, and the off-stage microphone is used by the actress who plays Janaki to do her voice for the rest. This means that Nandini never needs to be seen on stage. Since her role is not really essential to the play except in so far as it is important for Ramani to have a daughter of marriageable age in order to establish his own advanced age and the incongruity of his going on a honeymoon, it was easy to cut, and this simplified the production considerably. The other female role would have presented even more of a problem to stage because not only did it require a female actress, but one of a particular age and appearance.

Julie is an older half-white, half-Indian Australian woman who is staying at the bungalow in Ooty with them. The manager of the bungalow tells Ramani and Rukmini that she wants to marry an Indian man. Ramani is always lusting after her and being particularly stupid when she's around. There is an entire scene that was cut that involves Ramani taking her to Madras. The play is rewritten so that Ramani is always looking for her, but she's never around. When he does find her, it is off stage and can simply be related as a story to one of the other characters. This strategy allowed Kathadi to keep the story of a funny incident where Ramani sees Julie at the Botanical Gardens and hides because he has taken his dentures out because they have fruit stuck in them. He doesn't want her to see him toothless. The dentures are broken by some kids, and he needs new ones, which he asks the Maharaja's manager to procure for him. The Maharaja knows that he has special guests at the bungalow because his son and daughter-in-law are supposed to be there on their honeymoon. He is incredibly confused when the manager relays the request, because his young son, who had a full set of teeth when he set out for his honeymoon, shouldn't need a *pal set* ("tooth set") now.

There are several instances in this play that depict Ramani as a lecherous old man and are of questionable taste. Besides the whole Julie episode, the play opens with a scene where Ramani has gotten out of his bed, so his wife thinks he's up, but he's actually moved to his daughter's bed in the living room and fallen back asleep. When Rukmini scolds him, he jokes about how she shouldn't be too upset since he could have sleepwalked across the street and got into the neighbor's bed. He says, "What would that lady have thought about me then? Forget about me. What would her husband have thought about **her**?" (trans. Rudisill 2004, 2 from Mohan 1977). The misogyny and double standard are palpable here, and even more noticeable given recent media attention on recurring violence against women in India. Ramani's reputation, as a man, can not be overly damaged, no matter whom he sleeps with. But his neighbor's reputation would be destroyed, most devastatingly by her own husband, as the implication is that he would jump to the conclusion that she has cheated on him, when we know that in this hypothetical scenario it would have been Ramani who went across the street and climbed into her bed uninvited. While in this scenario, he is sleepwalking and therefore unaware of his actions, there is an element of victim-blaming and rape culture that makes it uncomfortable as well as funny. He keeps looking at the neighbor lady and talking about her, then trying to get on his wife's good side by comparing her favorably with the neighbor.

Funny Jokes from *Honeymoon Couple*

Honeymoon Couple is full of jokes that illustrate larger themes popular in the genre. One code-mixing joke that audiences find particularly funny in *Honeymoon Couple* and that is also directly related to the honeymoon concept is as follows. Ramani is trying to convince Rukmini to go on a honeymoon with him. He is getting very adamant and annoying, and finally she snaps and retorts, "Fine. Go on a honeymoon if you want to, but I'm not coming." To which he responds, "[d]on't you know anything? If I go alone that's not a 'honey' moon but a 'taṉi' moon (19). *Taṉi* means "alone" in Tamil and also happens to rhyme with "honey," making the joke funny on several levels. First is the cultural concept of a honeymoon, which has nothing to do with the literal meaning of the word. It implies a trip taken by a newly married *couple*. It is, by definition, not something that one does alone, so if Ramani were to go by himself, as Rukmini suggests, the trip would take on a completely different connotation. Second, the rhyme is clever and creates slippage between the two concepts of "honey" and "*taṉi*," which are set up as opposites although they are not. It also allows the two languages to blend together in a way that sounds natural to the ear and requires the listener to pay attention in order to catch the joke.

One recurring theme has to do with confusion about people's names. Naming is incredibly important in Tamil culture and can mark a person's religion, community, generation, and linguistic affiliation. Central to *Honeymoon Couple* is a joke about how confusing it can be when people have the same name and one person is mistaken for someone completely different. The protagonist Ramani's best friend at the office is named Rahottaman and it just so happens that there is a very rich maharaja who also lives in their neighborhood whose name is often shortened to Rahottaman. The maharaja Rahottaman owns a bungalow in Ooty and has a P.A. (personal assistant) named (surprise, surprise) Ramani.

This theme of confusion overlaps in this instance with jokes about doctors and anxieties about their incompetence and the effects it can have on people's lives. When Ramani sends his friend Rahottaman to pick up his heart x-rays from the lab, he is given Maharaja Rahottaman's x-rays to take to the doctor. The maharaja has serious heart problems and after seeing the x-ray the doctor fears for Ramani's life, telling his family to do anything he wants, or his heart may give out. The maharaja's P.A., on the other hand, is given Ramani's x-rays at the lab, and the confused doctor thinks there's been some kind of miracle.

Doctor jokes are always popular, and the doctor's office is the second most popular set in the sabha repertoire, right after the living room. Doctors are supposed to be the most educated people around, and the public trusts them with their health. The joke is usually about incompetent doctors, who have patients because of family connections or other non-merit-based reasons. There is an extended joke in *Honeymoon Couple* when we first meet the doctor, who has been informed that a patient has a pain in his mid-section. The doctor gets very excited about doing an "operation" to check it out since it has been awhile since he had the opportunity to operate. When the patient asks if he knows how to do this type of appendix operation, this dialogue ensues:

> DR.: Do I know? What is there to know? This is how you learn. Last year I did an appendix operation of this type on a patient. I forgot and cut his throat instead of his stomach.
>
> RAM: Ayyo . . .
>
> DR.: But see my luck: that guy had developed some growth in his throat and hadn't said anything to me. So I quickly cut away that flesh.
>
> RAM: Tell me the tonsil operation was successful . . .
>
> DR.: Why did you go and ask me that? That flesh that I cut away turned out to be that fellow's tongue. How's that? (trans. Rudisill 2004, 10 from Mohan 1977)

Similarly, Cho Ramasamy's *Cāttiram Coṉṉatillai* (*The Scriptures Don't Say So*) opens with an extended joke about how the doctor left a needle inside one of his patients after a stomach operation. When the patient's brother calls to tell him, the doctor accuses the patient of theft and demands the needle's return. Both of these examples exploit people's anxieties about the motivations of doctors, who make a living only when people are sick. They play on the fear that doctors actually *want* people to be sick and not get well so that they will have business and make money.

Crazy Mohan in particular is also fond of jokes about people with disabilities, though Cho Ramasamy and others include them as well. Common tropes are characters that are hard of hearing, have poor eyesight, a speech impediment, or some other affliction that can be exploited to humorous effect as they lead to misunderstandings. There are at least two instances of this in *Honeymoon Couple*. First, Ramani tells the story about how he married his wife Rukmini after his cross-eyed friend delivered his love letters to the Rukmini who lived in the house diagonally across from his instead of the one who lived directly across the street. Second, Ramani's work colleague Tanikatchalam has a stutter that Crazy Mohan shamelessly exploits for its humorous potential. This exchange is one example:

> RAM: Tanikatchalam . . . What have you named your new daughter?
>
> TANI: T . . . T . . . T . . .
>
> RAM: What, man? You named her Tea, Coffee?
>
> RAH: That's what happens with the 11th child. You don't know any more names. (trans. Rudisill 2004, 21 from Mohan 1977)

Even knowing he has a stutter, Ramani and Rahottaman don't have the patience for Tanikatchalam to finish his word. Ramani asks a simple question then interrupts to pretend he thought the "T" was the complete word. Of course, the letter is a homonym for the word "tea," which is not the girl's name. And tea pairs with coffee, as guests are usually offered the option. Rahottaman then cuts in to make fun of the man for having so many children, which is clearly uncommon, by saying he couldn't think of any other names, so had to resort to "Tea."

Another theme that is important to this community involves anxiety about money. The viewers of sabha theater almost without exception would say they were "middle class," a category that Sanjay Joshi argues is "primarily a project of self-fashioning" (2001, 2). This self-designation, as argued by Purnima Mankekar (1999) and Sara Dickey (2000b), is largely dependent upon appearances and possessions. In order to keep up appearances, therefore, many "middle-class" Tamils will cut corners in private, and if they are caught they will be exposed as "misers." Ramani laughs at his friend Rahottaman, saying, "[h]e's a bit of a miser. He isn't fit for enjoying life . . . If Rahottaman goes out somewhere and leaves the house, his son will be inside the house. If the son goes out, Rahottaman stays home. Why? Why? Because for the two men in that house, there is only a single veshti" (trans. Rudisill 2004, 16 from Mohan 1977). Generosity is one of the greatest Tamil virtues, even going back to the characteristics of the ancient Tamil kings, and miserly behavior is ridiculed and despised.

Many Indians struggle to maintain their middle-class status by saving money wherever they can, and Ramani and Rukmini are certainly in a precarious financial position. In a world where Tamil Brahmins respect those who opulently display wealth through physical possessions,[7] Rukmini is constantly worrying about money. As the realist in the family, she wonders how they will pay for their bills, take care of their son Dilip's college tuition and fees, and find their daughter Nandini a good husband if Ramani doesn't have a reliable salary. Ramani cannot seem to find the balance between being careful with money and being a miser, or between laudable generosity and opulence and private indulgence. He goes into a great deal of debt over expensive imported toiletries that not even his wife sees. The shopkeeper Chettiar exposes Ramani's unpaid purchases and they include

> CHET: Colgate Toothpaste—one dozen . . .
>
> RUK: One dozen toothpastes?
>
> CHET: Listen: Toothpaste: one dozen, giant size. He is the tooth-brushing demon. I have seen people destroyed by drinking . . . I've seen people destroyed by gambling. But *your* husband will be destroyed by brushing his teeth. (trans. Rudisill 2004, 15 from Mohan 1977)

These toiletries are considered luxuries, and Ramani is buying them in excessive amounts. The funny thing is, however, that they are not *visible* luxuries. A large part of middle-class identity has to do with status symbols and having things that people will *see* in your house or on your person that mark you as being of a certain status. As economist Thorstein Veblen pointed out in late nineteenth-century America, and is also true in India today, this "conspicuous consumption" is actually more important in the urban setting than the rural because in the rural setting everyone is already aware of each individual's economic status, whereas in the urban setting the respect that comes with wealth is often based on the perceptions of strangers. This is the reason that people in Chennai, as in other Indian cities, will go into debt over cars, motorcycles, television sets, refrigerators, and other expensive appliances. Ramani's bulk purchases of toothpaste, soaps, powders, creams, and razor blades are hidden away even from his *wife*, however, making him an object of ridicule, not respect.

There is also physical humor based on costume choices. An example of a specialized costume from *Honeymoon Couple* is that of the raja character, whose outfit is complete with ludicrously large jewels and a silly crown/turban. People laugh every time the raja makes an appearance not only because of his costume but also because of his entrance. The raja's personal assistant decided that the raja needed to be announced, so hired his talentless out-of-work cousin to head an orchestra that is assigned to march in front of the raja and play music (very badly). After the song, the assistant announces the raja using his full and very long name. He tries to do this all in one breath and always runs out of steam before he gets to the end.

Conclusion

These plays are viewed and discussed in the public forums of theaters and the press, as opposed to domestic practices, which take place within relatively more closed domains. This means that the debate about them and the families that they portray is open and can influence what is seen on stage. One reason why a joke can be funny in one socio-political context but not in another has to do with changes in public opinion. This has led to revision of plays in order to keep them contemporary as well as to include several significant shifts in style and content. Response to these jokes can also circumvent hegemonic ideas of good taste because laughter is spontaneous. There is no time to script a response or to formulate a position as audience members are prone to spontaneous laughter. This allows observers a more intimate look at taste than can be gained from the standard position on the most "legitimate" of the arts and their adherence to tradition.

The following chapter focuses on another crucial aspect of the sabha audience constituency: the economic marker of class. Most audience members consciously identify as being middle class, and one clear indication of this status is the hiring of servants. Most of the plays, however, erase this entire servant class of characters that members of the Tamil Brahmin community interact with on a daily basis. I analyze two sabha dramas from very different time periods (the early 1950s and the early 1990s) that share the plot device of a middle-class Brahmin husband masquerading as a servant. The situations and jokes in these two plays reveal the limits of proper middle-class behavior, especially when it comes to acceptable interactions between members of disparate economic classes.

CHAPTER SIX

Husband or Servant?

Masquerade and Middle-Class Identity

Most members of the educated middle-class community in Chennai have servants to help with household chores. It is a recognized marker of status to have someone else sweep your floors, do your laundry, clean your toilets, and possibly cook, drive, garden, and babysit. In this chapter, I investigate the middle-class identity that is being constructed through sabha theater by analyzing two famous sabha plays, written forty years apart, that address relations between members of the middle class and the servants with whom they interact daily. While middle-class men are also present, the focus is explicitly on interactions between middle-class women and male servants from the perspective of the employers. These plays explore servant-employer relations without crossing any real boundaries since in both cases the middle-class audience members know that the male "servant" is actually the husband in disguise.

Scholarship on the Indian middle class has exploded in the past twenty years along with the middle class itself, and while most of these books have focused on consumption (Brosius 2010; Lukose 2009) or politics and the economy (Fernandes 2006; Joshi 2001; Baviskar and Ray 2011), some are now starting to focus more on entertainment (Ganguly-Scrase and Scrase 2009; Donner 2011). Things are drastically different in the Chennai of 2022 than they were in either 1950, when the play *Undersecretary* was first written, or in 1993, when *Ci<u>nn</u>a Māp<u>ḷ</u>ē, Periya Māp<u>ḷ</u>ē* (*Younger Son-in-Law, Elder Son-in-Law*) was. In 1991, India adopted the New Economic Policy that opened the country up to more privatization, liberalization, and globalization. This had an impact by 1993, but nothing comparable to the situation more than a quarter of a century later when there are adults who have grown up with this as their entire experience. Middle-class identity, as Henrike Donner and Geert de Neve (2011) point out, depends on social and cultural capital as much as it does on economic assets. This means that both consumerism and the everyday practices and experiences of individual people contribute to the construction of middle-class identity, and I therefore address both in my examination of these two plays.

Undersecretary was adapted from Ramesh Mehta's Hindi version by actor Purnam Viswanathan shortly after he first saw it in Delhi in 1950 and is one of the earliest full-length comedy plays in Tamil. Viswanathan converted the background details (names, places, and so on) to Tamil and says that he made several more substantial changes while maintaining the integrity of the "whole theme of the play" and also published the script with Alliance Press (author interview, May 20, 2004) (see figure 6.1). Purnam

Figure 6.1. Cover of *Undersecretary* by Purnam Viswanathan. *Source*: Author's collection.

and later Y. G. Parthasarathy of United Amateur Artists made famous the role of Ramasamy, a clerk in a government office who masqueraded as a servant in his own home, allowing his wife's cousin to impersonate him as an "undersecretary" to fool her old school friend into thinking they are better off financially than they are. This play has not been done in many years but was performed more than four hundred times by Purnam and more than fifty by UAA, and is fondly remembered by theatergoers, especially for the late Chief Minister Jayalalitha's acting debut in the role of Kantha (see figures 6.2 and 6.3).

The story is that Ramasamy's wife Rajamma has recently renewed correspondence with her old school friend Pushpa who now lives in North India. When Pushpa tells Rajamma that her husband Gopal is a "deputy director," Rajamma builds up her own husband from a lowly clerk to an important government official, an "undersecretary." The lie would have passed harmlessly, but Pushpa and her husband just happen to be making a trip to Chennai and decide to visit. Rather than coming clean, Rajamma feels she must keep up her and her husband's prestige, so she rents fancy furniture and completely changes the house for the duration of their visit. She also arranges to hire the neighbor's servant Sauri to help their own servant Kali and make them look wealthier than they are. Ramasamy is not at all happy with his wife, feeling that there is no shame in being an ordinary clerk and that the house should match his status. He is overruled by Rajamma and her cross-cousin Shankar,[1] a bachelor who would be her perfect marriage partner, who has turned up unannounced from Bombay for a visit. But when Sauri gets sick and Kali has to rush home for a family emergency, it seems impossible to carry off since a respectable middle-class family cannot be without servants and they cannot afford to hire another one, even temporarily. Rajamma and Shankar suggest that Ramasamy himself play the role of the servant, while Shankar will pretend to be the undersecretary, as they have decided that his personality would play better in that role than her husband's. Under duress, after Rajamma threatens to run away since she can't face the shame of being exposed, he is compelled to agree to the plan, which they think that they can pull off for the single day that the guests will be there. There are a number of complications, but in the end, they are exposed by Gopal, who recognized Ramasamy from when they were childhood friends, and then confesses that his wife built him up in a lie as well and that he is not a deputy director. The lessons of the play address false prestige and the perils of pretending to be more important and wealthier than you actually are.

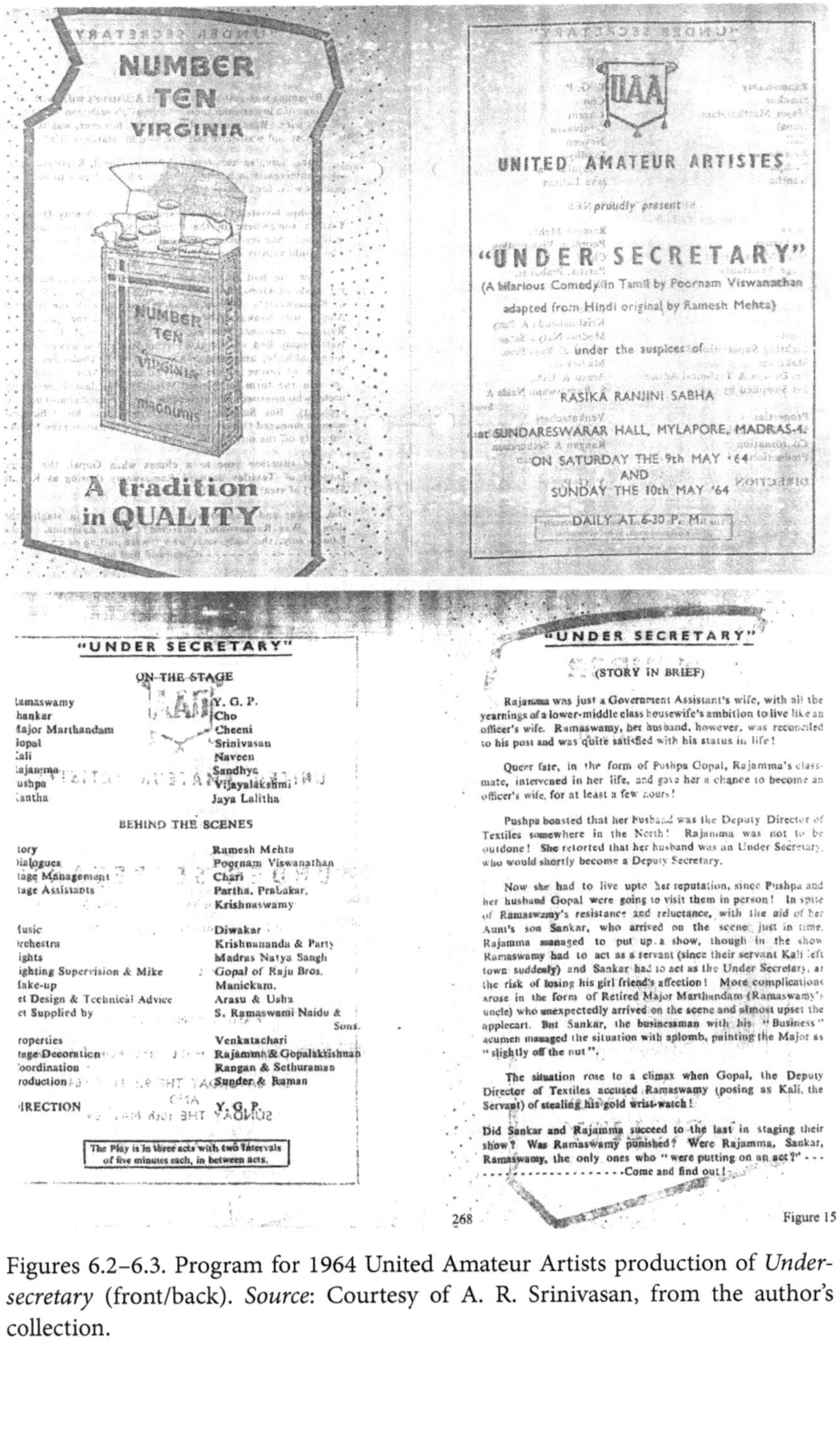

NUMBER TEN VIRGINIA

A tradition in QUALITY

UNITED AMATEUR ARTISTES

proudly present

"UNDER SECRETARY"

(A hilarious Comedy in Tamil by Poornam Viswanathan adapted from Hindi original by Ramesh Mehta)

under the auspices of

RASIKA RANJINI SABHA

at SUNDARESWARAR HALL, MYLAPORE, MADRAS-4.

ON SATURDAY THE 9th MAY '64

AND

SUNDAY THE 10th MAY '64

DAILY AT 6-30 P. M.

"UNDER SECRETARY"

ON THE STAGE

Ramaswamy	Y. G. P.
Shankar	Cho
Major Marthandam	Cheeni
Gopal	Srinivasan
Kali	Naveen
Rajamma	Sandhya
Pushpa	Vijayalakshmi
Kantha	Jaya Lalitha

BEHIND THE SCENES

Story	Ramesh Mehta
Dialogues	Poornam Viswanathan
Stage Management	Chari
Stage Assistants	Partha, Prabakar, Krishnaswamy
Music	Diwakar
Orchestra	Krishnananda & Party
Lights	Madras Natya Sangh
Lighting Supervision & Mike	Gopal of Raju Bros.
Make-up	Manickam.
Set Design & Technical Advice	Arasu & Usha
Set Supplied by	S. Ramaswami Naidu & Sons.
Properties	Venkatachari
Stage Decoration	Rajamma & Gopalakrishnan
Coordination	Rangan & Sethuraman
Production	Sunder & Raman
DIRECTION	Y. G. P.

The Play is in three acts with two intervals of five minutes each, in between acts.

"UNDER SECRETARY"

(STORY IN BRIEF)

Rajamma was just a Government Assistant's wife, with all the yearnings of a lower-middle class housewife's ambition to live like an officer's wife. Ramaswamy, her husband, however, was reconciled to his post and was quite satisfied with his status in life!

Queer fate, in the form of Pushpa Gopal, Rajamma's classmate, intervened in her life, and gave her a chance to become an officer's wife, for at least a few hours!

Pushpa boasted that her husband was the Deputy Director of Textiles somewhere in the North! Rajamma was not to be outdone! She retorted that her husband was an Under Secretary, who would shortly become a Deputy Secretary.

Now she had to live upto her reputation, since Pushpa and her husband Gopal were going to visit them in person! In spite of Ramaswamy's resistance and reluctance, with the aid of her Aunt's son Sankar, who arrived on the scene just in time, Rajamma managed to put up a show, though in the show Ramaswamy had to act as a servant (since their servant Kali left town suddenly) and Sankar had to act as the Under Secretary, at the risk of losing his girl friend's affection! More complications arose in the form of Retired Major Marthandam (Ramaswamy's uncle) who unexpectedly arrived on the scene and almost upset the applecart. But Sankar, the businessman with his "Business" acumen managed the situation with aplomb, painting the Major as "slightly off the nut".

The situation rose to a climax when Gopal, the Deputy Director of Textiles accused Ramaswamy (posing as Kali, the Servant) of stealing his gold wrist-watch!

Did Sankar and Rajamma succeed to the last in staging their show? Was Ramaswamy punished? Were Rajamma, Sankar, Ramaswamy, the only ones who "were putting on an act?" - Come and find out!

268 Figure 15

Figures 6.2–6.3. Program for 1964 United Amateur Artists production of *Under-secretary* (front/back). *Source*: Courtesy of A. R. Srinivasan, from the author's collection.

S. Ve. Shekher's 1993 play *Ci<u>nn</u>a Māpḷē, Periya Māpḷē* ("Younger Son-in-Law, Elder Son-in-Law"),[2] was performed over one hundred times in its first year and has been continually performed over the past thirty years by the polished troupe Natakhapriya in addition to being a very popular audiocassette (see figure 6.4) and then published as a book in

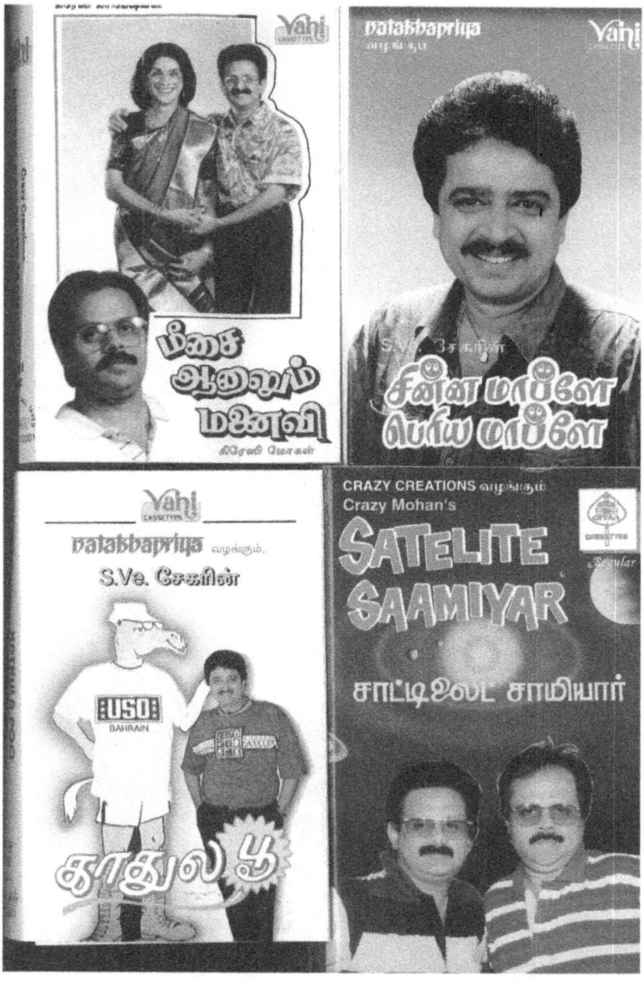

Figure 6.4. Audiocassette covers of S. Ve. Shekher's *Ci<u>nn</u>a Māpḷē, Periya Māpḷē* (top right), Crazy Mohan's *Mīcai Ānālum Ma<u>n</u>aivi* (*She's My Wife Even though She Has a Moustache*) (top left), Crazy Mohan's *Satellite Cāmiyār* (bottom right), and S. Ve. Shekher's *Kātula Pū* (bottom left).

2004 (see figure 6.5). This play, which echoes the 1975 Hindi film *Chupke Chupke* (*Hush Hush*), features comedian S.Ve. Shekher masquerading as an unmarried servant so that he can teach his new brother-in-law a lesson about the realistic boundaries of his influence. This play has built-in opportunities to rethink some socially repressive cultural norms, though it never actually lapses into didacticism or crosses any cultural boundaries with regard to inter-class relationships.

Figure 6.5. Book cover of S. Ve. Shekher's *Ci<u>nn</u>a Māpḷē, Periya Māpḷē*. *Source*: Author's collection.

Cinna Māpḷē, Periya Māpḷē is the story of a young couple, Jana (played by comedian S. Ve. Shekher) and Hema, whose love marriage is impeded by Hema's sister Savitri's husband, Dog Narasimhan, the *Periya Māpḷē* (older son-in-law) of the family. Dog is a detective ("Periya Zero Zero Seven," as he describes himself) in Hyderabad[3] and wishes for Hema to marry a police officer in Chennai, who could be useful to his career. Hema's father agrees to the love match even though Jana is a writer of Tamil dictionaries (educated, but with no prestige). Jana and Hema get married, and Dog orders them up to Hyderabad the very same day—canceling their "First Night" ceremony (the night of the wedding, when the marriage would traditionally be consummated). Incensed, and knowing that Dog Narasimhan and Savitri are looking for Tamil-speaking servants, Jana, the *Cinna Māpḷē* (younger son-in-law), heads up to Hyderabad alone, disguised as a cook. He manages to secure positions as both their cook and their driver. He is thus firmly established in the household when Hema arrives without her husband. They talk Jana's friend Kannan into pretending to be Hema's husband, a police officer, and the complicated masquerade is revealed when Dog Narasimhan botches a kidnapping case he has been working on and is saved and shamed by Jana. With Dog's acceptance of Jana into the family, and the kidnapped girl Nisha's return to her lover (Jana's friend Kannan), everything is resolved and all is well.

The sabha genre is targeted at the middle class and deals with issues relevant to their situation. They interact with servants every day, and these two plays address those relations in an unthreatening but not uncritical manner, through the device of the husband in disguise. The jokes point out class stereotypes and push the employer–servant relationship without threatening the status quo because the audience knows (although other characters do not) that the new servant is actually a member of the family and the husband of Hema/Rajamma. In this way, the plays give many humorous examples of how employers and servants should and should not behave and interact in a variety of stressful situations. These scenes highlight the ridiculousness of certain cultural attitudes and occasionally even stretch the boundaries of acceptable interactions between the different social and economic classes in India, particularly between middle-class women and their male servants.

Although it is easy to find the humor in these plays, especially in the false inversion of class relations, it is harder to understand the pleasure of the middle class in laughing at themselves in the form of the ridiculous employer in Shekher's play, which takes the side of the clever servant. The older *Undersecretary* does not challenge class relations as much as the more recent play, since Ramasamy in the role of servant is never in a position of power. This play instead uses Ramasamy's failings in contrast to the real servant's virtues to show the audience how the relations between the classes should be in a perfect world.

The Artists

S. Ve. Shekher is not primarily a writer, but an actor (see figure 6.6 for a photograph of the author with S. Ve. Shekher in 2004). The dialogues for his plays are written by a variety of people, each one doing just a few plays for him. This approach allows someone like Shekher to continue to update his plays based on current events. He says, "I give a lot of scope for improvisation. That day's main political happenings must be added to make the play live up to and relate to contemporary life" (Gopalie 2002, 228). An excellent example of this is the title change from *Ci<u>nn</u>a Māpḷē, Periya Māpḷē* to *CM-PM* and the political satire that accompanied the change.

Figure 6.6. Photograph of the author with S. Ve. Shekher at a performance of *Kātula Pū*, 2004. *Source*: Courtesy of S. Ve. Shekher.

The new title opened the way for jokes about the chief minister (CM) and the prime minister (PM) and their relative power that spoke particularly to Tamil voters in the late 1990s. In 1998, Tamilnadu Chief Minister J. Jayalalitha, in what Robert Hardgrave and Stanley Kochanek referred to as "a game of political extortion . . . held the BJP government . . . hostage" in order to get concessions for her state (Hardgrave and Kochanek 2000, 306–7). The ruling BJP was dependent on the AIADMK's eighteen parliamentary seats for its survival, and when Jayalalitha withdrew from the coalition in April of 1999, Prime Minister Atal Bihari Vajpayee lost the vote of confidence by one vote, the government fell, and new elections had to be held. In the play as well, it is the CM (younger son-in-law) who holds the power to topple the structurally dominant PM (older son-in-law). Like in the play, Tamils are predisposed to identify with and root for the underdog CM, as Jayalalitha was demonstrating not only her own personal power, but that of the state of Tamilnadu when she refused to remain in a coalition that wouldn't meet her demands.

Shekher is an actor who prefers live theater because that is where he can best utilize his gifts of improvisation and direct communication with audiences. He actually had his first acting experience in *Washingtonil Tirumaṇam.* He told an interviewer that he had gone to buy tickets for the play for his family "when the director, Nagarajan, made [him] do a female role in it" (Kumar 2006). Shekher's father S. Ve. Venkatraman also acted on stage and in films, and encouraged his son, who holds a diploma in mechanical engineering and a post-diploma in air conditioning and refrigeration, to pursue his performance career. Shekher started his own troupe, Natakhapriya, in 1974, which today commands higher rates from sabhas than any other in Chennai. Although he has a sense of humor both on stage and in person, when it comes to Natakhapriya he is completely professional and a perfectionist.

Natakhapriya's first play, *Avaṉ oru Taṉi Maram* (*He Is a Lone Tree*) was written and directed by Mouli, who had become well known through his association with United Amateur Artists,[4] and later formed his own troupe Mouli and Friends. He now works exclusively in the film world. Audiences attended the play because of Mouli and the fact that the lead actor was famous film comedian C. K. Nagesh. Shekher did the special effects and substituted for other actors if the need arose. It wasn't until 1976, when he began collaborating with writer Crazy Mohan, that Shekher started directing and really became a comedian in his own right. S. Ve. Shekher is an active personality in Chennai. He has a radio program (on

Radio Mircchi), a television show ("All in All Shekher" on Vijay TV), served as president of the Tamilnadu Television Artists Union,[5] is a member of the Central Board of Film Certification (aka the National Censor Board; he was appointed by Narendra Modi in 2015), has acted in over fifty films, and served as an MLA from the Mylapore constituency from 2006–2009 (for the AIADMK; now he is an active member of the BJP). He said in an interview that since his plays take place in the evenings, they would not interfere with his new responsibilities and might, in fact, allow him to better serve his constituency because "theatre can be used to share ideas and propagate issues."[6] Shekher also frequently appears solo as a guest for various corporate functions, judge for *Paṭṭimaṉṟam* debates,[7] or simply as a speaker for special events. Many other members of Natakhapriya are also involved in film and television.

There are many entertainments available in the city of Chennai, especially after the New Economic Policy of 1991, and attracting educated fans demands skillful marketing. As mentioned earlier, S. Ve. Shekher realized early on that markedly Brahmin dialect and subject matter would severely limit his audiences and so he broke from the norm by making a point of speaking standard Madras Tamil in his plays, keeping the families and themes as generic as possible, and employing both Brahmin and non-Brahmin actors (see figure 6.7 for a photograph of some of the actors and actresses who are part of Natakhapriya). Although he advocates for the Brahmin community in his political life, he has made it his business

Figure 6.7. Photograph of the Natakhapriya theater troupe with S. Ve. Shekher. *Source*: Courtesy of S. Ve. Shekher.

to appeal to the broadest audience base possible with his comedy. After breaking with the AIADMK in 2009, Shekher started the Federation of Brahmin Association for the Southern Region (FEBAS) with the goals of providing to the needy and deserving and achieving justice through convincing the state government to add reservations for Brahmins. Kathadi Ramamurthy, S. Raadhu, and other notable Brahmins from the sabha theater world attended his inaugural function.[8]

Shekher has succeeded more than any other performer in reaching audiences through the mass media of audiocassettes. Almost any cassette shop will sell his audiocassettes, and possibly one or two of Crazy Mohan's or Kathadi Ramamurthy's. A cassette is cheaper than even the cheapest seats at one of his shows and can be enjoyed countless times. One of the reasons these are so popular, more so than for other groups who have tried to break into the market is that he, like Purnam Viswanathan, was originally trained as an actor through radio. Shekher started his career in advertising and sound, and is a genius at editing, sound effects, and voices. Soon after he started his troupe, he also "became an approved artist of the All India Radio, in the Drama section. That was a great advantage for me. I learned all about voice modulation. How to play up or play down a sentence. Only Radio plays can give, as they survive only by sound [*sic*]" (Gopalie 2002, 219). He did a weekly radio program for years on Radio Mircchi in Chennai, on which he told jokes.

The style of Shekher's theatrical productions reflects this emphasis on the audio over the visual. He rarely distracts viewers from the dialogue by set or costume, notable even within the amateur aesthetic, using minimal sets and props and varying those and the costumes little from drama to drama. Actors actually face the audience most of the time they are speaking to one another and the theme music and sound effects kick in at opportune moments. Shekher is often criticized by other artists for keeping the microphones so visible on stage and directing the actors to just stand around them to talk. Figures 6.8 and 6.9 are photographs of Natakhapriya performing.

In contrast to this, Purnam Viswanathan is famous for his "natural acting" and in his dramas the actors face each other when they talk in their normal voices assisted by (relatively) unobtrusive microphones. Purnam's feeling is that when an actor delivers dialogues he doesn't need any artificial acting or expression. "Not acting is acting," he told me on May 20, 2004, but all the years of voice training and radio gave him remarkable projection, far superior to that of most sabha theater actors.

Figure 6.8. Photograph of S. Ve. Shekher's troupe members at a performance of *Kātula Pū* (*Flower in the Ear*), 2004. *Source*: Courtesy of S. Ve. Shekher.

Figure 6.9. Photograph of Natakhapriya performing, ca. 2004. *Source*: Courtesy of S. Ve. Shekher.

Undersecretary, much closer to the colonial and professional roots of the sabha genre than *CM-PM*, takes a lot of care with its single set of the ideal upper-middle-class living room, every detail described in the text.

Purnam Viswanathan was born in 1920 and grew up during the movement for India's independence. His father, a successful lawyer as well as a music and language enthusiast who had studied Sanskrit, felt that it was very important for all Indians to learn Hindi, which Purnam did enthusiastically. He was involved with scriptwriting and play production in high school and college, participating in primarily Hindi-language productions, along with a few Tamil and English plays. He took a job with All India Radio (AIR) in June of 1945 and worked for them in Delhi as a newsreader, translator, playwright, producer, actor, and talent scout. He told me that he was the one who read the first news of India's independence on AIR in 1947 and that in 1997 they invited him to announce the news again for the Golden Jubilee celebrations (author interview, May 20, 2004). During his time in Delhi, Purnam was involved with a small play production club called South Indian Theaters that did short plays in Tamil and Hindi. He trained Delhi Kumar and other Tamil actors in Delhi and also knew Y. G. Parthasarathy there.

In 1964 Purnam moved back to Chennai and quickly became an important figure in the Tamil theater scene. He did some work with Seva Stage on a contract basis and joined Triplicane Fine Arts during their production of Cāvi's *Washingtonil Tirumaṇam*. When their key artist died, the group was not maintained and Purnam went to Kala Nilayam with Marina and K. S. Nagarajan. This troupe mostly performed Marina's plays about middle-class Brahmin families, and Purnam made many of the roles famous, particularly that of the *atimpēr* (brother-in-law) in 1969's *Ta<u>n</u>ik Kuṭitta<u>n</u>am* (*Separate Family*). In the mid-1970s Kala Nilayam split. K. S. Nagarajan kept the troupe's name and continued its work, while in 1979 Marina started his troupe Rasika Rangam and Poornam, who had since retired from his work at AIR, started Purnam New Theater.[9]

Purnam New Theater primarily performed plays by Sujatha, who had given two plays to Kala Nilayam and enjoyed working with Purnam. Sujatha wrote ten plays for Purnam New Theater, the first being *Adimārkaḷ*, which was inaugurated October 11, 1979. They did one new play a year, and Purnam holds the exclusive rights to produce these plays.[10] Many of the actors in the new troupe were from Kala Nilayam, including Baladev, who later worked for the *Indian Express*, Ravi Jagannatha, Vishnu, and the

Figure 6.10. Photograph of the author with M. B. Moorthy and other members of Gurukulam Original Boys Company '95. *Source*: Author's collection.

actress Shobha. The late Viji Sulochana of Seva Stage, for whom Purnam had done contract work, was the primary lady artist in the beginning of Purnam New Theater. This troupe continued from 1979 until 1995, when Purnam dissolved it. At that time there were not as many opportunities to perform, he was seventy-five years old, and was busy with cinema commitments. Since they couldn't have Purnam New Theater without Purnam, M. B. Murthy, Gauri, and some of the younger actors from the troupe decided to re-organize themselves, with Purnam's blessings, as Gurukulam Original Boys Company '95. Figure 6.10 is a photograph of the author with several members of the Gurukulum Original Boys Company '95, including M. B. Murthy. They had to find new writers and all new plays because no one wanted to try to reprise Purnam's roles, feeling that they would only disappoint his fans.[11] This troupe has continued to produce new plays since Purnam's death in 2008 at age 87.

Employers and Servants

There are many perceived dangers inherent in the hiring of servants, and Sara Dickey has identified employers' most common worries with regard to prospective employees as including, but certainly not limited to, dirtiness, dishonesty, inappropriate involvement in family conversation, disrespect and subsequent gossip, and theft (2000b, 474). Each play addresses most of these areas, and in the process makes a statement about employer–servant relations. In the Natakhapriya play, Jana manages to make his employers appear classist, paranoid, cheap, and ignorant. In *Undersecretary*, middle-class pretensions themselves, not the characters, are ridiculed along with the material goods and status symbols that become so important in this play and in the lives of many Indians. Fancy silk saris and number of servants are continuous points of competition between the two couples. The set is elaborate, complete with plastic flowers in vases and big, intellectual-looking works of English literature.

Undersecretary, by juxtaposing two servant characters, one a "real" servant and one the educated husband in disguise, working together in the household, actually demonstrates how good servants should and should not behave. *Undersecretary's* humor comes primarily from the audience's knowledge of everyone's true identities and relationships and their unsuitability for the roles they are playing. Purnam felt that this narrative strategy, where the audience was taken into the writer's confidence and nothing was hidden from them, allowed them to participate more fully in the story (author interview, May 20, 2004). The clerk Ramasamy is a terrible servant, unable to even make coffee, and Shankar is a terrible government employee, not knowing the least thing about what they do and consulting with his "servant" on difficult questions.

One of the issues that Dickey mentioned, disrespect and subsequent gossip, can be extended to refer to the characteristic of "loyalty." The real servant Kali in *Undersecretary* is certainly a sympathetic figure, loyal to a fault (the middle-class fantasy servant) and dragged into all sorts of scrapes by his employers' attempts to cover up for Rajamma's lie. When he goes back to his village only to discover that his father is completely healthy, he rushes back to the city to help with the important guests. His employers have decided, however, that with Ramasamy already introduced to the guests as the servant Kali, his presence would be confusing so they give him some money to clear out for the rest of the day, explaining to their guests that his father is deathly ill. This seems like a great idea and an extra day's paid leave, so Kali goes to the park and plays cards with friends . . . where he is later "caught" by the guest Gopal and dragged home in disgrace. He puts up a good show, crying and begging not to be fired, thus allowing the "undersecretary" to show his compassion and forgiveness. The impersonator Ramasamy, however, highly annoyed that his wife has forced him into this humiliating situation, is far from the ideal loyal servant, agreeing almost at once to leave the house and go work for Pushpa and Gopal in Delhi for an extra ten rupees a month. Later, when the two "servants" are accused of stealing Gopal's watch, the real Kali politely denies the charges, saying, "I promise. I don't belong to that kind of race. I come from a good family. I've never even seen your watch." He remains loyal, opting to go to the police station rather than to confess his true identity to Gopal and betray his master. Ramasamy, on the other hand, still defiant and sulky, is far from subservient, actually being rude to Gopal, refusing to be questioned or searched, and eventually challenging him with the lie: "It's with me. I won't return it. What will you do?"

While the Ramasamys are lucky to have the model servant Kali working for them, the Narasimhans of *CM-PM* have been struggling to find good servants in Hyderabad. They have contacted their local Tamil Sangam to ask for assistance in finding a Tamil-speaking cook, necessary after the language difficulties they faced with their previous Telugu-speaking cook. In her essay on servants and their expatriate employers in Bangalore, Louise Kidder points out, "Hiring other people to do one's work has the potential for 'communication' problems built into every interaction, especially if one wants the other person to do it the 'right' way" (Kidder 2000, 213). This communication gap is naturally exacerbated when the employer and servant speak different languages. Knowing this, Jana decides that if Dog Narasimhan wants a Tamil-speaking cook, he'll get a *literary*-Tamil-speaking cook, whom he will likely have trouble understanding. Jana, an educated writer of Tamil dictionaries, is frequently able to confuse his boss by replacing loan words with their "pure Tamil" equivalents. The pure Tamil movement started with the Dravidian movement in the early twentieth century, and proponents tried to purge Tamil of "contamination" by other languages, but the results were often awkward, unwieldy, and difficult to understand.

Language jokes that play on words and slip between Tamil and English, Telugu, and/or Sanskrit continue throughout the play, and often take the form of insubordination between Jana and Dog, his new employer. It is clear from the play that Jana is by far the more educated man of the two, since Dog Narasimhan can't understand Jana's *ilakkaṇa* (literary) Tamil speech. For example, when Dog asks Jana why he hasn't made the coffee like he was supposed to, Jana says that there is no gas, using the Sanskritized form "*vāyu*" for gas. Dog misunderstands, thinking that Jana is complaining about his "*vayiṟu*" or stomach. The education levels of the two men represent an inversion of what would normally be the case, where the better-educated man would receive more respect and also be wealthier than the uneducated man (that is, hiring servants, not working as one).

Education level is raised in *Undersecretary* as well when Shankar scolds Ramasamy for sounding too intellectual to make a convincing servant. Ramasamy is unable to hide his education and intelligence, which are greater than those of Shankar, and this inversion, with the servant being better educated than his employer, is found to be humorous. The exchange foregrounds the fact that education level can be ascertained from the way a person talks, and that servants are expected to be a step below their employers. When Ramasamy asks Shankar if servants must be idiots, he is told that they can be intelligent, but still can't talk back to their employers. Ramasamy (and presumably the audience) suddenly realizes that many servants may be smarter than they are allowed for reasons of cultural propriety to appear. Audiences can read as much or as little into the plays as they like, taking pleasure in fantasy, revenge, storyline, character, theme, or simply in the acting skills of Purnam Viswanathan, S. Ve. Shekher, and their talented troupe members.

Money and education are certainly the biggest markers of class, but India has also had a history of dividing people based on rules regarding the sharing of food, according to caste status. *Ci<u>nn</u>a Māpḷē, Periya Māpḷē* deals with the anxiety about food and the sharing of food in Tamil culture by challenging cultural norms. The Narasimhans have complained numerous times to Savitri's father about their difficulties in finding good servants in Hyderabad. The Tanjavore cook requested by the Narasimhans in *CM-PM* would definitely be Brahmin, so the Narasimhans would eat food he cooked and be served by him, but for them to serve the servant food, regardless of his caste status, is an entirely different situation. The first time Dog and Savitri meet Jana, this tension is highlighted and challenged.

When Jana comes to apply for the open cook position, the Narasimhans think that the veshti-clad man entering their home so deferentially is the president of the Hyderabad Tamil Sangam coming to help them locate Tamil-speaking servants, and treat him according to his presumed status. When Jana tries to explain who he really is (pretending to be), knowing from their invitation to come in and sit down that there is some confusion, Dog Narasimhan says, "Who am I? I am an important detective in Hyderabad. I know everything." Jana's momentary fear that his new brother-in-law does in fact know who he is, is betrayed by the shaking in his voice when he says, "Do you know?" but it is quickly relieved. He is not recognized as either the new brother-in-law or the new cook, but as someone else, deserving of great respect. When Dog Narasimhan invites his prospective servant into his home and tells his wife to bring coffee for the man, it is clear that he has no idea what is actually going on. A prospective servant would normally be interviewed outside or just inside the door, not invited in and offered a seat or any refreshment.[12] Jana knows this unspoken rule well and protests, telling Savitri that he won't drink anything, "No coffee, no tea, thank you." So she brings him buttermilk, because she must offer this important guest something, and is puzzled by his response, "As soon as I come, you give buttermilk; you should not repent for that later." To which Dog Narasimhan replies, "What is there to repent for later? Nothing." It later comes out that Savitri has brought fresh buttermilk for Jana, not the old buttermilk that she has been serving her husband, and Jana politely offers his buttermilk to Narasimhan. Jana obviously looks uncomfortable and "afraid," so Dog Narasimhan goes overboard in politeness, telling Savitri not to threaten the man and urging Jana to please drink. But when the real president of the Hyderabad Tamil Sangam calls on the telephone, the detective is singing a different song, ordering Jana to get up, using non-respectful verb forms in sharp contrast to his former ingratiating speech. He then turns his wrath on his wife, yelling at her (even though he had told her to do it in the first place) for bringing buttermilk for the servant as though he were a guest.

This sequence touches on the stereotype of employers as petty, making their money off the poor[13] and trying to keep the material differences between themselves and their servants intact. Humorous situations in the play can be subtler than the language jokes, allowing the audience the option of simply laughing at the surface situation but inviting them to think more deeply about the flaws in the social structures that underlie these situations. Jana, to stop the fight, starts to leave, saying that once he earns the negligible cost of a glass of buttermilk he will send them a money order.

The question of food is also important in the Purnam Viswanathan play, but the concern in this case is about who can cook for the guests. The servant Kali normally cooks for the Ramasamys, so there would be no problem with his food. However, what should they do in his absence? Most men of Ramasamy's status would not know how to cook and would be dependent on their servants or wives even for a simple cup of coffee. So, when this clerk is put in the role of a servant and expected to make coffee for the guests, there is something of a crisis. Gopal is too polite to say anything, but he doesn't drink the coffee he is served. Shankar doesn't drink his, either, and makes the excuse that the *other* servant, stressing that they have more than one, usually does the cooking. Rajamma knows that her husband would rebel and reveal his true identity or carry out his threat to just boil whatever he finds in the kitchen and serve it as lunch, spoiling her charade, if she asked him to cook, and she certainly can't be seen doing her own cooking, with her class status as an undersecretary's wife and guests to entertain, so she decides to order out from a restaurant. Eating food from outside the home is often avoided by wealthy, upper-caste families for both pollution and health reasons, but under these circumstances it seemed to her the only workable solution.

After the buttermilk incident in Shekher's play, several more issues are addressed regarding the proper treatment of servants and the duties of the employer in this respect. The Narasimhans have been without satisfactory servants for a long time, except for the driver, who just left that morning. Savitri was upset at the driver because she said he only listened to her husband and didn't think he had to obey her orders. Of course, when Dog Narasimhan asked her why the driver left, she said, entirely self-righteously, that she had asked the man to wash her saris and blouses, but he refused to do it and walked out. Among servants, these pampered, middle-class housewives are thought to be very unrealistic and overly demanding. The stereotype of the rich Tamil woman being overly demanding of her servants is funny because of her ignorance of the servant's pride in his work and also of the proper division of labor. Even Dog Narasimhan knows better and is horrified at her behavior (that she doesn't see anything wrong) and yells at her, telling her that drivers don't know how to do laundry, and what are they to do now, since he doesn't know how to drive the car.

They decide to hire Jana as a cook, largely because he used her father's name as a reference, but do ask him a few basic interview questions before making that decision final. His responses to their questions are really funny because of their double meanings, speaking both to those who know his true identity (the audience) and those who don't (his new employers) at the same time. For example, he says of his cooking that he will cook like Nala of *Mahabharata* fame, whose wife was able to recognize him through his amazing food, and within half an hour of eating his cooking they will know the result and not be able to sit still, but will be running around saying urgently "Who is the cook? Who is the cook?" The implied meaning is that he will cook so badly that they will be sick and running back and forth to the toilet, subtly inserting into the text references to the power dynamic between servant and employer, reminding the employers in the audience that they are dependent on their cooks' good judgment and graces for their very health. The Narasimhans, however, are so pleased at the thought of having a famous cook like Nala that Savitri says wistfully, "Now, if only we could find a driver just like him, it would be great." This is a wonderful opportunity for Jana, who knows how to drive and by taking this job will be able to pick up his wife Hema at the train station when she arrives and fill her in on how things are going before she has to interact with her sister and brother-in-law. In addition, it is an opportunity to make Dog Narasimhan dependent on him in a different way. Dog Narasimhan asks him for references, and his response is this long history of drivers in his family:

> JANA: One of my ancestors drove (*ōṭṭu*) the chariot for Arjuna.
>
> DOG: For Arjuna?
>
> JANA: Yes. We are related to Krishna.
>
> DOG: Ah-ha.
>
> JANA: My great-grandfather drove (*ōṭṭu*) the tonga for the king of Arcot.
>
> DOG: Oh-ho.
>
> JANA: My grandfather drove (*ōṭṭu*) a horse cart on Wall Tax Road.[14]
>
> DOG: Very good.
>
> JANA: My father, when he had no other work, swatted (*ōṭṭu*) flies.
>
> DOG: Ah.
>
> JANA: Now I will drive (*ōṭṭu*) the car for you.
>
> DOG: Very good, very good.

The joke here lies in the use of the same verb (*ōṭṭu*) in wildly different contexts, but the Narasimhans don't seem to notice Jana's last reference to his father and find the resume more than satisfactory, hiring him as both driver and cook on the spot.

Jana continues to create conflict throughout *CM-PM* with his negotiation of wages and a dismissal policy, by sitting too close to his wife, lying about Savitri putting kumkum[15] on his forehead, and being overly friendly with the Narasimhans' distinguished guests. These scenarios highlight potential problems with servants, particularly those with unmarried male servants, yet all take place in a socially acceptable manner within a family. S. Ve. Shekher, playwright T. Durai Raj (T. D. R.), and the Natakhapriya troupe stretch the boundaries between the social and economic classes in India and remind employers both of their mutually dependent relationship with their servants and of the fact that they are actually not so different from the lower classes, whom they should treat with respect since the consequences of their actions can never be known in advance.

First Night and Dirty Jokes

Shekher also makes a point of pushing the boundaries of conservative Brahmin culture by including some characters and jokes in his plays that could be considered vulgar or inappropriate. For example, his 1991 play *Yāmirukku Pāyam Ēn?* (*Why Fear When I Am Here?*) introduces the character of a young girl who flirts with every guy she sees and acts very immodestly and inappropriately. *CM-PM*, which premiered a mere two years after *Yāmirukku Pāyam Ēn?*, included several suggestive scenes about the first night of a young couple's marriage. This may be one reason that Shekher's plays appeal to younger audiences more than most other sabha plays except for, perhaps, Crazy Mohan's, who has also attracted younger members to the sabhas that regularly sponsor their performances. This is atypical, since most sabhas have very few patrons from younger generations. Shekher's audiences tend to be from a younger, more global, and less conservative generation than typical sabha-goers. They have grown up with films that promote the idea of an "arranged love marriage," which entails "matrimony between a mutually acceptable and consenting couple that has been facilitated by the couple's parents,"[16] instead of placing the two concepts in direct opposition to one another. Middle-class youth are, as I say elsewhere about *desi* romance readers, "educated in English and comfortable with the changes globalization has brought to India, such as the growing acceptability of male and female co-workers drinking together at bars and clubbing, and couples having sex and even living together before marriage" (Rudisill 2018, 757). Perhaps that is why they are more permissive with their senses of humor and open the space for Shekher to push boundaries and address the traditionally restricted topic of sex. This space is limited, though, as older, more conservative Brahmin sabha members make up the bulk of theater-goers, and I saw Shekher scold an actress for acting too sexy in a 2003 performance of *Eppavum Nī Rājā* (*You Are Always a King*). "It is okay for some TV serials," he told her, "but drama is directed at families and needs to be clean and modest."

First night provides a special space to discuss sex not only in the theater, but in film as well. In his 2003 book *Indian Popular Cinema: Industry, Ideology, and Consciousness,* Manjunath Pendakur discusses the various components of a typical "first night" ritual that include not only the flowers, food, and milk mentioned in Shekher's play, but also the centrality of the image of a bed strewn with flowers, the ritual teasing of the newlyweds before sending them into the room, and the singing of erotic songs outside the room once they are in it. This is the accepted pattern for a first night, but as Pendakur says, "[a]ll these cultural practices stood in contrast to the guarded sexuality of the bourgeois family" (2003, 136).

The same year that *Ciṉṉa Māpḷē, Periya Māpḷē* was inaugurated, India was rocked by the debate surrounding the sexually suggestive and therefore controversial Hindi song, "Choli ke peeche kya hai?" ("What's behind the blouse?"). Monika Mehta has enumerated three distinct voices that emerged from that debate, which are helpful in this discussion of first night. Some opposed the song as morally offensive and therefore contrary to Indian culture. Some defended the song as a traditional folk song sung by women and therefore an integral part of Indian culture. Third, and most interesting, is the position espoused by Arun Katiyar in an article he wrote for *India Today* in 1994. Mehta quoted this article, in which she said Katiyar "confirmed that 'folk traditions, especially in Punjab, Gujarat, Rajasthan, and Uttar Pradesh have spawned wicked lyrics' (Katiyar 1994). However, he added that the songs are sung in *specific contexts* such as pre-wedding ceremonies. In these ceremonies, he explained that when 'women sing what is commonly called ladies' *sangeet* [songs] in Punjab, it is done more in fun than as a come-on' (Katiyar 1994)" (Mehta 2001, 4). The point made here is that although these songs may be "wicked" or vulgar out of context, they are acceptable and "fun" when sung at a pre-wedding ceremony. If this is the case in real life, it makes sense that audiences would feel that sexual innuendo in the specific context of a first night scene in either a film or a play would be more permissible than outside of that context.

Traditionally, the first night of a marriage is when a newly married couple would have sex for the first time, and their elders have some responsibility to ensure that this happens by preparing the young people adequately. The elders also have a vested interest in the possible outcome of the event: grandchildren. The topic of sex, taboo most of the time, is central and auspicious on a first night. In fact, Pendakur writes: "First night scenes are often used in films as they allow some space to the filmmakers to represent sex. There may or may not be a song in the room. Inclusion of the song prolongs the sexually loaded scene and offers opportunities to the director that may be disallowed by the Censor Board in other situations" (2003, 136). The implication is that even in the eyes of the very strict Indian Censor Board, especially with regard to the topics of sex and modesty, there is something innocent and acceptable about an inexperienced couple preparing for their first night and consummation of their marriage. Regardless of the Censor Board, however, it is certainly true that audiences are much more permissive in their expectations when it comes to song sequences. Amita Nijhawan goes so far as to say that song-and-dance sequences are "spaces of articulation of female sexuality" because "Bollywood film and dance genres (have the potential to) construct new sites of sexual desire and female identity in India" (2009, 99). They certainly create the space for the good Tamil girl to wear western clothes and dance erotically with the hero, since these scenes are often conceptualized as dream or fantasy, and therefore not essential to the plot or reflective of the morality of the character.

CM-PM contains lengthy jokes about the "first night" of a marriage, and the innuendoes in the dialogue are unmistakable. There are two scenes in this particular play that center on the issue of first night, and both are significant in the clever way that Shekher alludes to the topic of sex while managing to keep the surface level of the conversation "clean," "healthy," and suitable for all ages. These concerns are central to this genre and its middle-class audience. The first takes place just after the marriage, fairly early in the play, when the groom Jana is heading toward the bedroom on his first night. He is stopped by his new father-in-law, Sonachalam, who tells him the following after a long, suggestive exchange:

SONA: Son-in-law, one *good news.*

JANA: What?

SONA: *First Night cancelled.*

JANA: Huh?

SONA: *Periya Māppiḷḷai's* order. (Shekher 2004)

The implication is that instead of going in to his new wife and beginning their life together with the consummation of their marriage, the young couple is expected to hop on the night train up to Hyderabad to "make *periya māppiḷḷai* happy" (*cantōṣapaṭaṇum*). Jana is incredulous that he is actually expected to forego relations with his new wife Hema on the "order" of the elder son-in-law. He says to his father-in-law, "What is this? Do I need to go and make the elder son-in-law happy? Are you saying I shouldn't go the distance of ten feet to where your daughter is and make her happy? Do I need to go to Hyderabad and make another man happy?" The sexual undertone of the verb is present because the audience knows exactly where Jana was headed before his father-in-law interrupted him with this news.

Just before Sonachalam tells Jana the "good news," it is made clear that he has not thought about what the marriage of his daughter will mean for her modesty and virginity. He sees his new son-in-law Jana walking by with a *sombu*, a particular size and shape of pot that will be filled with milk for the new couple to drink on their first night, and asks if he is going to the bathroom with it. This opens the floor for a joke about the water shortage in the city of Chennai,[17] that Jana may have to use milk to wash himself after going to the toilet, but he then explains himself pretty explicitly to his father-in-law, who immediately announces that first night is cancelled . . . and calls it "good news." Jana says, "How can you tease me with a question like this? Today is my first night! In a house with no women it seems like I have to make all the arrangements by myself. Oh! Did you put oil in the lamp? Inside, Hema is waiting for me with the pangs of separation." The scene ends when Hema finally comes out and says, "You're still standing right here talking?! How long do I have to wait for you?" and Jana replies in an angry, rhythmic rant, "You'll need to wait and wilt and shrivel up to nothing. First night cancelled!" This statement of Hema's is one of the very few times a female character says anything even remotely sexually suggestive in a sabha play. She has implied that she has been anticipating her first night with as much excitement as her husband. Though it is very subtle, it is still noteworthy, since it is far more taboo for a female to make a suggestive comment than a male.

Angry at the older son-in-law Dog Narasimhan "poking his nose into my first night bedroom," Jana heads to Hyderabad to pose as a cook in his brother-in-law Dog Narasimhan's house. Since he is playing the cook, he cannot play his rightful younger son-in-law role, so he enlists his friend Kannan to pose as his wife's police-officer husband. This situation led to the second first night scene, when the elder brother-in-law, thrilled at having a police officer for a brother-in-law, encourages the younger son-in-law imposter to celebrate his "first night" with Hema, his "wife," there in Hyderabad. He continually coaxes, "Please go in, *Māppiḷḷai*, please go," and his "servant" Jana keeps interfering. The audience knows that *he* is the true husband, though Dog believes him to be only a servant.

Dog is making all the preparations for the ritual with milk, flowers, fruit, and the oil lamp when the "servant" asks what the occasion is. When he is told that it is "first night," he asks, deliberately assuming that Dog is talking about his *own* first night, "why have you just been sitting around all these years?" When the elder son-in-law tells his "servant" that it's "first night," the servant says, "Why didn't anyone tell me?" And when Dog replies, "We need to tell *you* that? What are you going to do?" the response "[a]m I allowed to say that in your house?" is clearly a reference to the fact that *he*, not the imposter, is the true husband and therefore the girl's first night has everything to do with him. There are then jokes about why Dog doesn't have any children. He believes that his kids will come in a single litter of five or six . . . just like a dog's, but the most telling moment and one of the funniest sequences in the play is when he describes what the young groom can expect on his first night:

> DOG: *Māppiḷḷai*, Hema will come and fall at your feet.
>
> JANA: Aaah.
>
> DOG: Bless her. Take up the *sombu* full of milk. You drink half of it.
>
> KAN: And the remainder?

JANA: Make curd out of it.

DOG: Hey!

JANA: Okay, okay.

DOG: Give it to Hema, *Māppiḷḷai.*

JANA: Oh!

DOG: Then turn around and look. There will be fruit, snacks, and palm fruit on the table. Don't leave any of it! Eat it all without leaving any leftover. After a short while, you'll get a bit dizzy. Your head will spin. So after putting your head in Hema's lap, fall asleep!

KAN: Is that all?

DOG: That's all. What else would there be?

JANA: What is this? Now I see why there are no little critters to be found in this house!

This dialogue, obviously, is full of innuendoes. Anyone in the audience who has already experienced "first night" and many who haven't will know from the language and inflection that the true event of the evening is only briefly alluded to by the word "*mayakkam*" ("stupor," "intoxication") and the references to children.

The scene is tasteful in that it never mentions sex directly, but it is also vulgar on two distinct levels. First, the scene explores the emotions of a man watching his wife (with whom he has not yet had relations) being encouraged to have sex with someone else by her own brother-in-law, but this is mitigated by the implication that the brother-in-law doesn't actually know the facts of life. Second, it addresses the situation of a man watching his male servant get too close to his newly married younger sister-in-law. The burden of interpretation, as Shekher claims, can be placed on the audience, but the innuendo is unmistakable, passing only over the heads of the very young.

The sexual tension is also present in the older play *Undersecretary*, in which the cousin playing the role of the husband is put in an awkward position vis-à-vis both his married cousin Rajamma and Kantha, the girl he is trying to court while disguised as another woman's husband. At one point, Shankar scolds Rajamma for speaking to her husband, Ramasamy, who is supposedly her servant, using respectful language. Ramasamy, who is not happy about the way this whole scenario has played out, snaps at this point. He yells at Shankar for calling his wife "darling" and standing too close to her, insisting that Shankar stay at least four steps away from her at all times.

Conclusion

Both *Undersecretary* and *Ci̲n̲n̲a Māpḷē, Periya Māpḷē* cleverly exploit the uncomfortable relationship between a middle-class family and their unmarried (or so some of the characters think) male servant. There is opportunity built into each play for rethinking some social and cultural ideas about how servants and employers can and should interact with one another. Servant–employer relations are explored in these plays without crossing any real boundaries since in both cases the middle-class audience members know that the male "servant" is actually the husband in disguise. These scenes help to define the boundaries, particularly the sexual boundaries, between members of these different classes from the standpoint of the middle-class employers, whose class identity in part depends on keeping the social, cultural, and material differences between themselves and their servants intact. The middle-class members of the audience can simply laugh at the humorous surface situations, but there are deeper layers in the plays that address underlying social structures and relations.

The following chapter turns to yet another aspect of audience identity and looks at sabha plays as regional. Nearly all of these plays rely on insider jokes that may be social, political, or linguistic, and in the next chapter I further define one of the boundaries of sabha theater by analyzing Cho Ramasamy's play *Mohammad bin Tughlaq*, which has been successful both on sabha stages and to some extent in the broader arena of nationally known and respected modern drama.

CHAPTER SEVEN

Blurred Genres

Tamil Brahmins as Indian Intellectuals

> BATT: I have been amazed to hear of your proficiency in the Arabic and Persian languages.
>
> TUGH: Sometimes, if I think about it, I even amaze myself.
>
> BATT: It seems that you have a very high opinion of yourself.
>
> TUGH: We need to value good things wherever we find them. Should we not value them only if they are in ourselves?
>
> —From *Mohammad bin Tughlaq* by Cho Ramasamy

This sequence is from the opening scene of Cho Ramasamy's 1968 political satire *Mohammed bin Tughlaq* (see figure 7.1). Foreign intellectual Ibn Battuta[1] has appeared at Tughlaq's court and praised him for his language skills, piousness, and level of knowledge. Tughlaq clearly enjoys hearing himself praised and is pleased until Battuta begins questioning some of his choices as a leader and revealing his cruelty towards his people. I've chosen this passage to start the chapter because Tughlaq's arrogance and assurance in his own superiority is reminiscent of the Tamil Brahmin producers of sabha plays more generally. His line, "we need to value good things wherever we find them. Should we not value them only if they are in ourselves?" is a critique of false modesty. If you are the best and know it, you should say so. As a leader, we see that Tughlaq favors those who

Figure 7.1. Cover of *Mohammad bin Tughlaq* book by Cho Ramasamy, 1995. *Source*: Author's collection.

praise him and are loyal to him and executes or at least ridicules and punishes those who do not recognize his obvious superiority.

This chapter uses Cho's play to look closely at the divide within the Tamil Brahmin community itself in order to probe the blurred boundaries between the sabha theater genre and the pan-Indian modern theater genre, which appeals to many Tamil Brahmins as cosmopolitan urban intellectuals. Tamil Brahmins present themselves as modern, often claiming that existing Brahminical traditions were inherently modern, and as M. S. S. Pandian notes in his book *Brahmin and Non-Brahmin* (2007), they were less likely to identify as secular than the Karnataka Brahmins Ramesh Bairy interviewed. Showing the dual allegiances and varied tastes within the community thus encourages the development of a more fluid and modern understanding of a multifaceted Tamil Brahmin culture, which is heavily influential both in India and abroad.

In her comprehensive study of post-Independence Indian drama, Aparna Dharwadker (2005) has delineated a national canon of modern Indian plays. Her study of this constructed but constantly changing and expanding canon is informed by the list of plays and theater practitioners invited to participate in the Nehru Centenary Festival in 1989 as well as years of criticism and published dramas and interviews. Despite the attention afforded to these plays within India, Dharwadker's work is one of the first attempts to bring Indian theater into discussions of contemporary world theater. One of the explanations that she offers for the obscurity of Indian theater on the world scene is the "linguistic plurality of Indian theatrical practice" (2005, 2). While this is certainly the case, it is also true that the majority of plays recognized as belonging to the national canon are from only four out of India's many languages and theatrical traditions: Hindi, Marathi, Kannada, and Bengali. No Tamil plays or playwrights are included in the lists of major Indian playwrights, plays, directors, and productions, with the exception of a passing mention of Brahmin playwright Indira Parthasarathy. There is, then, parallel to the obscurity of Indian theater on the world scene (itself indicating a gap in the history of international theater), an obscurity of Tamil theater on the national scene that signals a gap in the history of post-colonial Indian theater and drama. While many Tamil Brahmins appreciate and enjoy sabha theater, they are not promoting it nationally or translating it so that other language speakers can access it. Why not? The fact that many people from the Brahmin community choose to become members of sabhas or attend sabha dramas is not to say that the plays themselves are considered ideal representations of Tamil Brahmin culture or of good taste. In fact, as discussed earlier, the discourse about the plays has created two factions within the Tamil Brahmin community, the most vocal of which dismisses them as "just comedy."

Another word that is often brought up in regard to sabha theater is "commercial," which is never said of the modern theater. This word, however, can have two meanings. First, it can imply a theater that is profitable and commercially viable. This is highly unusual in Chennai. The few troupes whose shows are profitable (Natakhapriya, Crazy Creations,

United Amateur Artists) have troupe leaders who are successful in the mass media fields of television and film. The mass media is where the money is, not the stage.[2] The other meaning of "commercial," and the one that is employed in most discussions of Tamil theater, is that of pandering to the masses and giving the audiences what they want, presumably compromising the players' artistic integrity. Comedian S. Ve. Shekher is very frank about his manipulation of plays to fit the audience. He uses improvisation based on his communication with the audience to follow what he calls the "script graph." He says that he never complains that the audience members are fools. They are very clever, and if they're not responding then he must not be communicating properly and needs to change something (author interview, July 8, 2003). Cho, in contrast, was proud of the fact that his plays still resonated with audiences exactly as they were written fifty years earlier.

Even given this attitude, having spent years in Chennai studying the vital Tamil-language theater traditions and audiences there, I am curious about why these plays, writers, productions, and directors have not become part of what is still in many ways a closed club based in Kolkata, Mumbai, and Delhi. There is an exceptional amount of Tamil regional pride in culture and performing arts—why doesn't this extend to theater? Tamil theater has its own long history and generic branches,[3] but the tradition of criticism and dramatic theory that sprung up around modern Indian theater simply did not materialize in Chennai, as Dharwadker's 2019 volume *A Poetics of Modernity: Indian Theatre Theory, 1850 to the Present* demonstrates. A few writers from the experimental theater such as N. Muthuswamy and S. Ramanujam tried to develop critical writing about theater, but it did not catch on. A consideration of Tamil drama and theater can add a lot to the discussion of modern Indian drama, both because it offers a glimpse into what is excluded from the canon and because it gives a sense of a regional theatrical identity and diversity in performance. The only Tamil playwright to have gained national recognition (Indira Parthasarathy) spent many years of his adult life in Delhi, interacting with modern theater practitioners there.[4] Other Tamil playwrights and directors have been invited to stage productions at the National School of Drama festival and are therefore possible contenders for canonicity. Without exception, their plays are serious, not comedic, and address social issues, usually through history or mythology. When they are performed in Chennai, these plays are performed for non-sabha theater audiences.[5] Dharwadker's work makes it clear that although there is a great deal of formal and linguistic diversity in the modern Indian dramatic canon, there is also a set of characteristics that bring these particular plays together and appeal to urban intellectuals, many of whom in Chennai are also Tamil Brahmins.

This chapter attempts to add a different kind of shading to Dharwadker's arguments about the characteristics of the Indian national canon by comparing one play that has been included with one that has been excluded. Cho Ramasamy's 1968 Tamil *Mohammad bin Tughlaq* shares more than just a title character with Girish Karnad's 1964 Kannada *Tughlaq*, a play that is firmly within the canon. This comparison of the two South Indian plays from the same political context in terms of content, style, and literary and performance histories is instructive in considering the reasoning behind the tacit exclusion of Cho's play (and by extension other Tamil plays) from the accepted canonical lists. The two playwrights, independently of one another, dramatized the same historical figure into the different genres of historical psychodrama and political satire. The two Tughlaq plays are very much of the same time, but they have different approaches and focus on different issues through their treatments of the same historical figure. They leave readers with very different visions of both Tughlaq's time and their own. Both plays allude to the national political situation, but Karnad's historical drama looks backward sympathetically, evoking the complex feelings associated with India's first prime minister, Jawaharlal Nehru, who died the year the play was written. Cho's political satire, on the other hand, expressed his fears about the authoritarian ruling style of Nehru's daughter, then-prime minister Indira Gandhi, which were justified several years after the play when she declared a national Emergency and abused her enhanced power. Cho's political satire reflects regional issues of 1960s Tamilnadu and has remained confined to a regional audience, while the numerous translations of Karnad's work have brought him international acclaim.

The Playwrights and Plays

Girish Karnad was born in 1938 in the town of Matheran outside of Bombay. He grew up in a community that spoke Kannada and Marathi but was educated in English. He aspired to be an English poet and was awarded a Rhodes Scholarship to study at Oxford. On the voyage there, however, he found himself writing a play—in Kannada. He had some exposure to the folk theater of *Yaksagana* and to Natak companies[6] as a child, but his main influences at the time were from the West: Shakespeare, Brecht, Ibsen, and Anouilh. His first play, written in 1961, had an Indian story but a Western form. He said of himself that "I had no theatrical form to turn to. This is a problem many Indian playwrights face today . . . A playwright needs a tradition he can call his own, even if it is only to reject it . . . I could only imitate Anouilh, for there was nothing to refer to: the natak companies and yaksagana seemed to belong to another world altogether. Nothing filled the void they had left" (1989, 334). Karnad's hybrid style, where he combines elements of Indian folk theater with western theater, has been considered emblematic of what modern Indian theater should be. He has been referred to as "the most significant playwright of the post-Independence Indian literature" (Dhanavel 2000, 11). Suresh Awasthi, who was both chair of the National School of Drama and general secretary of the Sangeet Natak Akademi, "locates the crucial starting point of the development of an Indian 'theatre of roots'[7] in B. V. Karanth's direction of a new play [*Hayavadana*] by Girish Karnad in 1972" (Banfield 1996, 136). Karnad stayed involved in playwriting and the theater until his death in June of 2019, but he made his living in television and film as a writer, director, and actor.

Karnad's play is set in the past and tells the story of Mohammad bin Tughlaq's rule as sultan. He holds many ideals at the beginning of the play, but as he becomes more involved in the politics of the country he loses them and grows more and more cynical. From the time he ascends the throne, Tughlaq is fighting rumors that he murdered his father and brother during prayer time in order to gain that position. As the story progresses he becomes less and less averse to using deception and subterfuge to continue to rule, eventually masterminding the murders of respected Muslim holy man Imam-ud-din, advisor Shihab-ud-din, and even his beloved stepmother. Parallel to Mohammad bin Tughlaq's story is the narrative of Aziz and Aazam, two men who follow the logic of Tughlaq's policies to the extremes and profit from each one. Their actions are a physical expression of the shifting morals of their sultan. The play ends with Tughlaq's recognition of how well he has been understood by the lowly Aziz and his surrender to sleep, which had eluded him for years. The sympathetic Tughlaq of Karnad's play is meant to evoke memories of Nehru.

Cho Ramasamy, on the other hand, set his play in the present and brought the historical figure of Mohammad bin Tughlaq to 1968. The playwright used Tughlaq to express his fears about Prime Minister Indira

Gandhi's authoritarian ruling style (author interview, June 4, 2008). In Cho's play, Tughlaq and his advisor Ibn Battuta ate some herbs that prevented their deaths, and remained shut up in a box for six hundred years until history professor Rangachari unearthed them in 1968. Rangachari brings them home to his family, which consists of his wife Srimati, their children Pattu and Indira, and Srimati and Rangachary's fathers. After learning about how the country has changed over the six hundred years they slept in the box, Tughlaq decides to run for public office. He quickly rises to become prime minister and uses his position to demonstrate the level of ridiculousness and corruption that the Indian government had reached, with little distinction between a democracy and a dictatorship. At the end of the play, Battuta reveals that he and Tughlaq are both imposters, but no one believes him or wants to risk change.

Cho Ramasamy was one of Tamilnadu's most important contemporary playwrights and thinkers until his death in 2016. He was born in Chennai in 1934 and studied in Mylapore, then at Loyola College, and in 1955 finished a B.L. degree at Chennai Law College. Cho served as legal advisor for the T.T.K. Company for many years starting in 1960 (see figure 7.2 for a photograph of Cho working in his office).[8] He started writing dramas in the early 1950s for his younger brother S. Rajagopal (also known as Ambi) and a group of his friends from Vivekananda College,[9] but was not part of their Viveka Fine Arts until later. In its early years the group staged plays by Devan and Koothapiran while Cho occasionally played small roles. He was primarily working with Y. G. Parthasarathy's United Amateur Artists at this time and acted as Shankar opposite J. Jayalalitha in Purnam Viswanathan's *Undersecretary*, discussed in detail in chapter 6. In 1958, Koothapiran decided to start his own troupe (Kalki Fine Arts), so Cho wrote *If I Get It* for Viveka Fine Arts, which was now actively looking for good material. Since then Viveka Fine Arts has exclusively done his plays, and he had acting roles in every one. In addition to his twenty-three plays Cho wrote six novels, many short essays, and the stories for fourteen films and four television programs. He also directed one film and four television programs in addition to acting on television and in more than 180 films.[10]

Even given this impressive vita, Cho's primary identity was not as a writer or an actor, but as a political commentator. In fact, in a review of Viveka Fine Art's Golden Jubilee celebrations in 2004, journalist Arup Chanda wrote, "Cho Ramaswamy is a familiar name, not only in Tamil Nadu but all over India. He is known more as a political commentator who edits a Tamil magazine, *Tughlaq*. But little do people know about Cho as a Tamil dramatist." In a 1982 survey, it was found that 95% of college-educated adults in Tamilnadu but only 38% of those unable to read had heard of him, and that the vast majority of those who had heard of him had good opinions about him (Siromoney and Varathiraj 1982). He was very active in the Brahmin community and explored caste issues in other plays, most notably *Cāttiram Co<u>nn</u>atillai*, in which the possibility is raised that a Brahmin boy was switched at birth with a Dalit one.[11] He also wrote a book called *Eṅkē Pirāmaṇa<u>n</u>?* (*Where Is the Brahmin?* See figure 7.3) in 1993, which was adapted as a television series that "personified the quintessential Tamil Brahmin. As the story pursues in the background, Cho acted as the voice of the upper elite in Tamil Nadu explaining aspects, importance and the practical use of the Hindu religion, cultural practices, rituals etc. But what he starkly also indulged in was questioning what the religion and culture meant in common sense and the current times" (Online Desk 2016). So even though he is familiar to most college-educated Tamils, it is the Brahmins that he most clearly speaks for and to.

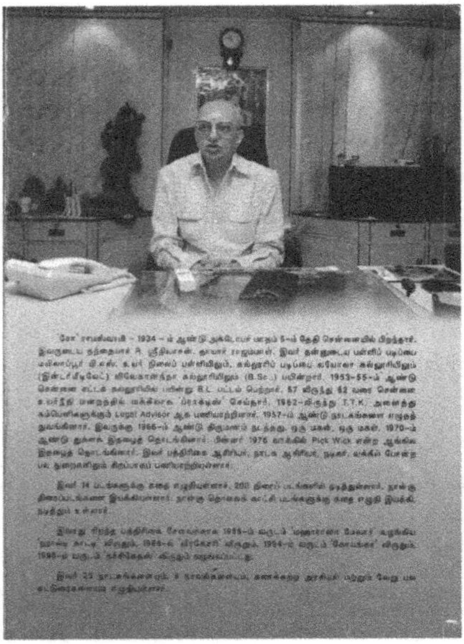

Figure 7.2. Back cover of *Eṅkē Pirāmaṇa<u>n</u>?* by Cho Ramasamy, 2007. *Source*: Author's collection.

Figure 7.3. Cover of *Eṅkē Pirāmaṇa<u>n</u>?* by Cho Ramasamy, 2007. *Source*: Author's collection.

Cho Ramasamy and the Tamil Middle Theatre

Cho has received occasional recognition outside of Tamilnadu. Like Komal Swaminathan (whose 1980 play *Taṇṇīr Taṇṇīr* [*Water!*] was translated into English by S. Shankar and made into a film by K. Balachander), Cho could be called a crossover playwright in Tamil. Shankar describes crossover plays, "which try to treat high-minded themes in a commercially viable format" and attempt "to straddle the gap between urban and rural audiences, between artistic integrity and popular reach," as part of the "Tamil middle theatre movement."[12] Both of these playwrights were popular with the sabhas, both plays were still being performed in the early 2000s, and I had the opportunity to see them staged. Their appeal, however, moves beyond the limited audiences usually found within the sabhas to the broader intellectual community in the city.

Both Cho and Komal Swaminathan are considered by academics to be among the great playwrights in Tamil, though on a somewhat lower level than writers like Indira Parthasarathy and N. Muthuswamy because of their more casual (spoken) language and broad appeal. Drama has been, in S. Shankar's words, "the least honored of the different genres in Tamil literary criticism" (2001b, 124). Writer and historian of Tamil literature M. Varadarajan writes that "[t]here are some valid reasons for neglecting plays in Tamil. . . . Since the Tamil language attained literary stature at a very early stage, it acquired certain rigid literary conventions. It was stipulated that works of literary merit should be written in chaste style devoid of regionalism and colloquialisms. But plays meant for acting were written in spoken but not in literary Tamil. Hence the plays in spoken language were detested by poets and scholars" (Varadarajan 1970, 269). This bias is still in evidence, and the more literary a play's language is, the more respected it tends to be in critical circles. R. S. Manohar's plays, for example, are in a much more formal, literary Tamil than those of Cho. Cho and Manohar are the only Tamils mentioned by theater scholar Farley Richmond in a long list of "India's leading directors" (Richmond 1990, 412).

Cho's comedy elicits something in between the respect granted to Indira Parthasarathy and the condescension expressed toward the work of Crazy Mohan. It has led critic N. S. Jagannathan to simultaneously denigrate and compliment him: "Now there are political plays of various kinds . . . We also have, admittedly at the level of low farce, plays in Tamil by Cho Ramaswamy that are extraordinarily effective in the exposure of the corruption of values in Indian politics" (1989, 107). "Low farce" or not, S. Shankar described Cho as a "distinguished playwright" and his political opinions and writing skill are well respected by the intellectual community in Tamilnadu.

Cho's plays are in closer conversation with the modern Indian dramatic tradition than most Tamil plays, and that is one reason that it is important to consider his work carefully in this context. Another reason is that his plays, though they are dated by their explicit parodies of Dravidian politicians, have stood the test of time and remain very popular in performance. Even in print many of Cho's plays sold out their first runs and have been reprinted. His most famous play, *Mohammad bin Tughlaq*, brought in packed houses in Chennai as late as 2008 when Viveka Fine Arts would perform it as a benefit for various charities. Most sabha troupes have either faded away entirely or have been replaced over the years. Only a few have adapted or somehow managed to remain relevant to the sabha audiences, and Viveka Fine Arts is one, though after Cho's death in December of 2016 at the age of eighty-two as well as Ambi's and Neelu's in 2018, this is unlikely to continue as the troupe did not take steps (like Stage Creations and other troupes have) to bring younger actors into the group to ensure continuity. See figure 7.4 for a photograph of Cho Ramasamy and R. Neelakanthan performing together.

Figure 7.4. Photograph of Cho Ramasamy and R. Neelakanthan in a performance of *Campavāmi Yukē Yukē* (*I Appear Age after Age*). *Source:* Courtesy of R. Neelakanthan, from the author's collection.

In her criticism of the scant scholarly work available on Indian post-colonial theater, Aparna Dharwadker makes two very important points. First, that "[f]or certain social groups in India . . . the colonial experience was one of privilege rather than subordination" (2005, 11). Most sabha theater practitioners fall into this category. Cho, for example, is at least a third-generation lawyer. Second, the majority of post-Independence theater practitioners were consciously trying to develop "a 'new' theatre for a new nation," writing about "the intersecting structures of home, family, and nation in the urban society of the present," not about the colonial encounter (2005, 11, 13). Like many of the modern playwrights whom Dharwadker discusses, Cho's emphasis is on the "postcolonial present" and his observation skills are the key to his success. He did not, however, employ realism to show Indian families and politics exactly as they were, but rather used satire and hyperbole to indicate the general direction in which he saw the family and nation to be headed.

This "shift from heroic self-praise to ironic self-reflexivity" (Dharwadker 2005, 180–81) was common among urban writers of the post-colonial period, and the increased use of irony and satire has been continually noted in discourses about India. Dharwadker discusses ironic and satiric plays that are *serious*, but satire is a device that can also be very funny and as such it is used in Tamil drama to great effect by Cho Ramasamy. Cho started his hobby by writing short comic skits for his brother and his friends in 1954 but didn't pen explicitly political plays until ten years later. His early plays were more in the style of social comedies. For example, his 1964 *Maṉam Oru Kuraṅku* (*The Mind Is a Monkey*) is a Tamil adaptation of George Bernard Shaw's *Pygmalion* that pokes fun at the pretensions of the Indian middle class. These first plays were not overtly political, and the audiences grew to love his keen sense of observation and his fast-paced dialogue. Cho was branded as a great comic writer several years before he started writing the political satire for which he eventually became known.

It was his *Campavāmi Yukē Yukē,* which also came out in 1964, that first brought Cho his fame as a political satirist. The title of the play is a line from the *Bhagavad Gītā*, and in the play, corruption is so rampant that Vishnu (as Krishna) is arrested and brought to court on a charge of murder. Sage Narada tells him that he can escape if he bribes the judge. This play was banned by the police because one of the character's names was actually the name of a real employee of the transport department who was concurrently in the news for his corrupt practice of accepting bribes.[13] Cho was asked to remove some sections and change the name of the character, but he refused and instead brought all his legal genius to bear on the court case. The case got a lot of press and went on for a month before Cho won. By then the audiences were lining up to see this play with its subversive reputation.

Over the next few years Cho developed his political satire and created the character of Mohammad bin Tughlaq with whom he has come to be identified. The 1968 play was made into a film in 1970, the same year he started his *Tughlaq* journal, through which he became known as a political commentator, then a DVD of the play was released in 2006 (see figure 7.5). The journal was started with the idea of criticizing whichever government

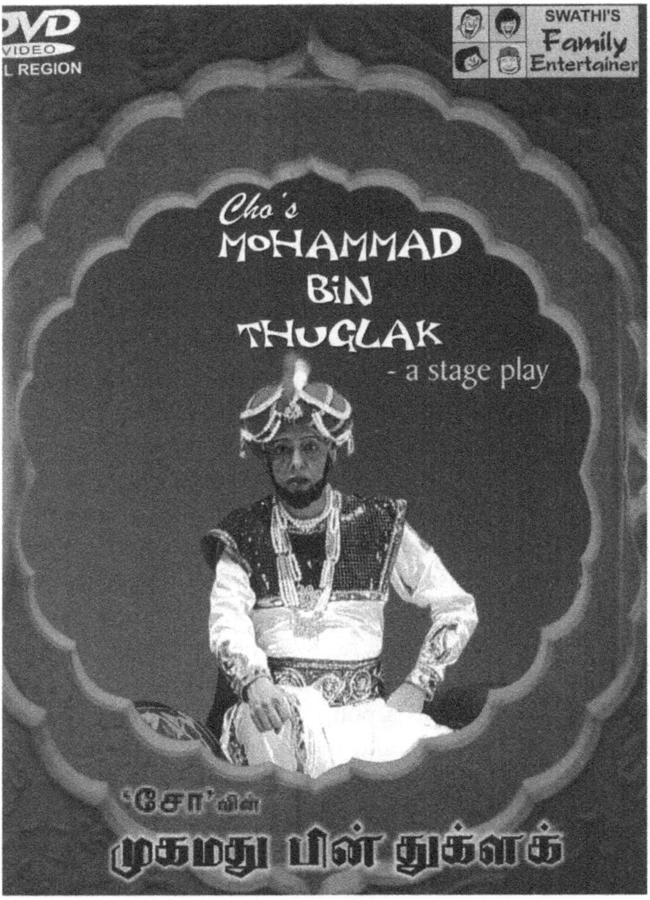

Figure 7.5. DVD cover for Cho Ramasamy's *Mohammad bin Tughlaq*, 2006. *Source*: Author's collection.

happened to be in power as well as all politicians, candidates, and policy initiatives. In one of his early issues Cho wrote in the "Dear Mister *Vācakarē* (Reader) . . . !" section that it is his duty to be the opposition: "I made it clear that I tell my personal opinion independent of affiliation with any party. Whichever party comes to rule, it is my responsibility to serve as the opposition party. 'Tughlaq's way is my way.' "[14] He wanted to make sure that the public knew about the issues and their options in elections, so he began each issue with an *eccarikkai* (warning). Cho spent his life criticizing politicians, then became one himself as a member of the national government's Rajya Sabha when he was appointed by President K. R. Narayan and served from 1999–2005.

The Tughlaq of Cho's play exploits the importance of name recognition in politics. There is a great deal of slippage between the identities of stars and politicians, who are so often the same. Cho himself, though he served for six years in the Rajya Sabha, is not considered a "politician" by many people because his position was an appointed, not an elected one. Although he voted on issues and was part of the central government, Cho never ran for office. This campaigning is where he finds politicians to be the most corrupt. His play *I<u>n</u>pakkanā O<u>nr</u>u Kaṇṭē<u>n</u>* (*I Dreamed a Sweet Dream*) is the story of a utopian community where everyone has a role and gets along beautifully until there are two candidates for one position. The resulting election leads to corruption and a complete disintegration of all the values of the society. Politicians, in Cho's view, tell the people whatever they think they want to hear, then ignore or renege on all campaign promises.

Farce, Satire, Psychodrama, and Tragedy

For the most part, the two Tughlaq plays use different devices, genres, and characterizations to focus on different concerns. What they share is a title character, a commitment to raising political awareness, and the device of farce. Cho's plays, which are not leftist, realistic, or necessarily progressive, as are most plays of the modern Indian dramatic canon, have been alternately described as "political satire" and "farce," terms that have different meanings and connotations, but are often linked in critical thought as well as in practice. There is a lot of overlap between the two concepts, but the major difference is that satire involves wit or humor and an object of attack. The satirist takes a high moral line and assumes "a special function of analysis, that is, of breaking up the lumber of stereotypes, fossilized beliefs, superstitious terrors, crank theories, pedantic dogmatisms, oppressive fashions, and all other things that impede the free movement of society" (Frye 1962, 19–20). Satire is associated with George Meredith's idea of "high comedy," which "evokes 'intellectual laughter'—laughter from spectators who remain emotionally detached from the action—at the spectacle of human folly and incongruity," while farce is associated with "low comedy," which "makes no intellectual appeal, but depends for its comic effect on violent and boisterous action, or slapstick" (Abrams 1962, 39–40).

Both satire and farce are routinely used to address serious issues and comment on politics. In his work on plays dealing with communism in Kerala, Darren C. Zook writes that politics are themselves so comical that even realistic dramatic portrayals of them are necessarily farces: "Political practice and rhetoric have become so comical and absurd that left-wing, socialist, and 'realist' dramas, if they are true to their task of representing the revolution as it is, must unwittingly and perhaps unwillingly tend toward a theatre of revolutionary farce (or farcical revolution)—or, indeed, a theatre in which farce and realism are indistinguishable" (2001, 176). In contrast to this view are the many serious plays such as Komal Swaminathan's *Water!* and Mahasweta Devi's *Mother of 1084* that have their roots in leftist politics. Zook accounts for Karnad's *Tughlaq* by arguing that "Karnad's play is not an antidrama but a complex farce (*prahasana vinod*) in which 'serious' political rule becomes increasingly indistinguishable from political charade and brute force masquerades as idealism in the hands of Muhammad Tughlaq, a fourteenth-century monarch of northern India" (Zook 2001, 188). The farcical scenes in Karnad's *Tughlaq* are part of what the playwright envisioned as the light, "shallow" comedy scenes interspersed with the drama of the main characters and their "deep" scenes, a technique he borrowed from the Parsi theater. Aparna Dharwadker calls Karnad's *Tughlaq* a "psychodrama" and talks about the "political and psychological ironies" (2005, 247) in the play, and that assessment seems much closer to the nature of Karnad's play than the designation "farce." Karnad sees Indian theater as jumping straight from the flat, generic characters of the folk theater to the psychological revelations of western theater, and his work tries to negotiate this divide as much as possible (see Karnad 1989). His characters may seem generic and predestined, but he emphasizes their choices and psychological growth.

Darren Zook understands that at the end of Karnad's play the clown (Aziz) and the king (Tughlaq) become impossible to distinguish from one another, and therein lies the farce: "The clown does not merely imitate the king—part of the power of farce is in recognizing the clown and the king as separate characters—but in fact elides with the king: the clown becomes the king and the king becomes the clown. And in that moment the possibility of clowning, or even of laughter, disappears" (2001, 189). He writes that he uses this example of Karnad's play in order to demonstrate that any political theater must be farcical, even outside of the Communist context of Kerala: "[t]he nonsensical reasoning through which Aziz, as the clown, justifies his heinous actions turns out to be synonymous with the reasoning through which Tughlaq has pursued his own political intrigues: government action is itself a farce" (2001, 189). The tragic figure of Girish Karnad's character Tughlaq does not fit into Meyer Abrams's definition of farce as "a type of comedy in which one-dimensional characters are put into ludicrous situations, while ordinary standards of probability in motivation and event are freely violated in order to evoke the maximum laughter from an audience" (1962, 39–40), though his minor character Aziz might.

Unlike Karnad's, Cho's play never separates the king and the clown. There is only Mohammad bin Tughlaq the clown/sultan. There is no psychodrama, no character development, no "deep" scenes. Still, neither theatrical category quite encompasses Cho's *Mohammad bin Tughlaq*, which stands at the intersection of farce and satire. It has the one-dimensional characters and nonsensical reasoning of farce combined with the incisive wit and corrective morals of political satire. Choice of descriptive terms does, however, make a difference in the minds of readers and viewers. Farce is usually considered "low" and satire "high" in the entertainment hierarchy. The use of the word "farce" makes Cho's work seem light and insubstantial, while "satire" praises him as a political thinker and mover.

Girish Karnad's Mohammad bin Tughlaq, with his internal struggle and increasing madness, is balanced by the comic character of Aziz. The two characters conflate in the end, when Tughlaq recognizes himself in Aziz and offers the man a government job. Aziz's cynical attitude toward politics and politicians is much closer to Cho's Tughlaq, and Karnad's splitting of this character adds depth to the portrait of Jawaharlal Nehru that is visible in his Mohammad bin Tughlaq. When they are escorting the people on their forced march to Delhi, Aziz says to his friend Aazam:

> Look at me. Only a few months in Delhi and I have discovered a whole new world—politics! My dear fellow, that's where our future is—politics! It's a beautiful world—wealth, success, position, power—and yet it's full of brainless people, people with not an idea in their head. When I think of all the tricks I used in our village to pinch a few torn clothes from people—if one uses half that intelligence here, one can get robes of power. And not have to pinch them either—get them! It's a fantastic world! (Karnad 1994, 190)

Cho's Tughlaq, like Aziz, works to manipulate the system; Karnad's Tughlaq *is* the system. Cho himself played the character of Tughlaq and continued to develop and expand that role through the *Tughlaq* journal. Even so, this character remains quite flat, never serious about anything except his own power and public image. This is exactly Aparna Dharwadker's assessment of Karnad's character Aziz: "In the character of Aziz the will to power is unhampered by any moral or psychological complexity, and the play's absolutist discourse of power comes appropriately from him, not from Tughlaq. . . . Tughlaq's self-reflexivity never produces this ironic clarity, and while Tughlaq is lost in epoch-making gestures, Aziz conducts his own micropolitics with singular success" (Dharwadker 2005, 254). It is notable that both Aziz and Cho's Tughlaq end the plays triumphant while Karnad's Tughlaq is "dazed and frightened, as though he can't comprehend where he is" (Karnad 1994, 221). Aziz and Cho's Tughlaq are the cynics, the keen observers and takers of advantage, and they are the comic element in both plays.

Aziz's definition of a king is what Karnad's Tughlaq does, without acknowledging it, but Cho's Tughlaq does openly. By means of allegory, Cho Ramasamy flattens and exposes the unapologetic authoritarian tendencies of then–prime minister Indira Gandhi, while Karnad complicates and sympathizes with her father, former prime minister Jawaharlal Nehru. Right up until the end when Aziz confronts him, Karnad's Tughlaq is still trying to justify his actions to himself and his advisors, holding vainly onto his idealism and asking "what gives me the right to call myself a King?" (Karnad 1994, 181). Aziz never has a question about this: "I am bored stiff with all this running and hiding. You rob a man, you run, and hide. It's all so pointless. One should be able to rob a man and then stay there to punish him for getting robbed. That's called 'class'—that's being a real king!" (Karnad 1994, 198).

When Aziz confronts Tughlaq with his actions, Tughlaq's first reaction is to yell at him: "Hold your tongue, fool! You dare pass judgment on me? You think your tongue is so light and swift that you can trap me by your stupid clowning?" (Karnad 1994, 217). But in the end, he admits that punishing the man he has publicly welcomed as a saint would not be a good idea and instead offers him a post as an officer in his army. He explains to his advisor Barani that "[i]f justice was as simple as you think or logic as beautiful as I had hoped, life would have been so much clearer. I have been chasing these words now for five years and now I don't know if I am pursuing a mirage or fleeing a shadow. Anyway what do all these subtle distinctions matter in the blinding madness of the day?" (Karnad 1994, 219). His uncertainty and complexity stand in clear contrast to the certainty and flatness of the Tughlaq in Cho Ramasamy's most famous play.

Political and Historical Context

Cho's political satire came at a time when the sociopolical situation in India was quite complex. After Independence (1947) and the celebration of Indian culture in the 1950s, the Congress Party, flush with the victory against the British, led the country in what amounted to a one-party system for a while with Jawaharlal Nehru serving as prime minister until his death in 1964. The end of his term was fraught with incidents that called into question India's moral superiority over the West as well as its policy of non-alignment. The early 1960s saw India at war with both Pakistan and China, and the Indian army invaded Portuguese Goa. Following Nehru's death, the Congress Party went through a succession crisis. Lal Bahadur Shastri, who became the next prime minister, died shortly thereafter, and Nehru's daughter, Indira Gandhi, took over the party and the country in 1966. Indira Gandhi's election, however, revealed deep divisions within the party. As she solidified her power, she pushed aggressive populist policies and further centralization of an Indian government that now placed a high value on personal loyalty to the prime minister and her unpopular initiatives. Conflict led to a split in the Congress Party in 1969, while the country as a whole was trying to resolve issues such as reservations for disadvantaged communities and disputes over state borders. The turmoil invited commentary on the government's policies and the political situation, a charge taken up by dramatists all over India.

The tenor of political drama changed during this period. The political personalities of the individual states that had been developing during Nehru's rule were clearly visible in the 1960s. These personalities influenced the types of dramas that were performed in different regions. As Communism gained support in West Bengal, for example, the traditional jatra theatrical form characterized by mythological and historical themes transformed into a social genre in the early 1960s. In the late 1960s and early 1970s jatra plays with titles such as *Marx, Lenin, Hitler*, and *Vietnam* were produced (see Sengupta 1984).

The Dravidian movement in Tamilnadu began much earlier, as discussed in chapter 2, but it was in the 1960s that it truly gained momentum and its candidates started winning elections. At the height of the Dravidian movement's rise to power, Cho Ramasamy proved that the tastes of the insular sabha audiences were broader than they had initially appeared. His work struck a chord with the population of a very politically literate state. The voting rate is remarkably high in Tamilnadu (around 73% in recent elections) and people pay attention to politics and the issues, in part because of the close ties in the state between politics and the media. Cho was overt about the political messages in his plays and had the political connections and legal knowledge to continue performances.

The discussion about the national language issue in scene seven is an excellent case in which Cho's ridiculous scenario is obviously close to the true political situation, and the solution he poses can be read as farcical, but it also forces the audience to think about the absurdity of a solution that addresses all concerns. The premise is that Tughlaq is learning the history of the past six hundred years, then running the country. He asks some of his many deputy prime ministers[15] to explain their positions on the issue, and while his responses and ultimate solution are comical, the arguments are pretty much exactly what the country was hearing from politicians in 1968. Govind, the Congress parody, says there is no issue: Hindi is the obvious choice. The political spin on this is that the majority of the country (and therefore the voters, especially in his region) speak Hindi, and they need to be appeased. The Communist says English is out of the question because it's foreign and "[w]e need to speak only in our mother tongue" (trans. Rudisill 2001, 40 from Ramasamy 1995a). This raises the obvious objection that Indians have many "mother tongues," so why should some get priority over others? Cho has Tughlaq voice a ridiculous solution to the problem that answers this objection: have a different national language each month, which doesn't give any single one priority over the others. The question of priority leads to the Dravidian representative saying that if we're going to give one mother tongue priority, let's make it Tamil, since that happens to be *his* mother tongue. Sastri, of course, tries to unite the country under Sanskrit, which has the obvious disadvantage of not really being a spoken language. Govind raises another objection to English, which is the fact that South Indians have an advantage in that language over those whose mother tongue is Hindi. Tyagarajan points out that if Hindi were the national language then Hindi speakers would have an advantage over South Indians. After weighing all of these concerns, which have no perfect compromise, and therefore haven't been satisfactorily solved in the real world, where English and Hindi are both considered "national languages," Tughlaq decides to make Persian the new national language. His rationale is that "Hindi speakers need to learn some new language. At the same time, it cannot be a language that South Indians know. We need to adopt some language like that as the national language. Therefore, let us take Persian as the national language. That solves the language problem" (trans. Rudisill 2001, 41 from Ramasamy 1995a). The satire addresses all concerns but does not take the issue or its real-world consequences seriously. It does not offer a feasible solution to a problem that was very contentious in the late 1960s when South Indians were immolating themselves to keep compulsory Hindi classes out of their schools (see Sumathi Ramaswamy 1997).

The language question, as Marguerite Ross Barnett rightly pointed out, could not have been solved at the state level, and the DMK had never made labor a priority, but "[s]ocial reform was both important to the party and a workable issue" (Barnett 1976, 263). Barnett lists untouchability and Adi-Dravida welfare; religious reform, anti-Hinduism, "anti-superstition"; and secularism as the top priorities of the new DMK government. Although Cho tackles all of these issues in one drama or another, his top priority was exposing corruption, especially within the DMK government itself.

R. Neelakanthan, an actor who was with Viveka Fine Arts from the beginning (see figure 7.6 for a photograph of him in costume), told me a story about a 1970 play of Cho's called *Eṉṟu Taṉiyum Inta Cutantira Tākam?*, which is a line from the nationalist poet Bharatiyar's poem that he translated as "[w]hen will we be released from thirst for independence?" The play was a success partly because it was highly critical of the ruling DMK government, a regional party of little interest to Indians in other states. The Congress Party of Tamilnadu and other opposition parties would arrange for the play to be performed at public meetings, to which Neelu said that goondas and rowdies would come from the DMK with eggs, cycle chains, and the like to frighten the artists. Madras City was

Figure 7.6. Photograph of R. Neelakanthan in costume during a performance of *Entru Thaniyum Intha Suthanthira Thaagam? Source:* Courtesy of R. Neelakanthan, from the author's collection.

fairly safe but outside the city the actors needed police protection to stage the play. For the first time in Tamilnadu's history, drama tickets sold on the black market at double their face value. The play was so popular that DMK leader M. Karunanidhi tried to counter with a play ridiculing Cho called *Nāṉē Aṟivāḷi* (*I Am a Most Intelligent Person*) that featured Cho as a buffoon. Karunanidhi's play, according to Neelu, was a failure and was only staged two or three times (author interview, April 14, 2004).

Cho's *Mohammad bin Tughlaq* is set in 1968 and deals with a number of regional and national issues over the course of the play. Some of these issues (corruption, national language, food shortages, unemployment, state border issues, and foreign policy) are directly confronted in the context of Tughlaq's meetings with various ministers in his government. Others, such as strikes, arranged marriage, sex education, and respect within the family, are indirectly addressed through the actions and interactions of Professor Rangachari and his family.

Cho's play *Tughlaq* parodies Dravidian politicians but moves beyond that narrow scope to poke fun at politicians from all parties as well as students, women, heads of household, Brahmins and democracies in general. It is a play that would work on a more national stage, because it functions as an exhortation to the people, the voters, to care about who is running their country and making decisions that affect their lives. *Tughlaq* shows the impact of policies on ordinary people and reminds viewers and readers that these things *do* matter. The most cutting criticism that the play makes is that people don't think. They don't force politicians to give them options. And when there are no options, and it really doesn't make a practical difference who is running the government, then the people are right to be apathetic. In response to one of the politicians in the play wondering how the people will react to some crazy policies the Tughlaq government is pushing, Tughlaq's confidante and advisor Ibn Battuta says: "They will think, 'If this government goes, what will the next government do for us?' Do you think that the people support us because they think that we are doing something for the country's well-being? 'No matter what government comes we will have the same fate.' Having thought this, these people won't say anything, just 'Let them be in the position. . . .' Only if the people *think* will a good government be formed. Until people realize that, there is no reason for people like us to worry" (trans. Rudisill 2001, 52 from Ramasamy 1995a). This defeatist attitude can sabotage a country and invite corruption, and it is clear that Cho wants his fellow citizens to take their part in India's democracy seriously and not underestimate their importance.

The Two Tughlaqs

Both Tughlaq plays addressed the political situation in the India of the mid-to-late 1960s, and both have also been prescient to some extent and remained relevant fifty years later. The main part of the historical Mohammad bin Tughlaq's story that Cho adopted as the basis for his character is the fact that he changed his capital from Delhi to Devagiri/Daulatabad and then back to Delhi. The character of Mohammad bin Tughlaq is someone who can change his mind at a moment's notice and not feel the need to consult anyone, let alone explain or justify himself, which is Cho's cynical vision of most politicians. The Ibn Battuta of the play has no problem with Tughlaq's changing the capital; his problem is with the forced move of the population to the new capital. Cho's Tughlaq has no regrets about these orders and atrocities (*akkiramaṅkaḷ*), as the traitor Asansha calls them, and is very flippant about the loss of life en route. He is concerned only with his own image and justifies the tragedy to scholar Ibn Battuta by citing "population control" as the "gain for the nation" in all of the shifting:

> BATT: You can move the capital if you want. But why did you tell the people of Delhi to go to Devagiri?
>
> TUGH: Shouldn't there be people in Devagiri?
>
> BATT: Then why did you tell all the Delhi people who were going to Devagiri to go back to Delhi again?
>
> TUGH: There wasn't enough food for them to reach Devagiri, and they had started to die. So I said that if they wanted to they could return to Delhi.
>
> BATT: Was there enough food for them to return to Delhi?
>
> TUGH: No. But then they died while returning.
>
> BATT: But then why did you tell them to return? They were going to die either way. You could have told them to go to Devagiri!
>
> TUGH: Therein you will see the brilliance of Mohammad bin Tughlaq! If they had died on the way to Devagiri, people would say that they died following the *Sultan's* wishes. But if they died on the way to Delhi, I had told them to go if they **wanted** to. So I can say that they died **then**, doing as they wished.
>
> BATT: In trying to change the capital, the people died. What is the gain for the nation in that?
>
> TUGH: The population reduced. (trans. Rudisill 2001, 8–9 from Ramasamy 1995a)

The flippancy and unconcern of Cho's Tughlaq is diametrically opposed to Karnad's Tughlaq and his reasoning for the change of capital. He says that he is changing the capital in order to "light up our path towards greater justice, equality, progress and peace—not just peace but a more purposeful life" (Karnad 1994, 149). He explains the decision in detail to his subjects, and explicitly tells them that they have the option to stay in Delhi, though one of the men in the audience immediately refers to the capital shift as "Tyranny! Sheer tyranny!" Tughlaq's response addresses the issue of communal relations, something that Cho's Tamilnadu-based Tughlaq (where the population is only about 6% Muslim and 88% Hindu) never worries about:

> I beg you to realize that this is no mad whim of a tyrant. My ministers and I took this decision after careful thought and discussion. My empire is large now and embraces the South and I need a capital which is at its heart. Delhi is too near the border and as you well know its peace is never free from the fear of invaders. But for me the most important factor is that Daulatabad is a city of the Hindus and as the capital it will symbolize the bond between Muslims and Hindus which I wish to develop and strengthen in my kingdom. I invite you all to accompany me to Daulatabad. This is only an invitation and not an order. Only those who have faith in me may come with me. With their help I shall build an empire which will be the envy of the world. (Karnad 1994, 149)

Never does Cho's Tughlaq display the sort of reasoning, character development, and internal struggle that forms the basis of Karnad's play. Karnad's Tughlaq is, in many ways, an idealist. He says to his advisors at one point, "[w]hat hopes I had built up when I came to the throne! I had wanted every act in my kingdom to become a prayer, every prayer to become a further step in knowledge, every step to lead us nearer to God" (Karnad 1994, 186). Over the course of the play we watch his descent into madness.

Cho's play, far from Karnad's serious, tragic story, has a ridiculous premise and jokes throughout to keep the audience laughing. Transplanted into the twentieth century, Tughlaq decides to take his dictator-like ruling strategy and see how it will work in a democracy. The opening scene, in the durbar of the historical Tughlaq, functions as an exposé of his character and policy. The stories first mentioned in this scene (movement of the capital, leather currency, summary execution of political opponents, and so on) are the ones that are later exploited by Tughlaq in his bid for power in the India of 1968. Tughlaq learns through his experiment that people will vote for a dictator using the democratic process.

It is not until the very last scene of the play that Cho brings the readers back into the realm of reality by revealing that Tughlaq and Ibn Battuta were actually just regular guys who faked their own deaths in order to impersonate the historical figures and through them teach the country a lesson. The lesson, as "Battuta" put it, "was to show these citizens just how easily they could be deceived" (trans. Rudisill 2001, 56–57 from Ramasamy 1995a), but it never gets across. We, the spectators, have seen how easily everyone was deceived, but the level of deception is so deep that the characters never see it themselves and never learn the lesson. These lessons are pitched at a national level, not a regional one, but the play is still inaccessible to a non-Tamil audience.

The themes of deception and impersonation are central to Karnad's play as well as Cho's. Karnad's clown character, Aziz, raises his status throughout the play, beginning life as a Muslim dhobi, then becoming a Brahmin, then a Muslim saint, and finally an officer of the army. Cho's Mohammad bin Tughlaq is actually an impersonation by a poor orphan who rises quickly to become the prime minister of India. Neither has any desire to give up his new status and the power that goes along with it. Aziz doesn't deny his low status when he talks to the sultan, but he certainly doesn't want to go back to it. Cho's Tughlaq won't even acknowledge his previous identity to his friend and fellow impersonator, continuing to call him Ibn Battuta to the end of the play:

> BATT: Battuta . . . what is this? . . . Battuta . . . Call me Raghavan. After acting and acting as Tughlaq have you become Tughlaq?
>
> TUGH: Yes. As far as I am concerned, you are Battuta himself. And I am Tughlaq.
>
> BATT: What are you saying?
>
> TUGH: After much thought we have done all this. But now I am the Prime Minister. If I say I'm not Tughlaq, then I won't be Prime Minister, either.
>
> BATT: So . . .
>
> TUGH: I have decided to continue to live as Tughlaq.

BATT: Mahadevan . . .

TUGH: Mohammad bin Tughlaq.

BATT: Hey! What is this injustice? When we started all this we made a vow at the Kali temple. Don't consider betraying the goddess . . . Mahadevan.

TUGH: If you call me Mahadevan one more time, you will invoke Mohammad bin Tughlaq's wrath.

BATT: Hey! Mahadevan!

TUGH: *I am not Mahadevan! Call me Mohammad bin Tughlaq. I am Mohammad bin Tughlaq, the Honorable Prime Minister of the sovereign Democratic Republic of India. Elected by the people, for the people, and working for the people.* (trans. Rudisill 2001, 57 from Ramasamy 1995a)

The politicians in Cho's play know that it is necessary for Tughlaq to be Tughlaq in order for their own power to remain intact. That is enough for them to kill any notions to the contrary, and Battuta, after revealing the original scheme to the people, is dismissed as crazy, his mind having cracked in the heat of Delhi. He is shouted down and the play ends with the rousing cry "Long Live Tughlaq! Long Live Tughlaq!"

Cho Ramasamy, though neither a revolutionary nor self-described realist, sees the humor of the current political situation, allowing viewers/readers to both laugh and realize how scarily close to reality these scenes are. He critiques society and politicians ruthlessly, but *Mohammad bin Tughlaq* still holds out some hope for democracy. The fifth scene of the play parodies all major parties in the context of a public meeting called to convince people to vote for the "all party alignment" candidate against Tughlaq. None of the candidates' parties are given by name, but they are transparent from the candidates' names and the speeches that they make. Govind (from the Congress) invokes Independence and says that they should win because they went to jail and have been known to the people for a long time. Sastri is obviously a Hindu nationalist entreating the people to study the *Bhagavad Gītā* and follow their dharma, throwing in a line about how he doesn't know much Tamil. Velayuttam is the Communist, making the argument that Tughlaq is an imperialist and will therefore be against the workers. Mr. Tyagarajan is the Dravidian politician, speaking eloquently and at length about how this land is the land of Kannaki, heroine of the Tamil epic *Cilappaṭikāram*. These politicians, we can surmise, would make the same speeches no matter what the occasion. At the end of each performance Cho makes a statement about the way politics have remained so corrupt and farcical that his plays are still relevant after all this time. He thanks politicians for that.

Both Tughlaq plays address the political situation in India during the second half of the 1960s. Karnad has written a historical play that alluded to the contemporary national political situation, an interpretation that was voiced by author U. R. Anantha Murthy, who in his introduction to the play wrote that "[a]nother reason for *Tughlaq's* appeal to Indian audiences is that it is a play of the sixties, and reflects as no other play perhaps does the political mood of disillusionment which followed the Nehru era of idealism in the country" (Karnad 1994, 143). Cho's play was also designed to reflect the issues and political mood of the 1960s, but in Tamilnadu in particular. The snapshots of politics Cho takes in scene five are funny, and would be to all Indians, but Tyagarajan is specific to Tamilnadu. This type of character and the insider joke about his flowery language may be partly why Cho the dramatist is still only a regional figure.

Crossover Audiences

Cho's play transcends the sabha theater that he is part of and shares characteristics with the plays of the modern Indian dramatic canon, as exemplified by Karnad's play. The intellectual Tamil Brahmin community appreciates both, though no one has tried to take Cho's play to a national audience. The plays and performances that are indisputably part of the modern Indian canon, however, reveal a conception of Indian "modern" or "post-colonial" theater that is not fully compatible with the sabha genre. Some of the gaps have to do with performance versus literary genres, comedy (especially language-specific jokes and regional humor) versus serious plays, translation, stage production quality, and performance rights.

Sabha theater differs from the plays in the national canon in that it is primarily a performance genre, not a literary one.[16] Dharwadker writes that "post-independence urban theatre . . . participates equally in the cultures of (print) textuality and performance" (2005, 4). Very few sabha plays are published. As explained earlier, sabha playwrights typically sell the rights to their plays, which are written for a specific troupe or actor, generally not even keeping a copy of the script for themselves. Cho's plays share more characteristics with the plays of the Indian modern canonical dramas as articulated by Dharwadkher (2005) than most sabha plays, as he is one of the few Tamil sabha playwrights who actually publishes his work. Cho's plays are published as literature and can be read and analyzed whether or not they are performed, though their primary existence has been on stage.[17] Part of the reason Cho is taken so seriously is that even though he writes in spoken language, he is, unlike most Tamil playwrights, a *writer*—his plays are published as literature and can be read and analyzed whether or not they are performed. They are published, however, in Tamil and by the local Alliance Press rather than being translated into English and published in anthologies of modern Indian drama or as individual plays through such prestigious publishing houses as Seagull and Oxford University Press. There is also a difference in performance practice as the plays of these modern Indian playwrights that are performed in Chennai are usually produced at different theater spaces than those that the sabhas use. These plays, like English-language plays, tend to utilize the Museum Theater, the Music Academy Theater, and the Alliance Française instead of the Narada Gana Sabha, Rani Seethai Hall, and Vani Mahal that the sabha plays like Cho's favor.

The distinction that Dharwadker makes between "performance-based" and "text-based" theater becomes difficult to maintain in the context of sabha theater. It makes sense that improvisational folk theater genres with their bright costumes and participatory music are performance-based, while the plays of Girish Karnad, for example, which are published in several languages and offer all sorts of opportunities for literary analysis, are text-based. There is very little, however, that is "performative" about sabha theater,[18] yet practitioners and audiences alike find that its value is almost purely in performance. This does not even need to be a live performance. The plays are primarily comedies, and the jokes also work on TV, film, and audiocassette. The audiocassette phenomenon demonstrates exactly how little is added to the play by the blocking, sets, costumes, or gestures. The general consensus is that it isn't necessary to actually *see* the performance, but that jokes are flat on the page and the play loses its dynamism in print. The actor gives inflection and timing to the script, and those are essential components of the humor.

This focus on humor and comedy plays may offer another hint as to why Tamil plays have not made it into the Indian canon, let alone gained much international recognition. None of the plays in the modern Indian canon are comedies, unlike the vast majority of sabha plays. Based on the trends in the film industry, where it is the parallel cinema movement that avoids song and dance sequences and deals with social issues that tends to receive critical attention and garners invitations to international film festivals, it is unlikely to be a coincidence that there are no riotous comedy plays in the national canon of dramatic literature in India. Additionally, the type of humor favored by sabha theater creates its own obstacles. In her study of Tamil humor, Gabriella Eichinger Ferro-Luzzi writes that "[i]f we count play with language to be a theme it outranks every other theme occurring in [Tamil] jokes" (1992, 3). These jokes do not translate very well and they are usually written with a particular actor in mind. Besides the language jokes, many Tamil sabha plays include humor based on events or circumstances specific to the city of Chennai, which may not be funny to audiences unfamiliar with the city and its history, politics, and culture.

These obstacles to translation and production by other troupes also help keep the sabha plays out of the modern Indian canon, which emphasizes an active translation and performance history for its plays: "[T]he last five decades have demonstrated that in Indian theatre the prompt recognition of new plays as contemporary classics does not depend so much on publication or performance in the original language of composition as on the rapidity with which the plays are performed and (secondarily) published in other languages. Such proliferation keeps a play in constant circulation among readers and viewers, creating the layers of textual meaning and stage interpretation that become the measure of its significance" (Dharwadker 2005, 75). Karnad's *Tughlaq* was staged in Kannada and Hindi in 1965, and soon after in Marathi and Bengali; the English translation came out in 1970. In contrast, Cho's play was first performed in 1968 but was not published in Tamil until much later.[19] My own English translation is the first of Cho's famous play and is not yet published or readily available. Very few other Tamil plays have been translated into English, Hindi, or other Indian languages,[20] and those very recently. Several of Indira Parthasarathy's plays have been translated since 2000, and Komal Swaminathan's 1980 *Taṇṇīr! Taṇṇīr!* became available to non-Tamil speakers as of 2001. None of these translated plays is a comedy, and each has roots in the leftist movement that so heavily influenced the majority of plays in the national canon.

The second part of Dharwadker's 2005 study is a series of readings of plays, which she has grouped together under a few headings in order to demonstrate the breadth of the canon. While there is some diversity, as plays may "draw on myth, history, folklore, sociopolitical experience, and the resources of earlier texts to reflect on culture, nation, gender, class, identity, experience, and modern citizenship in the postcolonial state" (Dharwadker 2005, 71), the striking similarity is that all the plays in her study are *serious* plays. Cho's *Tughlaq* is not serious, so it doesn't really fit.

Conclusion: Cho's Influence on Tamil Drama

In the late 1950s the drama scene in Madras changed with the start of theatrical patronage by the sabhas. The new system meant that it became "difficult to commercially stage plays in Madras without the support of [s]abhas, which can provide both resources and easy access to an audience through their members" (Shankar 2001a, xiii). That statement is as true today as it was when S. Shankar wrote it in 2001 and when Farley Richmond described the scene in 1990. Cho Ramasamy and Komal Swaminathan were some of the few playwrights to survive within the sabha system as well as outside of it. They both challenged what Shankar described as the "oppressive mediocrity and uniformity bred by the system" (2001a, xiv) and proved that the tastes of these middle-class Tamil Brahmin audiences were broader than they at first appeared. Like Swaminathan, Cho seems to be a crossover artist, with his brand of comedy earning good gate collection for sabhas all over the city and also earning the respect of a nationally recognized modern theater movement through critics like A. N. Perumal, Saktiperumal, and N. S. Jagannathan.

Tamil theater in general is still trying to overcome the low reputation that has stayed with it due to the public nature of performance and the low social status of the professional artists typically involved in it. The association of drama with popular social and political movements and political leaders such as former chief ministers M. Karunanidhi and C. N. Annadurai has helped its reputation. These high-profile playwrights have bestowed some legitimacy and efficacy on the dramatic form, which still plays a role as a vehicle for political opinion in the state through writers like Cho, but also through street dramas. People like Komal Swaminathan and Cho Ramasamy are helping Tamil drama to enter the world of modern Indian drama that has been primarily the provenance of Hindi, Marathi,[21] Bengali, and Kannada writers. Their plays are written in spoken, not literary Tamil and often in a marked Brahmin dialect, but they are recognized as addressing relevant issues in a popular urban context.

The idea of the gullibility of the people referred to in *Tughlaq* and the fear that they will imitate anything they see in the media is a very live issue in the Tamil Brahmin community. This is why it is so important to fans to keep repeating that the dramas are clean and healthy, unlike TV or cinema, and gullibility is something that Cho pokes a great deal of fun at. The premise of this play is that a college history professor, who should be well-educated enough to know that no magic herbs would keep Mohammad bin Tughlaq and Ibn Battuta alive in a box for six hundred years, believed just that. Professor Rangachari after his initial surprise that the two men speak fluent Tamil, raises no more questions as to the authenticity of their identity. He merely says that the miraculous herbs should be studied, prompting "Tughlaq" to throw them in the river, making this impossible. And with a historian, a Tughlaq expert, in fact, to vouch for his identity, the Mohammad bin Tughlaq of 1968 has all the credibility he needs to run for public office. The people in Cho's play simply shrug. Sometimes they riot, but they are appeased by empty promises, and the college students enjoy the time off to go to the cinema. The politicians simply raise their hands when so instructed, causing Tughlaq to comment: "Battuta! Do you see the state of the Parliament? People who are experts in raising their hands. It's enough if they say to. These people will raise their hands (shows his hand). They have taken the votes of thousands of people to come to Parliament and stand with their hands up. Traffic constables!" (trans. Rudisill 2001, 42 from Ramasamy 1995a) Compared to this conspicuous lack of suspicion in Cho's play, Karnad's Tughlaq faces suspicion on every side. Neither Hindus nor Muslims trust him, and even his advisors, friends, and relatives have their doubts and misgivings about his motives, policies, and everything else.

Cho's plays may be funny, but they are very serious in terms of their messages. Each joke has a keen observation behind it that readers/viewers can recognize, enjoy, and perhaps see themselves in. Not only is he one of the most popular dramatists the Tamil language has ever seen, he is one who is looked up to and emulated by many writers and performers. The national canon is continually adjusting to accommodate new work. And while Cho's plays are not new (the most recent being *Nērmai Uṟaṅkam Nēram* [*When Honesty Sleeps*] from 1982), they are still relevant. His recent death and the news stories that followed, detailing his close association with many influential politicians at both the state and national levels, have brought renewed interest in his work. If any sabha playwright can break into the national scene, it will be Cho.

Epilogue

Following Trends

The Future of Sabha Theater

Though it has lost the support it had in earlier decades, sabha theater is still evolving. Some of the old formulas still draw audiences, but many artists have realized that they need to do something different in order to keep seats in theaters filled and are actively working toward that goal. This involves strategies for both the retention of current audiences and the recruitment of new ones. Trends within this theatrical tradition can also indicate societal changes, as I address throughout, but especially in this epilogue.

Tamil Brahmins are still the primary target audience for sabha plays, as evidenced by Bombay Chanakya's 2020 advertisement for his play *Lakshmi and Kalyanam vs Kalyanam vs Kalyanam* (*Laksmi and Marriage vs Marriage vs Marriage*) as "a rollicking TAMBRAM [Tamil Brahmin] comedy on mistaken identity" (https://www.facebook.com/bombay.chanakya). However, there are two new demographics that sabha drama troupes are trying to bring into the theaters: members of the younger generations and residents of Chennai's outlying neighborhoods.

The younger generation of middle-class Chennai-ites generally prefers to attend films or go to the large air-conditioned malls that are cropping up all over the city or even go bowling or perhaps to an English-language play or a standup comedy show by comedians from their generation who share their experience. New strategies and incentives are required to bring them to the sabhas. They expect air-conditioning, standard in the malls and major cinema halls, so nicer theaters mean more audience members (but also more expense for both sabhas and ticket-buyers). Additionally, they are not interested in some of the tired old themes of the sabha dramas. The tale of the tradition-bound patriarch is not compelling for this generation. The slow tempos and poor production values of the plays, especially in comparison to the English-language productions, films, and standup comedy, are also deterrents to attendance.

Artists also take seriously the need to take their plays to more remote areas of the city in order to keep performing (see figure E.1 for a 2019 advertisement for a new sabha in southwest Chennai). Although many of the key artists and troupe leaders live in Mylapore or T. Nagar, many of their younger troupe members do not and performing closer to home would be more convenient for them. The same is true for audience members. Many people from the target Tamil Brahmin community have moved to the outlying areas in recent years. In Pallavaram, Tambaram, and Perambur, for example, they can own a house, whereas in the desirable, central, and therefore expensive Mylapore and T. Nagar neighborhoods they could only afford to rent. It is difficult to travel from the outlying areas of the city through traffic and pollution to attend a play, as well as expensive, so it is not a frequent undertaking. However, if there were plays presented in those neighborhoods, local residents might be inclined to attend. In 2008, I was present at an extremely well attended drama

Figure E.1. Rasamayee Sandhya Sabha poster, 2019. *Source*: Author's collection.

festival in the outlying area of Nanganallur, where they honored veteran theater artist K. S. Nagarajan. This neighborhood houses a number of new sabhas, and at least five hosted plays there in 2019, so it is clearly convenient for a number of Brahmins.

To retain current audiences, artists and sabhas are trying a number of strategies that may seem contradictory, but work toward the same ends. Many are reviving old favorites rather than developing new material. Audiences have shown their willingness to see plays multiple times and many express a preference for the tried and true over the gamble of a new production. Others are changing subject matter, aesthetics, and/or production values to provide an incentive both for new audiences to attend and for current or former audiences who have been bored by the stagnant state of sabha dramas to return to the theater. This may be especially important for plays staged in halls (for example, the R. R. Sabha and Mylapore Fine Arts Club) lacking the amenities of air-conditioning, good bathroom facilities, and quality refreshments. Most new theater troupes cannot afford to perform in the more expensive halls, so innovation is a particular concern for them.

Some artists claim that they have already seen the positive effects of their innovations. S. L. Naanu, a writer and actor who frequently works with Kathadi Ramamurthy, contrasted the dynamism of sabha drama with the monotony of television serials in his explanation of why he thinks theater audiences are improving. He told me in a July 12, 2003, interview that television had spoiled the drama audience for a while, but now television shows are monotonous. His impression is that television has saturated the market, so theater attendance and sabha membership have actually been improving in recent years. These new endeavors to challenge audiences and regain respect for the genre may be part of the renewed interest in theater that Naanu and others have perceived.

Innovation in the dramas is taking many forms and affecting all aspects of the production. There has been, in the years since I finished my fieldwork, a trend of reviving mythological and historical dramas. This was unsurprising given the number of theatergoers who expressed a longing for these earlier, and in their minds superior, plays. A related trend is the increase in the number of plays that are identified as having social or religious messages, which has continued to intensify with the continued rise of Hindu nationalism under Prime Minister Narendra Modi. I will briefly discuss a few plays that exemplify this trend, most of which attempt to combine the comedy that sabha theater is known for with a depth of social consciousness intended to engage and challenge audience members. More recent plays have included a number of biopics on the lives of saints that forego comedy to provide a more devotional viewing experience.

For years religion has been one of the major causes of division, war, and strife in our world. The United Amateur Artists drama troupe, which is one of the most active in Chennai, has made a tremendous effort with their 2004 play *Ubhadesam Seivathu UAA* (*Sermon Done by UAA*) to laugh about religious pretensions (see figures E.2 and E.3 for a double-sided advertisement for this play). The play, written by Venkat, demonstrates how the strict following of doctrines can interfere with common sense and basic human decency to everyone's detriment. In addition to the unusual theme, the play adopts a new type of format for the sabha genre and consists of several short skits followed by an hour-long show. This structure allows for the critique of a number of different religions as each small skit depicts a story or tale from a different religious or philosophical tradition in a humorous way. The longer piece demonstrates some of the difficulties and potential complications of the "vow of silence" and involves a lot of mime and physical humor that is also atypical of this predominantly verbal genre. The UAA has managed throughout its seventy-year history to continually reinvent itself and stay relevant to sabha audiences with its timely themes, slick productions, and innovative formats.

Most sabha dramas focus on the family, and references to religion are made in that context. Characters do pujas at home or go to the temple. Marriages take place and priests and holy men are consulted on a variety of topics. Prior to these family or social dramas, the Tamil stage was dominated by mythological and historical dramas. These dramas often told the stories of the gods and the lives of the saints and kings. What makes *Ubhadesam Seivathu UAA* so unique is not only the format, but the combination of these two types of play. The centralization of religion and didacticism recall the early mythologicals, and most audience members are familiar with at least one of the stories. These tales are told, however, not from the point of view of the gods, but from that of humans struggling to live their lives according to one of these philosophies. This human element allows for the portrayal of errors and misinterpretations that can be extremely comic. The play is a successful mix of the two styles of theater and keeps the audience laughing and thinking at the same time. Three of the five skits explicitly address Hinduism; one involves a discussion between religious leaders of Hinduism, Christianity, and Islam; and the final one is based on Zen Buddhist teachings. The skits are drawn together

Figure E.2. Advertisement for United Amateur Artists' play *Ubhadesam Seivathu UAA*, 2004 (side 1). *Source*: Author's collection.

★ING

Y.Gee.Mahendra, Typist Gopu, T.M.Subramanian, R.Purushothaman, A.Girish, K.Hussain, T.Ramanujam, R.Srinivasan, J.Subramani, P.Mahadevan, M.Nagalakshmi, B.Parameshwari(Revathi)

Suthradhari - ARS

BEHIND THE STAGE

Make-up	-	S.K. RAJENDRAN
Lights & Music	-	P.M. IBRAHIM
Lights Designed by	-	V. ARUN KUMAR
Scenes	-	PADMA STAGE KANNAN
PRO	-	S. JAGADEESAN
Publicity Design	-	Y.G. HARSHAVARDHANA & MADHUVANTHI ARUN
Stage Management	-	GOMEZ, KARTHIKEYAN, V. KANNAN
Co-ordination	-	Dr. (Mrs.) YGP, SUDHA MAHENDRA & YGR

The Senthur Offset ✆ : 26240203, 26270119

Figure E.3. Advertisement for United Amateur Artists' play *Ubhadesam Seivathu UAA*, 2004 (side 2). *Source*: Author's collection.

by veteran actor A. R. Srinivasan who acts as the narrator, or *sutradhar*, of the play. As such, he is merely an offstage voice, but one that prepares the audience for what is to come as well as hinting at the humor. During his opening speeches for each scene, well-lit posters of the various religious leaders are displayed on the corner of the stage the way they would be in a home or temple for worship purposes. This production detail had the effect of sobering the humor by reminding audience members of the philosophies and figures that are taken so seriously within the society.

The play opens with a skit called "Guru Sishyan" ("Teacher Student") about a religious teacher and one of his students. We are told by the narrator that this is one of many small stories (*ci<u>nn</u>a ci<u>nn</u>a pala kataikaḷ*) by means of which Sathya Sai Baba performs the miracle of helping his devotees easily reach the secrets of the Vedas. There are many lessons to be learned from this brief segment, but the primary one is that although it is true that the student should follow the words of his teacher, he must also use his common sense and not take everything the guru says literally.

The audience and press were very excited about this opening skit because of the set design. The bullock cart with moving clouds really looked like it was progressing across the stage, and therefore evoked nostalgia in the viewers for the mythological and historical dramas put on by R. S. Manohar and other professional troupes. Manohar was famous for his elaborate and "trick" sets, and actually stopped performing for many years after a back injury sustained from falling during a flying scene in one of his plays.

The plot is simple. Guru and sishya are traveling together on the bullock cart and the guru is sleeping with his head in the sishya's lap. He wakes up and searches for his *kamaṇṭalam*, a pot containing holy water that he will use for ritual purposes.[1] When he can't find it, he asks the sishya if he knows where it is. It transpires that the *kamaṇṭalam* has fallen in a ditch along the road a good while back but the sishya didn't want to stop the cart for fear of waking the guru over such a trivial thing. He explains to the guru: "You said not to wake you even if thunder fell . . . If I woke you when a *kamaṇṭalam* fell . . ." (Venkat 2004, 2). The guru tells him that in the future if anything falls off the cart he is to stop the cart and pick it up. So when the bullock defecates, the sishya stops the cart and collects the manure, keeping it right where it wakes the guru with its terrible stench. The cart driver, laughing at all of these proceedings, tells the guru that he needs to tell the sishya in no uncertain terms exactly what he should pick up and what he should not. The guru sees the wisdom in this and makes a list for the sishya of all the things on the cart that need to be collected in case of a fall.

At this point, the audience is laughing, anticipating the next segment of the story. The lights fade out and a loud noise is heard on the darkened stage. When the lights come up the guru has disappeared. The driver turns to the sishya and asks him about both the noise and the missing guru, to which the sishya replies, "[t]here is a relationship between the sound you heard and the fact that you don't see the guru. The guru fell off ten miles back" (Venkat 2004, 4). When the driver asks why the sishya didn't inform him, the man tells him, "[l]ook at this list. If anything from this list fell the guru said to pick it up. The guru's name is not on this list." The skit ends with the driver smacking himself on the forehead in disbelief.

The portrayal of the sishya is as an idiot, but there is an undercurrent of insubordination that runs behind his slavish obedience to the guru. There are implications of the guru's worldliness and impropriety in the text. After the guru writes the list, the cart driver turns to him with a dilemma: which of the two girls who have been offered to him should he marry? One is poor but beautiful and the other is ugly but rich. The guru tells him that "[t]oday money will come and tomorrow it will go—only beauty is permanent in this world. Therefore, marry the poor but beautiful girl" (Venkat 2004, 4). As soon as the driver respectfully agrees to follow the guru's advice, the guru tells him to give him the address of the ugly rich girl. The guru is forever calling his student an "idiot" (*a<u>r</u>ivili, maṭaiya<u>n</u>*) and asks rhetorically how he ever got such an idiot for a student. The student responds as if the guru really wanted an answer, explaining that the guru had compelled him to be his sishya since he was unable to find anyone else. The implication, of course, is that he is not much of a guru. He needed a student in order to be able to define himself as a "teacher" (guru) and there is the subtle accusation of coercion and self-aggrandizement in the sishya's comment. In contrast, there is nothing but respect in the sishya's voice. The subversion of the guru's instructions is a source of great humor, much appreciated by audiences.

Playwright V. Sreevatson's work has also broached the topic of religion and is quite innovative in the world of sabha theater. The troupe was in fact founded in order to counter what the members saw as stagnation in currently available dramas. Dummies Drama (aka Dummies Communications) started in 1998 as a new troupe and has continued to gain respect in critical as well as audience circles. Their first play, *Women's Rea*, followed the typical sabha style, but the plot, where a young man tells a prospective landlord, who doesn't like to rent to bachelors, that he is married and his wife has gone home to her parents for the delivery of their baby, is something new. When a woman shows up at his doorstep claiming to be his wife, the confusion really begins. For his second play *Kūttāṭi*, Sreevatson scoured Bharata Natyam schools all over the city looking for seven children to play the roles of students at a dance studio. They had to learn a short dance and perform on stage, a combination of the classical arts with the sabha theater that was, surprisingly, new given the proximity of classical dance and sabha theater and their shared patronage and performer populations.[2]

Vinodaya Chittam (*Contented Mind*), the play that Dummies Communications inaugurated in 2004, like UAA's, brought religion to the stage. This play was designed to teach lessons about detachment. The main character Parasuraman dies, then convinces Death to send him back to life. Death, in the guise of a friend's son, moves into Parasuraman's house and advises him on his life choices. At first, everything goes wrong for the man. He is passed up for a promotion, his wife gets sick, he spends all his money on medical bills, his daughter runs off with a young man, and his son loses his job in the US and returns home with a wife who dresses in revealing western clothes. In the second half of the play, everything goes right for him. He gets a better job than the one he'd been passed over for, his son gets his job back and has a doctor friend in the US who is a specialist and can cure the wife, and the daughter-in-law turns out to be a good Tamil girl who wears a sari beautifully and has a degree in mechanical engineering. Death lectures Parasuraman at this point that it is time to go and that he is not indispensable. Life is like a game in which the dead no longer participate, and he has to let go. At the end of the play, Parasuraman dies.

This play, with its overt message, was full of humor and the audiences, critics, and the judges at the Nataka Vizha of Karthik Fine Arts[3] really enjoyed it. Kausalya Santhanam called it "one of the best plays seen in recent times on the sabha circuit," and held it up as an example of "how it is possible to please the mainstream audience and yet make a detour from the tried and tired path" (Santhanam, May 21, 2004). It still centers on the family and the relations between its members and is full of jokes, but this play also deliberately deals with philosophical themes. Additionally, Dummies Drama departed from sabha standards aesthetically in terms of costumes, sets, and music. While most of the costumes were standard, Death was not given the elaborate kingly costumes usually seen on characters like Yama (the god of Death) in sabha plays. Instead, he was dressed in a stark black costume and given a fast, spare style of speech, which gave his character a very modern feel. It was in fact, highly reminiscent of Koothuppattarai's performance of N. Muthusamy's *Prahlada Charitram* that was directed by Israeli Gil Anon and staged at the Alliance Française in July of 2003 as well as at the National School of Drama Festival in Delhi. This, along with several other elements, improved the play's appeal to those intellectuals who tend to prefer "modern" dramas. In *Vinodaya Chittam*, there was a great deal of trouble taken with the sets, which were more elaborately designed and drama-specific than most sabha sets. While there was some recorded music, this play also included a live keyboardist who interacted with the players. The members of Dummies Drama have set high standards for themselves, and these little touches also raise the standards for all sabha dramas, which I expect will become more aesthetically and theoretically sophisticated in the future.

The last two plays of the Mahalakshmi Ladies Drama Group (MLDG) have centered on religious topics and have diverged significantly from their previous work in three major ways. *Sri Bodendhral* (2014) and *Bhaja Govindam* (2015) both have spiritual themes instead of dealing with women's issues, involve the dubbing of dialogue, and are not ticketed. Rather than selling tickets for these plays with the religious subjects, the troupe presents them for free and solicits donations from viewers. "Gnanam said at the curtain call . . . that though city sabhas funded the first few runs of the shows, people who watch it must do two things—spread the word even using Twitter, Facebook and WhatsApp and donate their mite" (Bombay Gnanam's New Play, 2015). The actors stand near the door with boxes in which people can drop their donations. People have been very generous with their donations, and the grand scale of the plays with their expensive, custom sets, costumes, and studio recordings has been manageable. The understanding of the importance of technology in advertising is ironic because Gnanam herself does not use any of these platforms; she doesn't even text message or email regularly.

The troupe came up with the idea of *Sri Bodendhral*, partly thanks to the influence of Gnanam's husband, as a way to mark their Silver Jubilee (twenty-five-year anniversary of their founding in 1989), and then were given the directive by Sri Jayendra Sarawati to produce a play about Adi Shankara. Gnanam puts it like this: "We had planned *Sri Bodendhral* and wanted to get the blessing of the Acharyas of the Sri Kanchi Kamakoti Peetam. But trepidation that the idea might not be received well prevented us from going to Kanchipuram. After mentally making the offering we went ahead with the play. On learning about it through Mutt sources, the Acharyas sent their blessings through a devotee" (Venkataramanan 2015). After that, the troupe did go to the mutt, where Sri Jayendra Sarawati gave Bombay Gnanam a book and told her, "Let this be your next subject." She says that "the title was hidden by the kumkum and when I gently pushed it to the side I realised it was Adi Sankara. We decided to enact the subject on a grand scale, costs notwithstanding. It is a privilege to showcase the life and teachings of one of the greatest Hindu savants" (Venkataramanan 2015). The new religious plays are receiving a lot of press and attention, all of it positive, and from the reviews both in newspapers and on individuals' blogs, it seems that the auditoriums are packed with viewers. *Sri Bodendhral* has been performed well over fifty times to date. The 2015 review of *Bhaja Govindam* in the Mylapore Times suggests that the subject matter of the play is one with which the audience is already familiar, confirming that the audience mostly consists of members of the conservative Hindu Brahmin community commonly associated with sabhas.

Bombay Chanakya has also been including religious themes in a few recent plays for his troupe Kalamandir. He describes his 2017 play *Makaḷir Kāval Nilaiyam* (*Women's Police Station*) as "Highlighting the life of Female Police officers with a story added to it based on REINCARNATION" (Bombay Chanakya Facebook). His 2019 saint biopic titled *The Life of Sri Bhagawan Ramana Maharishi* is another example of this trend. During the May 2020 quarantine, Chanakya coordinated a reading of a story from the religious epic *Mahabharata* called "Shikandi—the Avenger" with sixteen actors and actresses, each participating from his or her own home, as a tribute to K. Balachander. He has been very active, posting recordings of old plays on YouTube in recent months and leveraging social media to gain viewers.

These recent religious plays are right on trend with what has been happening in the sabhas over the last few years. Often the religious plays involve some humor (such as those staged by United Amateur Artists and Dummies Drama), but the Mahalakshmi Ladies Drama Group plays don't seem to be very funny, with audience members commenting things like "The huge hall [Narada Gana Sabha] was full and had in it devotees of this saint [Nama Bodendral] who were kept in their reverential mode throughout the event" (aarvalan 2014). One viewer said of *Bhaja Govindam*: "I must say I was transported to a world of piety, prayers, mantras, swamijis, philosophy, so much so, my evening was filled with a meaning and a purpose" (Rajaram 2015). However, Gnanam has not neglected her roots and still includes a social aspect by weaving in the story of a modern-day couple with the past narrative of the saint's life story. The idea is to take "the deep philosophy of Advaita" (Natarajan 2015b) and make it easy for ordinary people to understand and thus demonstrate its relevance to those living today.

The Tamil Brahmin community in Chennai is very conservative and most take their Hindu religiosity very seriously. They have a long history of questioning social mores that comes from the community's close association with the British during the colonial period. But when Hindu religious traditions were questioned and attacked in Tamilnadu, Brahmins were attacked along with them. Religion and the rituals that go along with it are part of Tamil Brahmin identity, and much of that is left to the women to uphold (see Hancock 1999). There is a very fine line between social conscience and religious practice, and the Tamil Brahmin community in Chennai must negotiate a balance between their modernity, characterized by high levels of education, ties to the West, and social progressiveness and reform tendencies with their tradition, characterized by religion, ritual, and social conservatism within their own families. This successful negotiation is demonstrated beautifully by the women of the Mahalakshmi Ladies Drama Group along with their families, friends, and fans.

Other plays discuss religious and philosophical themes, but also to look at current events in a more considered way than, for example, S. Ve. Shekher's improvised asides. One play that fits this description is Bombay Chanakya's 2004 *Niṟam Māṟum Nijaṅkaḷ* (*Truths that Change Color*), which directly addressed the events of September 11, 2001. This play, as I discuss elsewhere (Rudisill forthcoming), explores the long-lasting psychological effects of terrorism. An Indian girl studying abroad in the US lost her secret boyfriend, and her trauma affected her family and friends, and through their shared victimhood connected all Indians, including all who watch this play, to all Americans. I argue that by reframing the event in a way that local Indian audiences could relate to in a live theater medium, Chanakya has created a new entry point into 9/11 for Tamils distanced from the horror of the event by time, distance, and the mediation of the televised narrative.

These trends of trying to combine relevant social and political issues with family-oriented humor are one sign that artists are listening to the critics and the intellectuals in their audiences and trying to offer something different. This does not mean, however, that I think the "pure comedy" plays are being phased out. For the socially conscious plays to be "different," there needs to be a standard that they are different from, and comedy plays will continue to fill that role. They are still well-received by many, and the appeal of mindless entertainment, in like-minded company, especially after a long day at the office, is very strong. With such charismatic, established performers as S. Ve. Shekher, Crazy Balaji, and Bosskey filling that need, however, it is difficult for unknowns to break in as comedians. For unknown artists, intellectual appeal and innovations are more likely to bring recognition and respect from critics and help them make inroads with audiences.

I am confident that the sabha theater will continue on in the years to come, but there are likely to be some changes in both the dramas and the organizational structure of sabha patronage. Because the genre has been losing audiences in recent years, I think we'll continue to see more revivals of old classics as well as more innovative structures and themes in addition to more sophisticated staging in an attempt to draw audiences out of the cinema halls and the English-language plays to the Tamil-language theater. I also expect to see more plays explicitly focused on Hinduism, as these are more prestigious and acceptable to the conservatives that form the core of this audience, especially in the current political climate. I also wonder about how the new standup format will affect sabha plays, which may start doing more skit style comedy like the UAA play discussed above. Troupes are likely to continue their efforts toward combining what have been two separate threads of sabha theater—the comedic and the serious—into single performances, since each is struggling on its own. There will be some shifts in troupes as the founders of several well-known theater troupes have already or soon will be retiring or dying and new troupes spring up, but I doubt there will be much change in the number of active troupes in the city over the next ten years.

I also do not expect the amount of money in theater to change a great deal, so the dependency on sabha patronage is likely to continue. I think the Nanganallur drama festival of 2008 is merely the beginning of a trend of either new sabhas appearing or established ones beginning to look for alternative spaces in a variety of neighborhoods in which to stage plays in an effort to cut down on the expenses of hall rentals, allow for smaller audiences, and attract younger people and those in the outlying neighborhoods to performances. The Priya Cultural Academy, with zero members, may be an organizational model for other sabhas to follow.

With no membership to account to, no fixed schedule (for example, a play promised every second Thursday) and therefore no fixed overhead, this sabha has the freedom to sponsor whatever they happen to have the money for. The downside, however, is that the organizers need to spend a lot of time wooing corporate sponsors, advertising in order to sell tickets, and accepting whatever dates the different halls happen to have available.

The memberless sabha model could also resemble the seasonal sabha that is so common in the classical music genre and the single weekend performance that is common in the English-language theater in Chennai. These would be difficult adjustments for the theater artists to make. They are used to performing year-round and one of the major landmarks of sabha dramas is the number of times they have been performed. There are usually celebratory functions held when a play is staged for the hundredth or five hundredth time, for example, and single weekend performances would preclude this tradition. The changes in sabha theater that are explored throughout this book are concrete examples of the way users of culture can affect the products that they consume, and I am excited to see how the emphasis of the dramas continues to shift in the future.

Appendixes

Appendix A

Prices of Hall Rental in Chennai in 2001[1]

HALL	(APPROXIMATE) NO. OF SEATS	(APPROXIMATE) RENT PER SHOW (in Indian rupees)
1. Anna Auditorium*	1604	5000
2. Bharathiya Vidya Bhawan	500	2500
3. German Hall	600	3500
4. Kalaivanar Arangam*	1040	4000
5. Kamaraj Memorial Hall	1720	10000
6. Krishna Gana Sabha*	900	1350
7. Music Academy	1693	9000[2]
8. Museum Theatre	500	3000[3]
9. Mylapore Fine Arts Club*	1000	2000
10. Narada Gana Sabha*	1040	7000
11. N. K. T. Kalamandapam	Open Air	
12. Raja Annamalai Hall*	880	3500
13. Rani Seethai Hall*	640	3500
14. Rama Rao Kala Mandap	800	7000
15. R. R. Sabha*	980	1400
16. Sankaradas Auditorium	1014	2500
17. University Centenary Auditorium	25000	
18. Vani Mahal*	1000	3000

*These halls are commonly used for sabha drama performances.

Prices of Hall Rental in Chennai in 2007[4]

HALL	(APPROXIMATE) NO. OF SEATS	(APPROXIMATE) RENT PER SHOW (in Indian rupees)
1. Anna Auditorium*	1600	7000
2. Bharathiya Vidya Bhawan	500	7500
3. Bharathiya Vidya Bhavan (Mini Hall)	98	1800
3. German Hall	650	3500
4. Kalaivanar Arangam*	1040	12500
5. Kamaraj Memorial Hall	1700	23000
6. Krishna Gana Sabha*	750	10000
7. Music Academy	1600	17500
8. Museum Theatre	550	8000
9. Mylapore Fine Arts Club*	1000	3050
10. Narada Gana Sabha*	1080	11224
12. Raja Annamalai Hall*	880	7235
13. Rani Seethai Hall*	640	5700
14. Rama Rao Kala Mandap	865	7000
15. R. K. Swamy Hall	210	3400
16. Sivagamy Pethatchi Auditorium	450	7000
17. Vani Mahal*	840	12000
18. Vani Mahal (Obul Reddy Hall)*	230	6000

*These halls are commonly used for sabha drama performances.

Appendix B

Sabhas That Regularly Sponsor Dramas

In 1992:[5]

1. Nungambakkam Cultural Academy
2. Prabhat Cultural
3. Rageswari Fine Arts
4. Sri Kapali Fine Arts
5. Friends Cultural Academy
6. Narada Gana Sabha
7. Brahma Gana Sabha
8. Om Vigneshwara Cultural Academy
9. Sri Krishna Gana Sabha
10. Kalarasana
11. Sree Vaari Fine Arts
12. Madras Social and Cultural Academy
13. Chromepet Cultural Academy
14. Ten Stars Academy
15. Shastri Bhawan Fine Arts
16. Sri Parthasarathy Swami Sabha
17. Swapnam
18. Venu Gana Sabha
19. Salangai Arts
20. VGN Cultural Academy
21. Rasika Ranjani Sabha
22. Mylapore Fine Arts Academy
23. Bharat Kalachar

24. Mylapore Arts Academy
25. Shobana Cultural
26. Sri Thyaga Brahma Gana Sabha
27. Abbas
28. Golden
29. Senthil Fine Arts
30. Priya
31. Sri Devi
32. Karthikeya
33. Popular
34. Padhmalaya
35. Evening Entertainers
36. Kartik Fine Arts
37. Favourite Cultural Academy
38. Elango Kalai Manram
39. Friends Paradise
40. Nagarathar Cultural Academy
41. AAA
42. TVK Cultural Academy
43. Alankar
44. Esther Fine Arts
45. Angel
46. Thiruvalluvar Kalai Manram
47. Balajee Fine Arts
48. Youth Paradise
49. ARFI
50. Mullai Kalai Manram
51. Balamurugan Gardens Thuraippakkam
52. Tamilnadu Eyal Isai Nataka Mandram
53. Jupiter Cultural Academy
54. Nataka Mandir
55. Sumangali
56. Aroobam
57. Sai Arts Club
58. Bhavan's Fine Arts
59. Tiam House
60. Kalaranjini
61. Raju
62. Welcome Fine Arts

63. Mugavai
64. Alandur
65. VKR Exnora Cultural Academy
66. Amara Gana Sabha
67. Kalavagini
68. Perambur Sangeetha Sabha
69. Tamilnadu Cinema Kalai Mandram
70. NKT
71. Southern Arts
72. Kolam
73. Kolam Yavanika
74. Kalalaya
75. Gowri
76. Raju Cine Dramalaya
77. Mathi Arts
78. Gokul Arts
79. Tamilannai Cultural Academy
80. United India Sports and Recreation Club
81. Kolam Aikya
82. Sri Semmanari Andavan Trust
83. Classic Creators
84. Marrumalarchi Arts Academy

In 2004:[6]

1. Kalarasana
2. Sri Parthasarathy Swami Sabha
3. Abi
4. Sri Devi Fine Arts
5. Narada Gana Sabha
6. Southern Arts
7. Shastri Bhawan Fine Arts
8. Brahma Gana Sabha
9. Rasika Fine Arts
10. Sri Krishna Gana Sabha
11. Mylapore Fine Arts Club
12. Abbas
13. Alandur Fine Arts
14. Aaha

15. Kartik Fine Arts
16. Welcome Fine Arts
17. Chromepet Cultural Academy
18. Bharat Kalachar
19. Sri Thyaga Brahma Gana Sabha
20. Prabhat
21. Abhinaya
22. TVK Cultural
23. Arasu Arts
24. Priya Cultural Academy
25. Sree Vaari Fine Arts
26. Hamsadhvani
27. Rasika Ranga
28. South Zone Cultural Center
29. Nungambakkam Cultural Academy Trust
30. Vani Mahal
31. Madhu Enterprises
32. Rasika Ranjani Sabha
33. Elango
34. Tamilnadu Cinema Kalai Mandram
35. Mayura Cine Tel
36. Naadakakkaaran
37. L. Ve. Creators
38. TNCA
39. SVS
40. Nataka Academy
41. VKV Visions
42. Sri Muthukrishna Swami Mission Trust

In 2019:[7]

1. Abbas Cultural
2. Bharat Kalachar
3. Brahma Gana Sabha
4. Roshini Fine Arts
5. Almighty Sree Vaari Fine Arts
6. Astral Creations (aka Rasamayee Sandhya)
7. Bharatiya Sanskriti
8. Chennai Art Theatre

9. Chromepet Cultural Academy
10. Dasha Arts Madurai Kannan
11. Imayam
12. The Indian Fine Arts Society
13. Kartik Fine Arts
14. Sri Parthasarathy Swami Sabha
15. Mudhra
16. Mylapore Fine Arts Club
17. Nanganallur Fine Arts
18. Narada Gana Sabha
19. Naveen Fine Arts
20. RR Sabha
21. Sridevi Fine Arts
22. Sri Thyaga Brahma Gana Sabha
23. TVK Cultural Academy
24. United Visuals
25. S.V.Ramani Music & Arts Academy
26. Vasantham

Appendix C

Honeymoon Couple

A Kathadi Ramamurthy play written by Crazy Mohan in 1977

Translation from handwritten Tamil manuscript
by Kristen Rudisill in 2004[8]

Scene 1

PLACE: Ramani's House

CHARACTERS: Rukmani, Dilip, Nandini, Ramani, Rahottaman

(Morning time. Ramani is sleeping in a chair, covered with a blanket. Rukmani comes in.)

RUK: Nandini! Get up. It's late. (Looks inside.) Dilip! Come on! (Dilip comes.) Did you bathe?

DIL: Oh, I brushed my teeth, bathed, *and* said my morning prayers!

RUK: You are ready. Your dad got up, too, brushed his teeth, and left. But Nandini is still sleeping! Nandini! Wake up!

(Nandini calls from inside.)

NAN: Hey, Mom! Why are you yelling so much? I already got up, brushed my teeth, and bathed. I'm ready for the morning.

RUK: Nandini! Are you ready? And Dilip, you're also up! Then who is sleeping here?

DIL: Yes. Nandini is ready. Mom, you are, too. I am also ready. Then who is lying here?

RUK: Yes. This is like a big Quiz Program. Take away the blanket and then you'll know! Take it!

DIL: (taking the blanket) Hey! . . . Dad!

RUK: Do you see this, Dilip? He got up from there, came here, and lay down! What's he smiling about?

DIL: If you smile in your sleep, it means God is showing you flowers.

RUK: Why, he's getting up!

(Ramani gets up.)

RAM: Rukmani! I was lying down inside in the bedroom! How did I get here?

RUK: I woke you up there. Then you came here to Nandini's bed and lay down!

RAM: Are you so smart? You woke me up at dawn and I was half asleep. I came into the living room and saw this chair and laid down here. And that's not all—I could have gone straight to the neighbor's bedroom and lay down. What would that lady have thought about me then? Forget about me. What would her husband have thought about **her**?

DIL: Dad, you were smiling in your sleep. What did God show you?

RAM: He showed me a purple flower. Hey, why were you sitting holding your nose for ten minutes this morning?

DIL: If you do that, your intelligence will grow.

RAM: Your intelligence will grow? If you look at the grades you got in math this term, you'd never know your intelligence was growing!

DIL: Dad, I've been telling you for a week that today is the last day to pay my college fees. Give me money.

RAM: Don't worry, Dilip! Inside the bureau on the bottom shelf on the left-hand side in the back is a gold chain of your mother's . . .

RUK: Ayyayyo! That chain is the only thing not pledged! Would you give it also to the pawn shop?

RAM: Why are you so hasty? I've already pledged that chain and taken 400 rupees for it. You take 200 rupees from that and give me the remaining 200 for my expenses. (Dilip leaves.) Rukmani! Do you remember one thing?

RUK: Do I remember?

RAM: What?

RUK: You still haven't brushed your teeth!

RAM: Not that. When I came to look at you for marriage you sang a song. A good song. A rare raga! What was it called? . . . Oh, yes! Bukhari!

RUK: Dear Lord! That's not Bukhari, some non-vegetarian raga. What are you babbling about? Go brush your teeth.

RAM: No, really . . .Bukhari . . .

RUK: Idiot. Not Bukhari. *Mu*khari.

RAM: Oh . . . Mukhari.

RUK: I didn't know then that if I sang the Mukhari Raga, full of sorrow and pathos, in that auspicious hour that my whole life would become Mukhari also.

RAM: Rukku, Rukku. How old are you now?

RUK: Why ask so suddenly now?

RAM: You first then I'll tell you.

RUK: What? I'm 38.

RAM: I'm telling you truthfully, Rukku. No one could say you look more than 28.

RUK: Oh, go on . . .

RAM: Rukku . . . How old is the lady across the street?

RUK: Yes . . . I also have been watching. For two days, what is this? You keep talking and talking about the lady across the street. Why?

RAM: (immediately) Do you doubt me? I'm just making a comparison . . . She is about your age, but she looks like a 60-year-old woman.

RUK: Yes . . . Now what is your sudden obsession with age?

RAM: Nothing . . . Rukku . . . You asked why I was smiling in my sleep this morning . . . I dreamt that you and I were going on a honeymoon.

RUK: You have a daughter who's old enough to be married! Don't you have any shame? Dreaming about going on a honeymoon!

RAM: Why is that so crazy? It just came to me in a dream. What could I do? I sleep for that. If you prepare and think, "I shouldn't see all these kind of dreams," you can sleep . . . What dreams will come? Very rare dreams . . . Do you know where you and I went on our honeymoon? Simla. There is a Hotel Paradise there with twenty floors. One room had been reserved for us, Rukmani and Ramani, on the 18th floor.

RUK: Why—was your dream in black and white or color?

RAM: It was in good Eastman color, crazy girl. As if we could get prints at Gemini Color Labs. I was wearing double knit pants and a terracotta colored shirt. You weren't wearing this kind of cotton sari, but a georgette chiffon sari.

RUK: What was the design on the pallu?

RAM: Who do you think is paying attention to all that? Why don't you listen to me fully? You and I were sitting on the 18th floor in an air-conditioned room, then you said that you wanted ice cream!

RUK: So you immediately pledged the gold chain I'd brought from my parent's house to buy ice cream for me. So . . .

RAM: For shame. I had bundles and bundles of notes in my pockets.

RUK: Why?

RAM: Because in my dream last night someone came and gave it to me to go on the honeymoon.

RUK: Oh. So this is a conclusion of last night's dream . . .

RAM: Listen . . . I was having a rare and beautiful dream . . . at that time, your father came and spoiled it.

RUK: My father?

RAM: You asked for ice cream and I immediately rang the bell to tell the boy to bring ice cream. Immediately the door opened and the hotel server came. As soon as I saw him come smiling, I couldn't control my laughter. Full six feet tall, absolutely black—your father! Why had he come to Simla? Must be my bad karma.

RUK: Enough. Just so you can insult my father you tell some stupid lie and say you had some *dream*. It's 7:30 . . . you haven't gone to office . . . there is still a little time before your friend Rahottaman comes. Go bathe and you can be on your way.

RAM: Rahottaman won't come today because there is office leave.

RUK: Leave? Why would there be leave today?

RAM: Today is Gokulakshmi, Krishna Jayanti.

RUK: Krishna Jayanti? That was last week. It's over.

RAM: Crazy woman . . . It was over last week for Ram, but for our company manager Jagannathan . . . Raoji . . . for all Madhvas . . . *today* is Krishna Jayanti.

RUK: Why do you tell these lies only to not go to the office? Yesterday I went to your manager's house since his wife had been inviting me to come home for a long time. If it had been Krishna Jayanti wouldn't she have put out Krishna's little footprints? I looked but didn't see anything.

RAM: Fool. The manager lives in a Housing Board building on the 15th floor. If she started to put Krishna's footprints from the ground up to their portion on the 15th floor it would be impossible. So just for ritual's sake she would put one in the puja room—you wouldn't have seen it.

RUK: I don't believe you. You are always taking leave from office. One day they will just send you home.

RAM: He won't send me—definitely won't send me. It should be like this, Rukku: One day you wake up in the morning and look in the paper. It should be there that, "No one needs to come to office." It should be. Ayyo . . .

RUK: Why are you talking like this? If you don't go to the office, what about money? If there's no money, how can we take care of our children?

RAM: This office, money, all these are things created by us . . . So what if there's no money? "The one who planted the tree will provide the water."

RUK: Nevermind about the tree . . . it will draw up water from the earth. But you are just some small shrub earning a 1500 rupee a month salary and will just . . . disappear.

RAM: Okay. Just leave it. Today I have office leave. Shall we go for some matinee show? I'll go and bathe, then come. Did you cook something good, Dear?

RUK: Do you really have office leave?

RAM: Okay, Dear. If you doubt me, we will take this under consideration. Every day my friend Rahottaman comes to collect me to go to the office.

RUK: Yes . . .

RAM: He won't come today. Suppose he comes . . . then the office must be open today. All right?

(Ramani goes to bathe and Rahottaman comes in.)

RUK: You? He said you wouldn't come today!

RAH: I won't come? What is this nonsense?

RUK: He said the office was closed today—leave . . .

RAH: Office leave? What's today? Why should there be leave?

RUK: He said your manager Jagannathan Rao . . . celebrates Krishna Jayanti today.

RAH: He would say that . . . you believe what he says. If today is Krishna Jayanti, tomorrow he'll say that it's Ramadan in Jagannathan's house if it seems like you'll believe it and he'll get to take leave!

RUK: What about later . . . you won't come . . . How dare he tell me that if Rahottaman comes it will mean that there is office today?

RAH: *Now* I understand—this is why he told me I didn't need to come today!

RUK: He told you not to come?

RAH: Yes, Rukmani. He told me yesterday, "Rahottaman, you don't need to come tomorrow. I will come straight to the office." I didn't listen to why . . . He said you have some uncle in Mambalam?

RUK: Yes. Sambasiva Uncle . . . my mother's younger brother. He has great affection for me; even at this age he comes daily from Mambalam to see me.

RAH: Well, he won't come visit you any longer.

RUK: Why not?

RAH: Yesterday morning at 10 o'clock he had a sudden heart attack and died.

RUK: What nonsense! Sambasiva Uncle died yesterday morning at 10 o'clock? I saw him yesterday evening!

RAH: You saw him in the evening?! I didn't know all that . . . yesterday morning 10 o'clock . . . What to say? If you saw him yesterday evening— Ramani said that and left. That jerk.

RUK: He's getting worse and worse. What bald-faced lie won't he tell to get out of going to work?

RAH: Thieving rascal! He told me your uncle had died and today you had to go see your aunt and five cousins to offer your condolences.

RUK: That's also a lie. My aunt died at 10.

RAH: What is this, Rukmani? You're confusing me. Your aunt died at 10? Then how did she have five children?

RUK: Ayyo. My aunt died when **I** was 10.

RAH: That liar! He tried to deceive me . . . Rukmani, go call your husband and tell him he's bathed enough. NO. You wait here. **I'll** go and call him. That cheat . . .

(Ramani comes out drying his hair with a towel.)

RAM: What, Rukku? Is breakfast ready? Which film should we see today?

RUK: A Thousand Lies.[9]

RAM: "A Thousand Lies"? That's an old film! Okay, if that's what you want. Where is it playing?

RUK: Truth Theater.[10]

RAM: "A Thousand Lies" at Truth Theater? Listen to that Rukku! You said "A Thousand Lies" is playing at the *Truth* Theater . . . that's not funny.

RUK: A few people are just like that. From the outside they look like truthful people, but inside their hearts are a thousand lies.

RAM: Rukku . . . Don't talk with Dilip so much . . . you are starting to speak philosophically, too.

RUK: Oh. So the office is really closed today?

RAM: Crazy woman. If I had to go to the office today, Rahottaman would have come by this time. He didn't come, so there is office leave.

(Rahottaman comes up behind him.)

RAH: Say that to me one more time.

RAM: Rahottaman didn't come, so there is office . . . (turns around) You . . . you . . . Rahottaman.

RAH: I'm not God. You lying rascal. You lied about office leave. According to that . . . Krishna Jayanti at our manager's house?! (in Ramani's voice) That's not it, Rukku, darling, this is Gokulakshmi, Sita, Murugan, anyone . . . .

RUK: And he said you told him that Sambasiva Uncle died?

RAM: Yes, dear. Sambasiva Uncle is gone. He said . . . Che! That's not right . . .

RAH: Rukmani, it's not good for this Ramani to waste time like this. He's frequently taking leave from the office . . . He's taken all his leave plus 20 or 25 days with loss of pay. And he *still* takes leave! Soon he'll have to give a salary to the company! (Takes a diary out of his bag.) Ramani, look at this.

RUK: What is this?

RAH: Diary. I've written in this when Ramani has taken leave . . . and why . . . and having taken the leave, where he goes. I've taken notes on all this. This is my personal diary.

RAM: If you're writing all about other people's affairs, how can it be a "personal diary"?

RAH: Listen to what I've written: January 15, half day leave. Reason: Sambasiva Uncle died of typhoid. March 8: Sambasiva Uncle died of pneumonia. May 6: The same Sambasiva Uncle who died of pneumonia has died again. June 2: Sambasiva Uncle has died a natural death. Now it seems like the fellow doesn't know any more disease names than that.

RUK: Good Lord! What would Sambasiva Uncle think if he knew about this?

RAH: The same Sambasiva Uncle has died 4 times. Lazy, lying fellow. Start for the office now.

RAM: Rahottaman. I'm going to office. Why are you worrying that I won't? It seems like you must have been an Ayah in a past life, escorting children to and from school.

RUK: If you keep taking leave like this, they will send you out.

RAH: That's exactly why he does it, Rukku. If he resigns, he's afraid of how much you will scold him. So he does this, then what can they do but send him packing?

RAM: Go, Rukku. I'm fed up with this office life.

RAH: He said the same thing to me. Do you know what this man wants? It should be office leave every day. Then he said he would take you to a film or drama and enjoy life. And you know what else he's been saying? Now he's dreaming daily about taking you on a honeymoon.

RAM: Hey! Sh! Don't say all that . . . I'm embarrassed.

RAH: Beats me. 45 years old and this shy . . .

RUK: Daily you are dreaming about going on a honeymoon like this . . . for just one day why don't you lie down and dream about going to the office . . .

RAH: Okay, okay, it's late. Let's see about getting on our way.

RAM: . . . ! . . . ! Please. . . . I was already thinking of today as a holiday in my mind. Don't spoil my mood—from today I'll come regularly to the office . . .

RAH: I will kill you. Let's go.

DILIP: Dad, here's your tiffin box.

RUK: Buttermilk rice with pickle. Eat well!

RAM: Get out, Rukku. I'm bored with eating this buttermilk rice. Why don't you make poori or chapatti for a change?

RAH: I have poori and chapatti. This is just some excuse. Come on, let's go.

RAM: Today it was in the paper . . . did you see it? There's going to be a big thunderstorm today. Should we go to the office in all this rain?

RAH: I have an umbrella. Let's go.

Appendix D

Mohammad bin Tughlaq

A 1968 play by Cho Ramasamy

Translated by Kristen Rudisill in 2001[11] from the book published by Alliance in Chennai, 2nd printing 1995.

Scene 9

PLACE: Prime Minister's Office

CHARACTERS: Ibn Battuta, Tyagarajan, Tughlaq, Sastri, Govind, Velayuttam

BATT: Did you see how everyone was agitating about the language problem? How easily Tughlaq has solved everything.

TYAG: He promised he would change the law about national language. So the agitations have ceased.

BATT: Your people need a promise. Is that all?

TYAG: You need to fulfill that promise.

TUGH: Which promises have been fulfilled up till now? We start to make promises in elections, we come to power, we measure and calculate, distribute promises, then leave. The people are satisfied. *A successful democratic government is one which goes on making promise after promise.*

SAS: *But those promises must be kept.*

TUGH: *Yes. It shall be kept. A political promise shall always be kept as a promise and it shall always remain as a promise.*

TYAG: If you give a promise, you need to keep it. If you don't, this confusion will happen all over again in the South.

TUGH: Then I'll promise again.

BATT: The issue of the language problem has been solved. Your opinions on that are no longer necessary.

GOV: I agree with that. We've passed the law on national language. So what next?

SAS: If I could just say . . .

BATT: I have to keep reminding you constantly that you are one of 450 deputy prime ministers belonging to your party.

SAS: What is this? The language problem is solved, *Sir*! We all agree with that.

BATT: Next on Tughlaq's agenda is to wipe out corruption and bribery.

GOV: What is that, *Sir*?

BATT: Government officials collect bribe money to do things for ordinary people. That is against the law. This is bribery and corruption, isn't it?

GOV: Yes.

BATT: Tughlaq's plan is to wipe out all of this illegal activity.

GOV: How, *Sir*?

TUGH: I will wipe out illegal bribes by making bribes legal.

GOV: What?

TUGH: Yes. We need to fix the bribe amounts like we fix how much the salary should be for government officials and employees.

SAS: Ayyayyo! Have you suggested we award bribe money to *government officials*?

TUGH: We are awarding their salary money. Isn't that fair?

SAS: But aren't they getting their salary money lawfully?

TUGH: That's why I'm saying to make taking bribe money legal. Still, if the common people need something to happen it can be 20,000 for the *secretary*, 10,000 for the *undersecretary*, 5,000 for the *superintendent*, 1,000 for the *head clerk*, 100 for clerks, and 10 rupees for the peon. They can give money for this, or they can give jewels to the wives of this or that official.

GOV: What is this atrocity, *Sir*?

BATT: What's atrocious about it? It happens illegally, so why not have it happen legally?

SAS: All this is against the law, so how can it be in accordance with the law?

TUGH: What's wrong with it? Am I doing something that's never been done before? This strategy has been demonstrated by my predecessors before now. It used to be against the law to renounce the husband holding your hand; now divorce is legal. Black *market* business used to be illegal; now they have made *ration* shops legal. It used to be illegal to tell lies to deceive people; now elections are legal. *What was illegal yesterday is legal today. What is illegal today shall be legal tomorrow. The previous government made law an ass. My government shall make it a pig.*

GOV: *Sir*, are you going to fix the legal bribery *rate*?

BATT: There is no use in continuing to object to that. You need to go make it into law in *Parliament* using your votes.

GOV: Just one small amendment to that.

BATT: It can't be changed.

GOV: Oh no, it's not that. But could you please add some *rate* for *members* of *Parliament*?

TUGH: Oh!

BATT: We should do that *Sultan*.

TUGH: Okay.

GOV: In the same way, for *deputy prime ministers*, some *special* . . .

BATT: Will ministers take money from the people? I can't think about it.

TUGH: Yes. Ministers shouldn't take money from the people. We need to make some new arrangement. According to the legal *rate* officials take, they need to give a 25% share to the minister. That is the best way.

TYAG: I don't think the people will accept that bribe *rate* law or the legal share for ministers.

TUGH: The people of our country will accept anything.

TYAG: There will be public meetings in our country against this.

TUGH: There is no lack of those here. I have understood our country's people well. They will protest anything at first. But at the end of the day those objections will go. They will go without comment, thinking, "Whatever the government has done is okay, this is our fate."

TYAG: The next elections will come; you need to keep that in mind.

TUGH: The man who thinks about the next election is a proponent of politics; the man who thinks about the next generation is a proponent of leadership. I don't think about either—I'm a proponent of democracy.

GOV: Like *Sir* says, even though our people will object at first, they'll forget that later. We don't need to worry. Let's put this into law.

SAS: Next we need to deal with the food problem.

BATT: No need. Everyone who has tried that has had a miserable fate.

SAS: But if we don't deal with it immediately our country will have a miserable fate.

BATT: If we don't deal with the food problem that will be the country's fate. But even if we do, the fate will be the same.

TUGH: Even if we don't deal with them, some issues will solve themselves. The food problem is like that.

SAS: It would be good if we could somehow lower the unemployment rate.

BATT: How could we lower the unemployment rate?

GOV: We need to give everyone some job.

TUGH: I have already given positions to as many ministers as I could.

BATT: I have an idea. We can say frequently at public meetings that we need to reduce the unemployment rate. That's enough to satisfy our people.

SAS: Okay. That solves that problem. So far we've solved the language problem, bribery and corruption, food, and unemployment.

Gov: This is a great victory for our government. Other problems?

Tugh: You don't need to worry about any other problems. I will solve those.

Tyag: There are so many unsolved problems.

Tugh: Those are left for each government to inherit from the previous one. We will do that. *We should not act against our tradition and national practice.*

Tyag: In many places in the South there will be protests. What are you going to give to the South Indian people?

Tugh: Consolation.

Tyag: One other problem. There is an agitation that you need to give Tirupati to Tamilnadu.[12] One man has gone on a hunger strike. Another has announced that he is going to immolate himself. What are you going to do about this?

Tugh: *All right.* I'll give Tirupati to Tamilnadu.

Vel: If you give Tirupati to Tamilnadu, won't there be agitations in Andhra?

Tugh: I will give Tanjavore to Andhra.[13]

Gov: It seems like the food situation is still bad in a few states.

Tugh: That's why I have decided to go to America.

Sas: You're going to go to America? Why?

Tugh: Shouldn't I see America? I am going to meet the American president and talk about world problems. *I am going to discuss with the president of America about the problems facing this world.*

Tyag: Why should we worry about other countries' problems?

Tugh: It's not necessary to worry about other countries' problems, but there's no point in worrying about our country's problems. So what should I worry about?

Sas: All of us deputy prime ministers will also go abroad.

Batt: There aren't enough foreign countries for our deputy prime ministers to visit.

Tugh: *Let our deputy prime ministers visit the municipalities.*

GOV: The situation is that we need to listen to everything you say.

BATT: We don't say you need to listen. We just say to listen if you want to.

SAS: What is this, Sir? You have made us *deputy prime ministers*. So what is the meaning of this "listen if you want to"? How can we not listen?

BATT: Okay, today in *Parliament* the bill on bribery and corruption needs to be passed into law. We need to talk about unemployment like we discussed. We need to keep making promises if and when the language problem comes up again.

TYAG: But we can't say how people will react.

BATT: Yes we can. They will think, "If this government goes, what will the next government do for us?" Do you think that the people support us because they think that we are doing something for the country's well-being? "No matter what government comes we will have the same fate." Having thought this, these people won't say anything, just "Let them be in the position . . . ." Only if the people think will a good government be formed. Until people realize that, there is no reason for people like us to worry.

SAS: Shall I speak now?

TUGH: Let us adjourn the meeting.

SAS: Tughlaq's *durbar* is over.

TUGH: What did you say? Yes. This is definitely Tughlaq's royal court. What will you do? This is definitely Tughlaq's *durbar*. Everything will happen according to what I want. There is no room for anyone who opposes that. I don't need anyone to lift up their heads. I only need people to raise their hands. *Parliament is a place where people lift their hands up and put their heads down.*

Appendix E

Chennai Drama Troupes and Some Relations

What follows is a family tree of sorts. Most sabha drama troupes formed when an actor or writer within an existing troupe decided to branch out on his own. Because troupes tend to center around a single personality, it is difficult for actors or writers to reach their full potential from someone else's troupe. However, they learn many skills as well as lessons in dramaturgy and production from the leader of the troupe they started with, and this family tree attempts to make those relationships between troupes, which manifest themselves in the plays and the stylistic choices, easier to spot. The tree is not, however, absolute. Many writers, Venkat, for example, will write for several troupes (in his case United Amateur Artists and S. Ve. Shekher primarily) before starting their own troupes. In Venkat's case, running his own troupe proved to be too much and he went back to writing for other troupes and increasing his involvement in the television medium.

The dates are pulled from a variety of different sources and brought together in these charts, which I hope prove helpful. Some I got directly from troupe leaders or other actors, some from performance souvenirs or newspaper reviews, and some are from books such as *Tamiḻ Nāṭakamēṭ ai Muṉṉōṭikaḷ* ("Pioneers of Tamil Stage Drama"), edited by S. S. Ramar Ilango and *Tamiḻ Nāṭakam—Nēṟṟum Iṉṟum* ("Tamil Drama—Yesterday Today"), edited by K. Bhagavathy. Oftentimes the printed biodata of the actors will include dates that they were with certain troupes that allow for estimations. When I was unable to ascertain exact dates of a troupe's founding or demise, I have given an idea (for example, "Krishnan Nataka Sabha (c. 1930s–1960s)."

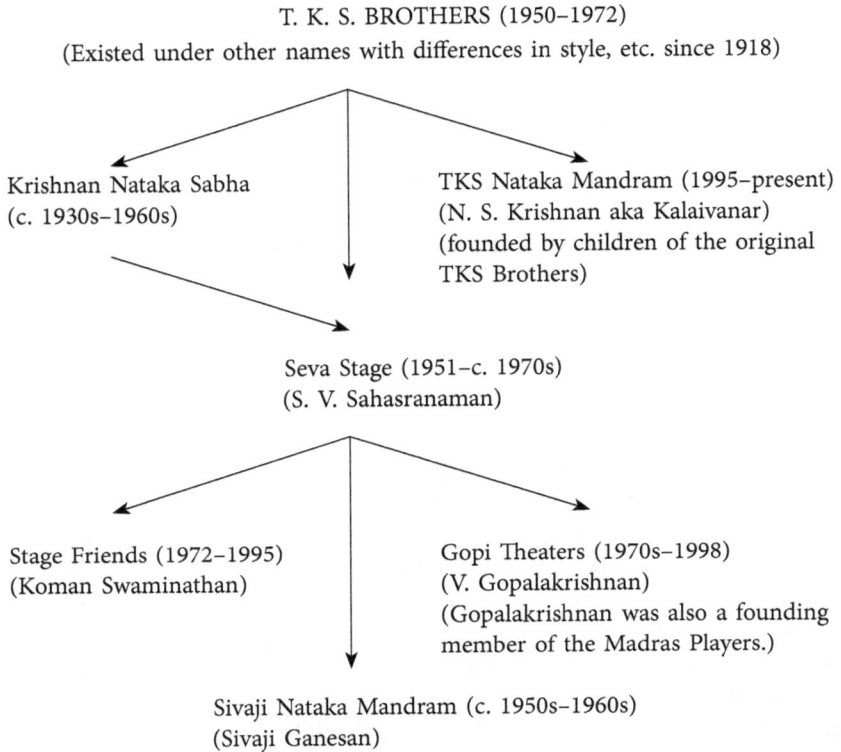

T. K. S. BROTHERS (1950–1972)
(Existed under other names with differences in style, etc. since 1918)

Krishnan Nataka Sabha
(c. 1930s–1960s)

TKS Nataka Mandram (1995–present)
(N. S. Krishnan aka Kalaivanar)
(founded by children of the original TKS Brothers)

Seva Stage (1951–c. 1970s)
(S. V. Sahasranaman)

Stage Friends (1972–1995)
(Koman Swaminathan)

Gopi Theaters (1970s–1998)
(V. Gopalakrishnan)
(Gopalakrishnan was also a founding member of the Madras Players.)

Sivaji Nataka Mandram (c. 1950s–1960s)
(Sivaji Ganesan)

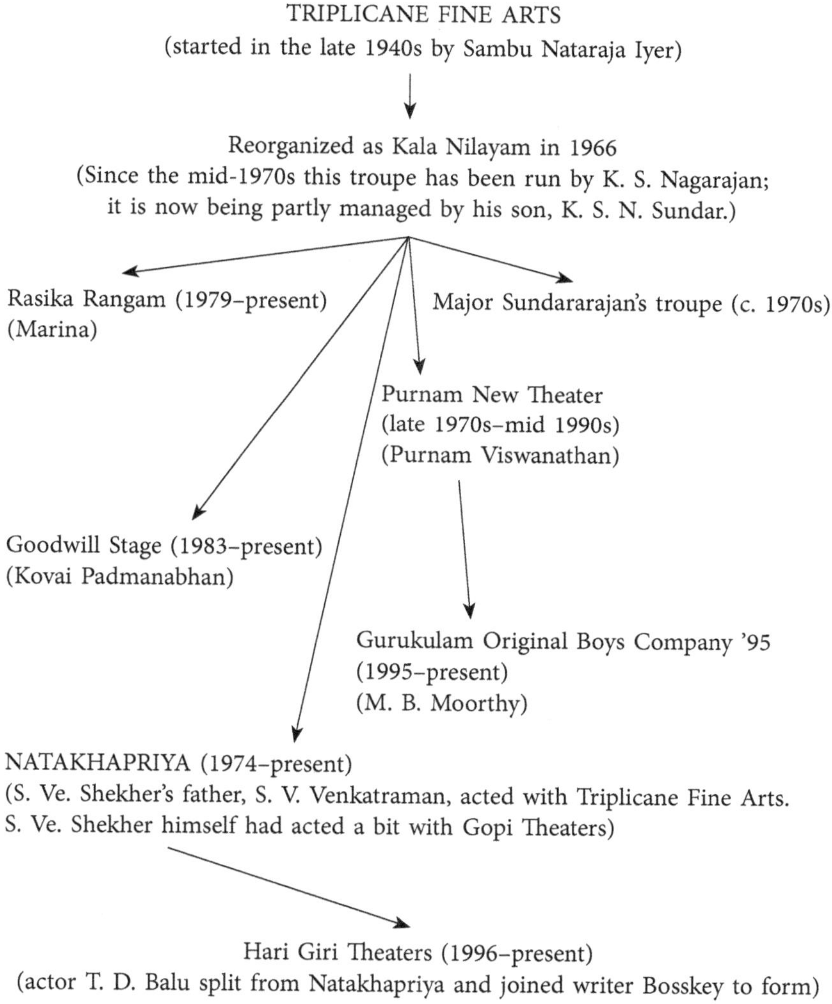
TRIPLICANE FINE ARTS
(started in the late 1940s by Sambu Nataraja Iyer)
Reorganized as Kala Nilayam in 1966
(Since the mid-1970s this troupe has been run by K. S. Nagarajan;
it is now being partly managed by his son, K. S. N. Sundar.)
Rasika Rangam (1979–present)
(Marina)
Major Sundararajan's troupe (c. 1970s)
Purnam New Theater
(late 1970s–mid 1990s)
(Purnam Viswanathan)
Goodwill Stage (1983–present)
(Kovai Padmanabhan)
Gurukulam Original Boys Company '95
(1995–present)
(M. B. Moorthy)
NATAKHAPRIYA (1974–present)
(S. Ve. Shekher's father, S. V. Venkatraman, acted with Triplicane Fine Arts.
S. Ve. Shekher himself had acted a bit with Gopi Theaters)
Hari Giri Theaters (1996–present)
(actor T. D. Balu split from Natakhapriya and joined writer Bosskey to form)

UNITED AMATEUR ARTISTS
(founded 1952 by Y. G. Parthasarathy and Padmanabhan (Pattu);
now managed by Y. G. P.'s son, Y. G. Mahendran)

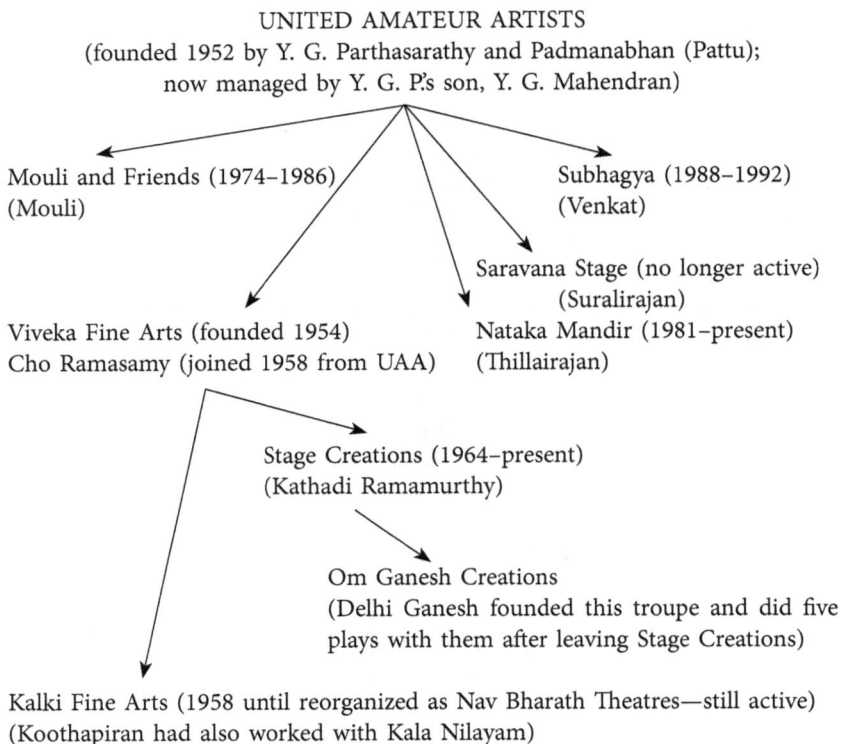

Mouli and Friends (1974–1986)
(Mouli)

Subhagya (1988–1992)
(Venkat)

Saravana Stage (no longer active)
(Suralirajan)

Viveka Fine Arts (founded 1954)
Cho Ramasamy (joined 1958 from UAA)

Nataka Mandir (1981–present)
(Thillairajan)

Stage Creations (1964–present)
(Kathadi Ramamurthy)

Om Ganesh Creations
(Delhi Ganesh founded this troupe and did five plays with them after leaving Stage Creations)

Kalki Fine Arts (1958 until reorganized as Nav Bharath Theatres—still active)
(Koothapiran had also worked with Kala Nilayam)

INDIAN NATIONAL ARTISTS THEATERS (c. 1954–1994)
(V. S. Raghavan)

Ragini Recreations[14] (c. 1960–1992)
(K. Balachander had done some acting and writing for INA Theaters before starting his own troupe)

Mali's Stage (at least from 2000–present)
(Mali)

Viswashanti (no longer active)
(Visu)

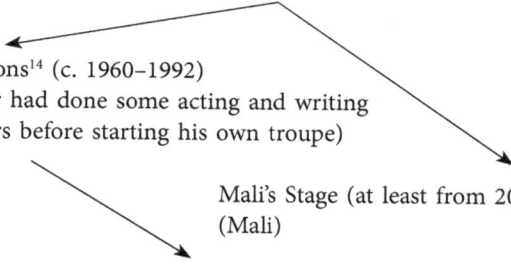

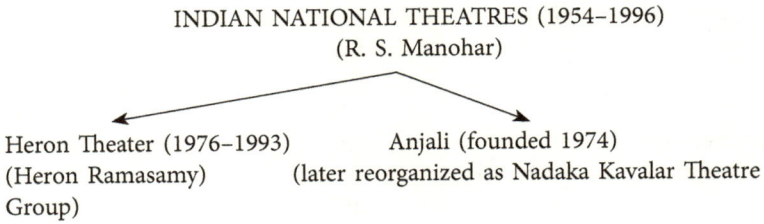

INDIAN NATIONAL THEATRES (1954–1996)
(R. S. Manohar)

Heron Theater (1976–1993)
(Heron Ramasamy)

Anjali (founded 1974)
(later reorganized as Nadaka Kavalar Theatre Group)

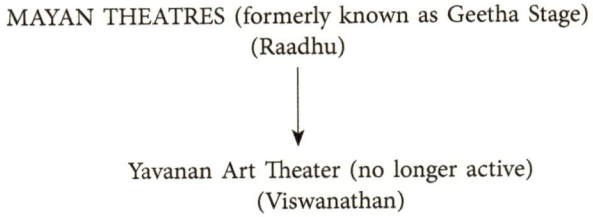

MAYAN THEATRES (formerly known as Geetha Stage)
(Raadhu)

Yavanan Art Theater (no longer active)
(Viswanathan)

OTHER NOTABLE TROUPES

1. Egmore Dramatic Society (no longer active)
2. Shantiniketan (Seshadri) (no longer active)
3. Mother Creations (C. V. Chandramohan)
4. Sathya Sai Creations (Karaikudi Narayanan)
5. Kalamandir (Bombay Chanakya)
6. Augusto Creations (Augusto)
7. Mahalakshmi Ladies Drama Group (founded 1989 in Bombay, moved to Chennai permanently in 1996, still active) (Bombay Gnanam)
8. Prayatna (K. Vivek Shankar)
9. Rail Priya (1994–present)
10. United Visuals (1994–present) (T. V. Varadarajan)
11. Dummies Communications (aka Dummies Drama) (1999–present) (V. Sreevatson)

Notes

Notes to the Introduction

1. All translations are mine unless otherwise noted. Anything in italics was in English in the original text.

2. See Hansen 2001. "These dramas are designated as *sabhai natak* in Urdu literary histories and have received ample treatment by Gupta (1981: 227–36), Husain (1990: 71–79), Rizvi (1957: 121–32), and Ibrahim Yusuf (1980: 52–71, 307–9)" (Hansen 2001, 108n22).

3. There are descriptions of many of these troupes in Saktiperumal 1979.

4. See Appendix A for a list of commonly used halls along with their amenities, capacity, and the price of an evening's rental in 2007.

5. See Ganesan, 2007 for more about this important actor's life and contributions to theater and film.

6. It began in a house in Georgetown, then moved to Victoria Public Hall (1902–1936), then to its current location on Mount Road. "In 1945, the Sabha built its own theatre, the New Theatre." Today, the club boasts rooms and suites, restaurants and a canteen, a permit room, banquet hall, health club, swimming pool, games and sports, a library, and yoga (see http://www.svsclub.net/home/history.html). When I went there, they pointed me to a photo of Mudaliyar on the wall but were at first confused when I asked about theater, with which they no longer have any connection.

7. See Ramakrishna 2006 for more information on Madras Players.

8. I use "insider theater" instead of "community theater" to refer to sabha theater because the latter term is used in the field to invoke applied, even radical forms of theater that tackle issues of socially and economically marginalized groups, which is not the case here.

9. There has been a lot written about how the current iteration of the caste system evolved and became normalized. Dirks 2002 is an excellent and informative source. Other resources include Dirks 1988; Beteille 1965; Bairy 2013; Chuyen 2005; Driver 1982; V. Geetha and S. V. Rajadurai 1998; Pandian 1990;

Pandian 2007; Fuller 1996; Fuller 1999; Fuller and Narasimhan 2007; Fuller and Narasimhan 2014.

Notes to Chapter One

1. See Anand 2003 on journalism and Hancock 1999; Singh 1976; Fuller and Narasimhan 2014; and Irschick 1986 on higher education.

2. In the audience survey that I conducted in Chennai, only 29.25% of respondents (of whom there were 253 total) said that they currently (71) or formerly (3) belonged to a sabha. I believe that this number is low because I got a very poor rate of response at most performances. The majority of my respondents came from attendees at S. Ve. Shekher plays (117 total, of which only 38 were sabha members) or from Kathadi Ramamurthy's Golden Jubilee, a special event that attracted many non-regular theatergoers (23 of the 82 respondents were sabha members, and 2 were press). S. Ve. Shekher fans are known for being fans of his, not necessarily of dramas in general. For this reason, fans will buy individual tickets to his performances when they want to attend (Shekher performs somewhere nearly every week), rather than joining a sabha, which will offer a variety of drama troupes along with other entertainments. Both S. Ve. Shekher and Kathadi Ramamurthy were incredibly supportive of my project and made a point of announcing the survey at their plays and requesting fans to respond. Shekher also invited me up on stage on occasion to do the same. This was much more effective than simply passing them out at the entrance and collecting them at the end, with only the tacit approval of the troupe. I did net 31 responses from the Kartik Fine Arts Annual Drama Festival, but again this was a special event that attracts many non-sabha members (only two of these respondents were sabha members). The responses from Crazy Creations and UAA performances were much more even, with 11 sabha members and 13 non-sabha members responding.

3. L'Armand and L'Armand wrote in 1978 that "[t]he largest number [of Madras sabhas] still are recognized as Brahmin organizations" (L'Armand and L'Armand 1978, 129).

4. See Weidman 2006 for an in-depth discussion on the use of the analogy of music to language and the way it played out in the debate between the Tamil music movement and the Brahmin music establishment. She reframes the debate in a footnote in this way: "These two choices—between voice as a cultivated, aestheticized instrument and voice as a representation of self—may be considered in relation to, respectively, Sanskritic rasa theory and Tamil bhakti discourse" (Weidman 2006, 310n2).

5. Early North Madras sabhas included the Krishna Gana Sabha (not the present-day one), the Bhagavath Katha Prasanga Sabha, the Bhakti Marga

Prasanga Sabha, the Punarvarasu Sabha, the Indian Fine Arts Society, and the Katchaleeswarar Gana Sabha.

6. The most famous of the sabha theater artists also live in these areas. S. Ve. Shekher, Crazy Mohan, Kathadi Ramamurthy, K. S. Nagarajan, V. S. Raghavan, and the Tamil Brahmin Association (TAMBRAAS) are all located in the Mylapore area. Y. G. Mahendran, A. R. Srinivasan, and Marina are all in T. Nagar. Kovai Pattu of Goodwill Stage still lives in Triplicane.

7. As you can see from the map (figure 1.1), this designation is no longer entirely accurate. The city has expanded since the 1970s to the south (Besant Nagar, Tiruvanmiyur, Nanganallur, Tambaram, etc.) making neighborhoods like T. Nagar and Mylapore seem "central" rather than "south." However, in Gopalie's estimation, as in that of many from his generation, "South" Madras is still north of the Adyar River.

8. Rumya Putcha writes about how Kuchipudi was compared to Bharata Natyam and at this juncture, found to be lacking, and thus "(mis)categorized as unclassical or folk" (2013, 91). She also points out that the delegation sent to represent Kuchipudi (and by extension the Telugu people) were chosen because of their English educations and conformity to a historical narrative yet to be written: the "institutionalization of a local tradition in order to impart it to middle-to-upper-class/caste girls from Telugu families" (101).

9. This is a characteristic of the Book-of-the-Month Club in the US that Janice Radway studied (Radway 1997, 5).

10. Lelyveld 1995, 57. He is quoting from H. R. Luthra, *Indian Broadcasting* (New Delhi: Publications Division, 1986), 105.

11. See figure 1.5 for the Income and Expenditure Report for the Narada Gana Sabha for the year ending March 31, 2003, which shows income in INR from subscriptions as 377,000, versus gate collections at 36,610, and music festival receipts far higher at 1,686,991. Expenditures for the music festival that year totaled 1,026,594.35 rupees while remuneration to artists was only 107,550 and hall rent/electricity 185,500 (Narada Gana Sabha's *Forty-Fifth Annual Report and Accounts* 2003, 25).

12. My interview with the secretary of the Priya Cultural Academy, May 12, 2004.

13. There has been a lot of scholarly writing in Tamil on these professional troupes (Annamalai 2001; Ashokmitran 1999; Bhagavathy 2000 and 2001; Gurusami and Dasarathan 2000; Ramaswamy, Murukesan, and Govindasamy 1999). See Gupt 2005 for more on Parsi Theater. Hansen (2020), Soneji (2017), and Mangai and Arasu (2009) address Parsi theater and influence in Tamilnadu in particular. Mangai and Arasu write, "While it is true that Parsi theatre gave a pan-Indian feel to popular drama, we learn that there were subtle differences within the way the adaptations were made in each region. In Tamil Nadu, the term Parsi has

become a generic term for a particular kind of drama which is predominantly musical with its attendant paraphernalia. It refers mainly to the techniques of visual bonanza. It also refers to comic interludes. It has come to refer to the importance of training. It connotes the shift to 'modern' entertainment offered within a time span. Parsi theatre stands at the threshold of the co-mingling of colonialism and modernism. In fact, both meant the same—colonial because of the proscenium arch, back curtain, set design, and other paraphernalia and modern because of the time span and stories that went beyond puranic tales. The irony is that it was this form that represented 'national' drama soon after independence" (2009, 116).

14. See Hanne de Bruin 1999 for more on *Kaṭṭaikkūttu.*

15. See Richmond 1990, 431. Richmond writes that R. S. Manohar estimated his cost to be 100,000 rupees per production (430). Komal Swaminathan's daughter estimated that when his social play *Taṇṇīr! Taṇṇīr!* (*Water!*) was first staged by his theater company, Stage Friends, that it cost around 50,000 rupees, an amount she thought was typical for that type of production (Shankar and Swaminathan 2001, 124). A typical sabha theater production, in contrast, costs closer to 2,500–5,000 rupees plus the theater rental (my estimation based on observation). This has gone up in the last few years, as hall rental rates have increased significantly in the past five years. For theater rental prices from 2007, see Appendix A.

16. Hari Krishnan talks about Bharata Natyam dance in early Tamil cinema and says specifically that "[t]he presence of courtesan genres in the drama thus also enabled their movement into the new spaces of the early cinema" (2019, 212).

17. For more on drama in this period and on the T. K. S. Brothers in particular, see Shanmugam 1967, which is the autobiography of Avvai T. K. Shanmugam.

18. Longtime sabha theater actor and director A. R. Srinivasan estimated that sabha dramas cater to a population of maybe thirty thousand middle-class, educated people. He contrasted this to Tamil films, which nearly the entire population of the state, including people of all different strata of society, watch. My interview, May 14, 2004.

19. I was told in an interview with T. K. S. Pughagherti that for one of their historical dramas they need to get 10,000–15,000 rupees in order to make it financially viable. He says that the sabhas offer only 3,000 rupees, so they rarely perform. It is particularly expensive for the T. K. S. Nataka Mantram because they have to hire all of their costumes for each production. The T. K. S. brothers had owned their own sets and costumes, but after T. K. Shanmugam died, his brothers were sad, quit performing, and disposed of all the sets, costumes, and other properties. R. S. Manohar owns his own sets and costumes, so he can afford to accept less payment from the sabhas. My interview with T. K. S. Pughagherti, May 8, 2004. S. Ve. Shekher told me that he thinks most troupes are paid between 5,000 and 8,000 rupees per performance. He and Crazy Mohan are paid more. My interview, July 8, 2003. Krishnamoorthy of Dummies Drama said in an interview

with Pushpa Narayan, "At the most, we get Rs. 2,500 per show from the Sabhas. Troupes like S. Ve. Shekar's get Rs. 15,000" (Narayan 2004). From what S. Ve. Shekher himself has said, I understand that his troupe makes a minimum flat rate of 25,000 rupees per performance.

20. Gopalie 2002, 37. These audiences were more likely to be non-Brahmin, and it is not surprising that they would prefer "pure Tamil." The Pure Tamil Movement was linked to the Dravidian Movement and is dated by most scholars to 1916. It promoted a decline in the use of foreign words, particularly those of Sanskrit origin (see Ramaswamy 1997).

21. Gopalie interview with Venkat, in Gopalie 2002, 260. Venkat clearly thinks that Cho and Manohar made more money from their plays than any other artists.

22. Mary Elizabeth Hancock found that social service, defined as "charitable activities for which the performer was not paid" (Hancock 1990, 56) is an important component of Tamil Brahmin identity. Nearly all of her Smarta Brahmin informants maintained ties with organizations that identified "social service" as a primary agenda. Many of the theater actors also promote themselves by referring to their charity work. S. Ve. Shekher, for example, has a sidebar on his website labeled "charity" that leads to a page describing all the contributions he has made to various charities, complete with a photo of himself giving blood (http://www.sveshekher.com/main.html viewed on December 2, 2005). Souvenirs and annual reports from every sabha and theater troupe that I have seen include enumerations of contributions to social service. The Mylapore Academy, in the *49th Year Celebrations Souvenir*, highlighting the motto "Service is our Religion," includes a page that lists the "main objects of the academy." Only three of these have to do with supporting the arts, while the other nine involve charity, the very first one reading, "To take an active interest in the civic, social, moral, and cultural welfare of the community and to promote practice of good citizenship" (Mylapore Academy 2003, 12).

23. There is no consensus as to when this took place. S. Ve. Shekher, in a July 8, 2003 interview, told me that the Federation of City Sabhas was founded in 1960 and mentioned a Federation of Amateur Drama Troupes that was founded at the same time. I have seen no other mention of this latter organization. K. S. Rajendran writes that the Federation of City Sabhas was founded in 1981 (1989, 155). S. Gopalie couldn't pinpoint a date, but because Komal Swaminathan was the power behind it, he believed the Federation of City Sabhas to have been founded in the mid-1970s (my interview, July 16, 2007). At any rate, it was powerful for many years. The Federation still exists in name, but according to Gopalie, the sabhas and troupes no longer feel any compulsion to follow its recommendations. (Quotation is from Gopalie 2002, 38, from an interview with Shri Srinivasan of Kala Niketan.) There is a website, but it has very little information on it, saying only that "The Federation was founded in the late 1970s by some of the prominent Sabhas in the City of Chennai." Eight sabhas are listed as members:

Brahma Gana Sabha, Hamsadhwani, Karthik Fine Arts, Narada Gana Sabha, Rasika Ranjani Sabha, Krishna Gana Sabha, Sri Parthasarathy Swami Sabha, and Sri Thyaga Brahma Gana Sabha.

24. Gopalie 2002, 17. While these numbers are not accurate, they do give a sense of both the general trend and the perception of the decline by the theater artists themselves.

25. Shekher says this used to be around thirty before TV became widespread in the late 1980s. My interview, July 8, 2003. It is clear that this number has dwindled further in the last fifteen years. Also, since the untimely deaths of Cheenu Mohan (May 17, 1956–December 27, 2018) and Crazy Mohan (October 16, 1952–June 10, 2019), Crazy Creations has continued performing, but not at the previous rate. The hundreth performance of *Crazy Premier League*, on July 1, 2019, was dedicated as a tribute to the playwright (see Kannan 2019).

26. Cited in Rajendran 1989, 85. At a March 14, 2004, performance of S. Ve. Shekher's *Alwā* at the Kalaivanar Arangam, there was a particularly riotous crowd with many young men in attendance. Shekher scolded them from the stage, telling them to go to the beach if they wanted to be rowdy. He then reminded them that he was being paid to perform and they had bought tickets, so they should listen to him.

27. See Fuller and Narasimhan 2014 for more on the Tamil Brahmin community's "distinctive identity and subjectivity" (229).

28. See Appendix B for a complete list.

29. Mayan Theaters and Poornam New Theater.

30. Balajee Construction Employees Welfare Association, Inter-Bank Drama Competition, Tamilnadu Kattai Koothu Kalai Valaroli Munnetra Sangam, Nandanam Ladies Association, Low Cost Health Care, L & T Recreation Club, TWAD Accounts Officers Association, Srinivasa Ladies Club, and the Federation of Sabhas.

31. These include the Malayalee Club, Ethiraj College Repertory Theatre, the Rajiv Gandhi Foundation, Pravin Joshi Theatre, the Alliance Francaise, Victoria Vidyalaya English School, Max Mueller Bhavan, and the Samskrita Ranga.

32. See Appendix B for a complete list.

33. Alpha to Omega Learning Center and the Lions Club of Padi Shenoy Nagar.

34. Dummies Drama, Gurukulam, Magic Lantern, Viveka Fine Arts Club, Natakapriya, Crazy Creations, Pareeksha Tamil Theatre Group, Hari Giri Theatres, and Raadhu.

35. Madras Players is now more active and new groups like Evam, the Center for Contemporary Culture, and the K. R. Rajaravivarma Alliance have sprung up. In addition are the old standbys such as the Alliance Francaise and the Max Mueller Bhavan as well as many college performances.

36. See Appendix B for the complete list.

37. Mahalakshmi Ladies Drama Group Trust, Mirrorz Theatre, Natakapriya Trust, OVM Theatres, Sellam Kalaalayam, Theatrekaran, and Theatre Marina.

38. One drastic change in 2019 compared to earlier years is the vast number of sabhas and other groups (I counted eighteen, all of which are new with the possible exceptions of Evam's Happy Cow and Evam Standup Tamasha, which may be related to the Evam that used to do English-language dramas) that are now sponsoring standup comedy, something I did not see at all before, and this is happening in English, Tamil, Telugu, and Hindi. There are also sketch comedy groups, improv groups, and regular open mics.

39. When I looked through the "Music of Madras" listings, I found a number of troupes I recognized still performing in 2019. There were also many I didn't recognize, which have clearly emerged in the last few years, including Prasiddhi Creations; SB Creations; Satyasai Creations; Sowmya Drama Troupe; Theatrekaran; Sallam Kalaayaam; Dasa Arts Madurai Kannan; TVK The Real Theatre People; Kalaivani Drama Troupe; S. Sruthi's Natya Nadha Nataka Sangamam; Legally Yours; Sairam Creations; OVM Theatres; Ajay Entertainers; Theatre Marina (not related to the playwright Marina); Sri Rajamathangi Creations; Visual Respiration; Best Arts; Arul, Janagi, Melody & Darshan; Mirrorz Theatre Productions; and artists Elango Kumanan, Coolevents Kumar, Santosh Rajan, Balasundaram, Anitha Santhanam of A Guduguduppukkari Production, John Pradeep, and Adhuthurai Baskar. These are not all from the sabha genre, but I would guess most are, and they are certainly all performing Tamil drama in Chennai.

40. Weidman 2006, 80. She cites the magazine *Sruti*, 2003, a special issue on the Madras music season, as noting that there were seventy-three organizations sponsoring concerts during the 2002–2003 season, up from seventeen in 1987–1988.

41. For example, Esther Fine Arts currently sponsors programs of film music and dance but no longer sponsors dramas.

42. The last census to enumerate the number of Brahmins in Madras City was in 1931 (after this date caste was no longer a census category), when 41,700 were identified. In 2011, the government conducted a socioeconomic and caste census (see *Economic Times*, September 5, 2010), but it only asked about scheduled caste and scheduled tribe status, so figures for a Brahmin population are not available. The most recent number comes from Fuller and Narasimhan, who estimate the maximum Tamil Brahmin population in the state of Tamilnadu to be 1.4 million people (2014, 5) out of a total population of about 67 million, so about 2%, heavily concentrated in the city of Chennai.

Notes to Chapter Two

1. See Soneji 2020 for information on intersections between Islam and South Indian raga-based music.

2. Geetha and Rajadurai (1998, 8) mention Grant-Duff, the governor of Madras, and Swami Vivekananda in particular.

3. See Pandian 1992 for a fascinating look at the intersections of M. G. R.'s politics and theater/film personas.

4. See Karunakaran 1978 and Karunakaran and Sivashanmugam 1981 for more on different Tamil dialects.

5. This number has now reached 69% per the 76th Amendment Act of 1994 (http://www.constitution.org/cons/india/tamnd76.htm).

6. Anil Seal's work shows the gains made by non-Brahmins: "Between 1879 and 1884 when the number of college students doubled, lower caste matriculates increased by 67 per cent while the Brahmins increased by 33 per cent" (107). He also points out that in 1879, Brahmins accounted for around 3% of the total population in Madras Presidency but made up 70% of college graduates. By 1884 this had dropped to approximately 60%.

7. The DK (Dravida Kazhagam) was a political party founded by Naicker in 1944.

8. Milton Singer estimates the *bhajana* groups to be 80% Brahmin, and with the possible exception of S. Ve. Shekher's audiences, I would estimate this to be about the average for sabha theater audiences as well.

9. This Tamil Brahmin association runs a service for arranging marriages. They keep the horoscopes of around five thousand Tamil Brahmins from around the world on file at all times. For a fee, they will provide a list of contact information for potential mates with compatible horoscopes who meet the criteria (age, location, salary, level of education, etc.) specified by the client. (Author interview at the TAMBRAAS main office in R. A. Puram, April 21, 2004.)

10. Specifically mentioned during the 2004 elections were the *anna daanam* (offerings of food) in temples scheme, moral lessons for children at renowned temples on weekends, the anti-conversion law, insistence on discussion of Godra in conjunction with discussion of Gujarat, the crushing of the public employees strike, and support of the majority (Hindus) over the minorities. In addition, many vote not *for* the AIADMK, but *against* the DMK, whose long-time leader M. Karunanidhi has displayed many "bouts of anti-brahmin rhetoric" (*Indian Express*, April 19, 2004).

11. I do not know if there was any conflict with him selling this play twice. He told Gopalie about TAMBRAAS and me about the film, though he did characterize the cinema sale as "backdoor."

12. See chapter 3 for a longer discussion about the role of the police in Chennai theater.

13. This summary is from the Kannada remake, which is said to be "a copycat of the original Tamil version." Found on http://www.musicindiaonline.com/ar/i/movie_name/8650/1/, viewed on May 21, 2007.

14. http://www.lolluexpress.com/idhu_comm.htm, viewed on May 21, 2007.

15. See Table 7, "Varna, Caste or Subcaste of Respondents: By Social Class" in Driver 1982, 242. "Lower class" was found to consist of 0% Brahmins, 32% Non-Brahmins, and 68% Adi-Dravida, Chakkiliyan, and Other; "middle class" was

21% Brahmin, 64% Non-Brahmin, and 15% Adi-Dravida or Other; and "upper class" was 39% Brahmin, 54% Non-Brahmin, and 7% Other.

16. An excellent illustration of this is the case of the "Vagina Monologues" in India in March of 2004. Eve Ensler, the author, went to India with Jane Fonda and Marisa Tomei to perform the play. They were very popular in Mumbai, a city that never thought to censor the performance. Chennai, however, had a different response. As of March 8, 2004, Ensler was scheduled to perform in Chennai on March 12, 2004, at the Music Academy with tickets already for sale (*Indian Express*, March 8, 2004). However, on March 11, 2004, an article appeared in the paper stating that "[t]he city police commissioner has refused permission to the organizers to stage the play." Police Commissioner R. Nataraj told reporters that he "found certain portions of it 'objectionable'" (Muthalaly and Karthik 2004). The police almost never reject scripts; most playwrights agree that it is usually just a formality and that the 1954 Tamil Nadu Dramatic Performance Act is outdated and should be repealed. (It was repealed in 2013.) In fact, Mitheran Devanesan of the Madras Players (a fifty-year-old troupe that is famous for its English-language performances, particularly of Shakespeare) says that he thinks that the only reason the act is still around is that "there is not enough unity among the theatre groups to make a common representation to have it repealed" (Muthalaly and Karthik 2004).

17. See, for example, Allen 1997; Gaston 1996; Weidman 2006; L'Armand and L'Armand 1978.

18. The other theater practitioners mentioned include Utpal Dutt, Vijay Tendulkar, Chandrasekhar Kambar, Shombhu Mitra, and Vijaya Mehta.

19. While Chennai is thought of as culturally conservative in general, that contrasts the city's reputation in the film industry, where "Both officials and directors told me [Monika Mehta] that producers often went to Hyderabad and Madras to obtain film certificates because these offices were more lenient with respect to representations of sex and violence" (Mehta 2011, 62).

20. One example discussed in detail by Rakesh Solomon is the Marathi play *Kichaka-Vadha* by Khadilker, which is a reading of the *Mahābhārata* story of the death of Kichaka that portrays the Gokhale-Tilak debate with Lord Curzon (Viceroy) as Kichaka.

21. See Hardgrave 1965, 1969, and 1979 and Hardgrave and Kochanek 2000 for more information on regional politics in India. See Hardgrave 1965 and Sumathi Ramaswamy 1997 for more information about language riots in Tamilnadu.

Notes to Chapter Three

1. See Hansen 2020 and Soneji 2017 for more on Parsi Theatre and its influence in Chennai.

2. My audience survey asked viewers to name or describe their favorite plays or performers. Comedy plays and troupes accounted for 630 out of 764

responses (some people listed more than one). Thirty-five responses either express a mixture of comedy and serious drama or were obscure or illegible. Of the ninety-nine people whose stated preference is non-comedy theater, eighty-one of them specified mythological or historical dramas by R. S. Manohar, the T. K. S. Brothers, Nawab Rajamanickam, Kittappa, and S. V. Sahasranaman.

3. K. P. Arivanatham, who began his theater career working with M. R. Radha when he was twelve years old, then went on to write plays for the T. K. S. Brothers and R. S. Manohar, told me that now plays are "*sumaa* ("just") satire, wits, jokes." Yes, the audience can be "jolly for a short time, but the mind doesn't have to work. No strain." He particularly mentioned Y. G. Mahendran, Kathadi Ramamurthy, and Crazy Mohan as artists of this lighter type. Similarly, Prasad, who produces a television program called "Tamil Oli" ("The Sound of Tamil") for the Tamil Television Network (TTN) and writes for the Tamil magazine *Kuṅkumam*, told me that popular theater in Chennai today is "pure entertainment based" and that there is no cultural progress. People just go to laugh at plays with S. Ve. Shekher, T. V. Varadarajan, and others like them. Unlike Arivanatham, however, Prasad mentioned Kathadi Ramamurthy (along with Purnam Viswanathan, Indira Parthasarathy, and K. S. Nagarajan) as having some social message in his work.

4. She tells a story to that effect on the video *Kalakshetra: Devotion to Dance* (1985).

5. On Sanskrit drama see Baumer and Brandon 1981. Modern playwrights have also copied this device resulting in such dramas as Girish Karnad's *Tughlaq*, which I discuss in detail in chapter 7. Unlike the Parsi theater model of "shallow" and "deep" scenes that Girish Karnad used in his 1964 play *Tughlaq*, the comedic (shallow) scenes of Special Drama interrupt the narrative, rather than link the serious (deep) scenes together (see Karnad 1994, 7–8).

6. Author interview, May 14, 2004.

7. Mathrabootham gained fame through his Vijay TV show, *Puthira Punithama?* (*Mystery or Sanctity?*), on which he answered viewers' questions about sex (see Venkatraman 2001). He has also acted in a few Tamil films.

8. This title is obscure, but according to Sreevatson it is meant to refer to a Latin phrase meaning "intention to defraud."

9. Author interview with V. Sreevatson, October 23, 2003.

10. See Vindhan 1998 for more on M. R. Radha.

11. Richard Frasca, for example, in his research on *terukkūttu*, found that many drama troupes would let him record performances but not see the paper/palm leaf manuscripts that were the archive of the troupe, because those were what made their *terukkūttu* style unique and distinct from all the other troupes. "These manuscripts represented an organic link with previous generations of great *kūttu* teachers and artistes, a continuity that had to be maintained and guarded if a group was going to be successful in the rapidly modernizing India of today"

(1990, 39). Hiltebeitel 1988 and 1991 and de Bruin 1999 are also comprehensive studies of this folk genre.

12. Shekher is not a playwright, but owns the rights to the plays written for Natakhapriya, and decided to publish them all in 2004.

13. *Marriage Made in Saloon* was produced as *Poikkal Kudhirai* by K. Balachander, and Shekher directed his own play as the film *Krishna Krishna.*

14. V. Lakshmanan, secretary of Humour Club International, Madras Main Chapter, quoted in Vijayalakshmi 2003.

15. *Āyiram poy colliyāvatu oru kalyāṇattai cey.*

16. The *Natyasastra* (200 BCE–200 CE) was the first text to establish connoisseurship. For elaborations of *rasa* theory and details on appropriate responses to various types of performances, see Selby 2000; Ingalls 1965; Schwartz 2004.

17. See Aju James 2020 on standup comedy in Mumbai.

18. Quoted in Sudakar 1981, 91. My translation.

19. This is especially true of Crazy Creations. The writer (Crazy Mohan) and the lead male actor (Crazy Balaji) are actually brothers, and they refer to the troupe (Crazy Creations) and their closest fans and supporters as the "Crazy Family."

20. See Ramaswamy 1997 on Tamil and Deshpande 2007 on Marathi.

21. Since most plays are not published, many actors write out their individual parts in notebooks. I noticed at a Viveka Fine Arts rehearsal that many actors brought copies of the published book to refer to.

22. S. Ve. Shekher told me that it costs about 4,000 rupees to commission an artist to paint one of these curtains.

23. Author interview with A. R. Srinivasan, May 14, 2004.

24. This is very well documented. For examples, see Jordan 2003; Gaston 1996; Hansen 1992; Seizer 2005.

25. Sangita Shresthova suggests watching the "Mukabla Humse Nakara" song-and-dance from the film Prince (1969), where the plot of a friendly dance competition allows for "a brilliant display of Hindi cinema's interpretation of Indian and non-Indian dance movements for specific characters in the narrative" (2011, 28).

26. Author interview with R. Neelakanthan, October 29, 2003.

27. Ibid.

28. Pritham Chakravarty, who acted with the troupe Shantiniketan as a child, told me that she was paid 30 rupees per show. By the time she stopped around age fifteen (1978 or so) she was paid 500 rupees for a sabha play in Chennai and more if it was outside the city (interview, February 28, 2004). Kamala Kamesh, an older actress, told me that she used to receive 100 rupees per play and agreed with Pritham that the going rate is now 500 rupees for an evening performance (interview, April 22, 2004). Male actor Kaladhar Parthasarathy told me that he receives only 100 rupees for an evening show in Chennai compared to 500 rupees

for an out-of-station performance and 1,000 rupees a day for television (author interview, August 16, 2003).

Notes to Chapter Four

1. I use the phrase "cultural performance" in the way that Mary Hancock does (Hancock 1999). She expanded Milton Singer's conception (Singer 1959), which included the more obvious secular performances found in theaters, concert halls, radio programs, and films as well as private and public religious rituals, to include things such as dress, diet, and home décor.

2. I am working primarily from the 1999 novel, which is pretty faithful to the *Āṉanta Vikaṭan* version, but also from my performance notes and a recording of the first fourteen episodes of the 1995 television serial. This recording was provided to me by actor R. Neelakanthan, who plays the groom's father on television and was an active member of the stage troupe Viveka Fine Arts until his death in 2018. He did not act in the stage version of *Washingtonil Tirumaṇam* with Goodwill Stage.

3. No one ever suggested that she go to India to fulfill this desire. The ideal is that wealthy people, especially women, do not travel for their shopping or entertainment. They pay the salesmen and performers to come to them. This may be one reason why the marriage had to take place in Mrs. Rockefeller's hometown, rather than her traveling to India to observe a wedding. At the end of the novel, she does offer to fly to India to personally conduct the marriage of Lali and Panju, who were so helpful to her with this marriage.

4. This is different from Fredric Jameson's (1989) idea of "nostalgia for the present," where there is less concern for creating a usable record of traditions for posterity and more of a focus on reifying the present as a nameable, datable, historical period. Rather than being concerned with the attributes of a particular time period, cultural expressions of pre-emptive nostalgia express the fear of loss of "tradition" and celebrate the ideal way things *should be*, not the way things stereotypically *are*.

5. Members of a tribe of traditional trappers and hunters in Tamilnadu.

6. A "lingam" is an aniconic representation of the god Siva.

7. Design in rice flour often done outside the entrance to a building (called a *rangoli* in North India).

8. Most saris are six yards. The nine-yard sari is worn exclusively by Brahmin women in Tamilnadu, and by very few of the younger generation, except perhaps for marriage.

9. One of my favorite images from my fieldwork is from a very elaborate ceremony held by some Brahmin friends to celebrate the construction of their new home behind the Music Academy. There were many priests involved in the

function, and every one of them carried a cell phone. These phones were hung around their necks or tucked into the waistband of their veshtis and were constantly being used. On this auspicious day there were a number of functions to coordinate and traditionally dressed priests with their sacred threads, topknots, and markings of ash and kumkum were busy coming in and out as needed and sending one another text messages.

10. A double-reed woodwind instrument that is considered to be auspicious and often found at temples and weddings.

Notes to Chapter Five

1. This is an approximate date for the tenth play produced by Kathadi Ramamurthy for his troupe Stage Creations. Ramamurthy originally thought it was earlier, but it has to be after 1976, when Crazy Mohan wrote *Crazy Thieves in Palavakkam* for S. Ve. Shekher and earned his nickname, and before 1979, when he founded his own troupe Crazy Creations. See appendix C for my translation of the first scene of *Honeymoon Couple.*

2. See appendix E for a partial family tree of sabha drama troupes. Kathadi Ramamurthy, for example, left Viveka Fine Arts, to which Cho Ramasamy had come from United Amateur Artists. In 2004, at age sixty-seven, Kathadi celebrated fifty years of acting and forty years of his troupe Stage Creations (founded 1966) with a festival put on by the troupe and Raadhu's Nataka Academy. The celebrations included eight nights of dramas from May 1–4 and 6–9, 2004. (See figures 5.4 and 5.5 for the program of this celebration.) In 2016, he celebrated sixty years of acting and fifty years of Stage Creations.

3. http://www.crazymohan.com/index.htm, viewed May 28, 2007.

4. This role was originally played by Sambu Nataraja Iyer, who handpicked Kathadi to play his role when he decided to revive the play. He says, " 'I have nothing to lose really. Either way, I will be praised for this decision. If Kathadi does a good job, I will be praised for the selection. If he does a poor job, people will praise me saying that no one can match Nataraja Iyer.' He came back after the play and patted Kathadi on the back with the words 'you have played it much better than I did. I am proud of you.' Those were unforgettable words of praise for Kathadi, one he still cherishes" (Prabhu 2014).

5. See Kevin Calcamp (2016) for more on this phenomenon between Hollywood and Broadway.

6. January 19, 2004, at function for Hamsadhwani's inauguratory drama, *Kalyāṇattil Kalāṭṭā* (*Wedding Fiasco*) by Raadhu with Kathadi Ramamurthy in the role of the boy's father.

7. A good example is Purnam Viswanathan's *Undersecretary*, which is discussed in chapter 6. This is also evident in the fantasies of cinema. Peter Manuel

wrote that in films "it is not the poor that are celebrated, but rather synthetic, urban, Westernized luxury. In this sense the films can be seen as responses to a mass desire for escapism, and as reflections of the ideology of the affluent corporate producers" (1988, 160).

Notes to Chapter Six

1. Her mother's brother's son (see Trawick 1990 on Tamil kin relations).

2. The story and dialogue were written by T. D. R. (T. Durai Raj) and the special effects, script editing, and direction are by S. Ve. Shekher.

3. Hyderabad, the capital of what is now Telangana State (which was the capital of Andhra Pradesh until that state split in two in 2014), is a Telugu-speaking area that can be reached by an overnight train from Chennai.

4. He wrote the famous plays *Flight 172* (1970) and *Hare Rama Hare Krishna* (1971) while he was with them. Mouli is one of the rare playwrights who kept the rights to his plays. His brother S. B. Kanthan is the director for sabha drama troupe Crazy Creations.

5. Rangarajan 2003. He had been president of the organization for eight years as of November 2003.

6. http://mylaporemla.blogspot.com/2006/06/s-ve-shekher-is-mylapores-mla.html, viewed June 18, 2007.

7. John Bernard Bate describes them as debates on "pre-determined topics on everyday life or literature" in which "two sides take opposing positions and argue several rounds, frequently involving comic asides and jabs at their opponents, which are finally resolved in a long (1–2 hour) summation of the argument and problem being debated by the 'Judge' (*nītipati*) or 'Mediator' (*naṭuvar*) of the proceedings" (2000, 10–11). I went to see Shekher present to a group of shopkeepers in Madurai who were learning about a new Cadbury Bourn Vita product they would be selling and when he was the announcer for the Miss Sahodaran transgender beauty pageant.

8. In fact, he doesn't think he has the unequivocal support of the Brahmin community. He said of his close margin of victory in the election over the DMK candidate, actor Napoleon, that "the Lok Paritran candidate seems to split the votes. Votes from the Brahmin community, the educated and of the young seem to have gone to the Lok Paritran candidate" (*Mylapore MLA*. http://mylaporemla.blogspot.com/2006/06/s-ve-shekher-is-mylapores-mla.html, June 1, 2006. Blog viewed on June 17, 2007). More recently however, he has been an active advocate for Brahmins, founding the "Federation of Brahmin Association" and sending a mass email through his MLA account on March 30, 2009, that read "Federation of Brahmin Association Founder President S Ve Shekher & Sree Raadhu met Tamil Nadu Honourable CM Dr. Kalingar & gave the representation for 7% reservation

to Brahmins in Tamil Nadu for social justice. Receiving the memorandum, CM said that he will consider and do the needfull [*sic*]. FEBAS will support Brahmin candidates only irrespective of parties or to the party which supports the reservation to Brahmins of Tamilnadu. S Ve Shekher will go for campaign after Tamil New Year to reach all Brahmins in Tamilnadu."

9. Author interview with M. B. Moorthy, May 16, 2004.

10. A few of the plays are *Oru Kolai, Oru Prayanam*, which is actually two short plays with an intermission; *Anpulla Appa*; *Uruvan Patukal*; *Dr. Narendra*; *Adimehal*; *Maratal Varum*; and *Unjal*, which was a play based on *Death of a Salesman* that was done on stage then appeared on TV in 1990 or so. Purnam's daughter Uma called it a "very touching story" in which Purnam plays the head of family with plans for various projects he's trying to earn 15,000 rupees for. She related that after seeing the play, her sister came and brought Purnam the money the next day (My interview, May 20, 2004).

11. My interview with M. B. Murthy and other members of Gurukulam, May 16, 2004.

12. Personal conversation with Dr. Sankaran Radhakrishnan, July 2002.

13. See Rachel Tolen (2000) on moneylending practices between employers and servants.

14. A famous street in north Madras city.

15. Dried and powdered turmeric mixed with slaked lime.

16. http://www.doubletongued.org/index.php/dictionary/love_cum_arranged_marriage/. Accessed March 2, 2022.

17. See Krishnakumar 2001 and Selby 2001 on the Chennai water supply.

Notes to Chapter Seven

1. Ibn Battuta is also a real historical figure. He was a fourteenth-century Islamic scholar and explorer.

2. Delhi Ganesh, a film actor who used to do stage plays with Kathadi Ramamurthy (and did perform for Kathadi's 2004 Golden Jubilee), told me that "acting in one film is equivalent to acting in a thousand dramas" in terms of both publicity and remuneration. His opinion that no one stays with the stage because they prefer it over film is widely held. If those actors were called to the film world, he told me, they would "forget stage." Author interview with Delhi Ganesh, April 24, 2004.

3. There is too much literature to cite it all here, but Sivathamby 1981, Perumal 1981, Seizer 2005, Sundaram 2014, Rajendran 1989, Bhagavathy 2000 (especially Arasu's chapter), Ilango 1998, and Mangai 2015 offer a broad representation.

4. Only one Tamil play, Indira Parthasarathy's *Aurangzeb*, has made it into one of the anthologies of Indian drama that have been published. These include

G. P. Deshpande's *Modern Indian Drama: An Anthology* (2000), Erin Mee's *DramaContemporary: India* (2001), and *City Plays*, which Mahesh Dattani wrote the introduction for (2004).

5. Of the seventy-three performances at the 2004 National School of Drama Theater Festival I attended, there were three Tamil performances: Magic Lantern's translation/adaptation of a Dario Fo play, N. Muthuswamy's *Prahaladha Charitram* directed by Israeli Gil Alon, and Kalairani's *Varukalāmō*, a solo performance in Tamil and English. With the exception of Kalairani, these were multinational performances, and all had only brief runs in Chennai at the Alliance Française and more critical and international appeal than the regionally insular sabha plays that may remain in a troupe's active repertory for more than fifty years (See *National School of Drama's Sixth National Theatre Festival Performance Schedule* 2004). Kalairani's work is discussed in detail by Sameera Iyengar (2001).

6. Yaksagana is a folk-theater form from Karnataka that incorporates singing, drumming, dancing, words with gestural interpretation, and colorful costumes. "Natak company" refers to touring professional drama companies found throughout India who generally perform historical and mythological dramas for various village festivals.

7. "Theatre of Roots" refers to a movement in India theater to shift away from colonial influences by turning for inspiration to what were considered pan-Indian theatrical styles. Modern theater artists looked to incorporate Sanskrit drama and folk-theater conventions in their work in a nationalist project that was meant to develop an "Indian" theater.

8. Biographic information is from the book jacket of Ramasamy 1997.

9. D. Narayanswamy (also known as Naani), R. Neelakanthan (also known as Neelu), V. R. Srinivasan, J. Muthuswamy, Kathadi Ramamurthy, Sai Srinivasan, P. N. Kumar, and A. N. Radhakrishnan. This list is from the souvenir from the group's golden jubilee (Viveka Fine Arts Club 2004).

10. This information is from the book jacket of Ramasamy 1997.

11. My translation of an abridged version of this play with an introduction will be published in *Ecumenica* in 2022 (Part I in Spring and Part II in Fall).

12. Shankar 2001b, 123–24. Shankar wrote in 2001 that "*Water!* is certainly one of the more significant Tamil dramatic works of the twentieth century. It was, in addition, tremendously successful commercially—the most successful of Swaminathan's plays, it has been staged more than two hundred and fifty times and still finds the occasional production, both for urban and rural audiences" (Shankar 2001b, 123). K. Balachander's 1981 Tamil film *Thaneer Thaneer* that is based on the play and the publication of Shankar's translation have brought Swaminathan some international recognition, but he is not that visible on the Tamil scene any longer. Only one audience member cited him as their favorite writer on my survey, as opposed to forty-nine votes for Cho.

13. Author interview with R. Neelakanthan, October 29, 2003.

14. March 15, 1971, p. 4.

15. Tughlaq promised that any members of Parliament that joined his party would be appointed deputy prime minister. This resulted in Tughlaq's government boasting one prime minister and a total of 450 deputy prime ministers.

16. In her 2019 work on modern Indian drama, Aparna Dharwadker talks about "closet dramas," which are exclusively literary, and notes that there are many in Tamil, though none of these really made it into the national modern Indian canon, either. She mentions Pammala Sambanda Mudaliar in a list of "prolific playwrights whose drama becomes a mainstay of the 'amateur' theatre in their respective regions, gives them literary pre-eminence and great success in their language, but leads to little visibility on the national stage" (lvii–lviii). Other Tamil playwrights she includes here are "C. N. Annadurai (1909–1969) and M. Karunanidhi (1924–2018), whose entry into regional and national politics at the highest level was through populist social and political theatre, acting, and cinema in Tamil. The progressively most recent chronology of these authors indicates that 'literary' and 'closet' drama are not just phenomena of the colonial period but penetrate well into the post-independence era to constitute a visible though theatrically negligible creative practice" (lviii).

17. Several of Cho's plays, including *Mohammad bin Tughlaq* (1971), were also released as films. Following Viveka Fine Arts Golden Jubilee in 2004 five recorded stage plays were released on DVD and VCD. These were *Judgement Reserved*, *Nērmai Uṟaṅkam Nēram* (*When Honesty Sleeps*), *Mohammad bin Tughlaq*, *Campavāmi Yukē Yukē* (*I Appear Age After Age*), and *Cāttiram Coṉṉatillai* (*The Scriptures Don't Say So*).

18. One great example of performativity in this play is the stylized way that Cho walks as Mohammad bin Tughlaq. There is consistently an odd little hop in his step for this role that he doesn't use in any other play I've seen. I was greatly puzzled by this until I read in one of the histories of Tamil drama that in the older historical dramas of the nineteenth century the actors playing kings would rub jackfruit on the soles of their shoes to deliberately slow down their steps and lend them dignity. It is possible that Cho is imitating this practice in his portrayal of Mohammad bin Tughlaq.

19. I have not been able to find a first-run copy, but the second printing was in 1995. It is likely that the first printing was in the early 1990s, when some of Cho's other famous plays were first published.

20. With the possible exception of Malayalam.

21. See Gokhale 2000 for more on modern Marathi theater.

Notes to the Epilogue

1. It was also suggested to me in an interview that waking in the morning and looking for a pot of water could be interpreted as the guru needing to go to the toilet, which is another subtle opening for humor.

2. I've seen a few other plays (one by S. L. Naanu and one by T. V. Varadarajan) where main characters are classical musicians, but when they "play" music on stage they merely mime silently along to recorded music.

3. Two awardees were chosen for each category and this play won Best Drama as well as Best Actor (for Sreevatson), Best Director (for Giridhar), Best Story Dialogue (for Sreevatson), Consolation Actor (for Sridhar), Best Actress (Hemalatha), the Best Drama S. Ve. Shekher Shield, the Best Director K. Balachander Shield (for Giridhar), and the Best Actor Late Gopalakrishnan Shield (for Sreevatson). "KFA Nataka Vizha Results," *The Hindu*, May 21, 2004.

Notes to the Appendixes

1. This list is taken from *Natakapriya 4001* (A Souvenir on the Occasion of Natakapriya's 4001st performance), January 1, 2001.

2. I was told by K. S. Narayan on October 10, 2003, that the Music Academy rented for 30,000 rupees a day.

3. I was told by K. S. Narayan on October 10, 2003 that the Museum Theater rented for 12,500 rupees a day and he expected the rent to be raised to 18,000 rupees soon.

4. This list is taken from *Natakhapriya 5007* (A Souvenir on the Occasion of Natakhapriya's 5007th performance), January 1, 2007.

5. List compiled by the author from *The Hindu* events listings from 1992.

6. List compiled by the author from *The Hindu* events listings from 2004.

7. List compiled by author using website https://musicofmadras.in/.

8. With special thanks for the assistance of Pritham Chakravarty and Sankaran Radhakrishnan.

9. *Aiyram Poi* ("A Thousand Lies") is a real film from 1972.

10. This is "Satyam" Theater, one of the biggest cinema theaters in Madras.

11. With special thanks for the assistance of Sankaran Radhakrishnan and Sam Sudhananda.

12. Tirupati is a city in Andhra Pradesh that is home to the Tirumala Venkateswara Temple, considered one of the richest temples in the world and an important site of Vaishnava pilgrimage. It is approximately 50km from the Tamilnadu state border and when the state lines were redrawn along linguistic lines in 1956, dividing the former Madras Presidency into Tamil and Telugu, this city was a point of contention.

13. Tanjavore is in the middle of Tamilnadu, nowhere near the Andhra Pradesh border, so this is not at all practical.

14. Sometimes noted as "Ragini Creations."

Bibliography

English Sources

aarvalan. "Bodendral's Life Depicted." *Sabhash!* February 22, 2014.

Abrams, Meyer H. "A Glossary of Literary Terms" (1941). In *Satire: Theory and Practice*, edited by Charles A. Allen and George D. Stephens, 36–47. Belmont, CA: Wadsworth Publishing Company, 1962.

"AIADMK Legislators Being Held Captive, Tortured by Goons, Alleges Paneerselvam." *The Hindu*, February 13, 2017.

Allen, Charles A. and George D. Stephens, eds. *Satire: Theory and Practice*. Belmont, CA: Wadsworth Publishing Company, Inc., 1962.

Allen, Matthew Harp. "Rewriting the Script for South Indian Dance." *The Drama Review* 41, no. 3 (Fall 1997): 63–100.

Anand, S. *Brahmans and Cricket: Lagaan's Millennial Purana and Other Myths*. Chennai: Navayana, 2003.

Anderson, Benedict. *Imagined Communities: Reflections on the Origin and Spread of Nationalism* (new edition). New York: Verso, 2006.

Appadurai, Arjun. *Modernity at Large: Cultural Dimensions of Globalization*. Minneapolis: University of Minnesota Press, 1996.

Apte, Mahadev L. *Humor and Communication in Contemporary Marathi Theater: A Sociolinguistic Perspective*. Pune: Linguistic Society of India, 1992.

Arnold, Matthew. *Culture and Anarchy*. Edited by Samuel Lipman. New Haven, CT: Yale University Press, 1993.

Arokianathan, S. *Language Use in Mass Media*. New Delhi: Creative Publishers, 1988.

Arudra. *E. Krishna Iyer Centenery Issue*. Madras: Music Academy, 1997.

Bairy, Ramesh. *Being Brahmin, Being Modern: Exploring the Lives of Caste Today*. New Delhi: Routledge India, 2013.

Banerji, Arnab. *Contemporary Group Theatre in Kolkata, India*. London: Routledge, 2020.

Banfield, Chris. "Girish Karnad and an Indian Theatre of Roots." In *An Introduction to Post-Colonial Theatre*, edited by Brian Crow with Chris Banfield, 136–60. Cambridge: Cambridge University Press, 1996.

Barnett, Marguerite Ross. *The Politics of Cultural Nationalism in South India*. Princeton, NJ: Princeton University Press, 1976.

Baskaran, S. Theodore. *The Message Bearers: The Nationalist Politics and the Entertainment Media in South India, 1880–1945*. Madras: Cre-A, 1981.

Bate, Bernard. *Tamil Oratory and the Dravidian Aesthetic: Democratic Practice in South India*. New York: Columbia University Press, 2009.

———. *See also* Bate, John Bernard

Bate, John Bernard. "*Mēṭaittamiḻ*: Oratory and Democratic Practice in Tamilnadu." PhD diss., University of Chicago, 2000.

———. *See also* Bate, Bernard

Baumer, Rachel Van M., and James R. Brandon, eds. *Sanskrit Drama in Performance*. Honolulu: University of Hawaiʻi Press, 1981.

Baviskar, Amita and Raka Ray, eds. *Elite and Everyman: The Cultural Politics of the Indian Middle Classes*. New Delhi: Routledge India, 2011.

Belson, Ken, and Heather Timmons. "A Basketball Deal in India, Where Cricket in King." *The New York Times N.B.A. Blog*, June 21, 2010. http://offthedribble.blogs.nytimes.com/2010/06/21/a-basketball-deal-in-india-where-cricket-is-king/. Accessed June 21, 2010.

Beteille, Andre. *Caste, Class, and Power: Changing Patterns of Stratification in a Tanjore Village*. Berkeley: University of California Press, 1965.

Bhatia, Nandi. *Acts of Authority/Acts of Resistance: Theater and Politics in Colonial and Postcolonial India*. New Delhi: Oxford University Press, 2004.

Bhuvaneshwari, V. "Trading in Laughter." *Indian Express*, July 19, 2003.

Blackburn, Stuart. *Rama Stories and Shadow Puppets: Kambaṉ's Rāmāyaṇa in Performance*. Delhi: Oxford University Press, 1997.

Bombay Chanakya Facebook Page. https://www.facebook.com/bombay.chanakya. Accessed June 1, 2020.

"Bombay Gnanam's New Play 'Bhaja Govindam' Draws Big Audience." *The Mylapore Times*, April 4, 2015. [online] http://www.mylaporetimes.com/2015/04/bombay-gnanams-new-play-bhaja-govindam-draws-big-audience/. Accessed August 28, 2015.

Bourdieu, Pierre. *Distinction: A Social Critique of the Judgement of Taste*. Cambridge, MA: Harvard University Press, 1984.

Brians, Paul. *Modern South Asian Literature in English*. Westport, CT: Greenwood Press, 2003.

Brosius, Christiane. "The Gated Romance of 'India Shining': Visualizing Urban Lifestyle in Advertisement of Residential Housing Development." In *Popular Culture in a Globalized India*, edited by K. Moti Gokulsing and Wimal Dissanayake, 174–91. London and New York: Routledge, 2009.

———. *India's Middle Class: New Forms of Urban Leisure, Consumption and Prosperity.* New Delhi: Routledge India, 2010.

Bruin, Hanne de. *Kaṭṭaikkūttu: The Flexibility of a South Indian Theatre Tradition.* Groningen: Egbert Forsten, 1999.

Butcher, Melissa. *Transnational Television, Cultural Identity and Change: When STAR Came to India.* New Delhi: Sage Publications, 2003.

Calcamp, Kevin. "The Semiotics of Celebrity at the Intersection of Hollywood and Broadway." PhD diss., Bowling Green State University, 2016.

Caldwell, Robert. *A Comparative Grammar of the Dravidian or South-Indian Family of Languages.* 3rd ed. Edited and revised by J. L. Wyatt. New Delhi: Oriental Books Reprint Corporation, 1974.

Cawelti, John G. *Adventure, Mystery, and Romance: Formula Stories as Art and Popular Culture.* Chicago: University of Chicago Press, 1976.

Chaitanya, Krishna. "Indian Dance: Naïve Longings for Winds of Change." *Sangeet Natak* 83 (January–March 1987): 5–13.

Chanda, Arup. "Cho Ramaswamy 50 Years of Drama." *Tribune India*, July 11, 2004. http://www.tribuneindia.com/2004/20040711/spectrum/main2.htm. Accessed August 8, 2006.

Charukesi. "Sixty Years on the Stage—and Fifty Years of His Theatre Group." *Madras Musings*, February 1–15, 2017.

Chatterjee, Partha. *The Nation and Its Fragments: Colonial and Postcolonial Histories.* Princeton, NJ: Princeton University Press, 1993.

Chennai Online. http://www.chennaionline.com/musicseason99/sabhainfo.asp. Accessed November 30, 2005.

Chuyen, Gilles. *Who Is a Brahmin? The Politics of Identity in India.* Delhi: Manohar, 2005.

City Plays. With an introduction by Mahesh Dattani. Calcutta: Seagull Books, 2004.

Dalmia, Vasudha. *Poetics, Plays, and Performances: The Politics of Modern Indian Theatre.* New Delhi: Oxford University Press, 2006.

Dasarathan, A. *See* Gurusami, S.

Deivasundaram, N. *Tamil Diglossia.* Tirunelveli: Nainar Pathippagam, 1981.

Deshpande, G. P., ed. *Modern Indian Drama: An Anthology.* Delhi: Sahitya Akademi, 2000.

Deshpande, Prachi. "Narratives of Pride: History and Regional Identity in Maharashtra, India c. 1870–1960." PhD diss., Tufts University, 2002.

———. *Creative Pasts: Historical Memory and Identity in Western India, 1700–1960.* New York: Columbia University Press, 2007.

Devi, Mahasweta. *Mother of 1084.* [1974] In *Modern Indian Drama: An Anthology*, edited by G. P. Deshpande, 681–711. New Delhi: Sahitya Akademi, 2000.

Dhanavel, P. *The Indian Imagination of Girish Karnad: Essays on Hayavadana.* New Delhi: Prestige Books, 2000.

Dharwadker, Aparna. *Theatres of Independence: Drama, Theory, and Urban Performance in India Since 1947.* Iowa City: University of Iowa Press, 2005.

———. *A Poetics of Modernity: Indian Theatre Theory 1850 to the Present.* Delhi: Oxford University Press, 2019.

Dickey, Sara. *Cinema and the Urban Poor in South India.* New York: Cambridge University Press, 1993.

———. "Mutual Exclusions: Domestic Workers and Employers on Labor, Class, and Character in South India." In *Home and Hegemony: Domestic Service and Identity Politics in South and Southeast Asia*, edited by Kathleen M. Adams and Sara Dickey, 31–62. Ann Arbor: University of Michigan Press, 2000a.

———. "Permeable Homes: Domestic Service, Household Space, and the Vulnerability of Class Boundaries in Urban India." *American Ethnologist* 27, no. 2 (May 2000b): 462–89.

Dirks, Nicholas B. *The Hollow Crown: Ethnohistory of an Indian Kingdom.* Cambridge: Cambridge University Press, 1988.

———. "Recasting Tamil Society: The Politics of Caste and Race in Contemporary Southern India." In *Caste Today*, edited by C. J. Fuller, 263–95. Delhi: Oxford India Press, 1996.

———, ed. *In Near Ruins: Cultural Theory at the End of the Century.* Minneapolis: University of Minnesota Press, 1998.

———. *Caste of Mind: Colonialism and the Making of Modern India.* Princeton, NJ: Princeton University Press, 2002.

Donner, Henrike, ed. *Being Middle-Class in India: A Way of Life.* New York: Routledge, 2011.

Donner, Henrike, and Geert de Neve. "Introduction." In *Being Middle-Class in India: A Way of Life*, edited by Henrike Donner, 1–22. New York: Routledge, 2011.

Driver, Edwin D. "Class, Caste, and 'Status Summation' in Urban South India." *Contributions to Indian Sociology (NS)* 16, no. 2 (1982): 225–53.

Dummies Communications. Play advertisement. Chennai, 2003.

Dwyer, Rachel. *All You Want Is Money, All You Need is Love: Sexuality and Romance in Modern India.* London: Cassell, 2000.

Economic Times. "India to Conduct First Caste Census in 80 Years." September 5, 2010. http://economictimes.indiatimes.com/news/politics/nation/India-to-conduct-first-caste-census-in-80-years/articleshow/6525484.cms. Accessed September 27, 2010.

Fernandes, Leela. "Nationalizing 'the Global': Media Images, Cultural Politics and the Middle Class in India." *Media, Culture, and Society* 22, no. 5 (2000): 611–28.

———. *India's New Middle Class: Democratic Politics in an Era of Economic Reform.* New Delhi: Oxford University Press, 2006.

Ferro-Luzzi, Gabriella Eichinger. *The Taste of Laughter: Aspects of Tamil Humour.* Wiesbaden: Otto Harrassowitz, 1992.

Frasca, Richard Armando. *The Theater of the Mahabharata: Terukkūttu Performances in South India.* Honolulu: University of Hawai'i Press, 1990.

Frye, Northrup. "The Nature of Satire" (from *The University of Toronto Quarterly* 14 [October 1944]). In *Satire: Theory and Practice*, edited by Charles A. Allen and George D. Stephens, 15–30. Belmont, CA: Wadsworth Publishing Company, 1962.

Fuller, C. J., ed. *Caste Today.* Delhi: Oxford University Press, 1996.

———. "The Brahmins and Brahminical Values in Modern Tamil Nadu." In *Institutions and Inequalities: Essays in Honour of Andre Beteille*, edited by Ramachandra Guha and Jonathan P. Parry, 30–55. Delhi: Oxford University Press, 1999.

Fuller, C. J., and Haripriya Narasimhan. "Information Technology Professionals and the New-Rich Middle Class in Chennai (Madras)." *Modern Asian Studies* 41, no. 1 (2007): 121–50.

———. *Tamil Brahmans: The Making of a Middle-Class Caste.* Chicago: University of Chicago Press, 2014.

Ganesan, Sivaji. *Autobiography of an Actor.* Translated by Sabita Radhakrishna. Chennai: Sivaji Prabhu Charities Trust, 2007. (Tamil original, 2002.)

Ganguly-Scrase, Ruchira, and Timothy J. Scrase. *Globalization and the Middle Classes in India: The Social and Cultural Impact of Neoliberal Reforms.* London and New York: Routledge, 2009.

Gans, Herbert J. *Popular Culture and High Culture: An Analysis and Evaluation of Taste.* Revised and updated edition. New York: Basic Books, 1999.

Gaston, Anne-Marie. *Bharata Natyam: From Temple to Theatre.* New Delhi: Manohar, 1996.

Geetha, V., and S. V. Rajadurai. *Towards a Non-Brahmin Millennium: From Iyothee Thass to Periyar.* Calcutta: Samya, 1998.

Gilroy, Paul. "Sounds Authentic: Black Music, Ethnicity, and the Challenge of a Changing Same." In *Imagining Home: Class, Culture, and Nationalism in the Black Diaspora*, edited by Sidney Lemelle and Robin D. G. Kelley. New York: Verso, 1994.

Gokhale, Shanta. *Playwright at the Centre: Marathi Drama from 1843 to the Present.* Calcutta: Seagull Books, 2000.

Google Maps. Chennai Map. https://www.google.com/maps/place/Chennai,+Tamil+Nadu,+India/@13.0478221,80.06 85816,11z/data=!3m1!4b1!4m5!3m4!1s0 x3a5265ea4f7d3361:0x6e61a70b6863d433!8m 2!3d13.0826802!4d80.2707184

Gopalie, S. (aka K. S. Narayanaswami). "Metro Amateur Theatre (1965–1985): A Project Report." Senior Fellowship of Cultural Ministry, 2002.

Government of Tamil Nadu Law Department. *The Tamil Nadu Societies Registration Act.* Tamil Nadu Act 27 of 1975.

Gupt, Somnath. *The Parsi Theatre: Its Origins and Development.* Translated and edited by Kathryn Hansen. Kolkata: Seagull Books, 2005.

Hall, Stuart. "The Question of Cultural Identity." In *Modernity and Its Futures: Understanding Modern Societies*, edited by Tony McGrew, Stuart Hall, and David Held, 273–326. Cambridge: Polity Press, 1992.

———. "Introduction: Who Needs Identity?" In *Questions of Cultural Identity*, edited by Stuart Hall and Paul du Gay, 1–17. London: Sage, 1996a.

———. "The Question of Cultural Identity" in Modernity: An Introduction to Modern Societies edited by Stuart Hall and Paul du Gay, 596–634. Oxford: Blackwell, 1996b.

Hancock, Mary Elizabeth. "Women at Work: Ritual and Cultural Identity Among Smarta Brahmans of Madras." PhD diss., University of Pennsylvania, 1990.

———. *Womanhood in the Making: Domestic Ritual and Public Culture in Urban South India.* Boulder, CO: Westview Press, 1999.

Hansen, Kathryn. *Grounds for Play: The Nautanki Theatre of North India.* Berkeley, CA: University of California Press, 1992.

———. "The *Indar Sabha* Phenomenon: Public Theatre and Consumption in Greater India (1853–1956)." In *Pleasure and the Nation: The History, Politics and Consumption of Public Culture in India*, edited by Christopher Pinney and Rachel Dwyer, 76–114. New Delhi: Oxford University Press, 2001.

———. "Tamil Drama in Colonial Madras: The Parsi Theatre Connection." *South Asian History and Culture* (October 11, 2020): 1–20.

Hardgrave, Robert L., Jr. *The Dravidian Movement.* Bombay: Popular Prakashan, 1965.

———. *The Nadars of Tamilnad: The Political Culture of a Community in Change.* Berkeley: University of California Press, 1969.

———. *Essays in the Political Sociology of South India.* New Delhi: Manohar Publishers, 1979.

Hardgrave, Robert L., Jr., and Stanley A. Kochanek. *India: Government and Politics in a Developing Nation.* 6th ed. Fort Worth, TX: Harcourt College Publishers, 2000.

Harriss, John. "The Great Tradition Globalizes: Reflections on Two Studies of the Industrial Leaders' of Madras." *Modern Asian Studies* 37, no. 2 (2003): 327–62.

Higgins, Jon B. "From Prince to Populace: Patronage as a Determinant of Change in South Indian (Karnatak) Music." *Asian Music* 7, no. 2 (1976): 20–26.

Hiltebeitel, Alf. *The Cult of Draupadi,* Volume 1, "Mythologies from Gingee to Kurukshetra." Chicago: University of Chicago Press, 1988.

———. *The Cult of Draupadi,* Volume 2, "On Hindu Ritual and the Goddess." Chicago: University of Chicago Press, 1991.

Indian Constitution. http://www.constitution.org/cons/india/tamnd76.htm. Accessed November 16, 2005.

Indian Express. "Get Ready for *The Vagina Monologues*." March 8, 2004

———. "Why Brahmins Root for Jaya." April 19, 2004.

Ingalls, Daniel H. H. *Sanskrit Poetry from Vidyakara's "Treasury."* Cambridge, MA: The Belknap Press of Harvard University Press, 1965.

Irschick, Eugene. *Tamil Revivalism in the 1930s.* Madras: Cre-A, 1986.
Ivy, Marilyn. *Discourses of the Vanishing: Modernity, Phantasm, Japan.* Chicago: University of Chicago Press, 1995.
Iyengar, Geetha. "Sabhanayaka: M. Krishnamurthy, Parthasarathy Swami Sabha." 2003. http://carnatica.net/nvr/partha-sabha.htm. Accessed November 29, 2005.
Iyengar, Sameera. "Performing Presences: Feminism and the Theatre in India." Ph.D. diss., University of Chicago, 2001.
Jagadheesan, L. R. "Caste Politics." *Aside*, December 31, 1991, 8–11.
Jagannathan, N. S. "Interview with G.P. Deshpande." In *Contemporary Indian Theatre: Interviews with Playwrights and Directors. For the Festival of Contemporary Theatre held September 3–17, 1989, for Nehru's Birth Centenary*, 103–12. New Delhi: Sangeet Natak Akademi, 1989.
James, Aju. "Spaces of Laughter: Stand-up Comedy in Mumbai as a Site of Struggle over Globalization and National Identity." PhD diss., Bowling Green State University, 2020.
Jameson, Fredric. "Nostalgia for the Present." *South Atlantic Quarterly* 88, no. 2 (Spring 1989): 517–37.
Johnson, E. Patrick. *Appropriating Blackness: Performance and the Politics of Authenticity.* Durham, NC: Duke University Press, 2003.
Jordan, Kay K. *From Sacred Servant to Profane Prostitute: A History of the Changing Legal Status of the Devadasis in India, 1857–1947.* New Delhi: Manohar, 2003.
Joshi, Sanjay. *Fractured Modernity: Making of a Middle Class in Colonial North India.* New Delhi: Oxford University Press, 2001.
Kalakshetra: Devotion to Dance. Videocassette. Produced by Adam Clapham for Griffin Productions and directed by Anthony Mayer. Boulder, CO: Centre Productions, 1985.
Kannan, Ramya. "Crazy Humor Set to Stage a Comeback with a Bang." *The Hindu*, June 25, 2019.
Karnad, Girish. "Theatre in India." *Daedalas* 118, no. 4 (Fall 1989): 331–52.
———. *Three Plays: Naga-Mandala, Hayavadana, Tughlaq.* New Delhi: Oxford University Press, 1994.
Kartik Fine Arts. *15th Kodai Nataka Vizha Schedule.* Mylapore Fine Arts Auditorium. April 24, 2004–May 2, 2004.
Karunakaran, K. *Studies in Tamil Sociolinguistics.* Madras: Oppuravu Achagam, 1978.
Karunakaran, K., and C. Sivashanmugam. *Study of Social Dialects in Tamil.* Annamalainagar: All India Tamil Linguistics Association, 1981.
Karunanidhi, M. *Poompukar.* Translated by T. G. Narayanaswamy as *Tale of the Anklet.* Madras: Tamizhkani Pathippagam, 1976. (Originally published, 1967.)
"KFA Nataka Vizha Results." *The Hindu*, May 21, 2004.
Kidder, Louise. "Dependents in the Master's House: When Rock Dulls Scissors." In *Home and Hegemony: Domestic Service and Identity Politics in South and*

Southeast Asia, edited by Kathleen M. Adams and Sara Dickey, 207–20. Ann Arbor: University of Michigan Press, 2000.
Kochanek, Stanley A. *See* Hardgrave and Kochanek.
Krishnakumar, Asha. "Chennai's Agony: Water Supply." *Frontline* 18, no. 13 (June 23–July 6, 2001).
Krishnamurti, Yamini. *A Passion for Dance: My Autobiography.* With Renuka Khandekar. New Delhi: Viking Press, 1995.
Krishnan, Hari. *Celluloid Classicism: Early Tamil Cinema and the Making of Modern Bharatanatyam.* Middletown, CT: Wesleyan University Press, 2019.
Kumar, S. R. Ashok. "S. Ve. Shekher, Down to Earth and Intense." *The Hindu*, April 7, 2006.
L'Armand, Kathleen, and Adrian L'Armand. "Music in Madras: The Urbanization of a Cultural Tradition." In *Eight Urban Musical Cultures: Tradition and Change*, edited by Bruno Nettl, 115–45. Urbana: University of Illinois Press, 1978.
Lakshmana, K. V. "Sasikala's MLAs: 'Locked Up' in Luxury, 'Without' their Freedom." *Hindustan Times*, February 11, 2017.
learnnew. "One of the Best Tamil movies!" *Imdb.com*, March 18, 2003. http://www.imdb.com/title/tt0155180/. Accessed February 28, 2022.
Lelyveld, David. "Upon the Subdominant: Administering Music on All-India Radio." In *Consuming Modernity: Public Culture in a South Asian World*, edited by Carol A. Breckenridge, 49–65. Minneapolis: University of Minnesota Press, 1995.
Lukose, Ritty A. *Liberalization's Children: Gender, Youth, and Consumer Citizenship in Globalizing India.* Durham, NC: Duke University Press, 2009.
Mahalingam, N. *See* Mali
Mahtani, Minelle. " 'I'm a Blonde-Haired, Blue-Eyed Black Girl': Mapping Mobile Paradoxical Spaces among Multi-ethnic Women in Toronto, Canada." In *Rethinking Mixed Race*, edited by David Parker and Miri Song, 173–90. London: Pluto Press, 2001.
Mali. Unpublished materials. Biodata, list of plays, play summary. 2008.
Mangai, A. *Acting Up: Gender and Theatre in India, 1979–Onwards.* New Delhi: LeftWord Books, 2015.
Mangai, A., and V. Arasu. "Ushering Changes: Constructing the History of Tamil Theatre during Colonial Times through Drama Notices." In *Theatre in Colonial India: Play-House of Power*, edited by Lata Singh, 105–31. New York: Oxford University Press, 2009.
Mankekar, Purnima. *Screening Culture, Viewing Politics: An Ethnography of Television, Womanhood, and Nation in Postcolonial India.* Durham, NC: Duke University Press, 1999.
Manuel, Peter. "Popular Music in India, 1901–1986." *Popular Music* 7, no. 2 (May 1988): 157–76.
Marx, Nick, and Matt Sienkiewicz, ed. *The Comedy Studies Reader.* Austin: University of Texas Press, 2018.

Medhurst, Andy. *A National Joke: Popular Comedy and English Cultural Identities.* London: Routledge, 2007.

Mee, Erin, ed. *DramaContemporary: India.* Baltimore, MD: Johns Hopkins University Press, 2001.

Mehta, Monika. "What Is Behind Film Censorship? The *Khalnayak* Debates." *Jouvert* 5, no. 3 (2001): 1–9. http://social.chass.ncsu.edu/jouvert/v513/mehta.htm. Accessed January 11, 2002.

———. *Censorship and Sexuality in Bombay Cinema.* Austin: University of Texas Press, 2011.

Mitchell, Lisa. *Language, Emotion, and Politics in South India: The Making of a Mother Tongue.* Bloomington: Indiana University Press, 2009.

Mohan, Crazy. www.crazymohan.com. Accessed February 28, 2022.

Morcom, Anna. *Illicit Worlds of Indian Dance Cultures of Exclusion.* New York: Oxford University Press, 2014.

Mudaliar, Pammal Sambanda. "Over Forty Years Before the Footlights": Chapters I & IV. Introduced and translated by Venkat Swaminathan. *Sangeet Natak* 121–122 (July–December 1996): 25–39.

———. "Over Forty Years Before the Footlights": Part III & Chapter XXII. Introduced and translated by Venkat Swaminathan. *Sangeet Natak* 123 (January–March 1997): 25–44.

"Music, Dance, Drama Event Listing." *The Hindu*, February 1, 2004.

Music of Madras. https://musicofmadras.in/eventlisting_date.php?date=2019-10-28&oid=650. Accessed November 23, 2019.

Muthalaly, Shonali. "Fine Arts, But No Future?" *The Hindu*, October 23, 2003a.

———. "Museum Theatrics." *The Hindu*, December 10, 2003b.

Muthalaly, Susan, and Madhavan Karthik. "No *Vagina Monologues* in Chennai, Say Police." *Indian Express*, March 11, 2004.

Muthiah, S. "The Mount Road Congregations." *The Hindu*, July 30, 2003.

Mylapore Academy. *Mylapore Academy 49th Year Celebrations Souvenir.* Chennai, 2003.

Mylapore MLA. http://mylaporemla.blogspot.com/2006/06/s-ve-shekher-is-mylapores-mla.html, June 1, 2006. Blog viewed on June 17, 2007.

Narada Gana Sabha (Regd.) Forty-fifth Annual Report and Accounts for the Year Ending 31st March 2003.

Narayan, Pushpa. "They Have Enacted a Dramatic Success Story in Tamil Theatre." *Indian Express*, May 8, 2004.

Nataka Academy. *13th Nataka Utsav: Golden Jubilee Celebrations of Kathady S. Ramamurthy.* Narada Gana Sabha, May 1, 2004–May 9, 2004.

Natarajan, P. Telephone Interview. September 2, 2015a.

———. Email communication. September 3, 2015b.

National School of Drama's Sixth National Theatre Festival Performance Schedule. March 20–April 8, 2004.

Neelakanthan, R. Photograph of the actor in costume during performance of *Entru Thaniyum Intha Suthanthira Thaagam*? Given to the author by R. Neelakanthan, Chennai, 2004.

———. Photograph of Cho Ramasamy and R. Neelakanthan in a 2004 performance of *Campavāmi Yukē Yukē*. Given to the author by R. Neelakanthan, Chennai, 2004.

Nijhawan, Amita. "Excusing the Female Dancer: Tradition and Transgression in Bollywood Dancing." *South Asian Popular Culture* 7, no. 2 (July 2009): 99–112.

O'Shea, Janet. *At Home in the World: Bharata Natyam on the Global Stage*. Middletown, CT: Wesleyan University Press, 2007.

Online Desk. "Cho Ramaswamy: The Man Who Defied Many and Yet Defined Many." *The New Indian Express*, December 7, 2016.

Padmanabhan, Kovai. Photograph from Goodwill Stage performance of *Washingtonil Tirumaṇam* ("Marriage in Washington"), 1992a.

———. Photograph from Goodwill Stage performance of *Washingtonil Tirumaṇ am* ("Marriage in Washington"), 1992b.

———. Photograph from Goodwill Stage performance of *Washingtonil Tirumaṇ am* ("Marriage in Washington"), 1992c.

———. "Washingtonil Thirumanam Synopsis." Unpublished, 2008.

Pandian, M. S. S. "From Exclusion to Inclusion: Brahminism's New Face in Tamil Nadu." *Economic and Political Weekly* 25 (September 1–8, 1990): 1938–39.

———. *The Image Trap: M. G. Ramachandran in Film and Politics*. New Delhi: Sage, 1992.

———. *Brahmin and Non-Brahmin: Genealogies of the Tamil Political Present*. New Delhi: Orient Blackswan, 2007.

Parthasarathy, Indira. *The Legend of Nandan*. Translated by C. T. Indra. New Delhi: Oxford University Press, 2003.

Pendakur, Manjunath. *Indian Popular Cinema: Industry, Ideology and Consciousness*. Cresskill, NJ: Hampton Press, Inc., 2003.

Perumal, A. N. *Tamil Drama: Origin and Development*. Madras: International Institute of Tamil Studies, 1981.

Prabhu, S. "Kathadi Ramamurthy." *The Hindu*, March 9, 2014.

Putcha, Ramya. "Between History and Historiography: The Origins of Classical Kuchipudi Dance." *Dance Research Journal* 45, no. 3 (December 2013): 91–110.

Radway, Janice. *A Feeling for Books: The Book-of-the-Month Club, Literary Taste, and Middle-Class Desire*. Chapel Hill: University of North Carolina Press, 1997.

Rajaram, B. "Bhaja Govindam by Bombay Gnanam: Overwhelmed by Spirituality and Devotion." *Beautiful Times*, 2015. [online] Available from: http://beautifultimes.in/2015/06/bhaja-govindam-by-bombay-gnanam-troupe-audience-was-overwhelmed-by-spirituality-and-devotion/. Accessed August 28, 2015.

Rajendran, K. S. "Drama and Society: A Study of Tamil Dramatic Performances (1870–1980)." Thesis presented to the Tamil Nadu Council of Historical Research, March 1989.

Ram, Anjali. *Consuming Bollywood: Gender, Globalization, and Media in the Indian Diaspora.* New York: Peter Lang, 2014.

Ramachander, S. "The Narrow Road to the North." *The Hindu Business Line, Internet Edition*, April 30, 2004. http://www.thehindubusinessline.com/life/2004/04/30/stories/2004043000090200.htm. Accessed November 29, 2005.

Ramakrishna, P. C., ed. *Bring Down the House Lights: Fifty Years of the Madras Players.* Chennai: The Madras Players, 2006.

Ramaswamy, Sumathi. *Passions of the Tongue: Language Devotion in Tamil India, 1891–1970.* Berkeley: University of California Press, 1997.

Rangarajan, Malathi. "TV Actors' Unions—Standing Asunder." *The Hindu*, November 28, 2003.

———. "It is a 'Golden' Milestone." *The Hindu*, October 20, 2016.

———. "The Nawab's Protégé." *The Hindu*, January 19, 2017.

Rasamayee Sandhya Sabha advertisement. http://www.chennaidecemberseason.com/2019/11/margazhi-madhyam-2019.html. Accessed February 25, 2021.

Richmond, Farley P. "Characteristics of the Modern Theatre." In *Indian Theatre: Traditions of Performance*, edited by Farley P. Richmond, Darius L. Swann, and Phillip B. Zarrilli, 387–462. Honolulu: University of Hawai'i Press, 1990.

Roshne B. "Detective Sambu Back on the Job After 20 Years. *The New Indian Express*, June 30, 2016.

Rudisill, Kristen. "Bharata Natyam and Terukkuttu: E. Krishna Iyer's Revival Efforts" in *Sagar* 10 (2003): 1–16.

———. Photograph of the author with M. B. Moorthy and other members of Gurukulam Original Boys Company '95. Chennai, 2004.

———. Photograph of the author with S. Ve. Shekher at a performance of *Kātula Pū*. Chennai: February 22, 2004.

———. "Evolution of the Mahalakshmi Ladies Drama Group 1989–2015." *Samyukta: A Journal of Women's Studies* 16, no. 2, special issue on Women in Indian Theatre (July 2016): 134–56.

———. "Full-Blooded Desi Romance: Contemporary English-Language Romance Novels in India."*Journal of Popular Culture* 51, no. 3 (June 2018): 754–75.

———. *The Scriptures Don't Say So*, Part I. [Abridged translation of Cho Ramasamy's *Cāttiram Coṉṉatillai.* Madras: Alliance, 1995, with introduction]. *Ecumenica* 15.1 (Spring 2022): 1–53.

———. *The Scriptures Don't Say So*, Part II. [Abridged translation of Cho Ramasamy's *Cāttiram Coṉṉatillai.* Madras: Alliance, 1995, with introduction]. *Ecumenica* 15.2 (Fall 2022).

Sambamoorthy, P. *History of Indian Music.* 2nd ed. Madras: Indian Music Publishing House, 1982.

Sangameswaran, K. T. "Police Nod Not Required for Plays: High Court." *The Hindu*, January 24, 2013.

Santhanam, Kausalya. "Caught in the Formula Trap." *The Hindu*, May 18, 2001.

———. "When Will They Try to Be Different?" *The Hindu*, May 10, 2002.

———. "Outdated Ideas, Antiquated Scenes." *The Hindu*, January 24, 2003.

———. "Voice of the Woman in Mainstream Theatre." *The Hindu*, May 23, 2003.

———. "Hooked on Humour: Is Comedy in Theatre Seeing a Resurgence?" *The Hindu*, September 8, 2003.

———. "Undiminished Passion for the Stage." *The Hindu*, October 10, 2003.

———. "Is Drama Left Out of the Celebration?" *The Hindu*, December 1, 2003.

———. "Life Painted with Wit and Humour." *The Hindu*, April 16, 2004.

———. "Very Little to Rave About." *The Hindu*, May 14, 2004.

———. "Lofty Theme Tackled Well." *The Hindu*, May 21, 2004.

———. "A Trip Down Nostalgia Lane." *The Hindu*, Aug. 5, 2005.

Sanyal, Sanjeev. *The Indian Renaissance: India's Rise After a Thousand Years of Decline.* New Delhi: Penguin, 2008.

"Sasikala Holding AIADMK MLAs Hostage: Madras HC Seeks Report." *India TV Politics Desk*, February 10, 2017.

Schein, Louisa. "Performing Modernity" in *Cultural Anthropology* 14, no. 3 (1999): 361–95.

Schwartz, Susan L. *Rasa: Performing the Divine in India.* New York: Columbia University Press, 2004.

Seal, Anil. *The Emergence of Indian Nationalism: Competition and Collaboration in the Later Nineteenth Century.* Cambridge: Cambridge University Press, 1968.

Seizer, Susan. "Dramatic License: Negotiating Stigma On and Off the Tamil Popular Stage." Ph.D. diss., University of Chicago, 1997.

———. *Stigmas of the Tamil Stage: An Ethnography of Special Drama Artists in South India.* Durham, NC: Duke University Press, 2005.

———. "Legacies of Discourse: Special Drama and its History." In *Theatre in Colonial India: Play-House of Power*, edited by Lata Singh, 70–104. New York: Oxford University Press, 2009.

Selby, Martha. *Grow Long, Blessed Night: Love Poems from Classical India.* New York: Oxford University Press, 2000.

———. "City Scan of Chennai (Madras)." *Persimmon: Asian Literature, Arts, And Culture* 1, no. 3 (Winter 2001).

Sengupta, Rudraprasad. "Viability of Professional Theatre in West Bengal Today." *Sangeet Natak Akademi* (December 1984).

Shankar, S. "Introduction" to *Water!* by Komal Swaminathan, viii–xxxi. Calcutta: Seagull Press, 2001a.

Shankar, S. and Komal Swaminathan. "*Water!*: A Tamil Play by Komal Swaminathan." *Asian Theatre Journal* 18, no. 2 (Fall 2001b): 123–73.

Shekher, S. Ve. http://www.sveshekher.com/main.html.
———. *Ellarum Vaanga* (*Everyone Is Welcome*) and *Alwaa*. Poster for performances held at the Dubai Folklore Society Theater on May 7, 1999.
———. Photograph of S. Ve. Shekher and Narendra Modi, 2016
———. Photograph of Natakhapriya performing, 2018.
———. Photograph of Natakhapriya troupe members at a performance of *Kātula Pū* (*Flower in the Ear*), 2004.
———. Photograph of S. Ve. Shekher's 50th Blood Donation, 2005.
———. Photograph of members of Natakhapriya drama troupe, 2018.
Shresthova, Sangita. *Is It All About Hips? Around the World with Bollywood Dance*. Los Angeles, CA: Sage Publications, 2011.
Singer, Milton B. *Traditional India: Structure and Change*. Philadelphia: American Folklore Society, 1959.
———. *When a Great Tradition Modernizes: An Anthropological Approach to Indian Civilization*. New York: Praeger, 1972.
Singh, A. *Neighborhood and Networks in Urban India*. Delhi: Marwah, 1976.
Singhal, Arvind, and Everett M. Rogers. *India's Communication Revolution: From Bullock Carts to Cyber Marts*. New Delhi: Sage, 2001.
Siromoney, Gift, and Johnson Varatharaj. "Relative Popularity of Political Leaders in Tamil Nadu: Results of a Statewide Public Opinion Survey." *MCC Magazine*, Vol. LI (1982): 47–48. http://www.cmi.ac.in/gift/Surveys/surv_relative.htm. Accessed February 28, 2022.
Sivathamby, K. *Drama in Ancient Tamil Society*. Madras: New Century Book House, 1981.
Solomon, Rakesh. "Culture, Imperialism, and Nationalist Resistance: Performance in Colonial India." *Theatre Journal* 46 (1994): 323–47.
Soneji, Davesh. *Unfinished Gestures: Devadasis, Memory, and Modernity in South India*. Chicago: University of Chicago Press, 2012.
———. "*Indra's Court* in Madras: The Parsi Theatre and the Cosmopolitan Origins of Modern Tamil 'Musical Drama.'" Unpublished paper presented for the 46th Annual Conference on South Asia. Madison, WI, October 2017.
———. "Resounding Islam: Occluded Histories of Modern South Indian Raga-Based Music." Paper presented at UCLA Center for India and South Asia, February 6, 2020.
Sreelalitha, W. "Kovaiyil Nadagam." *The Hindu* (Coimbatore), April. 12, 2008.
Srinivas, M. N. *Social Change in Modern India*. Berkeley: University of California Press, 1966.
Subramanian, Lakshmi. *From the Tanjore Court to the Madras Music Academy: A Social History of Music in South India*. New Delhi: Oxford University Press, 2006.
Subramanian, Narendra. *Ethnicity and Populist Mobilization: Political Parties, Citizens, and Democracy in South India*. Delhi: Oxford University Press, 1999.

Subramanyam, K. N. "Traditional Tamil Drama and the Present Impasse." *Sangeet Natak Akademi Journal* 4 (March–April 1967): 27–36.

Suguna Vilasa Sabha. http://www.svsclub.net/home/aboutus.html. Accessed December 11, 2019.

Sundaram, Dheepa. "Aesthetics as Resistance: *Rasa*, *Dhvani*, and Empire in Tamil 'Protest' Theater." PhD diss., University of Illinois at Urbana-Champaign, 2014.

Swaminathan, Chitra. "Landmark Show." *The Hindu*, May 11, 2001.

Tamilnadu Societies Registration Act, 1975. (indiacode.nic.in › bitstream › tn_societies-registration-act-1975). Accessed November 23, 2019.

Tewari, Ruhi. "Socio-Economic Caste Census Data to be Released by Sept." *Indian Express*, April 29, 2013. http://www.indianexpress.com/news/socioeconomic-caste-census-data-to-be-released-by-sept/1109038/. Accessed July 24, 2013.

Thirumalai, M. S. *Aspects of Language Use: A Case Study of Tamil*. Annamalainagar: All India Tamil Linguistics Association, 1983.

"Thuppariyum Sambu (Tamil Edition)." *Amazon.com*. https://www.amazon.com/Thuppariyum-Sambu-Tamil-Devan-ebook/dp/B07RNMF1CL. Accessed February 28, 2022.

Tolen, Rachel. "Transfers of Knowledge and Privileged Spheres of Practice: Servants and Employers in a Madras Railway Colony." In *Home and Hegemony: Domestic Service and Identity Politics in South and Southeast Asia*, edited by Kathleen M. Adams and Sara Dickey, 63–86. Ann Arbor: University of Michigan Press, 2000.

Trawick, Margaret. *Notes on Love in a Tamil Family*. Berkeley: University of California Press, 1990.

Turner, Victor. *The Anthropology of Performance*. New York: PAJ Publications, 1988.

Uberoi, Patricia. "Imagining the Family: An Ethnography of Viewing *Hum Aapke Hain Koun . . . !*" In *Pleasure and the Nation: The History, Politics and Consumption of Public Culture in India*, edited by Christopher Pinney and Rachel Dwyer, 309–51. New Delhi: Oxford University Press, 2001.

United Amateur Artists. *Golden Jubilee Souvenir 1952–2003*. Chennai: The Senthur Offset, 2003.

———. *Souvenir 1996*. Chennai, 1996.

———. *Under Secretary*. Performance program. May 9–10, 1964.

———. *Ubhadesam Seivathu UAA: A 5 in 1 Comedy*. Advertisement for play performed as part of the UAA Golden Jubilee, 2003.

Varadarajan, M. *A History of Tamil Literature*. New Delhi: Sahitya Akademi, 1970.

Veblen, Thorstein. *The Theory of the Leisure Class: An Economic Study of Institution*. With introduction by C. Wright Mills. New York: Mentor Books, 1953. (Originally published, 1899.)

Venkataramanan, G. "On the Trail of Adi Sankara." *The Hindu*, March 12, 2015.

Venkatraman, Janaki. "Vexed on Sex? Ask Dr M." *Outlook*, April 9, 2001.

Vijayalakshmi, B. "They Swear by Therapeutic Value of Humour Seriously." *Indian Express*, August 28, 2003.
Viswanathan, Purnam (adaptation from Ramesh Mehta's Hindi version). *Under-secretary*. Chennai: Alliance Press, 1992.
Viveka Fine Arts Club. *Golden Jubilee 2004*. Chennai, 2004.
Weidman, Amanda J. "On the Subject of 'Classical' Music in South India." PhD diss., Columbia University, 2001.
———. *Singing the Classical, Voicing the Modern: The Postcolonial Politics of Music in South India*. Durham, NC: Duke University Press, 2006.
Weinstein, Jay A. *Madras: An Analysis of Urban Ecological Structure in India*. Beverly Hills, CA: Sage, 1974.
Yusuf Ali, A. "The Modern Hindustani Drama." *Transactions of the Royal Society of Literature*, 2nd s. (1917): 35, 79–99.
Zarrilli, Phillip. *The Kathakali Complex: Actor, Performance, and Structure*. New Delhi: Abhinav, 1984.
———. "Kathakali." In *Indian Theatre: Traditions of Performance*, edited by Farley P. Richmond, Darius L. Swann, and Phillip B. Zarrilli, 315–57. 1st Indian edition. Delhi: Motilal Banarsidass, 1993.
———. *Kathakali Dance-Drama: Where Gods and Demons Come to Play*. London Routledge, 2000.
Zook, Darren C. "The Farcical Mosaic: The Changing Masks of Political Theatre in Contemporary India." *Asian Theatre Journal* 18, no. 2 (Fall 2001): 174–99.

Non-English Sources

Annamalai, C. *Tamil̲ Nāṭakam Cila Āḷumaikaḷ* ("A Few Personalities of Tamil Drama"). Chennai: The Parkar, 2001.
Arakappan, A. *Tamil̲nāṭaka Mē̲n̲maikku Nāṅku Yōca̲n̲aikaḷ* ("Four Thoughts for the Excellence of Tamil Drama"). In *Irupatām Nū̲r̲r̲āṇṭut Tamil̲ Nāṭakaṅkaḷ* ("Twentieth-Century Tamil Dramas"), edited by M. Ramaswamy, K. Murukesan, and P. Govindasamy, 296–300. Chennai: International Institute of Tamil Studies, 1999.
Arasu, V. *Tamil̲aka Vīti Araṅkam: Mu̲n̲n̲eḷumpum Vivātaṅkaḷ* ("The Street Stage of the Tamil Land: The Rise of Debates"). In *Tamil̲ Nāṭakam—Nē̲r̲r̲um I̲n̲r̲um* ("Tamil Drama—Yesterday Today"), edited by K. Bhagavathy, 1–12. Chennai: International Institute of Tamil Studies, 2000.
Ashokmitran. *Muppatu Varuṭaṅkaḷukkup Pi̲r̲aku Tirumpip Pārkkaiyil* ("Reflections Thirty Years Later"). In *Irupatām Nū̲r̲r̲āṇṭut Tamil̲ Nāṭakaṅkaḷ* ("Twentieth Century Tamil Dramas"), edited by M. Ramaswamy, K. Murukesan, and P. Govindasamy, 301–8. Chennai: International Institute of Tamil Studies, 1999.

Auclair, Christine. *Ville à vendre: Voie libérale et privatization du secteur de l'habitat à Chennai (Inde.)*. Pondicherry: Institute Français de Pondichéry, 1998.

Bhagavathy, K., ed. *Tamil̲ Nāṭakam—Nēr̲r̲um In̲r̲um* ("Tamil Drama—Yesterday Today"). Chennai: International Institute of Tamil Studies, 2000.

———. *Tamil̲ Mēṭai Nāṭaka Varalār̲u* ("The History of Tamil Stage Drama"). Chennai: International Institute of Tamil Studies, 2001.

Cāvi. *Washingtonil Tirumaṇam*. Chennai: Narmada Publishers, 1999.

Gupta, S. *Parsi thiyetar: Udbhav aur vikas* ("Parsi Theatre: Origin and Development"). Allahabad: Lokbharati Prakashan, 1981.

Gurusami, S., and A. Dasarathan. *Nāṭakamum Nāṭaka Kampen̲i An̲upavaṅkaḷum*. ("Dramas and The Experiences of Drama Companies"). Chennai: International Institute of Tamil Studies, 2000.

Husain, M. S. *Indar-sabha ki parampara* ("The *Indar Sabha* Tradition"). Delhi: Simant Prakashan, 1990.

Ilango, S. S. Ramar. *Tamil̲ Nāṭakamēṭai Mun̲n̲ōṭikaḷ* ("Pioneers of Tamil Stage Drama"). Chennai: International Institute of Tamil Studies, 1998.

Kriyāvin̲ Tar̲kālat Tamil̲ Akarāti (*Modern Tamil Dictionary*). Madras: Cre-A, 1992.

Marina. *Tan̲ik Kuṭittan̲am*. Madras: Alliance, 2007 (First printing, 1974).

Mohan, "Crazy." *Honeymoon Couple* [in Tamil]. Unpublished manuscript, 1977. Translated by Kristen Rudisill as *Honeymoon Couple* (Unpublished manuscript, 2004).

———. *Satellite Cāmiyār*. Crazy Creation's Audiocassette. Chennai: Gitaa Cassettes, 1992.

———. *Alāvutīn̲um 100 Vātt Palpum* (*Aladdin and the 100 Watt Bulb*). Audiocassette. Chennai: Vani Cassettes, 1993a.

———. *Ayya, Amma, Ammamma* (*Father, Mother, Grandmother*). Crazy Creations Audiocassette with Kathadi Ramamurthy and Delhi Ganesh. Chennai: Vani Cassettes, 1993b.

———. *Mīcai Āṉālum Man̲aivi* (*She's My Wife Even Though She Has a Moustache*). Crazy Creation's Audiocassette. Chennai: Vani Cassettes, 1996.

———. *Jurassic Baby*. DVD. Chennai: Swathi's Family Entertainment, 2006.

Natakhapriya 4001 [in Tamil]. (A Souvenir on the Occasion of Natakhapriya's 4001st performance.). January 1, 2001.

Natakhapriya 5007 [in Tamil]. (A Souvenir on the Occasion of Natakhapriya's 5007th performance.) January 1, 2007.

Natakhapriya 5600 [in Tamil]. (A Souvenir on the Occasion of Natakhapriya's 5600th performance.) May 7, 2010.

Ramamurthy, Kathadi. *Honeymoon Couple*. DVD. Chennai: Swathi's Family Entertainment, 2007.

Ramanujam, C. *Nāṭaka Kaṭṭuraikaḷ* ("Drama Essays"). Chennai: Kaavya, 2003a.

———. *Navīn̲at Tamil̲ Nāṭakam* ("Modern Tamil Drama"). In *Nāṭaka Kaṭṭuraikaḷ* ("Drama Essays"), compiled by C. Annamalai, 57–68. Chennai: Kaavya, 2003b.

Ramasamy, A. *Tamiḻil Nāṭaka Eḻuttum Pārvaiyāḷarkaḷum* ("Works and Audiences of Drama in Tamil"). In *Tamiḻ Nāṭakam—Nēṟṟum Iṉṟum* ("Tamil Drama—Yesterday Today"), edited by K. Bhagavathy, 106–18. Chennai: International Institute of Tamil Studies, 2000.

Ramasamy, Cho. "Dear Mister *Vācakarē*." *Tughlaq* (March 15, 1971): 4.

———, director. *Mohammad bin Tughlaq*. Prestige Productions, 1971. 2 hrs., 14 min.

———. *Iṉpakkaṉā Oṉṟu Kaṇṭēn*. Madras: Alliance, 1994.

———. *Mohammad bin Tughlaq*. [in Tamil] 2nd Printing. Madras: Alliance, 1995a. Translated by Kristen Rudisill as *Mohammad bin Tughlaq* (Unpublished manuscript, 2001).

———. *Cāttiram Coṉṉatillai*. Madras: Alliance, 1995b. Translated by Kristen Rudisill and published as *The Scriptures Don't Say So*, Part I. [abridged with introduction]. *Ecumenica* 15.1 (Spring 2022): 1–53. And *The Scriptures Don't Say So*, Part II [abridged with introduction]. *Ecumenica* 15.2 (Fall 2022).

———. *Maṉam Oru Kuraṅku*. Madras: Alliance, 1997. Translated by Kristen Rudisill as *The Mind Is a Monkey* (Unpublished manuscript, 2002).

———. *Mohammad bin Tughlaq*. [in Tamil]. DVD. Chennai: Swathi's Family Entertainment, 2006a.

———. *Nērmai Uṟaṅkum Nēram* (*When Honesty Sleeps*). Chennai: Alliance, 2006b (First printing, 1996).

———. *Eṅkē Pirāmaṇaṉ?* (*Where Is the Brahmin?*). Chennai: Alliance, 2007 (First printing, 1993).

———. *Nērmai Uṟaṅkum Nēram* (*When Honesty Sleeps*). DVD. Chennai: Swathi's Family Entertainment, 2009. 1 hr., 52 min.

Ramaswamy, M. *Tamiḻil Cōtaṉai Nāṭakaṅkaḷ* ("Experimental Dramas in Tamil"). Chennai: Sahitya Akademi, 2001.

Ramaswamy, M., K. Murukesan, and P. Govindasamy. *Irupatām Nūṟṟāṇṭut Tamiḻ Nāṭakaṅkaḷ* ("Twentieth Century Tamil Dramas"). Chennai: International Institute of Tamil Studies, 1999.

Rizvi, M. H. *Urdu drama aur istej* ("Urdu Drama and Stage"), pt 2, *Lakhnau ka awami istej: Amanat aur Indarsabha* ("The People's Stage of Lucknow: Amanatt and the *Indar Sabha*). Lucknow: Kitab Ghar, 1957.

Saktiperumal. *Tamiḻ Nāṭaka Varalāṟu* ("History of Tamil Drama"). Madurai: Vancikko Pathipakam, 1979.

Shanmugam, Avvai T. K. *Nāṭakak Kalai* ("The Art of Drama"). Chennai: Published with the assistance of the Tamilnadu Sangeet Nataka Sangam, 1967.

Shekher, S. Ve. *Ciṉṉa Māpḷē, Periya Māpḷē* (*Younger Son-in-Law, Elder Son-in-Law*). Natakhapriya audiocassette. Chennai: Vani Cassettes, 1993a.

———. *Kātula Pū* (*Flower in the Ear*). Natakhapriya audiocassette. Chennai: Vani Cassettes, 1993b.

———. *Eppavum Nī Rājā* (*You Are Always a King*). Natakhapriya audiocassette. Chennai: Vani Cassettes, 1995.

———. *One More Exorcist.* Ticket from a performance at the Kalaivanar Arangam in Chennai. July 29, 2001.

———. *Kuḻantacāmi* (*Child Guy*). Natakhapriya audiocassette. Chennai: Vani Cassettes, 2002.

———. *Ciṉṉa Māpḷē, Periya Māpḷē* (*Younger Son-in-Law, Elder Son-in-Law*). Chennai: Alliance, 2004.

Sudakar, M. V. *Marināvin Nāṭakaṅkaḷ* ("The Dramas of Marina"). Chennai: Puram Publications, 1981.

Tangarasu, M. *Tamiḻil Sabha Nāṭaka Marapu* ("The Sabha Drama Tradition in Tamil"). In *Tamiḻ Nāṭakam—Nēṟṟum Iṉṟum* ("Tamil Drama—Yesterday Today"), edited by K. Bhagavathy, 86–95. Chennai: International Institute of Tamil Studies, 2000.

Thuglak. www.thuglak.com/thuglak/. Accessed February 27, 2022.

Venkat. *Ubhadesam Seivathu UAA.* Unpublished manuscript, 2004.

Vindhan. "*Naṭika Vēḷ* M. R. Radha" ("'King of Acting' M. R. Radha"). In *Tamiḻ Nāṭakamēṭai Muṉṉōṭikaḷ* ("Pioneers of Tamil Stage Drama"), edited by S. S. Ramar Ilango, 125–34. Chennai: International Institute of Tamil Studies, 1998.

Index

Abraham, Itty, 118
Abrams, Meyer, 199
actors: amateur, 27, 35, 39, 87, 95, 103, 106, 110, 111, 137; backgrounds of, 5, 68, 87, 137; Brahmin, 67, 166; charity work by, 267n22; comic, 83, 140; donations collected by, 223; English, 82; female roles played by male, 109, 125; in films, 32, 34–35, 51, 60, 88, 103, 108, 139, 190, 277n2; improvisation by, 165; material written for, 211, 212; microphones used by, 95, 167; moving or standing by, 95, 279n18; non-Brahmin, 103, 166; paid (or not), 31, 36–40, 110, 273–274n28, 277n2; performances emphasized by, 94; in politics, 59–60, 75; professional, 110, 213; in radio, 111, 167, 169; reputations of, 27, 31, 84; sabhas and, 41; sabha vs. folk theater, 88, 106; in television, 35, 51, 103, 108, 190, 274n28; threatened, 204; training for, 107, 167; troupes centered on, 91, 93, 255; younger, 194, 216
actresses, 65, 88, 103, 106, 140, 170, 178, 224; amateur, 111; dancers vs., 110; limited numbers of, 110, 125, 149; in male roles, 108, 112; off-stage roles for, 149; pay for, 110, 273n28; professional, 41, 110; in radio, 111; reputation of, 108–109, 111; roles for, 111; in television, 109, 110, 111; touring, 111
Adimārkal, 169
Adimehal, 277n10
ADMK, 65
Adyar, 20–21, 50
aesthetics, 20, 217. *See also* sabha theater: aesthetic of
AIADMK (All-India Anna DMK), 54, 60, 64, 66, 165–167, 270n10
Aladdin and the 100 Watt Bulb (*Alāvutīnum 100 Vātt Palpum*), 17, 47
Alliance Française, 211, 223, 268n31, 268n35, 278n5
All India Radio, 26, 77, 167, 169
Almighty Sree Vaari Fine Arts, 136
alphabets, 133–134
Alwā (*Halwa*), 10, 268n26
amateur aesthetic, 91, 106–108, 112–113, 167
amateurs, 71–72. *See also* actors: amateur; actresses: amateur; troupes: amateur
amateur theater, 2, 5, 27, 35, 102, 279n16

Americans, 225, 253; audiences of, 46; basketball and, 17–18; as characters in plays, 13, 117–118, 122–130; as characters on television, 128, 129; culture of, 25, 83, 145; modernity of, 120, 122
Anderson, Benedict, 56, 57
Andhra Pradesh, 76, 253, 276n3, 280n12
Annadurai, C. N., 55, 59–60, 63, 78, 213, 279n16
Annamalai Mandram, 22
Anon, Gil, 223, 278n5
An̲pulla Appa, 277n10
anti-Brahmin movement, 48, 54–56, 58, 60, 63–65; decline of, 79; non-Brahmin movement and, 61; revival of, 65; sabha plays respond to, 79; TAMBRAAS and, 66
Appadurai, Arjun, 123
Apte, Mahadev, 103, 144
Ārambam (*Fresh Beginnings*), 97
Arasu, V. 24, 68, 265n13
Arivanatham, K. P., 272n3
Arnold, Matthew, 74
Arokianathan, S., 77, 102
associations, 2, 24; actors, 75; arts, 51; Brahmin, 65–67, 167, 265n6, 270n9, 276–277n8; dramas sponsored by non-sabha, 48–49, 268nn30–34; neighborhood, 18; political, 61; of sabhas, 41, 268n30. *See also* organizations; sabhas
Atiruṣṭakāran (*Lucky Guy*), 95
audiences: actors face, 122, 167; Bourdieu on, 43; Brahmin, 22, 29, 38, 55–56, 64, 69, 90, 93, 102, 124, 213, 215, 224, 270n8; Chennai (*see under* Chennai); classical performing arts, 26, 28, 46, 48, 83, 89, 98; connoisseur, 11, 44, 46, 83, 98; conservative or traditional, 97, 224, 226; critics and, 83, 221–222; crossover, 210–212; detached, 83, 198; diaspora, 49, 79, 101; educated, 42, 44, 49, 75, 79, 95, 100, 103, 118; elite, 5, 8, 10, 12, 19–20, 28, 85, 98; expectations of, 7–8, 97, 125; experimental theater, 5; family, 87–88; film, 4, 12, 32, 35, 45, 78, 87, 101, 108, 109; interpretation by, 87, 96–97, 173, 182; laughing, 4, 12, 43, 46, 83, 89, 98, 102, 144, 151, 155; limited (or not), 48, 55, 95, 102–103, 166–167; linked to venue, 82; local vs. tourist, 26; middle-class, 49, 79, 88, 90, 98, 155, 163, 179, 213; modern theater, 5, 223; noisy, 45–46, 95; non-Brahmin, 22, 68, 87, 267n20; non-sabha theater, 46, 188; participation by, 82, 96–97, 118, 125; patronage system and, 25; retention of, 217–218, 226; sabha (*see* sabha plays: audiences for); silent, 44–45; surveys of, 264n2, 271–272n2, 278n12; Tamil-speaking, 26–27, 77–78, 134; television, 51, 123, 131, 217; tourist, 26, 28, 129; village or rural, 85–86, 278n12; younger, 98, 177, 215–216, 226, 268n26
audiocassettes, 8, 46–47, 73, 167, 211; actors use, 107; covers of, 47, 161
auditoriums. *See* halls
Augusto, 51, 261
authenticity, 70, 130
Avan̲ oru Tan̲i Maram (*He Is a Lone Tree*), 165
Awasthi, Suresh, 190
Ayya, Amma, Ammamma (*Man, Mother, Grandmother*), 47, 135

backward castes, 63–65
Bala Shanmugananda Sabha, 75

sold to, 67, 270n12; politics and, 60, 65, 66, 279n16; song and dance in, 212, 266n16, 273n25; theater contrasted with, 88, 100–102, 214. *See also* films
Ci<u>nn</u>a Māpḷē, Periya Māpḷē (*Younger Son-in-Law, Elder Son-in-Law*), 13, 157, 178, 183; as audiocassette and book, 161; buttermilk scene in, 174, 175; employers in, 163, 171; first night in, 85; food in, 173–174; plot of, 162–163; popularity of, 161; title of, 164. See also *CM-PM*
classical dance or dancers, 4, 11, 18, 28, 37, 52, 69–70, 74, 109; amateur, 38, 72; audiences for, 26, 83, 89; caste and, 24, 72, 85, 110; debut (*arangetram*) of, 1–2, 36; in plays, 110, 222; popularity of, 51; sabhas and, 25, 28, 52, 83, 99, 106; self-funding, 38; status of genre of, 46
classical music or musicians, 3, 4, 11, 18, 117, 227; amateur, 38; audiences for, 19, 20, 26, 45, 54, 83, 89; Brahmins and, 26, 68; in "culture" hierarchy, 74; defining, 19; in entertainment hierarchy, 42; films replacing, 36; history of, 26, 68; language of, 76–77; patrons of, 20, 24; perceived as stale, 101; in plays, 280n2; sabhas and, 28, 36, 37, 50, 51, 52, 99, 106; status of genre of, 46; self-funding, 38; "vulgar" music vs., 19–20. *See also* Chennai Music Festival
classical performing arts, 18, 22, 27, 42, 46, 96, 98–99; audiences for, 4, 26, 46, 48, 50, 51, 90, 98; Brahmins and, 11, 24, 25, 56, 69–70; jokes presuming knowledge of, 103; sabhas as patrons or sponsors of, 12, 18, 25, 28, 36–37, 42, 51; status and, 25, 42, 46, 70–71; "traditional," 70
CM-PM, 164–165, 169; first night in, 179–183; food in, 173–175; language in, 172–173, 175–177. See also *Ci<u>nn</u>a Māpḷē, Periya Māpḷē*
code-switching, 70–71, 91
comedians, 93, 99, 134, 135, 165, 215, 226
comedy: audiences for, 98, 167, 188, 215; belonging or exclusion and, 43, 56–57; caste-based, 57–58; classical arts vs., 12, 36, 71; combined with other genres, 217–218, 225–226; community for, 43; dialects in, 78; drawing-room, 82; English-language, 101; high, 198; history of, 31, 54, 58, 78, 79, 86; identity and, 52; "just," 86–87, 100, 187; low, 198; modern Indian canon and, 188, 210, 211–213; physical, 88, 106; popularity of, 271–272n2; "pure," 28, 83, 86, 226; as sabha genre, 82–83, 86, 95, 99, 108, 118, 134, 135, 211; "serious" works vs., 83, 86, 99, 210, 213; social, 195; social divisions and, 12, 57; standup or shows, 97, 100, 215–216, 226, 269n38; village, 48. *See also* farce; humor; jokes
commercial theater, 3, 5, 27, 31, 71; decline of, 31
Communists, 198, 199, 202, 209
community theater, 263n8
company dramas, 5, 35
concerts, 3, 5, 37, 42, 51; decorum at, 44–45; music season, 26, 28, 269n40; sabha, 29, 36
Congress Party, 55, 78, 201–203, 209; Brahmin support for, 58, 61–64;

Kumar, P. N., 109, 278n9
Kuppusamy Chettiar, Nalli, 24
Kūttāṭi, 222

L'Armand, Kathleen and Adrian, 19, 264n3
Lakshmi and Kalyanam vs Kalyanam vs Kalyanam, 215
Lalitha, Sri, 140
language or languages: communities and, 57; dialects or varieties of, 77, 193; national, 202–203, 204, 249–250; of plays in national canon, 187; plays published in multiple, 212; state boundaries and, 76; Tamil politics and, 61, 63, 76, 271n21. *See also* jokes: language
Life of Sri Bhagawan Ramana Maharishi, The, 224
lighting, 38, 82, 91, 108, 113
Lights On, 103
Lucky Guy (*Atiruṣṭakāran*), 95

Madras (city): *bhajana* groups in, 24; commercial theater in, 31; dance in, 85; demographics of, 20, 269n42; dialects of, 78, 102 (*see also* Tamil: Madras dialect of); history of theater in, 5, 31, 75, 213; music or musicians in, 19–20, 269n40; North, 20, 38, 109, 264n5; number of sabhas in, 35, 51; plays set in, 81, 150; South, 109, 265n7; term "classical" in, 70. *See also* Chennai
Madras (state or presidency), 55, 75, 76, 270n6, 280n12
Madras By Night, 103
Madras Mahajana Sabha, 19
Madras Players, 6, 256, 268n35, 271n16
Madras Social and Cultural Academy, 233
Magalir Kaaval Nilayam (*Women's Police Station*), 224
Mahābhārata, 75, 175, 224, 271n20
Mahābhārtattil Maṅkāttā, 107
Mahalakshmi Ladies Drama Group (MLDG), 96, 112, 125, 223–225, 261
Mahendran, Y. G., 45, 91, 111, 258, 265n6, 272n3
Mahtani, Minelle, 71
majlis, 2
Malayalam, 48
Ma<u>n</u>am Oru Kuraṅku (*The Mind Is a Monkey*), 32–34, 95, 195
Man, Mother, Grandmother (*Ayya, Amma, Ammamma*), 47
Mangai, A., 24, 68, 265n13
Mangala Bala Gana Sabha, 2
Mankekar, Purnima, 153
Manohar, R. S., 28, 39, 111, 112, 193, 220, 260, 266n15, 266n19, 267n21, 272nn2–3; language used by, 193
Marathi, 75, 103, 144, 187, 189, 212, 213, 271
Marina (T. S. Sridhar), 55, 91, 94, 169, 257, 265n6; language used by, 78, 102–103
marriage, 72, 111, 241; arranged, 177, 204, 270n9; of Brahmins, 13, 57, 118, 119, 130; expense of, 119, 121, 127; in films, 88, 120–121, 145; first night of, 85, 163, 177–181; importance of, 74; "in-laws' quarrel" in, 129–130; jokes about, 134; love, 163, 177; North Indian, 120; preparations for, 129; rituals of (*see* rituals); South Indian or Tamil, 117–120, 144–145, 159; as theme for plays, 90, 97–98, 128, 131; "thousand lies" and, 97, 140, 148–149
Marriage Fiasco (*Kalyāṇattil Kalāṭṭā*), 50, 131, 275n6

nationalism: arts and, 25, 69; cultural, 63; ethnic, 64; Hindu or religious, 58, 66, 85, 209, 217; Indian, 69; plays and, 75–76, 278n7; Tamil or Dravidian, 54, 63–64, 66, 69, 89, 99, 104
National School of Drama, 24, 188, 190; theater festival of, 223, 278n5
Neelakanthan, R. (Neelu), 95, 109, 194, 203–204, 274n2, 278n9
Nehru, Jawaharlal, 62, 76, 189–190, 199–202, 210
Nērmai Uraṅkam Nēram (*When Honesty Sleeps*), 214, 279n17
newspapers, 112, 224; American, 120, 128; event listings in, 8, 9, 24, 48–49, 269n39; *The Hindu*, 6, 8–9, 28, 37, 48, 84, 99, 140; *Indian Express*, 169; language of, 77; *Mylapore Times*, 224; *New York Times*, 17; *Swarajya*, 26
Nijhawan, Amita, 179
Nil Darpan ("The Indigo Mirror"), 74
Niram Mārum Nijaṅkaḷ (*Truths that Change Color*), 225
Nīyā Nānā (*You or Me?*), 98
non-Brahmin community, 19, 50, 52, 60–61; backward/forward split in, 63; dichotomy of Brahmin and, 60; political power of, 58, 64–65
non-Brahmin movement, 58, 60–61, 68, 120. *See also* anti-Brahmin movement
nostalgia, 58, 84, 102, 123, 131, 220; pre-emptive, 121, 274n4
novels, 77, 104, 191. See also *Washingtonil Tirumaṇam*: novel
N. S. K. Nataka Sabha, 2

One More Exorcist, 29, 83, 103
organizations, 1, 3, 18–19, 25, 39, 97, 269n40; Brahmin, 66, 264n3; classical music, 117; community, 18; militant, 62; neighborhood, 21; non-Brahmin, 60; social service, 267n22. *See also* associations; sabhas
Oru Kolai, Oru Prayanam, 277n10
OVM Theatres, 268n37, 269n39

Paṭi Tāṇṭiya Pati (*The Husband that Crossed the Threshhold*), 111
Padmanabhan (Pattu), 35, 258
Padmanabhan, Kovai, 257
Pandian, M. S. S., 61, 65, 186
Parama Rahasiyam (*Top Secret*), 81
Parsi theater, 5, 29, 72, 82, 198, 265–266n13, 271n1, 272n5
Parthasarathy, Indira, 5, 187–188, 193, 212, 272n3, 277n4
Parthasarathy, Kaladhar, 273–274n28
Parthasarathy, Mrs. Y. G., 22, 89–90
Parthasarathy, Y. G., 35, 38, 66, 90, 159, 169, 191, 258
Parvathi, S. N., 140
Pass Mark, 83
Patriotism (*Desa Bhakthi*), 75
patronage: Brahmin, 12, 19–20, 24, 58; of classical arts, 3, 70, 222; exclusions due to, 57–58; homogenization of plays and, 8; of music, 19, 20, 24, 42; non-Brahmin, 24; of plays, 28, 64, 82, 84–85, 89–90, 222; sabha, 3, 5, 8, 11–12, 18, 49–52, 58, 90, 213, 226; status and, 25, 42; taste-making and, 25; by younger people, 177. *See also* sponsors
Pendakur, Manjunath, 178, 179
performance genres, 210
performances: "authentic," 70; banned, 85; benefit, 72, 271n16; classical, 3, 11, 18, 25–28, 48, 74, 98; commemoration of anniversary,

respectability *(continued)*
music, 25; of classical arts, 11; of dancers, 26, 72, 85; of families, 159; of heroines, 109; of musicians, 26; of plays, 89
revivals, 50, 84, 107, 117, 140, 217, 226, 275n4; of traditional arts, 69–70, 72
Richmond, Farley, 8, 31, 98, 107, 110, 193, 213
rights (to plays), 67, 93, 94, 169, 210–211, 273n12, 276n4
rituals, 11, 13, 243, 274n1; Brahmin, 66, 121, 130, 192, 225; first-night, 85, 178, 181; inversion, 62; marriage, 34, 117–121, 123–124, 126, 128–131; pot used for, 220; televised, 131; tourism and, 129

sabhai natak ("sabha drama"), 2, 263n2
sabha plays, 2, 36, 54–55, 64, 263n2; audiences for, 5, 7, 22, 26, 35–36, 38, 57, 79, 83, 155, 179, 187, 202, 212, 215, 266n18; Brahmin-oriented, 22, 24, 69, 109, 117; conservative, 91, 96; complaints about, 11, 84, 86–87, 100–101, 217; defended, 87–90; Dravidian movement and, 58–59; declining numbers of, 48; families in, 107, 135, 222; features of, 99; influences on, 82; innovations in, 217–218, 221, 222, 226; language of, 56, 77–78, 102; marriages in, 90, 97–98, 131; new, 84, 218, 222; performances of, 94–95, 106, 211; plots of, 83, 91, 96–97; prescription for, 89; published (or not), 94, 140, 158, 161, 210–212, 249, 273n12, 273n21, 279n19; recorded, 94–95, 211; revivals of, 84, 117, 217; scenes in, 96; scripts for, 91–93, 107, 140; "serious," 83, 99, 100; sets of (*see* sets); social dramas as, 36; on television, 95, 136; themes of, 82, 90, 97, 102, 216–218; traditional values affirmed by, 96; translations of, 212; types of, 82–83; value of, 87, 89–90, 145
sabhas: age of members of, 100, 177–178, 215–216, 226; caste or class and, 11, 12, 19, 24, 26, 41, 50, 52, 69, 74, 155, 224, 264n3; in Chennai, 1, 3, 20–21, 38–39, 71, 109, 213, 215–217, 233–237, 264n3; conservative taste of, 74, 91, 109, 178, 224; decline of, 48–51; defined, 2; early, 264n5; finances of, 3, 41, 22, 29–31, 35–40, 42, 50, 51, 72, 165, 213, 266–267n19; future of, 224, 226–227, 269n38; history of, 2–3, 18–20, 22, 29, 49; members or memberships of, 18, 44–45, 74, 178, 187, 217, 226; neighborhoods of, 19–22, 38–39, 216; officials or secretaries of, 1–2, 8, 22, 25, 28, 36, 38, 39–41; performance types sponsored by, 3, 5, 22, 50, 83, 99, 193; power of, 1–2, 8, 12, 49, 213, 226 (*see also* patronage); precursors to, 18, 24; reputations of, 28, 45, 50, 52; scholarship on, 5, 51; seasonal, 51, 227; size or number of, 40, 41, 48, 51, 269n40; social service by, 39, 267n22; Tamilnadu Societies Registration Act and, 39–40; taste-makers, 18, 25, 42, 44, 52, 71
sabha theater: aesthetic of, 3, 4, 7, 11, 18, 31, 72, 82–83, 90–91, 106–107, 112–113; audiences for, 5, 7, 22, 26, 28, 36, 48, 82, 83–84, 100, 153, 226, 266n18, 270n8; boundaries of, 183, 186, 210; caste and, 11, 12,

Tamil Brahmins *(continued)*
as imagined community, 66; influence of, 13, 25, 41, 52, 187; as intellectuals, 13, 102, 186, 189, 210; marriages (*see* marriages); middle-class, 93, 135; modern, 11, 70, 71, 73, 129, 135, 186, 225; religion's importance to, 225; Tamil identity emphasized by, 55, 63, 68, 79, 102; as taste-makers or taste of, 25, 42–44, 48, 57, 71; traditional, 69–71, 112, 118, 122, 129, 135, 186, 225; urban, 13, 74, 93, 186. *See also* Brahmins; identity: Brahmin or Tamil Brahmin
Tamil Musical Dramas, 82
Tamilnadu Dramatic Performances Act of 1954, 91, 271n16
Tamilnadu Nadikar Sangam (Tamil Actors Association), 75
Tamilnadu: caste politics in, 55, 60, 63–66, 73, 82, 120; college-educated adults in, 192; comedians in, 99; communal issues in, 208; cultural trends in, 118; language politics in, 76, 104, 202–203; legislation in, 39–40, 91; performing arts in, 28; political parties in, 48, 55, 60, 64–65, 104; politics and dramatic arts in, 59–60, 65, 189, 202, 203–204; post-Independence or post-colonial, 2–3, 4, 6, 22, 24, 119; pre-Independence, 2, 5, 31; voting rate in, 202; youths in, 122
Tamil theater, 24, 31, 39, 91, 95, 102, 169, 187–188, 226; history of, 2, 3, 4–6, 158, 188, 218, 279n18; music festival and, 27–28; reputation or status of, 28, 187, 213; sabhas' impact on, 3, 39, 41, 48; scholarship on, 5, 188, 255. *See also* sabha theater
Tangarasu, M., 3, 95, 106
Ta<u>n</u>ik Kuṭitta<u>n</u>am (*Separate Family*), 169
Tanjavore (Tanjore), 19, 119, 173, 253, 280n13
Taṇṇīr Taṇṇīr! (*Water!*), 193, 198, 212, 266n15, 278n12
taste: bad or low, 87, 88, 150; Bourdieu on, 42–44; conservative or traditional, 69–70, 74; culture and, 74; factors determining, 46; "good," 18, 28, 44, 46, 48, 51, 52, 57, 74, 86, 155, 187; improving, 42; standard-setters for, 20, 25; theater humor and, 44, 48, 71; varied, 71, 187. *See also* Brahmins: as taste-makers; sabhas: as taste-makers; Tamil Brahmins: as taste-makers or taste of
"Teacher Student" ("Guru Sishyan"), 220–221
television, 3, 35, 46, 73, 89, 103, 109, 272n3, 272n7; plays' decline and, 48, 50, 217; plays shown on, 46; plays' superiority to, 64, 89; serials, 36, 90, 217. *See also* actors: in television; actresses: in television; *Washingtonil Tirumaṇam*: television serial
Telugu, 20, 64, 76, 103, 134, 172, 265n8, 269n38, 276n3, 280n12
temples, 20, 72, 270n10, 275n10; music for, 26; performances organized by, 49; in plays, 108, 209, 218; Tirupati, 253, 280n12
terukkūttu, 94, 272n11
Thangavelu, 99
theater: colonial-era, 2, 5, 24, 31, 58, 75; experimental, 3, 5, 6, 188; history of, 3–6 (*see also* sabha theater: development of; Chennai: history of theater in); intellectual

definition of, 5–6; international or world, 187; music and, 43, 51; performance- vs. text-based, 211; post-colonial or post-Independence, 3, 4, 6, 31, 22, 24, 187, 195, 210; serious, 71, 188; social, 31; song and dance in, 11; western, 5, 31, 190, 198. *See also* amateur theater; commercial theater; folk theater; insider theater; modern (Indian) theater; Parsi theater; professional theater; sabha theater; Tamil theater
theaters, 2, 32, 40, 108, 155, 215, 274n1; audience remains at, 82; cinema, 32, 280n10; neighborhoods of, 21–22; rental prices for, 231–232, 266n15, 280n3; sabha vs. non-sabha plays in, 211; troupes remain at 2. *See also* halls
theatre of roots, 190, 278n7
Theosophical Society, 19
Thirumalachariar, Manni, 18
This Is Our Man (*Itu Namma Āḷ*), 67
Thyagaraja Nagar (T. Nagar), 21, 22, 38, 216, 265nn6–7
Thyagaraja Sangeetha, 21
tickets, 18, 29, 37, 38, 41, 72, 227; black market, 204; Chennai Music Festival, 28–29; donations instead of, 223; expensive, 4, 215; individual, 264n2; sabhas' income from, 29, 36, 44
T. K. S. Brothers, 35, 75, 256, 266n17, 266n19, 272nn2–3
tourists, 26, 28, 118, 129, 131
tradition, 11, 123, 253: arts' adherence to, 155; displaced, 122, 131; fear of loss of, 274n4; folk, 178; glorified, 131; importance of, 69–70, 101; performed, 122; signs or markers of, 19, 20; as trope, 24
tragedy, 199, 207
Triplicane, 18, 20, 22, 38, 265n6
Triplicane Fine Arts, 22, 118, 169, 257
troupes: all-men, 99, 109; all-women, 112 (*see also* Mahalakshmi Ladies Drama Group); amateur, 3, 5, 35, 49, 72, 38, 72, 95, 111; changes in, 49, 226, 269n39; comedy, 76, 271n2; dialect used by, 31, 102–103; donations sought by, 223; Dravida Kazhagam, 55; as family, 103, 273n19; family tree and listings of, 255–261, 269n39; female artistes and, 109–111, 273n28; finances of, 35, 38, 40–41, 48–49, 54, 91, 187–188, 266–267n19; identity fostered by, 55, 102; leaders of, 41, 91, 188, 216, 255; longstanding, 6, 140, 161, 194, 223, 271n16, 275n2; mixed-caste, 68, 103; new, 38, 49, 91, 135, 139, 169, 217, 221, 226, 255, 269n39; performances per year of, 41–42; plays or repertory of, 94, 169, 211, 212, 278n5; playwright- vs. actor-centered, 91, 93; politics and, 59, 65; popular, 28, 36, 41, 65; pre-Independence, 2, 31, 49, 68; professional, 29, 31, 35, 49, 72, 75, 78, 84, 110, 220, 265n13; recruitment to, 72, 91, 103, 110–111; respectability of, 72; sabhas' relations with, 3, 38–39, 41, 49–50, 82, 264n2; self-sponsoring, 42, 48–49; sets rented by, 107; social service by, 267n22
Truths that Change Color (*Niṟam Māṟum Nijaṅkaḷ*), 225
Tughlaq (Cho play). See *Mohammad bin Tughlaq*
Tughlaq (journal), 196–197, 200
Tughlaq (Karnad play), 272n5; characters in, 199–201, 206–207; in modern Indian canon, 189, 210;

www.ingramcontent.com/pod-product-compliance
Lightning Source LLC
Chambersburg PA
CBHW021120270326
41929CB00009B/974
9781438489766